*V V*oolf *S*tudies *A*nnual

Volume 9, 2003

SPECIAL ISSUE

Virginia Woolf and Literary History

Part I

PACE UNIVERSITY PRESS ● NEW YORK

ISSN 1080-9317
ISBN 0-944473-62-8 (pbk: alk.ppr.)

Member

Council of Editors of Learned Journals

Contents

Woolf
Studies
Annual

Volume 9, 2003

VIRGINIA WOOLF & LITERARY HISTORY: PART I
Edited by Jane Lilienfeld, Jeffrey Oxford, and Lisa Low

GUIDE

REVIEWS

Abbreviations

AHH	*A Haunted House*
AROO	*A Room of One's Own*
BP	*Books and Portraits*
BTA	*Between the Acts*
CDB	*The Captain's Death Bed and Other Essays*
CE	*Collected Essays (4 vols.)*
CR1	*The Common Reader*
CR2	*The Common Reader, Second Series*
CSF	*The Complete Shorter Fiction*
D	*The Diary of Virginia Woolf (5 vols.)*
DM	*The Death of the Moth and Other Essays*
E	*The Essays of Virginia Woolf (6 Vols.)*
F	*Flush*
FR	*Freshwater*
GR	*Granite & Rainbow: Essays*
JR	*Jacob's Room*
L	*The Letters of Virginia Woolf (6 Vols.)*
M	*The Moment and Other Essays*
MEL	*Melymbrosia*
MOB	*Moments of Being*
MT	*Monday or Tuesday*
MD	*Mrs. Dalloway*
ND	*Night and Day*
O	*Orlando*
PA	*A Passionate Apprentice*
RF	*Roger Fry: A Biography*
TG	*Three Guineas*
TTL	*To the Lighthouse*
TW	*The Waves*
TY	*The Years*
VO	*The Voyage Out*

Virginia Woolf's Russian Voyage Out

Natalya Reinhold[1]

The modified title of Woolf's novel *The Voyage Out* figures in this article as a metaphor for Woolf's imaginary journey into Russian space. Unlike Rachel Vinrace's voyage to semi-imaginary Santa Marina, hers ended, we argue, in coming back home. In other words, I claim that Russian literature has a status of its own in the work of Virginia Woolf. How well is this claim justified?

The substantial Russian agenda in Woolf's work is one of the discoveries brought about by the "new books" published in the field of lupine studies in the 1970-90s.[2] When collected, Woolf's literary-critical heritage reveals an undeniable fact: she read the Russian authors extensively and wrote about them in her critical essays. Woolf speculated on Russian literature in her letters and diaries and collaborated in translating certain pieces of Russian writing into English. She made attempts to learn Russian. These facts cannot be explained away merely by the general interest of the English public in Russian arts and literature in the first quarter of the last century. Among the English writers of the 1910s and 1920s we

[1]The author's thanks go to Elizabeth Inglis, former Assistant Librarian in the Manuscript Section of the University of Sussex Library, for her help with the Virginia Woolf papers; Michael Bott and his colleagues from the archives of the University of Reading who helped her with examining the Hogarth Press materials; special thanks to Chatto & Windus for their kind permission to quote from the Hogarth Press papers; great thanks to the School of English of the University of Exeter, and the Open Society Institute (Moscow) for their financial support.

[2]See Russian themes in the following publications, most of which are referred to below (the list is by no means exhaustive): Woolf, Virginia. *The Waves. 2 Holograph drafts.* Trans. and Ed. J. W. Graham. London: The Hogarth Press, 1976; *Books and Portraits.* By Virginia Woolf. Ed. Mary Lyons. London: The Hogarth Press, 1977; *The Diary of Virginia Woolf.* Ed. Anne Olivier Bell; introd. Quentin Bell. 5 vols. London: The Hogarth Press, 1977-1984; *The Letters of Virginia Woolf.* Eds. Nigel Nicolson and Joanne Trautmann. 6 vols. London: The Hogarth Press, 1975-1980; *Melymbrosia. An Early Version of* The Voyage Out. By Virginia Woolf. Ed. with an Introduction Louise A. DeSalvo. Scholar's edition. New York: Public Library, Astor, Lenox and Tilden Foundations, 1982; *Virginia Woolf's Reading Notebooks.* Ed. Brenda R. Silver. Princeton: Princeton University Press, 1983; *The Essays of Virginia Woolf.* Ed. Andrew McNeillie. 6 vols. London: The Hogarth Press, 1986-; S. P. Rosenbaum, ed. *Women and Fiction. The Manuscript Versions of* A Room of One's Own. By Virginia Woolf. Oxford: Blackwell Publishers, 1992; *Virginia Woolf's* Jacob's Room: *The Holograph Draft: Based on the Holograph Manuscript in the Henry W. and Albert A. Berg Collection of English and American Literature at the New York Public Library.* Transcribed and Ed. Edward L. Bishop. New York, NY: Pace University Press, 1998.

can hardly find any other artist of her caliber (except for D. H. Lawrence) who was so creatively and professionally involved in working with Russian literature as was Woolf. This places her in the unique position of a modern English writer who worked professionally for years on Russian literary material.

Another issue of wider cultural interest is the role played by Woolf in developing English readers' awareness of Russian literature and social life. The lines of critical perception of the Russian writers, Tolstoy and Turgenev in particular, were first formulated by Matthew Arnold and Henry James,[3] who were followed by a younger generation of translators and critics like Constance Garnett, Edward Garnett, and others.[4] These lines persisted in English literary criticism till the end of the 1910s and the beginning of the 1920s, and then were drastically reconsidered by the modern generation of writers, including Woolf.

How far has the issue been studied? George J. Zytaruk in his *D. H. Lawrence's Response to Russian Literature* pointed out the biographical and professional links which Woolf had with S. S. Koteliansky, the Jewish Ukranian translator of Russian fiction, and it was Zytaruk who commented on the relation between Woolf's novels and the fact of her reading the Russians: "[her] own novels were undoubtedly shaped by her reading of the Russians" (Zytaruk 108). His statement, however, concerning the status of Russian literature in the work of Woolf is arguable: "there were [. . .] such writers as Virginia Woolf, who felt that, after the Russians had spoken, there was nothing left for English writers to say" (Zytaruk 37). As a matter of fact, the study of the corpus of Woolf's "Russian essays" reveals her growing disappointment with Russian literature,[5] and in what follows I would like to examine why this happened. I will look into the motives for Woolf's work with a language and cultural material other than English, and

[3]See Arnold, Matthew. "Count Leo Tolstoi." [1887] *Essays in Criticism*. London: Dent, New York: Dutton, 1964: 352-70; "De Maistre's Lettres et opuscules inédits." [1879] *Essays, Letters, and Reviews*. By Matthew Arnold. Collected and Ed. Fraser Neiman. Cambridge [Mass.]: Harvard University Press, 1960: 216-36; James, Henry. "Ivan Turgénieff." [1884] *Partial Portraits*. London and New York: Macmillan, 1888. Rpt. 1970: 291-323; *The Notebooks of Henry James*. Ed. F. O. Matthiessen and Kenneth B. Murdock. New York: Oxford University Press, 1961: 101.

[4]See, for example, Garnett, Richard David. *Constance Garnett: a Heroic Life*. London: Sinclair-Stevenson, 1991: 361-62; Garnett, Edward. *Turgenev: A Study*. With a Foreword by Joseph Conrad. London: W. Collins Sons & Co., 1917; Murry, John Middleton. *Fyodor Dostoevsky: A Critical Study*. London: M. Secker, 1916.

[5]See Bushmanova (Reinhold), Natalya. "Virdjinia Woolf o Russkoi Literature." [Virginia Woolf on Russian literature] *V Mire Otechestvennoi Klassiki*. [In the world of Russian classics] 2 vols. Moscow: Khudozhestvennaia literatura, 1987, 2:260-82; *Angliiskii Modernism: Psikhologicheskaia Proza*. [English modernism: psychological prose] By Bushmanova (Reinhold), N. Yaroslavl: University Press, 1992: 35-36, 53-56.

the practical ways she dealt with them. I will also address Woolf's role as inter-
preter and co-translator of Russian texts, as well as her critical and reader's
responses to Russian literature via reviews, references, and comments.

In a more general way, I will address contextually Woolf's life-long engagement with Russian literature, in the wake of the assumption that in her case, it
turned out to be a field of search for "the Other" and the discourse of modernity.
"Cultural Otherness" should be understood as the awareness of cross-cultural
space dividing English and Russian cultures, and differences in social institutions, life-styles, values, and historical context, as well as a writer's quest for a
broader, more culturally adequate and realistic societal perspective. (The latter,
for scarcity of space, will be hinted at rather than made explicit.) "The discourse
of modernity" denotes a combination of artistically shaped discourses, which are
either linked up with the social-cultural agenda of the turn of the century, or are
congenial to twentieth-century mainstream developments. Such broader cultural
perspective, as we shall see, brings out a remarkable message behind the
"Russian voyage out" undertaken by Virginia Woolf.

There exist seventeen published essays by Woolf specifically on Russian lit-
erary and social issues: "Tolstoy's 'The Cossacks'" (*E2* 76-80), "More
Dostoevsky" (*E2* 83-87), "A Minor Dostoevsky" (*E2* 165-67), "A Russian
Schoolboy" (*E2* 179-83), "Tchekhov's Questions" (*E2* 244-48), "Valery Brusof"
(*E2* 317-19), "A View of the Russian Revolution" (*E2* 338-41), "The Russian
View" (*E2* 341-44), "The Russian Background" (*E3* 83-87), "Dostoevsky in
Cranford" (*E3* 113-15), "The Cherry Orchard" (*E3* 246-50), "Gorky on Tolstoy"
(*E3* 252-55), "A Glance at Turgenev" (*E3* 314-17), "Dostoevsky the Father" (*E3*
327-31), "The Russian Point of View" (*CE1* 238-46), "A Giant with Very Small
Thumbs" (*E4* 416-19), and "The Novels of Turgenev" (*CE1* 247-53). Written
between 1917 and 1933, they present us with a fine picture of the writer, critic
and reader's reception of Russian literature in the shaping years of the late 1910s
up to the early 1930s. Besides these are a number of manuscript and typescript
versions of both published and unpublished pieces of writing related to the
Russian theme. These are her wittily entitled unpublished review "Tchekhov on
Pope: *The Rape of the Lock*,"[6] also three manuscript pages of the essay
"Tchekhov's Questions,"[7] two typescript drafts of "Uncle Vanya," and three
pages of notes in Woolf's handwriting on her Russian language studies dated
February 1921, entered in her notebook with the first sketch of *Mrs. Dalloway.*

---

[6]*The Virginia Woolf Manuscripts. From the Henry W. and Albert A. Berg Collection
at the New York Public Library*, Research Publications, 1993. Sussex Virginia Woolf
archive, M 121.

[7]Book B1.d: f. 36 verso, f. 37 verso. Sussex Virginia Woolf archive.

Besides, Woolf's letters, diaries and essays abound in literary and extra-literary references, allusions and comments on Russian authors, their books, lives and the social issues they raise.

As is clear from Woolf's "Russian reading list," it did not include Tolstoy and Dostoevsky, Turgenev and Chekhov alone, but also Sergei Aksakov and Valerii Brussov ("Valery Brusof" in Woolf's transliteration, typical of her time), who were not widely known in England at the turn of the century. Her knowledge of Russian fiction was not limited to one or two works of a certain novelist. She read and reread the whole of Turgenev as well as Tolstoy and Dostoevsky. Her interest in Russian culture was not narrow or purely literary. The disputes between the Slavophils and Westernizers, the biographies of the great writers, as well as the ethical problems raised by Tolstoy are frequently referred to in the pages of her diaries as, for instance, in the following entry of 6 January 1918:

> The talk [. . .] settled upon conscience: social duties, & Tolstoy. Gerald [Shove] read Tolstoy the other day [. . .] He thinks seriously of starting a nursery garden after the war, & threatens to give up their [his and Fredegond Maitland's] capital.
> 'What's the use of that? L. [Leonard] demanded. [. . .]We dont want people to live on 30/ a week.'
> 'Psychologically it may be necessary if one is to abolish capitalism' I remarked.
> 'I dont agree, ' said Alix. 'Besides who would he give his capital to?'
> 'In the ideal state everyone would have £300 a year' L. went on.
> [. . .] I still feel, however, that my fire is too large for one person. I'm one
> of those who are hampered by the psychological hindrance of owning capital.
> (*D*1 100-101)

To Woolf and the Bloomsbury circle Russian culture was not something merely exotic or fashionable. Rather, their interest corresponded to the general widening of the frontiers of European culture from the turn of the century on. For example, Roger Fry in his studies of folklore and national traditions in the art of different peoples became interested in Russian national art (*RF* 171). In particular, he was attracted by Russian painting of the beginning of the twentieth century and even tried to organize a joint exhibition of English and Russian artists at the Grafton Gallery in October 1912: "[. . .] so I conceived the idea of having the Exhibition divided 2 rooms to this English group and 2 rooms to the works of the younger Russian artists which I thought ought to be better known in England; I thought that this would be of great interest to English artists [. . .]" (*RF* 167).[8] John Maynard Keynes thought about Russia not only as his wife,

[8]Roger Fry realized his project, though "many of the Russian pictures failed to arrive upon the opening day" (*RF* 178).

Lydia Lopokova's native land but first and foremost as the birth-place of an unprecedented economic experiment (*D*3 43-44 n10-11).[9]

As for Virginia Woolf, she focused on creative issues and the differences of the national and historical backgrounds. She was obviously intrigued by the density of life experience she found in Russian fiction, by what in the work of Dostoevsky and also Chekhov looked like a peculiar neglect of social hierarchy in favor of being and sensibility,[10] as well as freedom from conventions of content and form—all of which, in her opinion, the English fiction of her time lacked. For some time Woolf used Russian literature as a means of identification of her priorities in writing. In her essay "More Dostoevsky" (1917) she stressed the author's remarkable rendering of certain emotional states: "Alone among writers Dostoevsky has the power of reconstructing these most swift and complicated states of mind, of rethinking the whole train of thought in all its speed, now as it flashes into light, now as it lapses into darkness" (*BP* 118-119). To her mind, Dostoevsky's method sets writing free of its attachment to what she called "the old tune," that is, conventional ways of depiction. It breaks the stereotypes of the reader's response. In this way it even promotes the development of a

---

[9]Keynes, John Maynard. *A Short View of Russia.* London: The Hogarth Press, 1925.

[10]Cf. "To him [Dostoevsky] a child or a beggar is as full of violent and subtle emotions as a poet or a sophisticated woman of the world; and it is from the intricate maze of their emotions that Dostoevsky constructs his version of life" (*BP* 119). Woolf's sharp observation of the social aspect of Dostoevsky's work needs, in our view, an extra literary-historical comment by way of clarifying the background of Russian writers' focus on social justice in their treatment of the poor. For one thing, there existed in nineteenth-century Russian literature a long-term practice of detailed description of the common people in numerous *ocherki* ("essays") and *povesti* ("stories"). It began in 1845 with the publication of a two-volume collection of essays *Fiziologiia Peterburga* [Physiology of St. Petersburg]. One of the contributors, Russia's most influential literary critic Vissarion Belinskii, commented on its message by putting a rhetorical question, "Could there be anything of interest in an uncouth uneducated person?", and answering it in the affirmative: "Definitely! A person's soul, his mind, heart, passions, and inclinations, in other words, everything, like in any cultivated person" (Belinskii 345; my trans.). Another contributor to the above collection, Dmitrii Grigorovich, made a real discovery in his stories "Derevnia" [The Village], 1846, and "Anton Goremyka" [Anton], 1847, by focusing on Russian serfs and their awful lot. From that time on every Russian writer of merit, Turgenev or Tolstoy, Dostoevsky or Chekhov, made a special point of writing about common people, peasants in particular, without any social bias. On the whole, it was a humanist response to the atrocious conditions of life of the common people who were deprived of every human right. In contrast to European countries where social reforms,

human being, for it gives vent to feelings suppressed by long habit:

> We have to get rid of the old tune which runs so persistently in our ears, and to realize how little of our humanity is expressed in that old tune. Again and again we are thrown off the scent in following Dostoevsky's psychology; we constantly find ourselves wondering whether we recognize the feeling that he shows us, and we realize constantly and with a start of surprise that we have met it before in ourselves, or in some moment of intuition have suspected it in others. But we have never spoken of it, and that is why we are surprised. (*BP* 119)

It was the expression of fullness of being that Woolf held high in the work of Russian writers, in particular of Sergei Aksakov. Consider the terms in which she described his personality in the essay "A Russian Schoolboy" (1917): "[. . .] a man of extraordinary freshness and substance, a man with a rich nature, moving in the sun and shadow of real life" (*BP* 101). Woolf ascribed the fullness of Aksakov's "I" to his life amid nature, and to his unbounded expression of all the emotions and passions of a child. As for writing, Woolf thought spontaneity, sincerity and the sense of fullness of being in Aksakov's autobiography to be its strongest points.

---

however slowly, made their way under succeeding governments, social improvements in Russia had been dramatically procrastinated. As a result the position of peasants had been for decades similar to that of slaves. It is in the face of that gross social injustice that Russian writers took it upon themselves to draw public attention to the common people's hardships. Gradually what shaped itself as a literary tradition grew into a well-known *narodovol'cheskoye dvizhenie* ("populist movement") of the 1860s-1870s. The writers did not go unpunished for their fair and honest depiction of the poor and under-classed. As is known, Dostoevsky was sentenced to a four-year imprisonment in 1849 for his sympathy with revolutionary activities aimed at social reforms. Chekhov chose to travel all across Siberia to the Far East, to Sakhalin, to see with his own eyes the life of the exiled. That journey provided him with the material for one of his best books, *The Isle of Sakhalin* (1893-94) but it also cost him his health. To return to Woolf's view, the ease with which Dostoevsky and, for that matter, Chekhov see beyond social barriers is not a product of the above outlined literary tradition alone. It is also a trace of a peculiar norm which shaped itself in Russian society in the middle of the eighteenth century. As soon as a person of inferior social rank made his (sic) name as a writer all social impediments which, under different circumstances, might have proved to be insurmountable, came to be levelled. Nikolai Chernyshevskii described a typical case study in his essay of 1855: "A merchant from Kazan', one Kamenev, a newly fledged author of a published ballad, came to Moscow to pay a visit to Karamzin [outstanding Russian writer and historian]. This acquaintance immediately opened all the doors of Moscow literary *salons* to him. That happened forty years ago, at the time when merchants had been admitted to aristocratic houses only through the back-door, to display their goods or beg for their payment that was long overdue" (Chernyshevskii 378; my trans.).

No wonder, then, that she would emphasize Gorky's characterization of Leo Tolstoy as "a man-orchestra" in her essay "Gorky on Tolstoy" (1920). Here, in connection with the problem of having "a wonderful compass of voices,"[11] Woolf discussed a way of writing different from the one she found in Dostoevsky's fiction. Gorky's method of short notes not aimed at the exhaustive description of a person and thus close to reality seemed to her productive. For in life one usually perceives one's fellows in a fragmentary, note-like way:

> But Gorky's picture comes nearer than the others to completeness, because he makes no attempt to include everything, to explain everything, or to sum up all in one consistent whole. Here there is a very bright light, here darkness and emptiness. And perhaps this is the way in which we see people in reality. (*E3* 254)

Here one gets a direct parallel to Woolf's remarkable method of portraying a plurality of selves via fragmentary discourse in *Jacob's Room* (1922).

Similarly, in Chekhov's prose Woolf found a more rewarding strategy of writing than in the "well-made" stories and works of her contemporaries, Joyce included. In her essay "The Russian Background" (1919) she remarked that by means of "incomplete" stories Chekhov achieved a far-reaching, identity-enhancing result: "Almost all the stories in the present volume are stories of peasants; and whether or not it is the effect of this solitude and emptiness, each obscure and brutish mind has had rubbed in it a little transparency through which the light of the spirit shines amazingly" (*BP* 125).

Likewise, Woolf praised the English production of Chekhov's comedy *The Cherry Orchard* in the essay of the same title (1920) for conveying the writer's view of man penetrating beyond class divisions and the fixed notions of personal and social identity. She twice quoted Charlotte's remark about her having no passport and having forgotten her age. This "free" view of a human being generated in the English spectator, Woolf thought, an intoxicating feeling of freedom and fullness of life: "it [*The Cherry Orchard*] [. . .] sends one into the street feeling like a piano played upon at last, not in the middle only but all over the keyboard and with the lid left open so that the sound goes on" (*E3* 248).

It would be easy to see in this a mere fascination of the young writer with the then popular literature. However, what one finds in Woolf's Russian essays

---

[11]"It is easier to write tonight than to sleep. A wind which has been playing about all day, suddenly goes to work in dead earnest. It is battering at my windows pressing them as tight against the frame as possible, & then swerving aside so that the pane released from pressure rattles loose. The wind has *a wonderful compass of voices*" (*PA* 205; emphasis added).

is better defined as her interest in the "cultural Otherness" of experience as shaped in Russian literary texts. This approach distinguishes Woolf from numerous critical interpretations of her work as highbrow, idiosyncratic, and reader-unfriendly.[12]

Yet for all her great interest, Woolf never lost her sense of distance, being well aware of the fact that she was dealing with a specific cultural and social agenda. This explains why Woolf so often compared the Russian and English points of view[13] or put a Russian writer into the imaginary perspective of the English landscape.[14] In all her essays about Russian literature Woolf thought it necessary to project the English reader's point of view:

> In reading him [Dostoevsky], therefore, we are often bewildered because we find ourselves observing men and women from a different point of view from that to which we are accustomed. (*BP* 119);

> [. . .] here is a new country, people said, and therefore its literature must be different, if it is true literature, from any other. They sought out and relished in Chekhov and Dostoevsky those qualities which they supposed to be peculiarly Russian and therefore of peculiar excellence. They welcomed joyously an abandonment to emotion[,] an introspection, a formlessness which they would have detested in the French or in the English. People drank tea endlessly and discussed the soul without stopping in a room where nothing could be seen distinctly; such was our supposition. (*BP* 109)

Much of Woolf's speculation on the differences in cultural identities and writing between English and Russian literature went into her essay "On Rereading Meredith" (1918). Though Meredith might seem to English readers of the 1910s and 1920s who were engrossed in Russian novels somewhat old-fashioned, nevertheless she advised them to read deeper into Meredith's work. Relating it to the Russian novels she singled out Meredith's mode of writing as a most significant feature that distinguished him from Dostoevsky, whom she saw as completely absorbed in the ideology of his theme:

> They [Russians] accumulate; they accept ugliness; they seek to understand; they penetrate further and further into the human soul with their terrible power of sustained insight and their undeviating reverence for truth. But Meredith

---

[12]This view of Woolf takes its origin, to a great extent, in the works of F. R. Leavis and his critique of Bloomsbury.

[13]See, for example, "A Russian Schoolboy" (*BP* 101-105) and "The Russian Background" (*BP* 123-125).

[14]Cf. "Dostoevsky in Cranford" (1919): "How, one asks, would Dostoevsky have behaved himself upon the vicarage lawn?" (*BP* 120)

takes truth by storm; he takes it with a phrase, and his best phrases are not mere phrases but are compact of many different observations, fused into one and flashed out in a line of brilliant light. (*GR* 50)

Woolf emphasized the necessity for modern English writers to draw upon their national cultural identity which, to her, was linked with such imaginative and intellectual power (*GR* 51).

It seems but natural, in a view of Woolf's long-term practice of reading and writing on Russian books, that she came to collaborate with S. S. Koteliansky[15] in translating Russian texts. Their work began in 1919[16] and was carried through mainly via the Hogarth Press, with Leonard Woolf acting as a conduit between the two for twenty odd years.[17] The following passage from Koteliansky's letter of 14 February 1923 is representative of the tone of their correspondence, and the pace at which translation was accomplished: "If you like it [A. B. Goldenveiser's *Near Tolstoy*] (and I think that a very interesting book could be made of it—perhaps by condensing it to half its, Russian, size), and you also like the Rosanov

[15]S. S. Koteliansky's role as a Russian literary consultant, translator and conduit, who taught Russian to English writers and inspired them to "English" his translations, is a well-known story. See Zytaruk, ed. (i-xxx); Zytaruk (44-45); Woolf, Leonard. "Kot". *The New Statesman and Nation*, XLIX (February 1955): 170-72; Berberova, Nina. *Zheleznaia Zhentschina*. [The Iron Lady] *Druzhba narodov* (September, October, December 1989):145, 179, 125-26; Bushmanova (Reinhold), Natalya. "Perevodchik i mezhkul'-turnoe prostranstvo (Neizvestnye stranitsi russko-britanskikh literaturnikh sviazei)". [Translator and the intercultural space: Some unknown aspects of English-Russian literary relations] *Vzaimosviazi i Vzaimovliianie Russkoi i Evropeiskoi Literatur: Materialy mezhdunarodnoi nauchnoi konferentsii 13-15 noiabria 1997 v St Petersburgskom Universitete.* [Interconnections and mutual influences of Russian and European literatures: Proceedings of the international conference held at St Petersburg University 13-15 November 1997] St Petersburg: St Petersburg University Press, 1999: 71-77; Rogachevskii, Andrei. "Samuel Koteliansky and the Bloomsbury Circle (Roger Fry, E. M. Forster, Mr. and Mrs. John Maynard Keynes and the Woolfs)." *Forum for Modern Language Studies*, 36:4 (October 2000): 368-85; Marcus, Laura. "On Not Knowing Russian" (paper read at the 11th Annual Virginia Woolf Conference at University of Wales, Bangor, 2001).

[16]See Virginia Woolf's letter of 4 April 1919 to Koteliansky in the Manuscript Student's Room of the British Museum Library (MS48974, No 285). Both first met on 15 January 1918 when S. S. Koteliansky came to the Woolfs to dinner (*D* 1 106 fn 24).

[17] See MS48974 in the Manuscript Student's Room of the British Museum Library, No. 286 of March 1921; 287 of 25 June (1921?); p/c of 9 March 1923; 124 of 27 November 1927; 159 of 9 April 1932; 164 of 10 July 1933; 166 of 13 July 1933; 168 of 21 August 1933; 249 of 19 July 1937; 251 of 23 July (1937); 284 of 8 January, n. d.

book,—then perhaps Virginia would like to do with me the Rosanov book, and you–the Goldenveiser? See that in about five or six weeks we could have both books ready for the press—."[18] Yet hardly any description of Woolf's co-translation practice exists apart from the one given by Leonard Woolf:

> Mrs Woolf did not know Russian. We taught ourselves a little Russian in order to understand Koteliansky's problems in translating. The procedure was that Koteliansky translated the Russian book into very bad English by double-spaced lines, so that Mrs Woolf went through the text with him, sentence by sentence, and then put the translation into good English. (Kirkpatrick 85)

For all its brevity, Leonard Woolf's note contains two statements which are relevant to the study of Woolf-cum-Koteliansky co-translation work. One concerns Koteliansky's habit of translating "the Russian book into very bad English." The other is about Virginia Woolf's teaching herself a little Russian. The phrase about Koteliansky's "very bad English" points to one of the basic aspects of translating into the second language: a non-native speaker provides a word-by-word rendering of the source text for the partner who, being a native speaker, should produce a target text. Taken in this perspective, Koteliansky's and Woolf's co-translation activities look like a perfectly normal case, with Woolf acting as a native speaker. Non-translator, she, nevertheless, could do her own stint in translation as a professional writer. The second of Leonard Woolf's statements needs added information. What could "teaching ourselves a little Russian" mean? Three pages of Woolf's notes dated February 1921 (*L2* 459n3) found in her manuscripts[19] make it clear that she had some experience in reading Russian. The notes in question come in her notebook after the "First Sketch of Mrs Dalloway," preceding the manuscript version of *Mrs. Dalloway*, dated 9 November 1922. The first two pages and part of page 3 are pencil-notes; the rest is done in ink. The notes preserve Woolf's attempt to write two cyrillic letters Й and Н.They include phonetic rules about pronouncing Russian vowels. They also contain a grammar exercise obviously coming from a textbook, for Woolf transliterated the Russian words *pervoe uprazhnenie* ("the first exercise") and

---

[18]Hogarth Press archive No 38 in the University of Reading Library. See, also, Koteliansky's letters to Leonard Woolf of 23 February 1923 (Hogarth Press No 595), of 20 March 1923? [Ibid.], of 22 March 1923 (No 493), of 14 April 1934 (No 130), Leonard Woolf's letter to Koteliansky of 22 February 1923 (No 595).

[19]*The Virginia Woolf Manuscripts. From the Henry W. and Albert A. Berg Collection at the New York Public Library*, Research Publications, 1993. Manuscripts, Reel 6, M15-M 26 (the Manuscript Department of the Sussex University Library).

uchebnik ("a course book"). There are also grammar rules about the negative particle ne ("not"), and information on the Russian declension system entered into the notebook. Obviously Woolf made an effort to write cyrillics and to pronounce Russian words, to transcribe them into English and to sort out certain morphological and syntactical cases. Who gave her the Russian textbook becomes clear when the notes are related to Woolf's letter to Koteliansky of March 1921: "Dear Mr. Koteliansky, [. . .] We are taking our Russian. The aspects seem to me very interesting—that is not to say that I understand them at all" (*L2* 459). In her letter of 25 June 1921 she again refers to her Russian studies: "Then I hope we shall see you: but you will not find that I have learnt Russian" (*L2* 476). In principle Koteliansky-cum-Woolf's role in the co-translation process is in accord with the English and Continental practice of literary translation accomplished by two persons, the source text translator and the maker of the target text. The fact that Woolf thought it necessary to learn something of the language she was putting into English (the notes precede in time Koteliansky-cum-Woolf's translations of Dostoevsky, Tolstoy and Goldenveiser) characterizes her as being fully aware of both the stylistic and the socio-cultural implications of such translation strategy.[20]

All of this makes the task of textual examination of Woolf's translation strategies an urgent one. A provisional comparative study of the Russian source text, Koteliansky's word-by-word translation and the target text has long existed with researchers as an idea. It has not been carried out only because of the absence of manuscript versions as textual products of the collaboration between Koteliansky and Woolf, as was remarked by G. J. Zytaruk in his introduction to *The Quest for Rananim* (xxvii-xxviii). The manuscript versions of her and Koteliansky's translations have not yet been located.[21] Still, something can be done by way of investigating Woolf's writing technique by comparing the draft versions of her sketch "Uncle Vanya," where the plot of Chekhov's play is repro-

---

[20]See Dostoevsky, F. M. *Stavrogin's Confession and the Plan of the Life of a Great Sinner.* With Introductory and Explanatory Notes. Trans. from the Russian by Virginia Woolf and S. S. Koteliansky. Richmond: The Hogarth Press, 1922; *Tolstoi's Love Letters.* With a Study on the Biographical Elements in Tolstoi's Work by Paul Biriukov. Trans. from the Russian by S. S. Koteliansky and Virginia Woolf. Richmond: The Hogarth Press, 1923; Goldenveiser, A. B. *Talks with Tolstoi.* Trans. by S. S. Koteliansky and Virginia Woolf. Richmond: The Hogarth Press, 1923; Hogarth Press archive 493 on *Tolstoi's Love Letters,* and 595 on *Talks with Tolstoi.*

[21]Cf. S. P. Rosenbaum's letter of April 1997 written in reply to the author's question about a possible location of ms. versions of V. Woolf-cum-Koteliansky's translations: "I have no idea where the manuscripts might be if they survived. I suspect they have not."

duced to build up a picture of the reception of Russian issues by an English spectator.[22]

Though the exact date of its composition is unfixed (the editor of *The Complete Shorter Fiction* gives 1926-1941 for all shorter pieces of Woolf's writing), it is probable that it was composed between 1926 and 1933, when Woolf was reconsidering her view of Russian fiction and identifying Turgenev as the most satisfactory Russian writer in a number of critical reviews.[23] The form of a concise, suggestive and aphoristic sketch describing the reception of Chekhov's play *Uncle Vanya* at one of the London theatres resembles Turgenev's *Poems in Prose* (1882).[24]

Comparative study of its two typescript versions and the final text [B.10 b)] may provide an adequate way of defining Woolf's strategy in writing about cross-cultural issues. The first point to identify is the early and the late Ts variants [B10 b3)] vs Draft 3.

Though both drafts are almost the same length, the typescript B10 b3), beginning with the words "We shall rest," seems to be the earlier. First, because it is more heavily revised than the other piece: fourteen phrasal corrections versus four deletions, respectively. Second, punctuation is more careless in the "We shall rest" piece than in the other draft, which is typical for the early stages of Woolf's working on a piece. Third, there are many more details in the "we shall rest" piece than in the other variant, which, again, is characteristic of the initial stages of Woolf's writing. Some of these details, which are all gone from the final text, are traces of reading ("[Wordsworths lakes]," "[Countess Tolsyoys last diaries?]," "[Did you read how] she lay out in her nightgown on the [. . .] damp earth?"), others are critical remarks ("Is [it going to end on that note]?", "Is that the message of the play?", "[Is it Tchekoves time?]"). Fourth, the identity perspective of the "We shall rest" piece is not clear. The "we" of the female viewer ("And is that also true of us?") changes into "I" ("as we hear the tinkling bells vanish, I shall turn to my husband"), which gradually transforms into "she"

[22]B.10b) Unfinished drafts of stories or sketches: "Uncle Vanya." 2 typescript drafts, corrected by Virginia Woolf, 6 pp. in the Manuscript Department of the Sussex University Library. For the transcript, see the Appendix. For the published text, see Woolf, Virginia. *The Complete Shorter Fiction of Virginia Woolf.* Ed. Susan Dick. London: The Hogarth Press, 1985: 241.

[23] "A Giant with Very Small Thumbs" (1927) (*E*4 416-19), "The Novels of Turgenev" (1933) (*CE*1 247-53).

[24]See one of the English translations of Turgenev's work as *Poetry in Prose: Russian Reader.* Ed. B. A. Rudzinsky. Glasgow and Edinburgh: John Menzies, London: H.S.Marshall, 1916 (?).

("Dreadfully she replied"). "They" and "we" are used without the speaker's and the addressee's perspectives being clearly defined. Such vagueness of identity reminds one of Woolf's diaries, providing a provisional background for "a wonderful compass of voices." Fifth, the image of "a ginat fountain pen filler" seems to be a trace of the writer's self-reflection that usually occurs at the initial stage of writing, and is afterwards deleted. Such are the arguments in favor of the "we shall rest" piece as the earlier draft.

The cross-cultural aspect of the sketch is revealed by relating the first and second versions. In the early piece the comparative perspective is introduced by means of someone asking oneself: "We shall rest -- we shall rest?", "And is that also true of us?", "Do we hear the tinkling bells vanish down the road also?", "<But we have not> we do not even load the pistol?" The questions of a self-critical type enhance the view in the draft of the Russians as a great "race" at disbelieving palliatives and taking death as the ultimate meaning of everything: "Dont they see through all time? [all times?] All the little barriers we have put up," "the plain pure cold water thats all thats lft [. . .]." In contrast to the first draft, the second piece (Draft 3) is foregrounded through stressing the aspect of the perception of Chekhov's play by a London female spectator. The first half of the sketch up to, "And is that also true of us? she said," is her inner monologue. The distance between the personages'—the husband's and the wife's—views, and the invisible author's is hinted at in the end by the English spectators' misunderstanding of the Russian play and their ultimate indifference towards its subject. For example, the husband's response is inadequate, or perhaps shows his feeling of superiority, in the remark, "A very depressing play" being accompanied with the epithet "smiling": "he said to her smiling." The wife's missing the whole point comes out in the final remark, "Dreadfully" [depressing] "especially [. . .] if ones not even tired." The latter comment on the key phrase in Chekhov's play (Sonya's remark beginning with the words "We shall rest" from Act 4 has been entered into all Russian dictionaries of quotations) is curtailed as the stress is laid on the physical meaning of the word "rest," whereas the connotations attributed to it by Sonya, are Christian ("rest" implying "after death"). Also in contrast to the early draft which emphasized the sense of disturbance the Russian play evokes in the English spectators, the second piece explicates the reception of the Chekhov play as depressing, morbid and alien to the English ("Its a most depressing play", "arent they morbid, the Russians?", "A very depressing play", "Dreadfully she replied").

In the final text the English and the Russian points of view are still further foregrounded, thus contributing to a balanced picture. The Russian perspective is given intertextually, through rendering the key points of the plot of Chekhov's play *Uncle Vanya*: [in the order of events] "[. . .] he tried to shoot him; he suddenly rose erect, reeled up the st<a>i[a]rs and got his pistol. He pressed the trigger. [. . .] Then a shot rang out. [. . .] now he's shot him [. . .] but the shots missed. The old villian with the dyed whiskers in the check ullster isnt hurt a bit.... 'Let it all be forgotten, dear Vanya. Let us be friends as of old,' <he's saying.> [. . .] 'We shall rest' the girl was saying now. as she clasped Uncle Vanya in her arms. [. . .] the curtain fell." The perspective of the English reception of Chekhov's play is pointed via providing the speculation and comments on it as the London woman's direct speech: " 'Dont they see through everything --- the Russians? [. . .]' she was thinking at the play. " The woman is also shown as comparing the English and the Russian points of view: " 'And is that also true of us?' she said [. . .]; 'Do we hear the bells tinkling away down the road [too]?'<">she asked, and thought of the taxis and omn<i>buses in Sloane Street [. . .]." The details of the English landscape are well sorted out. Left are only those describing civilization ("taxis and omn<i>buses"), social status ("for they lived in one of the big houses in Cadogan Square"), and loyalty to the British Monarchy ("they stood [_____]still for a moment in the gangway, while they played God Save the King"). Compare the last with the second version from which the stress on loyalty is absent: "she added following up t [ ] him up the gangway while they played [ ]od save the king and eveybody stood upright... ." Because of foregrounding and neatly chosen details, the picture described in the final text is balanced and suggestive. The English reception of Chekhov's play is given via a spectrum of opinions about the Russians: they see through to the core of things; the English love palliatives; the Russians are capable of a resolute action; the English civilized landscape is altogether different from that of peasant backward Russia. The discourse is thus worked into an interplay of two "voices," one of Chekhov's play and the other of a London female upper-middle-class spectator with reactions not uncommon to those belonging to her class. The author's point of view is emphatically impersonal, "above and beyond" the voices, to be guessed at perhaps only from a slightly critical and ironic note which refers both to the Russian and the English ways. Suggestive is the inadequacy of the Russian ability to see everything through, to act resolutely and yet have all their efforts spent in vain ("The old villain [. . .] isnt hurt a bit...."; "It came to nothing anyhow"). Equally suggestive are the details pointing at the civilized, healthy, undisturbed ways of life of the English. Impartiality of the point of view characteristic of modernist writing is achieved by Woolf, as is shown by the study of the drafts, via her working through the dramatic interplay of two "voices" or perspectives, critically evaluated and foregrounded. Thus this example of Woolf's strategy as a modernist should be related to her practice of writing in terms of a "compass of voices" which is argued for here as part of the discourse of modernity in her work.

This brings us to another important aspect of Woolf's writing on the Russian theme: its intertextuality. On the whole the first draft reads as a variation on certain key phrases or episodes in the Russian text. It is worth emphasizing that it begins with a quotation from Chekhov's play *Uncle Vanya* ("We shall rest—we shall rest?" [B10 b 3)]), which gradually grows into a motif in the piece. For example,

> Uncle <V>anya she cries, *we shall rest;* and once said, you know, just as you know that a drop once heard, another drop must fall; measured; as from a ginat fountain pen filler [. . .] (emphasis added).

Or, take another instance of intertextuality in the early draft: " *'Let [ ]e take you in my ar[ ] dear Vanya and let us embrace before we part,'* —thats all that came of it (emphasis added)." Taking a piece of translation from the Russian and building on it, or incorporating it into her own discourse is a remarkable feature of Woolf's manner. Supported by her habit of co-translating Russian texts with Koteliansky, it constitutes a substantial layer of intertextuality in her writing. This, in its turn, signals a certain amount of the nineteenth-century sub-forms in Woolf's work; for example, the above-mentioned genre of "poems in prose" created by Turgenev. Woolf's work related to the Russian theme was one of the means of enhancing the cultural and ideological background of her writing via intertextuality.

To sum up *en passage*, Woolf's writing strategy in "Uncle Vanya" is that of a critical description of the English view, against the Russian view, both foregrounded. That this strategy reads as a way to overcome a certain social stiffness by taking on other cultural voices, however distant in time or locality, seems to be a predictable development of Woolf's early intention to have "a wonderful compass of voices." Woolf's approach to the source text is set on achieving impartiality in treating different points of view, and her strategy tends to be culturally non-bracketing. Also, with her, writing includes a substantial "rewriting" input. This is the case of shaping the discourse of modernity by using the texts and genre sub-forms already existing in other languages and cultures. Also, Woolf tends to reveal essentials in the source text by focusing on the issues of being, men's and women's relationships ("[Did you read Countess Tolsyoys last diaries?]" "[Did you read how] she lay out in her nightgown on the [. . .] damp earth?"), and cognition ("Dont they see through everything --- the Russians? all the little disgu<i>s[i]es we've put up?"). With Woolf, translation and cross-cultural work is a search for a writing mode which would involve "cultural Otherness." In this respect Woolf's translation and (re)writing practices belong to modernity with its focus on developing cultural text.

What could then be the sources of Woolf's interest in Russian literature? Who could be a possible mediator for Woolf's voyaging out in the "intercultural space"?[25] Koteliansky certainly was a remarkable cultural conduit, who for several decades played a significant part in the Russian section of the Hogarth Press: out of eleven publications of translations from Russian, six were accomplished in cooperation with him.[26] But despite this fact, Koteliansky could hardly have made Woolf interested in translating Russian writers if she had had no interest of her own.

There is a strong likelihood that one of the closest English sources of her enthusiasm for Russian literature, apart from the general atmosphere of reading and commenting on Russian works,[27] was Jane Harrison, the Cambridge classical scholar. Woolf's co-translation activities and the Hogarth Press archives reveal facts connected with Jane Harrison and the Russian issue. The Hogarth Press published two works by Jane Harrison linked with Russia. One is the first English translation of *The Life of the Archpriest Avvakum by Himself* (1924), made from the seventeenth-century Russian by Jane Harrison and Hope Mirrlees.[28] The other is Jane Harrison's *Reminiscences of a Student's Life* (1925), which includes chapters devoted to her family's links with Russia, her meeting Turgenev in Cambridge, and to her own journey to St Petersburg.[29] Woolf's letters and the Hogarth Press archive papers also reveal other links between Woolf and Jane Harrison, which serve to justify this suggestion. One of the first mentions of Jane Harrison occurs in Woolf's letter to Violet Dickinson of 22 October 1904 (*L1* 145). By 1908 the figure of Jane Harrison had become firmly established in Woolf's mind as one of brilliant Cambridge scholarship (*L* 1 351). In 1919 Woolf reviewed the poem *Paris* by Hope Mirrlees, Jane Harrison's favorite student.[30] Meeting the scholar in person in Paris in July 1923, she was fascinated by "this gallant old lady, very white, hoary, and sublime

[25]Iser, Wolfgang. "On Translatability: Variables of Interpretation." *The European English Messenger*, (IV/I 1995):32:38.

[26]See in the Hogarth Press archives: 1922-1955, in the University of Reading Library, No 38 (Bunin, Ivan. *The Gentleman from San Francisco*. 1922-1951); No 72 (Dostoevsky, F. M. *Stavrogin's Confession*. 1947-1952); No 595 (Goldenveiser, A. B. *Talks with Tolstoi*. 1923-1943); No 130 (Gorky, Maxim. *Reminiscences*. 1928-1953); No 483 (Chekhov, Anton. *Notebooks*. 1944-1948); No 493 (Tolstoi, L. N. *Tolstoi's Love Letters*. 1923).

[27]Woolf first read *Le Crime et le Châtiment* by Dostoevsky in September 1912 upon Lytton Strachey's advice. See her letter to him of 1 September 1912 (*L2* 5).

[28]*The Life of the Archpriest Avvakum by Himself*. Trans. Jane Harrison and Hope Mirrlees. London: The Hogarth Press, 1924; repr. 1963. See No 7 *Avvakum Life of Archpriest* in the Hogarth Press archives.

[29]Harrison, Jane. *Reminiscences of a Student's Life*. London: The Hogarth Press, 1925: 44, 125-126.

[30]See Mirrlees, Hope. *Paris*. The Hogarth Press archives: 1922-1955, No 282.

in a lace mantilla [. . .], partly for her superb high thinking agnostic ways, partly for her appearance," as she wrote to Jacques Raverat in the letter of 30 July 1923 (*L3* 58-9). It is no accident that Woolf twice referred to Jane Harrison in *A Room of One's Own*,[31] for in her she saw embodied a woman's new life-style, something exceptionally challenging—the English woman scholar, an agnostic who shared with her knowledgeable student not only a joint literary project but also a lodging. There can even be proposed the hypothesis that the two Cambridge papers Virginia Woolf was going to read in spring 1928 (Rosenbaum xv), but which were postponed till 20 and 25 October 1928,[32] were written and delivered with an eye to paying tribute to Jane Harrison, who had died on 15 April 1928. Perhaps Woolf felt that she owed something to Harrison, who had exclaimed upon their meeting in Paris in 1923: "Alas [. . .] you and your sister and perhaps Lytton Strachey are the only ones of the younger generation I can respect. You alone carry on the traditions of our day" (*L3* 58). At any rate, such an intention would have been in accord with the essay speaker's statement that "we think back through our mothers if we are women" (*AROO* 114), however little we can trust Woolf's speakers. What the Hogarth Press archive materials make clear is that Jane Harrison had cherished a long-term interest in Russian culture as the inheritor of Greek cultural and religious roots; her Russian contacts included Dmitrii Mirsky and the Remizovs.[33] Herself a Cambridge scholar, she constituted one of the figures in English university life of the time who propagated and developed scholarly and cultural links with Russia. It was her choice that the preface to the translation of *The Life of the Archpriest Avvakum* was written by D. S. Mirsky,[34] who also contributed a list of English subscribers to the trans-

---

[31]Cf. "[. . .] could it be the famous scholar, could it be J—H—herself?" (AROO 26); "There are Jane Harrison's books on Greek archaeology [. . .]." (119) See S. P. Rosenbaum's comment on these instances of Woolf's evoking the memory of "the famous scholar" as "anachronistic fantasy" (xxiv).

[32]See the unpublished letter of Virginia Woolf of 3rd August 1928 to Miss Phare which is kept in the family archive of Miss Katherine Duncan-Jones, who kindly permitted the author's quoting it: "Dear Miss Phare, Saturday October 20th will suit me for coming to Newnham, and I will keep that date free unless I hear from you to the contrary."

[33]See Hope Mirrlees's p/c to Leonard Woolf of 15 September 1924 in No 7 Avvakum in the Hogarth Press archives.

[34]See Hope Mirrlees's letter to Leonard Woolf of 8 August 1924: "We have a definite promise of an introduction by Prince Mirsky. He has not stated the length, but hopes to let us have it in the course of a week. [. . .] Prince Mirsky is going over the Ms with us at Pontigny" (No 7 Avvakum in the Hogarth Press archives). Also, see D. S. Mirsky's letter to Leonard Woolf of 3 October 1924, and Jane Harrison's letter of 10 December 1924 to Leonard Woolf (No 7 Avvakum in the Hogarth Press archives).

lation, which includes a few English university scholars of merit.[35] And it was she who in 1915 read a paper on *Russia and the Russian Verb: A Contribution to the Psychology of the Russian People* at the Heretics in Cambridge. All these facts show that Jane Harrison, with her great scholarly enthusiasm for the Russian language, history and culture, could hardly fail to inspire Woolf with an interest in Russian literature, their being connected by so many family, university and professional links. It certainly needed some such figure (a weightier one than Koteliansky) to imbue Woolf with an interest in Russian material. An indirect proof towards this is found in her above quoted letter to Koteliansky of March 1921. There she mentions the "aspects" which "seem to [her] very interesting" (*L2* 459). The aspects of the Russian verb were discussed at length by Jane Harrison in her *Russia and the Russian Verb*. There she remarked:

> The singular, the characteristic trait of the Russian language is, not that it has a perfective [aspect]—we all have that—but that it clings to the imperfective, at all costs, even at the cost of having laboriously to create a new form. [. . .] perfectiveness leaves, for the Russian, an aching void, and instinctively he fills it by a new and tougher suffix, [. . .] which is indomitably imperfective. The Russian hungers for durée. (Harrison 10)

The parallel between Woolf's interest in the "aspects" and Harrison's original paper on the aspects of the Russian verb is, of course, of a secondary kind. It nevertheless points at Woolf taking after Harrison as a sort of expert on Russian matters. What also holds true is that Woolf's many-faceted work with Russian literature, supported by the Hogarth Press publications of the English translations of Russian works, served to further develop the English-Russian university tradition, which goes back to Victorian times. As such, it formed a part of Woolf's diverse work as an essayist and critic who, among others, shaped the English critical discourse of modernity.

Put in a broader cultural perspective, the study of Woolf's strategy of writing associated with Russian fiction makes it clear that whatever experience of Russian literature Woolf had as reader, critic or translator, she was using it to fill up what to her seemed to be a vacuum in contemporary English writing (*CE*2 122). It was "a wonderful compass of voices" which she could not find in her own literature but which she did discover, first in Dostoevsky and later in Turgenev, and used in her own way and for her own purposes in her novels. Being open-minded about "cultural Otherness" and flexible about rewriting foreign texts (both features belonging to the culture of modernity), she,

---

[35]See the list of subscribers in Mirsky's hand attached to his letter of 3 October 1924 (No 7 *Avvakum* in the Hogarth Press archives).

nevertheless, tried these things only with the aim of stretching the possibilities of English prose still further. It is here that Woolf found herself to be a "voyager out." Russian literature constituted a challenging stimulus to her creative search.

Allusions to the Russians occur in many of Woolf's novels. These concern literary, cultural and social issues raised by Tolstoy, Dostoevsky, Chekhov and other Russian writers. As such they were part of the culture of the 1910-20s, being as much socio-cultural markers as "the Russian ballet."[36] There are at least two ways of approaching Russian allusions in Woolf's early work. (For lack of space here is given a brief outline of what, we argue, is a significant aspect of her novelistic discourse.) One is placing them in terms of concrete source texts and interpreting them as inclusions in the target texts. The other is identifying those aspects of Woolf's writing techniques which could be treated as parallel to the Russian writers' strategies. On the level of inclusions indirect allusions to Pierre Bezukhov and to Gogol's "Shinel" [The Overcoat] occur in *Melymbrosia*.[37] There are comments on Dostoevsky's *The Idiot* and Tolstoy's *War and Peace* as well as extensive intertextual inclusions from Tolstoy's social works in the final text of *Night and Day*.[38] Also, direct and indirect references to Chekhov are found in *Jacob's Room* (*JR* 230, 235).[39] On the level of writing technique there

[36]See Haller, Evelyn. "Her Quill Drawn from the Firebird: Virginia Woolf and the Russian Dancers," in Gillespie, Diane F., ed. *The Multiple Muses of Virginia Woolf.* Columbia: University of Missouri Press, 1993:180-226.

[37]There are certain hints in the description of Terence Hewet's appearance which show that his character may be built on Pierre Bezukhov (*MEL* 78-79). Hewet's imaginary novel, which he describes to Rachel, may have been prompted by Gogol's famous story "Shinel," with the reservation that Hewet's fictitious novel is absolutely English and comic (*MEL* 153).

[38]Russian literary allusions in *Night and Day* include direct references to Dostoevsky and Tolstoy (*ND* 323). There are also some implications in the novel pointing at Tolstoy's ideas of truth and societal falsity standing behind Katharine's speculations on marriage and family relations (*ND* 196-99). These ideas form the background to the new relations, devoid of straightforward jealousy and aggressiveness, between the two women, Mary and Katharine (*ND* 257). Another group of allusions deals with the socio-political issues of democracy, equality and education, as well as political activities involving conspiracy, all of which at that time may well have a Russian background to them or, at least, certain associations (*ND* 331-32).

[39]There is also found an intertextual allusion to Chekhov in the following observation: "It's not catastrophes, murders, deaths, diseases, that age and kill us; it's the way people look and laugh, and run up the steps of omnibuses" (*JR* 133). Cf. "People are having dinner, just having dinner, but at this very moment it is their happiness that is at stake and their life that is getting broken" (Ars 521; my trans.). The final scenes of the novel contain clichés of Russian (mainly Tolstoy's) ideas about love and the soul put into the mouth of Sandra Wentworth Williams (*JR* 230-31).

are deducible certain aspects of Woolf's discourse which could run parallel to what she found in Russian fiction. For example, the abrupt opening in *Jacob's Room* may be owed to Woolf's reading of Tolstoy's *War and Peace*[40] or Chekhov's stories.[41] The fragmentariness of its discourse and the explication of the view that you cannot get a whole picture, only separate details of it, though being a technical modernist device, may well correspond to Woolf's ambition to get the essence of being onto the pages of her writing, which she found so satisfactorily supported by Gorky's "Recollections of Leo Tolstoy." Also, the submerging of links between episodes in *Jacob's Room*, which makes Woolf's writing non-transparent and tense, correlates with her above mentioned essay "More Dostoevsky" with its call for new "tunes" in fiction (*BP* 119).

These are mostly found in Woolf's later work. One of the striking cases is the ambivalent treatment of a Russian theme in *Orlando* (1928). The protagonist's "I" there is shown as split up between romantic "ideal" love for a "young, slender, seductive" girl Sasha (*O* 303), and her shock at finding Sasha grown into a "fat," "lethargic" "apparition of a grey woman in fur" "who, leaning over the banks of the Volga, eating sandwiches, had watched men drown." (303) As if predicting *A Room of One's Own*, a split of consciousness is described in *Orlando* in terms of a modernist critical view of culture. For centuries the position of women had been ambiguous: portrayed as angels, they had existed under conditions of material and social inequality and suppression. Hence the monsters or *Doppelgängers* in a woman's guilty subconscious. That this cultural-historical comment is directly referred to the Russian character is, in our view, particularly interesting. No doubt Woolf's modernist view of culture was influenced by her "Russian voyage out." No doubt her experience of Russian literature came under her critical analysis as a writer of modernity.

Woolf took as much from reading, commenting on and translating Russian texts as was needed for her writing. Her distancing herself from Russian literature after a certain period of time was in this respect predictable.

The latter tendency in her work took the upper hand by the end of the 1920s. The change, or rather the choice, manifested itself, among other things, in the priority given in 1933 to Turgenev, whom earlier, in 1920, she had called "the least great of the Russian trinity" in the essay "English Prose" (*BP* 126). Now Woolf found Turgenev to be of those rare artists who managed to combine European and Russian cultural identities, civilization and freedom, spontaneity and imper-

---

[40]Cf. the opening scene of *War and Peace*. Starting with *Jacob's Room*, Woolf would stick to the abrupt beginning, followed in *Mrs. Dalloway* and *To the Lighthouse*.

[41]See the positive evaluation of Chekhov's seemingly illogical composition in the essay "The Russian Background" (*BP* 123).

sonality of writing: "[. . .] his novels are still so much of our own time; no hot and personal emotion has made them local and transitory; [. . .] because he chose to write with the most fundamental part of his being as a writer; nor, for all his irony and aloofness, do we ever doubt the depth of his feeling" (*CE*1 253).

The main reason for Woolf's reconsidering her views of Russia at the end of the 1920s may have been a social-political one,[42] but there were also more concrete motives for her revaluation of Russian fiction. Additional biographical evidence about Leo Tolstoy and Fyodor Dostoevsky published in English in the 1920s enabled Woolf to form a more balanced judgment of the Russian writers; for instance, Tolstoy's attitude to women's issues. That there was a certain uniformity of thinking behind Virginia and Leonard Woolf's critical evaluations of Tolstoy's treatment of his wife becomes explicit when Woolf's early draft of "Uncle Vanya" is matched with Leonard Woolf's article "A Fly Is Struggling in the Web," in which he presented *The Diary of Tolstoy's Wife, 1860-1891*, and *The Diary of Dostoevsky's Wife* to English readers.[43] Knowing Virginia Woolf's habit "to interpret the opinions of great men not only by what they say, but by what they do" (*AROO* 81), we can measure the degree of her critical judgment of Tolstoy's and Dostoevsky's views of women.

To sum up, this critical survey of Woolf's Russian texts has revealed two tendencies: one of transcending the boundaries of English literature to experience "cultural Otherness," and the other of combining her searching as a modern writer with the English literary tradition. Certainly, this "voyaging out" and "coming back home" metaphor does not exhaust the Russian chapter of Woolf's work. It has served the purpose of this article—to give the reader a clear view of the ways Woolf's "Russian lessons" matter. This done, further research is timely and indispensable, to explore the field in all its richness and diversity.

[42]Post-revolutionary terror, exiles and impending repression; see Woolf's observation made during her meeting with Prince Mirsky before his leaving for Soviet Russia in 1932, which turned out to be prophetic: "Mirsky [. . .] [has] been in England, in boarding houses for 12 years; now returns to Russia 'for ever.' I thought as I watched his eye brighten & fade–soon there'll be a bullet through your head" (*D*4 112). Upon his return to the USSR Mirsky was arrested in 1937 and put in the gulag where he died early in June 1939. See Biryukov, Alexandr. *Poslednii Ryurikovich*. Magadan, 1991:47-61. Quoted from Mirsky, D. S. *Stikhotvoreniia; Statii o Russkoi Poezii*. Compiled and ed. G. K. Perkins and G. S. Smith; with an Introduction, G. S. Smith. Oakland, California: Berkeley Slavic Specialties, 1997:14.

[43]Cf. the above quoted passage from the early draft of "Uncle Vanya": "[Did you read Countess Tolsyoys last diaries?] <It reminds me of the> [Did you read how] she lay out in her nightgown on the [. . .] damp earth," and the following extract from Leonard Woolf's article which reads as an extension or illustration of the above reference:

Appendix

Virginia Woolf's spelling, punctuation and typewriting are reproduced as they are in the typescript drafts. The line arrangement and paragraphing, though not the page division, are also followed. When too big for the width of the page, the lines are indented. Woolf's insertions above, below or within lines are represented by being enclosed in angle brackets. The insertions usually appear after the cancellations that they replace. Pencil notes are enclosed in braces.

The following conventions are used in the transcription:
<example> = insertion
<example?> = uncertain insertion
[_____] = illegible cancellation
<example [example]> = cancellation within insertion
[ ] = a letter missing
{example} = pencil note in the margins
{example?}= uncertain pencil note

"It is clearly a terrible thing to marry [. . .] a great Russian novelist. On January 19th, 1891, when Sophie Andreevna Tolstoy was in her forty-seventh year and had been married to Tolstoy for nearly thirty years, she sat down one evening to write her diary, and this is what she wrote:—

'I am still ill—my stomach and feverish condition are the same. As if in a dream, I taught the children music for two hours, and corrected the long proof of 'The Kreutzer Sonata.' It amazes me how much good work I can do. Only it's a pity that I never had an opportunity of applying my abilities to something higher and worthier than mere mechanical labour [. . .].

There is such an obvious thread connecting the early diaries with 'The Kreutzer Sonata': and a buzzing fly is struggling in the web–and the spider had sucked its blood [. . .].'

'A buzzing fly is struggling in the web,' describes the wife of Dostoevsky as well as the wife of Tolstoy. Their fate was the same; only the social class from which they came and their characters were different, and so while the spider sucked the blood of the jealous countess, the naïve typist escaped." Woolf, Leonard. "A Fly Is Struggling in the Web." The *Nation and Athenaeum* (November 1928): 294.

B.10 b)   UNFINISHED DRAFTS OF STORIES OR SKETCHES:
Uncle Vanya. 2 Ts drafts, corrected by VW, 6 pp.

1 Ts draft

Uncle Vanya
"Dont they see through everything --- the Russians?
all the little disgu<i>s[i]es we've put up? Flowers against
decay; gold and velvet against poverty; the cherry
trees, the apple trees -- they see through them too, "
[_____] she was thinking at the play. Then a shot rang
out.
    "There! now he's shot him. Thats a mercy. Oh but
the shots missed. The old villian with the dyed whis
kers in the check ullster isnt hurt a bit.... Still
he tried to shoot him; he suddenly rose erect, reeled
up the st<a>i[a]rs and got his pistol. He pressed the
trigger. The ball lodged in the wall; perhaps in the
table leg. It came to nothing anyhow. "Let it all be
forgotten, dear Vanya. Let us be friends as of old," <he's saying.>
....Now theyve gone. Now we hear the bells of the
horses tinkling away in the distance. And is that
also true of us?" she said, leaning her chin on her
hand and looking at the girl on the stage. "Do we
hear the bells tinkling away down the road [too]?<">
she asked, and thought of the taxis and omn<i>buses in
Sloane street, for they lived in one of the big
houses in Cadogan square.
    "We shall rest" the girl was saying now.
as she clasped Uncle Vanya in her arms. "We shall
rest" she said again. Her words were like drops
falling -- one drop, the<n> another drp. "We shall rest
she said again. "We shall rest Uncle Vanya."
And the curtain fell.
"As for us" she said, as her husband helped her on
with her cloak, "We've not <even> loaded the pistol.
We're not <even> tired"
    And they stood [_____] still for a moment in the
gangway, while they played God Save the King.
"Arent the <R>ussians morbid?" she said, taking his arm.

Uncle Vanya.   B 10 b 3)

We shall rest -- we shall rest? Is [it going to end on
that note]? Is that the message of the play? The
Russians are a most disconcerting race, <t>he Russians
of Tchekovs time. [Is it Tchekoves time?] Is it not all
time? Dont they see through all time? [all times?]
All the little barriers we have put up. <F>lowers against
decay; gold and velvet against poverty. The chirping
branches of the cherry tree; of the apple tree.
even them, nature given, and thus so valid, so
solid, they see through too. [Wordsworths lakes; they
see through too; and the glories of the east.]
Uncle <V>anya she cries, we shall rest; and once said,
you know, just as you know that a drop once heard,
another drop must fall; measured; as from a ginat
fountain pen filler; another drop of desprair; dis
tilled; the plain pure cold water thats all that
s lft of crushed fllwers; gold and velvet; cheery tree
and apple trees ground to powder. <We shall rest.>
          [We shall rest, Uncle vanya.] The pistol went
off its true. He tried to shoot the old villain with
the dyed whiskers in the check ulster. He suddenly
[solidified]<rou?> from the curly vapours of indiff[ ]erence,
indolence. <?> He pressed the trigger. And the ball
lodged perhaps in the parr[ ]ts cage; pe[ ]haps in the
table leg. <all he?> "Let [ ]e take you in my ar[ ] dear Vanya
and let us embrace before we part, -- thats all that
came of it. Let We shall rest Uncle [ ]anya
And is that also true of us? she asked, leqning her
chin on her hand, looking at the girl on the stage who
has now clasped Uncle <V>anya in her arms. and they
hear the bells of the horses tinkle away in the
distance. Do we hear the tinkling bells vanish down
the road also? she thought. [A r are we worse off
even than they are]<We who live in Cadogan Square.>....We shall rest shes
saying to
the Uncle. Shes on her knees now.
[Because] <But we have not> we do not even load the pistol? No; as we hear
the tinkling bells vanish, I shall turn to my husband.
and say, <">How morbid the Russians are?<">

[Did you read Countess Tolsyoys last diaries?] <It reminds me of the>
[Did you read how] she lay out in her nightgown on the <She fired a toy pistol
        And he went away.>
damp earth?<And he> She fired a pistol she thought, and he too, when he stole
away. <But> Even if the shot
lodged only in the table legs, both <they> of them loaded
a pistol and fired. Whereas we,
<">We shall rest, <Uncle?> we shall rest" [she said]. And here the
curtain came down.
"A depressing play he said handing her her coat.
"Dreadfully she replied. [As for] <Especially [for that]> us she added turning
to go, [we're not] <who aren't> <if we? not> even tired.

Draft 3

Its a most depressing play --- arent they morbid, the
Russians? Dont they seem to see through everything --
all the little disgusises weve put up? Flowers against
decay; gold and velevt against poverty. the chirping
branches of the apple trees of the cherry trees ---
even them, nature given, and thus, one would hope,
so enduring, and protective; they see through too.
 There! hes shot him! That a mercy. Oh but the shot
missed. The old villain with the dyed whiskers in the
check ulster isnt hurt a bit... Still he tried to
shoot him --- he suddenly rose erect and reeled up the
stairs and got his pistol. He pressed the trigger.
The ball lodged perhaps in the parrots cage; perhaps
in the table leg. It came to nothing either. "[ ]et it
all be forgotten, my dear Vanya;;; Let us be freinds
as of old..." Now theyve gone. Now we hear the bells
of the jorses tinkle away in the diatnce. And is
that also true of us? she said, leaning her chin on
her hand and looking at the girl on the stage who had
now clasped Uncle vanya in her arms.   {tinkling}
Do w[ ] hear the tinkling bells vanish down the road
too she thought; and thought of ambulances in Sloane
street; for they lived in Cadogan <s>quare.
We shall rest she was saying to uncle vanya as she
clasped his arms. Just as one knows that a drop

once falled means another drop; another drop from a
measured glass; distilled; full of despair;
a durop of the pure cold water thats crushed from
from flowers; flowers, velvet and gold, cheery trees
and apple trees --- we shall rest she said again.
Now shes on her knnees.
[But] as for us, we have not even loaded the pistol...
        We [shall rest she says again.]
        Turning to her husband, she said,
        [Arent <But> the [ ]ussians morbid?]
        It [reminds me] of the Tolstoys. She fired a   toy
pistol, to try and kill herself. And he drove away.
["Very morbid"] he answered her still looking at the
stage.
"We shall rest --- shall rest" the girl said again.
And here the curtain came down.
{Not a?} "A very depressing play" he said to her smiling, as
he handed her her coat.
"Dreadfully she replied. especially she added
following up t[ ] him up the gangway while they played
[ ]od save the king and eveybody stood upright, if ones
not even tired.

*The author's great thanks go to the Special Collections of the University of Sussex
Library, and the Society of Authors as the Literary Representative of the Estate of Virginia
Woolf for their kind permission to publish a full transcription of the typescript draft of
Virginia Woolf's "Uncle Vanya" (Monk's House Papers B.10 b).

Works Cited

Ars, G. "Iz Vospominanii o Chekhove." [From my recollections of Chekhov]
    Teatr i Iskusstvo [Theatre and arts] (1904: 28):521.
Belinskii, V. G. "Vzgliad na Russkuiu Literaturu 1847 goda." [A glance at the
    Russian literature of 1847] *Izbrannye Aesteticheskie Raboty* [Selected works
    on aesthetics]. Ed. N. K. Gey. 2 vols. Moscow: Iskusstvo, 1986, 2:322-409.
Chernyshevskii, N. G. "Ocherki Gogolevskogo Perioda Russkoi Literatury:
    Statia Vos'maia." [The essays of the Gogol's period in Russian literature:
    Eighth article] *Izbrannye Proizvedeniia* [Selected Works]. Minsk, 1954:117-
    405.

Gillespie, Diane F., ed. *The Multiple Muses of Virginia Woolf.* Columbia: U of Missouri P, 1993.

Harrison, Jane Ellen. *Russia and the Russian Verb: A Contribution to the Psychology of the Russian People.* Cambridge: W. Heffer and Sons, 1915.

Kirkpatrick, B. J. *A Bibliography of Virginia Woolf.* Rev. ed. London: Rupert Hart-Davis, 1967.

Mirrlees, Hope. Letter to Leonard Woolf of 8 August 1924. No 7 *Avvakum.* The Hogarth Press archive of the University of Reading Library.

Rosenbaum, S. P. , ed. *Women and Fiction. The Manuscript Versions of* A Room of One's Own. By Virginia Woolf. Oxford: Blackwell Publishers, 1992.

Woolf, Virginia. *Books and Portraits.* Ed. Mary Lyons. London: The Hogarth Press, 1977.

——. *Collected Essays.* Ed. Leonard Woolf. 4 vols. London: The Hogarth Press, 1966-67.

——. *The Diary of Virginia Woolf.* Ed. Anne Olivier Bell. Introd. Quentin Bell. 5 vols. London: The Hogarth Press, 1977-1984.

——. *The Essays.* Ed. Andrew McNeillie. 6 vols. London: The Hogarth Press, 1986 -.

——. *Granite and Rainbow: Essays.* London: The Hogarth Press, 1958.

——. *Jacob's Room.* London: The Hogarth Press, 1935.

——. *The Letters of Virginia Woolf.* Eds. Nigel Nicolson and Joanne Trautmann. 6 vols. London: The Hogarth Press, 1975-1980.

——. *Melymbrosia.* An Early Version of *The Voyage Out.* Ed. with an Introduction by Louise A. DeSalvo, scholar's edition. New York: Public Library, Astor, Lenox and Tilden Foundations, 1982.

——. *Night and Day.* Harmondsworth: Penguin Books in Association with the Hogarth Press, 1974.

——. *Orlando: A Biography.* New York: Harcourt, Brace and Company, 1929.

——. *A Passionate Apprentice: The Early Journals, 1897-1909.* Ed. Mitchell A. Leaska. London: The Hogarth Press, 1990.

——. *Roger Fry. A Biography.* London: The Hogarth Press, 1940.

—— *A Room of One's Own.* London: The Hogarth Press, 1929.

——. "Uncle Vanya." B.10 b) Unfinished drafts of stories or sketches: "Uncle Vanya." 2 typescript drafts, corrected by Virginia Woolf, 6 pp. in the Manuscript Department of the Sussex University Library.

——. *The Virginia Woolf Manuscripts from The Henry W. and Albert A. Berg Collection at the New York Public Library,* research publications, 1993. Manuscripts, Reel 6, M15 - M26.

Zytaruk, George J. *D. H. Lawrence's Response to Russian Literature.* Mouton: The Hague-Paris, 1971.

——, ed. *The Quest for Rananim: D. H. Lawrence's Letters to S. S. Koteliansky, 1914-1930.* Montreal and London: McGill-Queen's University Press, 1970.

Three Guineas, Two Exhibits: Woolf's Politics of Display

Amy M. Lilly

In a recent article on Virginia Woolf's participation in anti-fascist activities, David Bradshaw notes that, "by the beginning of 1935 Woolf had become involved in the arrangements for an anti-fascist exhibition and at the end of February 1935 she confessed [in her diary] to being 'plagued by a sudden wish to write an Anti-fascist Pamphlet,'" (Bradshaw I, 6). The Anti-Fascist Pamphlet eventually turned into *Three Guineas*; the anti-fascist exhibition was the "Cambridge Exhibition on Fascism and War," conceived and mounted by the Cambridge Anti-War Council. Though Bradshaw probably did not mean to imply a causal connection between Woolf's involvement in the exhibition and the writing of her polemic, his comment nevertheless raises the question of what Woolf gained from her experience with this exhibition, and how it might pertain to her 1938 work.

Woolf's anti-fascist pamphlet plays with modes of exhibition in several ways: it poses as a pamphlet accompanying the exhibition of English patriarchal society, whose penchant for self-display is exploited to the full in the original text with the inclusion of five photographs of figures of patriarchy exhibiting the uniforms, decorations and plumes that signify their power. Its narrative guise of epistolary correspondent, responding to letters by analyzing their contents and implications and drawing connections between them and other objects on display, is also the narrative analogue for the guide at an exhibition, shaping a viewer's response to a certain series and arrangement of images—a voice that reads very similarly to the one Woolf used in her catalogue forewords to Vanessa Bell's 1930 and 1934 exhibitions. If there is an exhibition guide to *Three Guineas*, however, there is also a behind-the-scenes exhibition organizer, who emerges in the gap between the photographs reproduced in the text and photographs merely described during the narration. The fictional narrator repeatedly bids "you" (that is, not just the man and two women to whose letters she responds, but we the readers of the polemic) to examine with her the Spanish Civil War photographs of "dead bodies and ruined houses" which are "all this time piling up on the table" (74) of the fictional exhibit, yet she never alludes to the existence of actual photographs (those of British men in power) in the book. Only that latter part of "you," the readers of the meta-text *Three Guineas*, is able to see the actual photographs included in the text, which Woolf the silent exhibition organizer places strategically throughout—without ever acknowledging that those photographs of "dead bodies and ruined houses" so often referred to in the text are nowhere represented. This is a work, in other words, in which the fictional narrator-guide and the actual author, present as exhibit organizer, both make their appearances, while remaining distinct from each other. It is a gap that draws attention to itself, and therefore to the text *as* an exhibition, by deliberately eschewing and subverting our expectations as viewers.

For all this, the Cambridge exhibition and Woolf's level of engagement in it receive short shrift in as recent a study as Nigel Nicolson's biography for the Penguin Lives series (2000), in which he writes, "To please Leonard, she canvassed support for an anti-Fascist exhibition, probably unaware that it was Communist-inspired" (Nicolson 144). Less apt to take Woolf's own dismissive comments about her involvement in political activities to heart, Hermione Lee has argued that the Cambridge exhibition was a political enterprise in which Woolf took especial interest, closely questioning one of the exhibition's organizers, Princess Elizabeth Bibesco, on why feminism would be out of place in such an exhibit,[1] contributing her own money to help fund it, and writing rather unsuccessfully to friends for additional financial support, including Clive Bell and Robert Trevelyan. Both refused, objecting to the project's unacknowledged Communist agenda and backing (Lee 673-4).

Beyond this biographical account of her involvement, however, little discussion of the exhibition exists. Having located the catalogue to the exhibition, a small text-only pamphlet of seven pages entitled "Explanation,"[2] I would like to

[1]The letter Bibesco wrote in response (dated 1 January 1935), which I address below, is one of the items Woolf pasted into her scrapbooks for *Three Guineas*. These scrapbooks are housed in the University of Sussex manuscript collection (Monks House Papers B.16f., Vols. 1, 2, and 3); catalogued in Brenda Silver, *Virginia Woolf's Reading Notebooks* (Princeton, NJ: Princeton UP, 1983), pp. 255-314; and can now be viewed online in complete digital facsimile, due to the efforts of Merry Pawlowski and Vara Neverow, at <http://www.csub.edu/woolf_center>.

[2]A copy can be found in the British Library under "Cambridge: Miscellaneous Institutions and Societies," a collection of papers and pamphlets issued by the Cambridge Anti-War Council, all of which I mention here. There are four: "What Is the Cambridge Anti-War Council?" (1933); "Cambridge Anti-War Exhibition," a pamphlet which includes a page on "special private view" and an "Explanation" (1933); a folding advance-advertising pamphlet entitled "A Cambridge Exhibition on Fascism and War, To Be Organized by the Cambridge Anti-War Council" (1935); "Cambridge Exhibition: Fascism and War," a pamphlet which includes a page on "special private view" and an "Explanation" (1935). I would like to thank Anthea Butler for her crucial help in finding these documents, the British Library for permission to quote from their catalogue, and the University of Iowa for awarding me the Stanley Fellowship and the T. Anne Cleary International Dissertation Research Fellowship to complete this research.

flesh out the significance of this exhibit for her polemic, closely reading that 1935 text against what Woolf refers to as her own "pamphlet." In what follows, I argue that the form Woolf's polemic takes, its marshaling of "evidence" in the shape of a collage of documents and visual images, specifically engages with, and challenges, the Cambridge exhibit's material displays as well as its ideological underpinnings. In addition, I examine the polemic in light of the Cambridge exhibit's relation to a neighboring anti-fascist exhibit dedicated to the arts, suggesting that Woolf's knowledge of both exhibits may have contributed to *Three Guineas*' deliberate slippage between visual media—paintings and photographs, sketches and newspaper excerpts. Calling attention to this aspect of the work, I argue that it demonstrates Woolf's awareness of the manipulations and limitations inhering in the exhibition venue, whether it frames its contents as "art" or as "fact," and the processes by which each category of exhibit shapes and scripts viewer response.

Emily Dalgarno's *Virginia Woolf and the Visible World*, a recent study of Woolf's work in relation to visual media through a cultural studies lens similar to mine, offers a particularly thorough examination of the photographs in *Three Guineas* in the context of press photography during the Spanish Civil War. Yet this focus, I believe, places an artificial limit on the visible world within the polemic, which encompasses not only press trends and photography but, equally, references to painting and sketching.[3] Jane Goldman's *The Feminist Aesthetics of Virginia Woolf* does consider the extent of Woolf's investment in, and responses to, a range of exhibitions, but her focus is entirely devoted to art; the Cambridge exhibit is left out of consideration, no doubt for reasons, discussed further below, of its categorization apart from "art." Woolf's polemic is particularly attentive not just to all forms of visual media but to their modes of

[3]Dalgarno's focus on the photographs is among a number of studies on Woolf's attitudes toward photography: see also Julia Duffy and Lloyd Davis, "Demythologizing Facts and Photographs in *Three Guineas*," a Kristevan reading of the photographs' function as miming patriarchal "factual" discourse in order to undermine it; and Diane F. Gillespie's "'Her Kodak Pointed at His Head': Virginia Woolf and Photography" for a comprehensive survey of photographic instances and mentions in Woolf's diaries, letters, and fiction. Like Duffy and Lloyd, Gillespie also analyzes the use of photography in *Three Guineas* as Woolf's appropriation of a patriarchal, objectifying medium in order to objectify the patriarchy itself. Both of these articles make points related to my reading—Duffy and Davis argue that the "truth value" of photographs is culturally determined rather than absolute (134), Gillespie that Woolf "seems to have recognized," at least early on during her own experiments with amateur photography, the possibilities for aesthetic form in the photographic medium (115)—but ultimately these analyses, like Dalgarno's, privilege photography and Woolf's use of it as an isolatable and distinct phenomenon, a focus I attempt to rework here by noting the slippages of medium in Woolf's polemic.

display, to the extent that her argument hinges on ways of seeing.[4] This is not surprising, given her interest in the relationship between the literary and visual arts, as elaborated in Diane Filby Gillespie's *The Sisters' Arts*, as well as her considerable exhibition-goings and commentaries during the thirties.[5] Drawing on a cluster of seminal theoretical texts in the field of museum and exhibition studies, I argue that Woolf's own exhibition of visual media that is *Three Guineas* constitutes an integral strategy of its argument, one that reveals the political investments inhering in the exhibition form in order to expose the politics at work in English patriarchal society.

The exhibit to which Woolf lent her aid, the "Cambridge Exhibition on Fascism and War," was launched first in Cambridge at the University's St. Andrew's Hall, November 4-9, 1935, by the Cambridge Anti-War Council, and then moved within the week to London, where it ran from November 13-17, 1935 at 27 Soho Square.[6] The exhibit had a documentary and informative aim,

---

[4]I use this phrase with reference to Svetlana Alpers's article "The Museum as a Way of Seeing," the opening essay of one of museum studies' recent pivotal texts, *Exhibiting Cultures*. Alpers argues that "everything in a museum is put under the pressure of a way of seeing" which renders all museum contents objects of art offered up for attentive looking, whether their creators intended that or not (30). Woolf is intensely interested in this way of seeing—what Alpers calls the museum effect—both demonstrating how far it can be expanded and questioning the kind of viewer it elicits.

[5]Gillespie's book explores the "raidings" Woolf regularly made on Vanessa Bell's medium, and Woolf's growing recognition of the similar challenges each sister faced in her medium. As a sampling of Woolf's exhibition-related activities in the 1930s, Woolf wrote the catalogue forewords to her sister's 1930 and 1934 exhibitions; she wrote the address for a memorial exhibition of Roger Fry's paintings in 1935 (she was working on her biography of Fry and *Three Guineas* simultaneously); she attended an exhibit of Walter Sickert's paintings in November 1934, which led her to write "Walter Sickert: A Conversation," also published with variations as "A conversation About Art"; and in the same month she attended a private showing of Man Ray's photographs, as a guest of poster artist McKnight-Kauffer, whose role in the Cambridge exhibits is detailed further on.

[6]The "Explanation" pamphlet I refer to in this essay was written for the exhibit that took place in Cambridge. I have not been able to get hold of a copy of a sister one written for the London exhibit. Therefore I am surmising that the London exhibition Woolf writes about, apparently a project of the Cambridge Anti-War Council, and the Cambridge exhibition described in the "Explanation," definitely a project of the Cambridge Anti-War Council, are the same. Woolf herself never connects her exhibit with the Cambridge Anti-War Council; Quentin Bell's biography of Woolf (II, p.187) seems to be the source for that. Bradshaw cites an advertisement for an exhibition, reproduced in Radford and Morris' book on the Artists' International Association, and identifies it as the one Woolf

chronicling the origins and history of fascism using "historic" photographs, documents, newspaper clippings, and sketches. The exhibit's "Explanation" pamphlet provides a summary of the information covered in each of the exhibit's eight sections, which were titled: (1) Italy: Fascist Origins; (2) Italy: Fascism a State Power; (3) Germany: Fascism Comes to Power; (4) Germany: Fascism in Power; (5) Semi-Fascism: Austria and Spain; (6) Embryo-Fascism: Can Fascism

---

talks about in her diaries and letters. The advertisement, apparently issued by the AIA, reads, "Cambridge Anti-Fascist Exhibition: While the [AIA] 1935 Exhibition is open, a further exhibition will be on view at 27, Soho Square (adjoining). This will be an exhibition of documentary evidence, photographs, charts etc. showing the growth, the rise to power and the fight against Fascism. (Lectures will be given every Monday, Wednesday and Friday at 3 p.m.)." It is Bradshaw who specifies the dates of this exhibit, 13-27 Nov. 1935. If we accept that the London exhibit Woolf writes about is indeed a project of the Cambridge Anti-War council, then it seems reasonable to infer that Woolf's exhibit is the London showing of the Cambridge exhibit described in the "Explanation." The same organization could not have come up with a completely new "anti-Fascist exhibition" that differed substantially from the one described in the catalogue for the Cambridge event; the dates of the showing in Cambridge and the showing in London are too close to admit changes. The description in the advertisement of the nature of the London exhibit matches the more elaborated description given in the "Explanation" pamphlet of the Cambridge exhibit. And the precedent of turning original Cambridge Anti-War Council exhibits into traveling ones had already been set by the organization's earlier, 1933 exhibit, which according to *its* "Explanation" pamphlet, traveled to numerous other galleries around England to be shown, among them one in London. Nevertheless, none of the lists of organizers in all the Cambridge Anti-War Council material I found includes a Princess Elizabeth Bibesco, a Ralph Wright, a Mr. Bluit, or a Lord Ivor Spencer-Churchill, all of whom Woolf writes about as organizers and committee members with whom she discussed the exhibit. The only way I can account for this is to suggest that these committee members acted as temporary London contacts for the Cambridge Anti-War Council.
Additionally, Woolf indicates in one letter the possibility that the exhibit would not be launched in London at all for lack of funds: "From what I hear, I think it doubtful that they [will] get enough money to hold the Exhibition. Many people hold off because they think it absurd not to expose the other tyrannies at the same time. What a horror it all is!" (to Robert C. Trevelyan, 27 Feb. 1935; *L*5 374). She mentions the exhibit only twice after that point in her letters, once on 19 March to call it a "fiasco" (379) and finally on 3 April to say "Lord Ivor [Churchill] tells me the other Fascist Exhibition [i.e. the Cambridge one] has been proved a Communist plot; and I'm to have my five pounds back. But I forgot if I told you" (382). Both of these comments suggest that the exhibit may not have occurred at all in the end. However, whether it occurred or not, Woolf was still involved in assessing its proposed contents while it was being planned and while she was thinking up *Three Guineas*; and in any case, if indeed it was finally dropped altogether, the failure of any attempt to relate women's predicament to fascism would likely have spurred her all the more to write her own anti-Fascist pamphlet.

Come in Britain?; (7) Fascism and Militarism: Fascism and Culture; (8) The Anti-Fascist Movement.[7] The subtitling of the section on Fascism in Britain as "Embryo-Fascism" points directly toward Woolf's startling use in *Three Guineas* of the metaphor of eggs being shaken out of respectable English newspapers to signify the presence in England of proto-fascist tendencies. "There," she asserts in the second Guinea, "is the egg of the very same worm that we know under other names in other countries. There we have in embryo the creature, Dictator as we call him when he is Italian or German, who believes that he has the right . . . to dictate to other human beings how they shall live" (*TG* 96).

For Woolf, of course, these "other human beings" are women. The exhibit's advance-advertising pamphlet did announce the intention to show, among other objectives, "Its [Fascism's] Policy toward Culture, toward Women and Youth," but in the final event, evidence of attention to women's situation under Fascism shrinks to two references: Section Four on Germany mentions that women are excluded from employment under the Nazis in order to reduce unemployment; Section Seven on culture describes women as being forced to "revert to a mediaeval role." The absence of a separate section on women comes as a surprise in part because exhibition organizer Bibesco assured Woolf that it would be there. In response to Woolf's inquiries about why the "woman question" was being ignored in the show, Bibesco writes, "There will of course be a section dealing with women under the Nazi regime."[8] It is also surprising because the

---

[7]Originally, nine sections were projected in the advance-advertising pamphlet: (1) The Post-War World; (2) Italy: The First Chapter; (3) Italy: The Corporate State; (4) Germany: The Rise of Hitler; (5) Nazis in Power; (6) Fascism and Culture; (7) Fascism and War; (8) Can Fascism come in Britain?; (9) The Anti-Fascist Movement. In its final form, the exhibit somewhat changed shape, leaving out the introductory survey of the post-war world, adding a new section on the expansion of fascist influence beyond Italy and Germany, and fusing the section on war with that on culture. Just as the advance-advertising pamphlet promised a separate section on "Fascism and War" which was absent in the event, similarly, the exhibit next door was originally entitled "Artists Against War and Fascism" on its call for submissions poster (see reprint in Morris and Radford 29), but the final title placed "Fascism" ahead of "War." In the case of both exhibits the effort to de-emphasize anti-war sentiments can be attributed to the growing disagreement within the Left over Britain's official policy of non-intervention.

[8]Bibesco's letter continues, "I am afraid that it had not occurred to me that in matters of ultimate importance even feminists could wish to segregate and label the sexes. It would seem to be a pity that sex alone should be able to bring them together." Woolf copies this quote into her diary and calls it a "teasing letter" in an entry dated six days after Bibesco's letter (*D4* 273). But she also saved Bibesco's handwritten letter in her folders of materials collected for the writing of *Three Guineas*, which suggests that she saw more than lightheartedness in it. Brenda Silver proposes that the Bibesco letter may have

Cambridge Anti-War Council included at this time representatives from four different women's organizations: the Romsey Lab. Women's Section, the Central Women's Co-op. Guild, the N.U.R. Women's Guild, and the A.S.L.E. & F. Women's Guild.[9]

The feminist agenda was apparently considered secondary to the overriding concern of presenting the narrative of Fascism's development with "historical" accuracy and documented evidence. Viewers are repeatedly asked in the "Explanation" to note examples of this, from "historical photographs of 1920 and 1921 and the March on Rome" and "historic photos of Kapp Putsch" to a "photocopy of [the] telegram calling off martial law and summoning Mussolini to Rome" and "the photostat of the Indictment in the Leipzig Trial, which was not communicated to the defence, but which was secretly photographed at great personal risk and smuggled out of the country." Clearly, authenticity was a priority for the "Explanation" writers, and this emphasis on the historical accuracy of the displayed documents acts to substantiate an overall emphasis on an authoritative narrative of history, one in which fascism could be understood linearly, as a development through chronological time and a succession of discrete geographical units. This exhibition method was of course not a novel one; as museum historian Philip Fisher states, the museum, evolving out of singular sites of meaning like the royal home or the cathedral, reordered their extracted works in a linear, usually chronological, fashion so that the idea of a museum became synonymous with "pure path," incurring an understanding of a "single, linear motion of history" (Fisher 9).

Three Guineas may be seen to take a generic formal cue from the Cambridge exhibit's range of "documentary" evidence, using the same juxtaposition of photographs, narratively sketched scenes such as the bridge scene, excerpts from biographies and histories, newspaper excerpts, and government

---

spurred Woolf to complain in a letter to Ethel Smyth (8 January 1935), "[N]ever do I get any letter . . . of pure affection. All the rest implore, command, badger, worry. Here's Lady Rhondda, heres a man who wants a puff, and woman who wants a preface; and that d——d ass Elizabeth Bibesco" (Silver 271; *L5* 361). Quite apart from the issue of affection, the specificity of Bibesco's response—addressing women solely under the Nazi regime, as if the treatment of women under fascism was an issue only in Germany—must have irked Woolf and fueled her argument in *Three Guineas* for a recognition of how irrelevant national borders are to the treatment of women under any form of patriarchy.

[9]As listed in the 1935 advance-advertising pamphlet. The Central Women's Co-operative Guild, considered the women's counterpart to the male-dominated British trade union movement from the early thirties on, is cited by Jessica Berman as an organization "close to Woolf's heart and politics" (Berman 109).

publications.[10] Yet as a whole, the polemic deliberately upsets the form of a traditional exhibit, in which fixed objects on display are arranged in a linear, teleological order to be followed by individual viewers who pass from one to the next, as in the Cambridge exhibition's consecutively numbered sections. Instead, the exhibit that is *Three Guineas* often loops back on itself rather than adhering to a linear order, returning once again to Whitaker's Alamanack or the teachings of St. Paul or the biography of Sophia Jex-Blake, as Woolf's argument requires.[11] It also undermines the typical linear order of exhibited objects by requiring the reader to move imaginatively between two simultaneous exhibits, as mentioned above: one actual though never directly alluded to, namely, the five actual photographs, the other a fictional exhibit of freely discussed but unrepresented photographs, sketches, and images.

As demonstrated in the description of the photostat of the Leipzig Trial Indictment—"secretly photographed at great personal risk and smuggled out of the country"—the "Explanation" was concerned to stress not just the authenticity of the exhibit's materials but also their extreme rarity, the thrilling combination of risk and luck that has made them available to the public for viewing. Indeed the Cambridge exhibit's largest draw was predicted to be its final section, "The Anti-Fascist Movement," which was conceived from the start as the culmination of the exhibit precisely because its materials had supposedly narrowly escaped destruction. "An offer has been made of two valuable collections of material on present-day Germany and Italy, much of it consisting of 'inside' documents, illegal material, etc., of a quite sensational kind," the advance-advertising pamphlet

[10]Woolf's own method of collecting and organizing materials for *Three Guineas*—by pasting various items for display (articles and photos clipped or torn from newspapers, reviews of her previous books, and so on), singly or with two or three in juxtaposition, into the pages of three bound notebooks, each of which she headed with an index of its contents—also mimics this exhibitionary method. Unfortunately, there is no way to identify when Woolf began work on these notebooks, as Silver points out: it could have been any time between 20 January 1931, when she suddenly conceived of a "sequel" to *A Room of One's Own* "to be called Professions for Women perhaps" while in her bath (*D*4 6), and the publication of *Three Guineas* in 1938 (Silver 255-56).

[11]It is for this very reason that critics have often had so little patience with *Three Guineas,* from Woolf's younger contemporaries Nigel Nicolson and Quentin Bell to Valentine Cunningham, who judges it "skittishly wayward" and "vexingly round about" in his study *British Writers of the Thirties* (70). Shari Benstock has noted what she calls the text's elliptical tendency in *Textualizing the Feminine. S*he provides an extended reading of the relationship between the polemic's form and its feminist politics through the ellipsis (both the textual dots and the trajectory of the shape in space), identifying it as "the primary structuring device of the text" (124). Benstock, however, ultimately privileges the "rhetoric of scent" (and its elliptical leakings) over the pictures and photographs that Woolf "shoves under [patriarchy's] nose" (157).

promised. The "Explanation" elaborates on these collections in its final section, using even more dramatic language:

> Driven underground, the opposition reverts to novel and illegal methods of propaganda—propaganda which carries for its agents the constant risk of torture or death. This Section contains a unique collection of illegal literature and propaganda-devices in contemporary Germany and Italy, Austria and Spain. For obvious reasons such propaganda is hard to trace and receives little publicity: to the general public abroad its mere existence is hardly known. Yet despite the fact that its devotees need to have something of the character of martyrs of persecuted sects in the Middle Ages, this opposition-activity continues and is strong. In countries like France and Britain propaganda against Fascism is at a more primitive stage, if open and legal. (1935 "Explanation")

The Cambridge exhibition's culminating display, then, draws upon the properties usually attributed to a traditional, highly acclaimed art exhibition: its materials are "valuable" and rare; its collectors are daring and, as connoisseurs, can bring to the public works to which they would not otherwise have access, being "hard to trace." The modern museum's authority, in Eilean Hooper-Greenhill's theory, in fact rests in its development, in England, in tandem with the nineteenth-century traveler who brought back artifacts as signs of conquest; the establishment of museum collections is no less "a form of symbolic conquest" (Hooper-Greenhill 18). The Cambridge exhibit's guide-writers implicitly draw attention to precisely this vestige of authority by pointing out the difficulties undergone to amass its materials, materials whose "mere existence" would be unacknowledged were it not for these professionals' efforts.

In addition, if the creators of these anti-fascist materials are "martyrs of persecuted sects in the Middle Ages," their works are by implication holy relics, and should be revered as such. Through the language of the "Explanation," then, the exhibit's culminating display attempts, ironically, to construct of its viewing audience a kind of cult of the anti-Fascist. This cult is implicitly characterized as synchronic and transhistorical, in opposition to the cult of Fascism which the exhibit meticulously historicizes and demystifies in the first seven sections, having shown its spread linearly through successive countries.[12] The aura of

[12]It should be noted that this last section of the Cambridge exhibit, dedicated to anti-fascism's "martyrs," ironically makes reverse use of one of Fascism's main ideological instruments, the exhibiting of its own history and artifacts as mythic objects of quasi-religious veneration. The final room of the hugely successful 1932 Exhibition of the Fascist Revolution in Rome, for example, was called "The Martyrs' Shrine" (see Schnapp and Stone on this exhibition; see Gentile for an extended discussion of Italian Fascism's envisioning of itself as a political religion). One of the items that the Cambridge exhibit soberly documents, Mussolini's first newspaper articles, were cast as the mythic origins of fascist ideology in the regime's first large-scale exhibitions (see Braun 134-45).

reverence with which Section Eight's works of anti-fascist "propaganda" are presented and meant to be viewed is a direct manifestation of what one museum critic has termed the museum ritual. "Like most ritual space," Carol Duncan writes, "museum space is carefully marked off and culturally designated as reserved for a special quality of attention" akin to reverence, and is often signified by an architecture that resembles older ritual sites like Greek and Roman temples (8). What the Cambridge exhibit, being temporary, lacked in architectural signs of ritual, its "Explanation" made up for in descriptive metaphors.

Woolf, however, categorically rejects the museum ritual, subverting the elevated nature a traditional exhibit accords its objects by stressing the opposite nature of her exhibits.[13] The narrator of *Three Guineas* repeatedly reminds her readers and her addressee(s) that the sources of "evidence" she places before them have not been obtained under "risk of torture and death" but are universally available, readily accessed, and already widely distributed. "Let us go into greater detail and consult the facts which are nowadays open to the inspection of all who can read their mother tongue" (128). Each time she turns to the evidence of biography, she reminds us that it is evidence that "anyone who can read English can consult on the shelves of any public library" (44) or even "the shelves of your own library" (128). (Indeed the emphasis she places on English as the shared "mother tongue" is perhaps better understood in light of the Cambridge exhibit's numerous German and Italian documents, preserved in their original languages in order to stress their authenticity, but also thereby emphasizing fascism's "otherness.") The unrepresented photographs she discusses are not smuggled illegally out of another country but sent gratuitously, she mentions several times, every week by the Spanish Government. Likewise, the included photographs, while of recognizably famous men of the time,[14] are identified not by name but by generic title and so seem to come from a stockpile of such images. Finally, the documents she uses, like Whitaker's Almanack, are not "inside" documents but public ones which "even outsiders can consult" (49).

[13]Christine Froula has also noted, though in an anthropological context, a subversion of the "sacred" and the ritualistic in *Three Guineas*, arguing convincingly that Woolf recognizes the oppression of women as the ritualized destruction of a scapegoat, carried out as a way of structuring and maintaining hierarchies within a society. For Froula, Woolf revises rather than rejects out-of-hand the idea of the sacred, seeing its spirit as a capacity within all human beings to envision a shared world (48).

[14]In "Name That Face," Alice Stavely identifies the subjects of four of the photographs—"A General," "A University Procession," "A Judge," and "An Archbishop"—and speculates that the remaining one, representing merely a row of heralds in the place of the monarch they announce, gestures at once toward the recent abdication crisis and the instability of the old order (5).

Woolf constructs her exhibit in opposition to the Cambridge exhibition's culminating display, as ubiquitous and pervasive rather than select and rare, demonstrating that politics are at work in every viewable object—if only it is put on exhibit.

Woolf thus refuses to elevate her own status as daring critic and connoisseur by way of emphasizing the select nature of her materials, as did the "Explanation" writers; but, one might say, she borrows that authority by transferring it to the *arrangement* of her materials.[15] Indeed from first sight such disparate, everyday materials seem to require no less than a connoisseur and keen critic to draw them together meaningfully. Anticipating the expectations of any exhibit-goer, she asks, "What connection is there between the sartorial splendors of the educated man and the photograph of ruined houses and dead bodies?" (39). To make such connections is precisely the exhibit organizer's job; and who, we might ask in turn, would be able successfully to connect these displayed items other than Virginia Woolf?

The fact that the Cambridge exhibit's rhetoric aggrandizes the aura of its materials and organizers by drawing on art museum ideologies is a particularly interesting feature, given that the exhibit seems to have defined its identity in part by way of differentiating itself from an art-only exhibit being held simultaneously next door. At 27 Soho Square, the "Cambridge Exhibition on Fascism and War" adjoined the space being used for "Artists Against Fascism and War," the second major exhibit of the Artists' International Association (AIA).[16] Similarly entitled, the two exhibits seem to have been intended to complement each other in the growing anti-Fascist cause while maintaining implicit boundaries. Woolf was not directly involved in the artists' exhibit as she was in the Cambridge one, and it is unclear whether she attended it; but her involvement and ties with the AIA itself, in addition to references in her letters and diaries, indicate that she was likely as aware of the artists' exhibit as the Cambridge one. The AIA was

[15]In this, her most convincing work fusing art and politics, Woolf famously laments the use of that thoroughbred horse, the art of literature, to propound political opinions, which would result merely in mules. Marcus' now landmark reading of Woolf's position on art and politics—that Woolf nevertheless sees the production of "mules" as occasionally necessary—is relevant here: the "mule" of photographs and pictures on display is balanced by the thoroughbred's managing of these plodding materials in such illuminating ways and to such startling purposes.

[16]See the reproduction of the publicity advertisement in Morris and Radford (30).

the organization at whose request Woolf would write "Why Art Today Follows Politics" for the *Daily Worker* in December 1936.[17] While she was canvassing financial support for the Cambridge exhibit (whose support committee as listed in the "Explanation" includes E. M. Forster[18]), Duncan Grant, along with four other AIA members, was calling for submissions to the artists' exhibit. Vanessa was probably a member of the AIA herself by this time; she is certainly a member by the outbreak of the Spanish Civil War eight months later.[19] I suggest that Woolf also implicitly links the two exhibits in a letter to Quentin Bell dated 3 April 1935: "Lord Ivor [Churchill] tells me the other Fascist Exhibition has been proved a Communist plot; and I'm to have my five pounds back" (*L5* 382). This "other" one is the Cambridge exhibit to which she contributed a bit of her own money; and since Quentin Bell would be elected to the AIA within a year and become its chair within two years, the unspecified first exhibition of Woolf's sentence most likely refers to the AIA's. In Woolf's diary entries during this time (February 1935), she is recording both lunch with Ralph Wright, a Cambridge exhibit organizer, and dinner with Herbert Read and Henry Moore, both AIA members and Britain's preeminent art critic and sculptor, respectively; the latter would show his work at the AIA exhibit. She was immersed in both worlds.

The "Artists Against Fascism and War" exhibition billed itself, like the Cambridge exhibit, as extra-ordinary, but it posed as art rather than documentary. It was advertised and acknowledged as the first of its kind in England, insofar as

[17]Retitled as "The Artist and Politics" in *The Moment and Other Essays* (in *Collected Essays* II 230-232).

[18]For Merry Pawlowski, Forster is one of three of Woolf's male modernist contemporaries whose exchanges with her spurred her to formulate the ideas of *Three Guineas*. From the late 1920s, Pawlowski suggests, Forster and Woolf's mutual disagreements over "the representation of life in art," combined with Forster's misogynist privileging of homosexual bonding over sapphism, point toward growing disagreements over how to fuse art and politics and Forster's eventual dismissal of Woolf's 1938 polemic (Pawlowski 61).

[19]See Morris and Radford (2). Before resigning in 1949, Vanessa Bell's involvement in the AIA was regular: she donated paintings to the December 1936 exhibition "Artists Help Spain"; she showed again at the February-March 1939 exhibition "Art for the People"; and she contributed prints to the Everyman Prints series put out by the AIA during wartime (Morris and Radford 30-82). In a letter dated 10 October 1936 she mentions to her son Julian that his brother Quentin has been elected to the "Artists International Committee," and she tries to discourage Julian from contemplating joining the International Brigades in Spain by citing the case of AIA member and graphic artist Felicia Browne, killed in Spain in August 1936. In the same letter, she mentions that she and Duncan Grant have just been selected to write the preface to a memorial catalogue of Browne's drawings (Bell 425), published before the year's end as *Twenty Drawings by Felicia Browne Killed in Defense of the Spanish Republic*.

it constituted a large-scale exhibition with explicit political intent and international representation. It did bring together the work of widely divergent English artists and works by French, Dutch, Polish, and Russian artists (Radford 45-47). British artists' work ranged from that of established, traditional painters new to the AIA—Augustus John showed a portrait of King Feisal and Laura Knight a painting of a female representing Dawn [20]—to original AIA members Cliff Rowe and Peter Peri who showed paintings and sculpture fashioned specifically for this exhibition, with titles like "Canvassing the Daily Worker" and "Against War and Fascism."[21] Within the frame of this exhibition, though, such works signified as art rather than propaganda. Abstract art and political cartoons were hung together: the international sections included among their long lists cubist painter Fernand Léger and sculptor Ossip Zadkine, while the vestibule housed newspaper drawings from the *Left Review* (Morris and Radford 29). The point was to unite under the single aegis of anti-fascism (and, subordinately, anti-war sentiment) all that counted as "art."

However, the apparently clear separation between the artists' exhibition and the documentary exhibition blurs somewhat under scrutiny: the program cover of the "Explanation" for the Cambridge Anti-War Council's exhibit was designed by E. McKnight Kauffer, a member of the AIA; a set of cartoons mentioned on the private viewing advertisement for the Cambridge exhibit which were "specially lent by Low" are in all likelihood the work of prominent AIA cartoonist David Low; and the Cambridge exhibit even included drawings by an AIA artist among its collection of evidence comprising Section Three ("Germany: Fascism Comes to Power"):

> NOTE especially photostat of the Ernst Document (Ernst was a storm-trooper shot on June 30th, 1934, and is alleged to have left this document confessing Nazi complicity in the Reichstag fire); drawings by R. Boswell of the Artists' International; historic photos of Kapp Putsch and Munich rising 1923; whips and cudgels actually used by storm-troops. (1935 "Explanation")

[20]Woolf read Dame Laura Knight's autobiography *Oil Paint and Grease Paint: An Autobiography of Laura Knight* (London: Nicolson & Watson, 1936) and quotes from this text in *Three Guineas,* Chapter 3, note 39.

[21]Cliff Rowe helped to found the AIA; other founding members include Misha Black, Pearl Binder, James Boswell, and James Fitton.

"R. Boswell of the Artists' International" is probably a mistype for James Buchan Boswell, the only Boswell listed at this point in the AIA literature,[22] and a specifically graphic artist who helped to found the AIA in 1933 and contributed caricature drawings regularly to the *Left Review*. Though we cannot know the content of these drawings from the "Explanation" pamphlet, their inclusion indicates that artists' rendering of events is intended to play a documentary role in this context, providing as much persuasive and evidential weight as photographs taken on the scene or the military instruments "actually used by storm troops." Next door at the AIA exhibit however, as we have seen, such *Left Review* drawings counted as "art." Similarly, if the Cambridge exhibit framed its photographs ("historical photographs of 1920 and 1921 and the March on Rome"; "historic photos of Kapp Putsch") as transparent evidence of political history, the same medium could be read as "art" next door, where the AIA exhibit devoted a section, among its rooms of paintings and sculptures, to photographs of working class life, including a collection by Edith Tudor-Hart. Thus, duplicating displays of visual media—photographs and sketches, the types of visual media that Woolf employs most commonly in *Three Guineas*—the two exhibits nevertheless insisted that the same media be read differently by virtue of their context.

It is instructive to look at an art historian's explanation for this separation. On the basis of extensive interviews with still-living members of the AIA, some of them original members, Robert Radford carefully establishes the boundary between the AIA and university-based Leftist organizations, under which category the Cambridge Anti-War Council would fall:

> The establishment of Communist Party cells at Oxford and Cambridge Universities has been frequently commented on, and the views and attitudes of the radical element of this generation are glimpsed from such incidents as the famous resolution of the Oxford Union that: 'this house would in no circumstance fight for King and Country,' or, as Anthony Blunt summed it up: 'About every intelligent young man who came up to Cambridge joined the Communist Party.'

> But it must be emphasized that the inception and growth of the AIA had little direct connection with this radical activity at the Universities which remained for the most part as philistine as ever in their disposition towards the Fine Arts, and whilst Blunt and A. L. Lloyd entered the AIA ambit occasionally, in the role of speakers and critics, and whilst AIA Propaganda material was used at Cambridge [footnote], the inauguration of the body [of AIA] was entire-

[22]In addition to Morris and Radford's *The Story of the AIA: Artists International Association 1933-1953*, see Radford, *Art for a Purpose: The Artists' International Association, 1933-1953*. Margot Heinemann briefly addresses the AIA in "The People's Front and the Intellectuals" (165).

ly the product of the grass roots experience of young artists and designers, generally working in London. (15)

Radford downplays the overlap, relegating to a footnote the information that "a
photograph of posters for an anti-War exhibit at Cambridge University, described
as by the Artists' International 'Revolutionary group of England', appears in
International Literature, 1 (7), 1934" (38 n5). *International Literature* (1932-
45) was published monthly in Moscow in English by the International Union of
Revolutionary Writers, and their obvious approval of the AIA's "revolutionary"
qualifications suggests that at least from the outside, the AIA was seen as fundamentally Communist.[23]   In fact, the "Explanation" pamphlet from the
Cambridge Anti-War Council's *first* exhibit, the "Cambridge Anti-War
Exhibition" (Nov. 13-18, 1933 with a second showing Nov. 21-24, 1934) demonstrates that the relationship between the Cambridge Anti-War Council and the
AIA was significantly more cooperative than Radford acknowledges: the 1933
exhibit was designed and mounted by Misha Black, one of the AIA's founding
members; its program cover was designed by another of the founders, Cliff
Rowe; and the exhibit also incorporated a set of lithographs by Paul Nash, an
early member of the AIA who exhibited at the first of its exhibitions ("The Social
Scene," September-October 1934) and helped put out the call for submissions for
the second (i.e. "Artists Against Fascism and War").

Radford's differentiation between the two groups is based on a confluence of
assumptions about divisions between art, politics, and class: the University
types, too influenced by their higher class background to see that art may encom-
pass much more than the narrow category of "Fine Arts," were also too caught
up in being "radical" and joining the Communist party; the AIA was a movement
originating in working London, a product of the people, so to speak, whose first
allegiance is to "art" (for them, presumably, a much more informed and wide-
ranging concept) and who were therefore less inclined to be found joining the
Communist party or committing their time to party-based political activity.
Assuming that this view is not merely Radford's but the predominant view of the
original AIA members from whom he gathered his material, we might conclude
that the AIA's "Artists Against Fascism and War" exhibit maintained an emphasis, despite its polemical title, on the showing of its contents as "art"—as objects

---

[23]In this light, AIA member Clive Bell's fury at Woolf's being caught up unawares in
a Communist organization's exhibition (the 1935 Cambridge one) seems somewhat puzzling. In her diary Woolf mentions Bell's "absurd pompous letter" to the exhibition
committee chairman, written after receiving Woolf's letter of request for money (*D*4 280).
His attitude, however, seems to have been a prevalent one among AIA members, according to Radford's summary of those he interviewed.

meriting appreciative viewing rather than espousing political views—albeit in this new, more inclusive, less "philistine" conception of art. The separation between the 1935 Cambridge and AIA exhibits, despite sharing similar and in some cases identical visual displays, may thus be seen to uphold this assumption: despite appearances, art-enhanced politics and politically-charged art are ultimately distinctive and distinguishable.

Woolf, however, is a self-declared "outsider," lacking any inhibiting investments in distinctions between what is and is not "art" in the world of visual media. Her project in *Three Guineas* is precisely to undermine such distinctions; to assert that politics and aesthetics cannot possibly be separated; to reveal that the visible world is simultaneously both inherently political and inherently aesthetic, insofar as we recognize it so. According to the logic of her argument, it is in designating or framing certain parts of the visible world as "merely aesthetic," as the polemic's narrator puts it (112), or on the other hand as incontrovertibly factual (the narrator of *Three Guineas* returns incessantly to "the facts"), that a kind of calcification of the vision and understanding occurs, an inability to move beyond passive appreciation of either the "truth" value or the "aesthetic" value of a given image's circumscribed meaning. Woolf's approach to visual media in *Three Guineas* focuses on destabilizing one's way of seeing by pointing to an image, making much of the medium through which the image takes form, and then displacing or changing that medium. The slippages in media identified above between the Cambridge exhibit and the AIA exhibit thus offer a suggestive background with which to understand Woolf's idiosyncratic use of visual media.

While, as discussed above, *Three Guineas* draws its form from the Cambridge exhibit's range of documentary evidence, the polemic's individual exhibits are often construed not just as evidence but as "art," recalling and crossing over into the realm of the artists' exhibit. While photographs are plausibly defined as "pictures of actual facts," biographies and histories are referred to pointedly as "pictures of other people's lives and minds" (20). At times, the "facts" of history are figured in visual, even suggestively painterly terms, as with "Arthur's Education Fund," a phenomenon of past British history in which daughters sacrificed education, travel, and pleasure so that sons could receive those benefits: very quickly this "solid fact" (whose name, of course, Woolf has garnered from a work of fiction) takes on visual contours as a "voracious receptacle" which "cast[s] a shadow over the entire landscape" of university buildings (12) in a kind of de Chirico-esque narrative painting. Always, what is at stake is not the images themselves but the "angle" (22) from which they are viewed, the way in which the significance of each item on exhibit changes depending on the frame. "Though we see the same world, we see it through different eyes," the narrator famously states (22), so that the image of Cambridge itself appears as "noble courts and quadrangles" to the male viewer but so many "cold legs of mutton" to the female viewer (12).

As if in direct response to the unacknowledged imbrications of the Cambridge and AIA exhibits and their artificial framing devices—this exhibit is "factual," that one "artistic"—Woolf plays with the framing device for each of her exhibits in ways that continually destabilize the authority and significance with which they are vested by virtue of that frame or form. One method she employs to this end is a continual disruption of our understanding of "fact." In her first discursive Guinea, the narrator proposes that, by way of beginning to "help you, Sir, to prevent war," she might contribute money to the woman treasurer asking for funds to rebuild a women's college. But first, the value of education must be established, and to do so, "biography," earlier qualifying as "pictures of people's lives and minds," is now made to serve as factual evidence marshaled for the purpose of "proving" education's worth (45). The culminating biographical sketch is of Mary Astell's effort, 250 years before, to start a women's college, an idea she is forced to abandon because of opposition from the Church. Despite the obvious culpability of a (male) institution to thwart women's efforts to gain an education—the very point, indeed, of the inclusion of this story—the statement which concludes this foray into "biography" acting as "fact" casts blame on the form, on the status of these biographical excerpts *as* "facts": it is the idea of facts which has failed us, not the institution of the Church.

> But these facts, as facts so often do, prove double-faced; for though they establish the value of education, they also prove that education is by no means a positive value; it is not good in all circumstances, and good for all people; it is only good for some people and for some purposes. [. . .]

> Such at least would seem to be the answer of biography—the oracle is not dumb, but it is dubious. As, however, it is of great importance that we should use our influence through education to affect the young against war we must not be baffled by the evasions of biography or seduced by its charm. (48)

By the end of this conclusion, the evidence of biography is no longer a fact to be depended on but its complete opposite, something charming and evasive against which one should be on one's guard. Tongue in cheek, Woolf's narrator brushes her own (extremely disturbing) previous evidence aside in distinctly feminized terms (it seduces, charms, evades) and advises her male addressee to turn to "history" instead, here described as "that record of the public life," the "considered opinions of bodies of educated men" like the male addressee himself, conveyed "through the mouths of Parliaments and Senates" (49). She builds up expectations—"But, you will interpose, what are these facts? these historical but deplorable facts?"—only to fill the bill with a continuation of the same story of women's efforts to build a women's college: which is to say, the same "facts," now posing as "impartial and disinterested" "history" rather than "double-faced" biography. In a final undermining of the authority of historical "facts" in this representative passage, she renders her "history" in storybook language: "Then a second house [for a women's college] was taken, a better house this time, though it is true that the water rushed through the dining-room in stormy weather and there was no playground" (50). She is, of course, appearing to collude with, then undermining, the assumptions of her highly educated male addressee, who imagines that "history" and its authoritative "facts" reign in one display case, subjective biographical images in another. In *Three Guineas*, "facts" are often merely shifting signifiers; even the presumably incontrovertible evidence of Whitaker's Almanack, a government-published list of occupations and salaries, is an exhibit apt to change merely when examined through "a stronger pair of glasses" (86).

Thus, when the narrator, pointing to the Spanish Civil War photographs for the first time, asserts that photographs are "simply statements of fact addressed to the eye" (20), the statement is clearly meant to be seen as strategic rather than transparent. This is confirmed when she suggests that we consider the custom of men going off to work while women wait at home, and presents it, too, as a photograph which she "lay[s] before" us (34)—as if this were no less tangible a piece of documentary evidence than the journalists' photographs of the remains of bombed houses in Spain. That no photographic lens could capture a centuries-old tendency in the world of professional, public life as she describes it is irrelevant; the "procession of the sons of educated men" crossing the bridge between the private and the public worlds is, she reasserts in the second Guinea, "a photograph that . . . [women] have often looked upon" (90).

It is this very "photograph," however, which undergoes a series of medium transformations that suddenly illuminates its viewing conditions as crucially important. The passage begins by animating the "photograph" that was previously laid before us:

> Close at hand is a bridge over the Thames, an admirable vantage ground for such a survey. The river flows beneath; barges pass, laden with timber, bursting with corn; there on one side are the domes and spires of the city; on the other, Westminster and the Houses of Parliament. It is a place to stand on by the hour, dreaming. But not now. Now we are pressed for time. Now we are here to consider facts; now we must fix our eyes upon the procession—the procession of the sons of educated men. (110-111)

With its iconic architecture and the other signifiers of the tourists' London—the river and the bridge (inevitably referencing London Bridge)—the image evokes a postcard photograph—though not entirely stilled—and thus the sense of an exhibited picture. As the text continues, the procession of men is likened to a "caravanserai crossing the desert," a Napoleonic image evocative of a Romantic painting; rerendered a photograph ("a site, merely") and, in the same breath, equated with a "fresco scrawled upon the walls of time":

> There they go, our brothers who have been educated at public schools and universities, mounting those steps, passing in and out of those doors, ascending those pulpits, preaching, teaching, administering justice, practising medicine, transacting business, making money. It is a solemn sight always—a procession, like a caravanserai crossing a desert. [. . .] It is a solemn sight, this procession [. . .] But now, for the past twenty years or so, it is no longer a sight, merely, a photograph, or fresco scrawled upon the walls of time, at which we can look with merely an aesthetic appreciation. For there, trapesing along at the tail end of the procession, we go ourselves. And that makes a difference. We who have looked so long at the pageant in books, or from a curtained window . . . need look passively no longer. (112)

Woolf is thus explicitly condensing patriarchal public power into an image on exhibit, one to be gravely admired: a "solemn sight." Such a construction, she makes clear, has induced a particular way of looking in the spectator: a "passive" contemplation of the image's "aesthetic" merits. In this sense her analysis anticipates Pierre Bourdieu's theoretical concept of the "pure" gaze as instrumental in contributing to, even producing, an object's value. Bourdieu traces this gaze directly to the workings of museums:

> There is in fact every reason to suppose that the constitution of the aesthetic gaze as a 'pure' gaze, capable of considering the work of art in and for itself, i.e. as a 'finality without an end', is linked to the *institution* of the work of art as an object of contemplation, with the creation of private and then public galleries and museums, and the parallel development of a corps of professionals appointed to conserve the work of art, both materially and symbolically. (36)

In the same way, Woolf links the pure gaze at work in society's glance to the institution of patriarchy, and its wish to project itself as admirable in its intricate workings. Institutional patriarchy, as her scenario implies, is well served by the pure gaze it fosters, for such a way of seeing naturalizes its workings, disarms attempts to change it, and, most crucially, renders it timeless. Yet in a deceptively simple move, Woolf dismantles this gaze by reframing it within a different vantage point, that of "now, for the past twenty years or so"—revealing the procession scene to be not "merely aesthetic" but explicitly political. The temporal frame with which she disrupts the gaze is post-1919, the year English women were granted by act of Parliament the right to earn their livings in the professions. With this shift in frames, the image changes from a "photograph, or fresco" frozen in time to a work of visual art continuous with life, in which the (female) viewers simultaneously constitute and animate the scene. Woolf's rejection of the function of this image of patriarchal power, as one fashioned for appreciative viewing by a collective female public, specifically recalls her objection to the Cambridge exhibit's possible exclusion of a section on women, the absence of which would have, of course, relegated women once more to the role of passive viewers of an all-male world. More importantly, the rhetorical move serves to align the naturalization of men's power in the public sphere with a particular view of the function of art, as immutable objects intended to elicit "aesthetic" appreciation from passive viewers. In Woolf's polemic, it takes the upsetting of the latter assumption to reveal the falsity of the first.

Woolf's implication in the "photograph, or fresco" passage, that the visual arts as framed by the exhibition form could be co-opted for political purposes to make patriarchal (and therefore proto-fascist) power seem natural, reveals a skepticism concerning exhibitions themselves. This skepticism is confirmed in her sketch of the ideal women's college, in which not only traditional attitudes to art are rejected but also the very concept of museums, since they encourage the "pure gaze" and thus foster the isolation and iconicization of artifacts belonging to a particular historical moment as timeless aesthetic objects. The suggestion for a museum-free women's college is given in the first Guinea, in the course of the narrator's letter responding to the woman honorary treasurer who has written asking for money to rebuild a women's college at Cambridge. The narrator stipulates the terms on which her guinea will be given to the treasurer:

> [Y]ou must rebuild your college differently. It is young and poor; let it therefore take advantage of those qualities and be founded on poverty and youth. Obviously, then, it must be an experimental college. Let it be built on lines of its own. It must be built not of carved stone and stained glass, but of some cheap, easily combustible material which does not hoard dust and perpetrate traditions. Do not have chapels. Do not have museums and libraries with chained books and first editions under glass cases. Let the pictures and the books be new and always changing. Let it be decorated afresh by each generation with their own hands cheaply. (61-62)

Like the "photograph or fresco" in which the revered and static artwork becomes the living scene of its observers-turned-participants, Woolf's alternative world depicted here is one in which the space of exhibitions and the space of everyday activity coextend. It is, as Erin Carlston has noted, Woolf's re-envisioning of the fascist ideal of the totally aestheticized life—by eliminating the authoritarian element (163).[24] Objects are transferred from the sterile isolation of glass cases to the creative hands of their observers, all within structures whose dominant quality is their transience, their "combustibility," their inextricability from historical and generational change.

As we have seen, such an ideal is constitutive of *Three Guineas* itself, insofar as the polemic is constructed as an exhibit of "evidence" taken from lived and living examples, a sort of counter-Cambridge exhibit which metaphorically replaces its glass cases with the everyday milieu of British society itself. The ideal also finds a crucial reiteration in the Society of Outsiders, Woolf's proposed solution to the question of how the daughters of educated men might help those men to prevent war. One of the central aspects of the proposed lifestyle of the Outsiders is in fact their adoption of a politically motivated aesthetic, one which directly endorses the idea of integrating museum exhibits and the everyday milieu:

> the outsiders will dispense with pageantry not from any puritanical dislike of beauty. On the contrary, it will be one of their aims to increase private beauty; the beauty of spring, summer, autumn; the beauty of flowers, silks, clothes; the beauty which brims not only in every field and wood but every barrow in Oxford Street; the scattered beauty which needs only to be combined by artists in order to become visible to all. (207)

From the representative of small commercial enterprise, the barrow on Oxford Street, to seasonal change, this is indeed the turning (inside) out of the contained, enclosed exhibit. It is worth noting, however, that even what seems to be simply the visible world, in this glimmer of a new vision, cannot be "visible to all" until it is properly combined in a display.

Woolf's ideal fusion of museum and life appears to rest on divesting history of its accrued traditions and artifacts. Hence displays in the experimental college by each generation are replaced by those of the next, and the materials of the Outsiders' aestheticized life are of the present moment, the passing season. Checking herself ironically with the unfeasibility of this solution, the narrator cuts short her letter to the woman treasurer of a woman's college, seeing in her

---

[24]Carlston provides an extended reading of the ways in which *Three Guineas* "engages with and attempts to redefine many of the categories and concepts that fascism, in the 1930s, had managed to make its own: the nation, the media, art, sexuality, motherhood" (155). Her discussion of the media and art is particularly useful for its careful assessment of Woolf's latent "impulse" to recuperate bourgeois notions of pure art and individual artistic genius, a tendency Carlston ultimately reads as suggestive of "socialist aesthetics in the tradition of Morris and Wilde" (163).

saddened face the knowledge that one cannot get anywhere in this world without the attributes a historically grounded institution affords: degrees, honors, recognition. Indeed, much of the productiveness of Woolf's argument comes from the tension she stages, rather than occludes, between the ideal of a life in which aesthetics are of the moment, incorporated into its very fabric, and the recognition that the museum space, while stultifying and artificially isolated, offers collective access to a sense of history and knowledge of that history. Thus the narrator can exhort her addressees to "Go to the public galleries and look at pictures" (148) at the end of the second Guinea, just as she has gone to biography and government publications, in order to learn how people in the past have determined, in this case, how best to approximate the ideals she lays out for the practices of the professions by women. The museum space does have its uses: not as a space for aesthetic contemplation or a source for incontrovertible, transparent fact, but as a space for—and here Diane F. Gillespie's term is appropriate—productive raidings.

At its best, Woolf's argument achieves a fusion between ideal and real, proposing a seemingly impossible aesthetic ideal, deliberately outlined as such, only to suddenly illuminate it as already extant--by finding "factual" evidence of its existence in metaphors of visual aesthetics. This is indeed how the third Guinea, proposing and outlining the binding agreements of the Society of Outsiders, gains its *éclat*. After asserting that its members will work but refuse monetary compensation, cease all competition, turn down all honors, and practice their professions "in the interests of research and for love of the work itself" (204), the narrator anticipates dismissal of such an idea as improbable, and then refutes our doubt:

> [W]hat chance is there, you may ask, that such a Society of Outsiders . . . can be brought into existence, let alone work to any purpose? Indeed, it would have been [a] waste of time to write even so rough a definition of the Outsiders' Society were it merely a bubble of words . . . Happily there is a model in being, a model from which the above sketch has been taken, furtively it is true, for the model, far from sitting still to be painted, dodges and disappears. That model then, the evidence that such a body, whether named or unnamed, exists and works is provided . . . by history and biography in the raw—by the newspapers that is, sometimes openly in the lines, sometimes covertly between them. (209)

The fusion of ideal and real is also at the same time a fusion between visual media, a blurring of the boundaries that distinguish factual print and aesthetic depiction. By casting newsprint, and the history and biography into which news stories will eventually coalesce, as the product of artistic endeavor, the passage succeeds in lending equal aesthetic *and* factual political reality to all media. It has the effect of dissolving the separation between the AIA's artists-only exhibit and the Cambridge factual exhibit. What this passage also makes clear is that Woolf's narrator is herself the artist, sketching furtively but from life, from the "body" of ongoing history that is sometimes dressed, sometimes nude—seen "sometimes openly in the lines, sometimes covertly between them." She thus stands as an example of that artist who facilitates the Society of Outsiders' totally aestheticized life, who combines the scattered beauty so as to make it visible to all. In a sense, this has been the project of *Three Guineas* all along: the artful selection and combination of apparent oddities and incongruencies pieced together to form a new artistic vision that is, fundamentally and inescapably, political.

Woolf's final exhibit in her polemic is thus appropriately an image of the narrator's own creation. Asking us to observe the Spanish Civil War photograph of dead bodies and ruined houses one final time, she points to a dramatic change it has undergone. "It is not the same picture," she observes. She has in fact recreated it as a mixed-media composition, seemingly wrought by the polemic itself:

> For as this letter has gone on, adding fact to fact, another picture has imposed itself upon the foreground. It is the figure of a man; some say, others deny that he is Man himself, the quintessence of virility, the perfect type of which all the others are imperfect adumbrations. He is a man, certainly. His eyes are glazed; his eyes glare. His body, which is braced in an unnatural position, is tightly cased in a uniform. Upon the breast of that uniform are sewn several medals and other mystic symbols. His hand is upon a sword. He is called in German and Italian Fuhrer or Duce; in our own language Tyrant or Dictator. And behind him lie ruined houses and dead bodies—men, women, and children. (257)

In a typical reversal, the narrator here renders the real-life fascist leader a prototypical figure—"the perfect type"—such as might be found in a painting belonging to an art-historical tradition, as, for example, Laura Knight's painting of the archetypal female representing Dawn in the AIA exhibit.[25] Thus the casting of a Hitler or a Mussolini in terms that evoke traditions preserved in art museums does not so much aestheticize political figures as reinforce, and remind us of, the political valence of the aesthetic exhibit. While the uniformed, bemedalled military figure inevitably recalls to the reader-viewer the first of the

---

[25]Gillespie similarly notes that Woolf's argument is enhanced by her decision to describe a "generic dictator" rather than including photographs of Hitler or Mussolini, as did Leonard in *Quack, Quack!* (1935): the latter method "allows us to blame the dictators, not ourselves" ("Her Kodak" 139). Though illuminating, the point leaves unacknowledged the ways this composition exceeds comparisons to photographs alone.

polemic's included photographs, that of the anonymous general, Woolf's language also denotes the painted image: "the hand upon the sword" signals a pose that recalls military portraits, with the military figure in the foreground against the requisite backdrop of war imagery—though in this case the backdrop, the black-and-white photograph, connotes ignominy rather than the glory that military portraits are meant to convey. And though not explicit, the posed, generic figure echoes the "body, named or unnamed" who earlier served as the elusive painter's model from whom a sketch of the Outsider's Society was taken. The echoing of media is of course deliberate, further diminishing the separation of self and other, fascism abroad and at home. *Three Guineas'* basic premise is thus given a visual embodiment, one that also constitutes its final display.

Such a mixed-media image, too, bursts the categories of documentary and artistic exhibitions, and resists inclusion in either, necessitating an entirely different "way of seeing" on the part of us, the visitors to Woolf's radical exhibit. As if to preempt our attempts to fit the composition into a pre-defined exhibition frame, she quickly intervenes, after giving its description, to guide us in our interpretation of it:

> But we have not laid that picture before you in order to excite once more the sterile emotion of hate. On the contrary it is in order to release other emotions such as the human figure, even thus in a crudely coloured photograph, arouses in us who are human beings. . . . It suggests that we cannot dissociate ourselves from that figure but are ourselves that figure. It suggests that we are not passive spectators doomed to unresisting obedience but by our thoughts and actions can ourselves change that figure. (258)

The "sterile emotion of hate" may have been Woolf's final assessment of the productiveness of the Cambridge exhibit, the only possible effect of an exhibit which was organized along predefined lines designating the visitor as reverent admirer of the anti-fascist cause and hater of fascism's adherents. In the passage above, Woolf's narrator aims at redefining the exhibition form so that the distance between exhibit and exhibit-goer is collapsed. Simultaneously the exhibit organizer, artist, and guide, the narrator's clinching argument rests on persuading us that the form of an exhibit, subjecting "passive spectators" to an authoritative arrangement of iconic images and evidence, must be transgressed in order to combat fascism in the real world.

The Cambridge exhibit and its silent relation with its neighboring exhibit, materially incestuous and yet, ideologically, clearly marked so as to be approached and regarded differently, may well have provided Woolf with a model to overturn in order to reveal the "invisible" presence of fascism within British society and history. By undermining the authority of the framing device of each exhibit—by forcing her readers continually to reconsider the exhibition

frame within which an item gains authority—she creates the destabilized conditions for a new exhibit, fascism as manifested in the patriarchal control of
women, heretofore unexamined as such because its "frame" (England, rather
than Germany or Italy) precluded such insights. Finally, the revisionist museum
strategies she adopts for her own exhibits, by which she divests them of any stable claim to a documentary, factual authority or, on the other hand, a "merely
aesthetic" frame, strips the reader's eye of a preconceived frame of reference,
and allows for the sighting of the everyday world as a crucial exhibit. It is this
strategy, too, by which Woolf may have overcome her frustration at not being
able to control what was being exhibited at the Cambridge exhibition: here, at
last and forcefully elaborated, is the completed section on Women and Fascism
that went neglected in the Cambridge Exhibition on Fascism and War.

Works Cited

Alpers, Svetlana. "The Museum as a Way of Seeing." *Exhibiting Cultures:*
     The Poetics and Politics of Museum Display. Ed. Ivan Karp and Steven D.
     Lavine. Washington, D. C.: Smithsonian Institution Press, 1991, 25-32.

Bell, Vanessa. *Selected Letters of Vanessa Bell.* Ed. Regina Marler. New
     York: Pantheon Books, 1993.

Benstock, Shari. *Textualizing the Feminine: On the Limits of Genre.* Norman:
     U of Oklahoma P, 1991.

Berman, Jessica. "Of Oceans and Opposition: *The Waves,* Oswald Mosley, and
     the New Party." *Virginia Woolf and Fascism: Resisting the Dictators'*
     Seduction. Ed. Merry M. Pawlowski. New York: Palgrave, 2001. 105-121.

Bourdieu, Pierre. *The Field of Cultural Production: Essays on Art and*
     Literature. Ed. Randal Johnson. New York: Columbia UP, 1993.

Bradshaw, David. "British Writers and Anti-Fascism in the 1930s, Part I: The
     Bray and Drone of Tortured Voices," *Woolf Studies Annual* 3 (1997), 3-27,
     and "British Writers and Anti-Fascism in the 1930s, Part II: Under the
     Hawk's Wings," *Woolf Studies Annual* 4 (1998), 41-66.

Braun, Emily. *Mario Sironi and Italian Modernism: Art and Politics under*
     Fascism. Cambridge: Cambridge UP, 2000.

Carlston, Erin. *Thinking Fascism: Sapphic Modernism and Fascist Modernity.*
     Stanford: Stanford UP, 1998.

Cunningham, Valentine. *British Writers of the Thirties.* Oxford: Oxford UP, 1988.

Dalgarno, Emily. *Virginia Woolf and the Visible World.* Cambridge:
     Cambridge UP, 2001.

Duffy, Julia and Lloyd Davis. "Demythologizing Facts and Photographs in
     Three Guineas." *Phototextualities: Reading Photographs and Literature.*
     Ed. Marsha Bryant. Newark: U of Delaware P, 1996. 128-40.

Duncan, Carol. *Civilizing Rituals: Inside Public Art Museums.* London:
     Routledge, 1995.

Fisher, Philip. *Making and Effacing Art: Modern American Art in a Culture of Museums*. New York: Oxford UP, 1991.

Froula, Christine. "St. Virginia's Epistle to an English Gentleman; or, Sex, Violence, and the Public Sphere in Woolf's *Three Guineas*." *Tulsa Studies in Women's Literature* 13 (Summer 1994): 27-56.

Gentile, Emilio. *The Sacralization of Politics in Fascist Italy*. Trans. Keith Botsford. Cambridge, MA: Harvard UP, 1996.

Gillespie, Diane F. "'Her Kodak Pointed at His Head': Virginia Woolf and Photography." *The Multiple Muses of Virginia Woolf*. Ed. Diane F. Gillespie. Columbia: U of Missouri P, 1993. 113-47.

———. *The Sisters' Arts: The Writing and Painting of Virginia Woolf and Vanessa Bell*. Syracuse: Syracuse UP, 1988.

Goldman, Jane. *The Feminist Aesthetics of Virginia Woolf: Modernism, Post-Impressionism and the Politics of the Visible*. Cambridge: Cambridge UP, 1998.

Heinemann, Margot. "The People's Front and the Intellectuals." *Britain, Fascism and the Popular Front*. Ed. Jim Fyrth. London: Lawrence and Wishart, 1985.

Hooper-Greenhill, Eilean. *Museums and the Interpretation of Visual Culture*. London: Routledge, 2000.

Lee, Hermione. *Virginia Woolf*. New York: Alfred A. Knopf, 1997.

Marcus, Jane. "'No More Horses': Virginia Woolf on Art and Propaganda." *Women's Studies* 4 (1977): 265-89. Rpt. in *Critical Essays on Virginia Woolf*. Ed. Morris Beja. Boston: G. K. Hall & Co., 1985. 152-171.

Morris, Lynda and Robert Radford. *The Story of the AIA: Artists' International Association, 1933-1953*. Oxford: Museum of Modern Art, 1983.

Nicolson, Nigel. *Virginia Woolf: A Penguin Life*. New York: Lipper/Viking, 2000.

Pawlowski, Merry M. "Reassessing Modernism: Virginia Woolf, *Three Guineas*, and Fascist Ideology." *Woolf Studies Annual* 1 (1995): 47-67.

Radford, Robert. *Art for a Purpose: The Artists' International Association, 1933-1953*. Winchester, Hampshire: Winchester School of Art Press, 1987.

Schnapp, Jeffrey T. "Epic Demonstrations: Fascist Modernity and the 1932 Exhibition of the Fascist Revolution." *Fascism, Aesthetics, and Culture*. Ed. Richard J. Golsan. Hanover: UP of New England, 1992. 1-33.

Stavely, Alice. "Name that Face." *Virginia Woolf Miscellany* 51 (Spring 1998): 4-5.

Stone, Marla. "Staging Fascism: "The Exhibition of the Fascist Revolution." *Journal of Contemporary History* 28.2 (April 1993): 215-44.

Woolf, Virginia. *The Diary of Virginia Woolf. Vol. 4: 1931-1935*. Ed. Anne Olivier Bell, asst. Andrew McNeillie. New York: Harcourt Brace Jovanovich, 1982.

———. *Three Guineas*. London: Hogarth Press, 1952.

"Queer Fish": Woolf's Writing of Desire Between Women in *The Voyage Out* and *Mrs Dalloway:*

Kathryn Simpson

I want you to imagine me writing a novel in a state of trance. . . . a girl sitting with a pen in her hand. . . . . . The image that comes to my mind when I think of this girl is the image of a fisherman lying sunk in dreams on the verge of a deep lake with a rod held out over the water. She was letting her imagination sweep unchecked round every rock and cranny of the world that lies submerged in the depths of our unconscious being. . . . And then there was a smash. . . . The imagination had dashed itself against something hard. . . . she had thought of something, something about the body, about the passions which it was unfitting for her as a woman to say. Men, her reason told her, would be shocked. ("Professions for Women")

"I'm a mermaid! I can swim . . . so the game's up." (*The Voyage Out*)

She wore ear-rings, and a silver-green mermaid's dress. Lolloping on the waves and braiding her tresses she seemed, having that gift still; to be; to exist; . . . all with the most perfect ease and air of a creature floating in its element.
(*Mrs. Dalloway*)

Fish, fishing, fins and mermaid metaphors for women's forbidden desires and creativity, and the connection between the two, are richly suggestive of women's same-sex desire in Virginia Woolf's writing.[1] In "Professions for Women," Woolf draws attention to the risk of censorship and censure consequent on a woman writer's "unchecked" forays into her psychic and erotic depths (7). She suggests the precarious balance the woman writer must maintain between allowing the rush of her imagination and her awareness of the consequences of the 'shocking' revelations about women's passions, bodily pleasures and erotic possibilities. The configuration of elements used to represent the connection between women's eroticism and literary creativity here (bodies of water, land/water borderline, fish and fishing) frequently recurs in Woolf's writing and repeatedly draws attention to the dilemma of speaking of women's passions, in particular the representation of desire between women, given the danger of social reprisal.

---

[1] As Jane Marcus, Jane Goldman, Ellen Rosenman and Deborah Wilson have also suggested.

In *Mrs. Dalloway* Peter Walsh calls the artists and writers whom Clarissa welcomes into her home "queer fish" (*MD* 86) and in this essay I want to explore the figure of the mermaid (a 'queer' fish indeed) as a complex and contradictory metaphor for representing desire between women in *Mrs. Dalloway* and in *The Voyage Out*. The land/sea borderlines that mermaids negotiate, and indeed their hybrid and border-crossing identities, can be read as one of a number of strategies for lesbian survival in a homophobic world in these novels. This slippery mermaid metaphor also signals the difficulties of writing openly about lesbian desire. The ambiguity and plurality of the cultural associations of the mermaid provide a tantalizing screen in *The Voyage Out* and *Mrs. Dalloway* for what in *Orlando* is referred to as the risky smuggling in of "highly contraband,", implicitly lesbian, material (*O* 166). Yet the mermaid figure also suggestively embodies, as indeed does the transsexual, transgressive figure of Orlando him/herself, the sexual allure of queerness.

Jane Marcus argues for the lesbian erotics of Woolf's creative process and identifies the figure of the mermaid as central to this,[2] claiming that "the underwater world of the woman artist's imagination suggests a submarine lesbian utopia where desire and writing are intimately connected" (155). Indeed, the literal and metaphorical bodies of water that pervade Woolf's writing create significant locations for the figuring of women's same-sex desire. Her writing in many ways seems to privilege the sea as a significant space for a renegotiation and a reconceptualisation of gender as more fluid and less rigidly defined, and for a revision of woman-centred sexuality which is potentially emancipatory. Culturally coded as a feminine and maternal space, the sea has become a site of freedom and possibility beyond the force field of patriarchy[3] and stands as the binary opposite of 'masculine' land and all it represents (reason, stability, patriarchal law, regulation of behaviors and identities, heterosexuality, civilization and empire). The sea figures the plural, fluid and unregulated realm of the pre-Oedipal and the semiotic, and so is a locus for the exploration and fulfilment of

[2]She argues that "[t]he muse of the woman writer, her guide into the unconscious realms of female sexual experience, is a mermaid. Their relationship, the writer as 'fisherwoman,' and the muse as diver, is distinctly lesbian" (151). In a more general consideration of the potential for animal imagery to function as a homoerotic code, Ruth Vanita similarly suggests that the mermaid's hybridity, the combination of "disturbing eroticism" with her "unavailability" for heterosexual reproduction makes her "an apt symbol for homoerotic desire" (237). Further, she suggests that the mermaid, along with other fabulous creatures, generally symbolizes creativity (238).

[3]As feminist theoreticians of space and territory suggest. In the words of one critic, the sea offers Rachel and Edna, the heroine of Kate Chopin's *The Awakening*, "the promise of unfettered possibilities outside patriarchy" (Vlasopolos 75).

unconventional, non-heterosexual desires and sexual drives, of erotic possibilities beyond those culturally prescribed. The recurrent image in Woolf's writing
of a fin *in* the water far out to sea figures the necessarily elusive process of representing such unconventional desires and passions and, indeed, can suggest the
homoerotic inspiration for Woolf's creativity.[4] Tracing the metaphor of the fin
in Woolf's writing, Deborah Wilson reads it as "a marker of lesbian desire" and,
pertinent to my exploration here, argues that "the fin . . . marks the hidden, the
unrepresentable, and interrupts the hegemonic surface to figure a subversive lesbian desire" (122, 126).

However, the sea as a metaphorically utopian space for women is also
fraught with dangers and the fantasy of escape or return to the sea can simultaneously threaten dissolution and death (*fin* indeed) in the form of non-identity, or
of an identity perceived as monstrously deviant and not fully human. Such an
escape can only ever be a fantasy since to move to this space 'outside' patriarchy
and phallocentric culture is to occupy a space already constructed by the dominant culture as dehumanized 'other.' As Juliet Mitchell spells out, "[y]ou cannot
choose the imaginary, the semiotic, the carnival as an alternative to the law. It is
set up by the law precisely in its own ludic space, its area of imaginary alternative, but not as a symbolic alternative" (cited in Russo 37). So what might seem
to be a feminine, fluid and liberating space for women can actually operate as a
trap.

Woolf's writing shows an awareness of the paradox of pleasure and danger
of such metaphorical spaces and her texts continually test the borderlines of culturally constructed identities and sexualities. In her writing, the transgression of
land/sea borders acts as a spatial metaphor for other boundaries being tested and
transgressed–notably those cultural boundaries which demarcate the permissible
sexual and artistic territory available for men and women to occupy. These borderlines are not merely sites of potential lesbian trespass on heterosexual male
territory, however, but the ever-shifting land/sea boundaries defy the binary logic
so fundamental to Western culture and to the structures of heterosexuality itself.
Refusing the logic of either/or, of fixed boundaries between stable oppositions,
these liminal spaces can be read as sites of queer resistance to heterocentric
imperatives. Occupation of these frequently erotically charged spaces offers
immense possibility for sexual and linguistic jouissance, for pleasure which

---

[4]The image of "a fin passing far out" is a phrase in Woolf's *Diary* specifically connected to her inspiration for *The Waves*, and for her tracing of the process of her own
creativity (113). It conveys her "curious state of mind" which follows a period of gloomy
solitude and contemplation, an experience she sums up as "a plunge into deep waters" and
"awfully queer" (*D3* 113, 112).

exceeds cultural norms in its privileging of 'both/and,' even as it simultaneously signals the difficulties of openly expressing such queer desires.

Located in the ambiguous borderline space between land and sea, human and animal, and masculine and feminine, the hybrid mermaid figure represents this testing and disruption of culturally constructed borderlines and the privileging of 'both/and.' In particular, the mermaid's 'femininity with a phallic tail' queries and queers the gender pairings so fundamental to the operation of patriarchal heterosexuality and her hybridity thus marks a refusal of heterosexual imperatives. Hybrid in still another way, the largely Celtic and Gaelic folkloric myth of the mermaid is often conflated with the Ancient Greek myth of the sirens and it is this composite figure of female allure and deviance which forms such a powerful source of male heterosexual fascination and anxiety.[5] Associated with freedom and mobility, and representing the powerful temptation of female sexuality, the siren-mermaid is a heterosexual male fantasy of the seductive power of women's unfettered sexuality.[6] Simultaneously, the mermaid's monstrous form embodies a fear of women's untamed and uncontained sexual energy and a transgression of bourgeois constructions of ideal femininity as sexually inactive and morally pure. Her possession of a phallic, impenetrable tail is the most obvious external sign of her monstrosity because it disrupts the gender dualism central to the hetero-patriarchal social order in its suggestion of active, 'virile' sexuality. Her tail also prevents the recuperation of this active female sexuality into the heterosexual reproductive matrix and so still further signals the resistance to this sexual economy. Although there is a wide range of accumulated cultural meanings and associations around the figure of the mermaid, all in some way are concerned with the issue of female sexuality as powerfully attractive yet potentially dangerous, excessive and deviant if not regulated or tamed by heterosexual restrictions. The siren-mermaid figure is, then, an apt metaphor with which to embody, yet not explicitly name, those lesbian desires so 'shocking' and unfitting for women writers to express.

---

[5]This conflation is apparent, for example, in Herbert James Draper's painting, *Ulysses and the Sirens* (1909). The painting alludes to Homer's epic poem, the *Odyssey*, and depicts Odysseus/Ulysses tied to the mast of his boat to prevent him from succumbing to the powerful allure of the sirens' song. Three sirens climb onto the boat and the last one has a tail just visible beneath the sea. Lynda Nead offers a more detailed reading of this painting (19). I am grateful to Mike Davis for calling my attention to this painting.

[6]As Nead points out, in the eighteenth century and increasingly in the nineteenth, "[t]he term 'siren' was a useful short-hand" for "the contemporary prostitute," connoting "one dominant view of the prostitute. . . . as a temptress, corrupted and corrupting, luring young men to their destruction and able to wreak terrible havoc on society" (11).

In the nineteenth century the mermaid became a pervasive figure in the visual arts and in literature.[7] Retaining her dangerous allure, the mermaid became more specifically identified with the sense of women's defiance of restrictive bourgeois gender definitions, sexual transgression and self-transformation. In her now classic text, *Woman and the Demon*, Nina Auerbach, like Lynda Nead, identifies the mermaid and other serpent women as central to the profoundly contradictory conceptualizations of woman in this period. She argues that far from being discrete stable categories, the dualistic definitions of women as angel/demon threatened always to collapse into one another (7-8). Whilst the angel-woman was ostensibly and publicly lauded, cultural iconography "slithered with images of a mermaid" (7), and the repressed disruptive power of the angel woman threatens always to erupt into something monstrously attractive.

Hans Christian Andersen's "The Little Mermaid," immensely popular in the Victorian period, acts in some ways as a counter to this sense of empowered female sexuality, evoking the severe restrictions on women felt necessary to keep them in their place. It clearly spells out the necessary sacrifices young women must make in the transition to ideal womanhood through a powerful tale focused on taming the danger that the mermaid represents and on channelling women's deviant sexual energy into the heterosexual romance script. The Little Mermaid must sacrifice her most precious gift, her voice, and separate herself from the female community of her fellow mermaids, in order to stand a chance of marriage.[8] In the context of the myths surrounding mermaids in general, the story is also, implicitly, a cautionary tale with its images of the non-human, monstrous feminine metaphor-

[7]As Nead's article makes clear, there was an explosion of interest in the siren-mermaid myths, which came to a peak in the 1880s, with the publication of a number of histories and mythologies (including that of Woolf's friend and mentor, Jane Harrison's, *Myths of the Odyssey In Literature and Art* [1882]), the regular reprinting of William Cowper's and Alexander Pope's translations of the *Odyssey*, and the "romantic and nationalistic revival of interest in folk traditions and Celtic and Gaelic mythology" (5, 15, 6, 7). In addition to the seven paintings Nead discusses in this article, there are numerous others which depict the figure of the siren-mermaid and which contribute to the ongoing debate about femininity and female sexuality. Auerbach, for instance, also discusses Edward Burne-Jones' "Head of a Mermaid" and "In the Depths of the Sea" (1887). In literature too there are numerous instances of the figure of the mermaid which contribute to this debate, such as Alfred Lord Tennyson's poems, "The Mermaid" and "The Sea-Fairies," in *Poems, Chiefly Lyrical* (1830), Elizabeth Gaskell's *Mary Barton* (1848), and William Makepeace Thackeray's *Vanity Fair* (1847-8).

[8]At the end of the nineteenth century, as Jack Zipes notes, the fairytale as a literary form for children was concerned with the control of desire and the imagination (25). It aimed to promote bourgeois values and mores, and to reinforce "the patriarchal symbolic order based on rigid notions of sexuality and gender" (25, 26).

ically representing 'Other' female figures, deviant women, who refuse to comply with dominant social and sexual norms and who are hence considered to be sinful, 'soulless' and less than fully human.

However, as Jack Zipes suggests, the symbolic and polyvocal nature of fairy tales, and the sometimes deliberately subversive intent of some of their writers open up possibilities for multiple interpretations that can also question the social values and mores the tales seem to be promoting.[9] Despite the tale's apparently conservative and heterocentric focus, the themes of "The Little Mermaid" also resonate with aspects of lesbian and gay experience. It is a tale of unrequited love, loss and sense of otherness, of longing and the willing self-sacrifice of independence and aspects of identity, of collusion in oppressive social structures and self-censorship experienced by many marginalized groups seeking social acceptance. It seems significant that the Little Mermaid's real motivation for marriage is not the completion of the heterosexual romance script, but the attainment of an immortal soul and the recognition of being perceived as fully human. It can also be read, as Ruth Vanita points out, as a "parable" in which "gay love is misread by its object as filial," where the Little Mermaid operates "as stand-in for the gay male" whose cross-dressing as female costs him his voice (237). In this reading, the Little Mermaid's dumbness is a metaphor for the love that dare not speak its name, and points to the silencing of homoerotic desires involved in the pretence of 'passing' as straight. Given Andersen's own ambiguous social (and sexual) position, Laura Sells suggests that the story can be read as "a personal narrative of the pleasures and dangers of 'passing'" (177). The pleasure and pain of such ambiguity and passing have relevance to the survival strategies figured by the mermaid in *The Voyage Out* and *Mrs. Dalloway*.

[9]The most popular and influential version of "The Little Mermaid" tale in the late twentieth and early twenty-first centuries is the Walt Disney film version, *The Little Mermaid*. Whilst it most obviously enforces conservative ideas about gender identity and women's roles, Disney's version of the tale continues to retain a degree of ambiguity and potential for transgressing the values and mores it seems to promote. Like Andersen's tale, Disney's film seems to reinforce the idea that the only acceptable route to maturity for women is through the loss of independence, agency and 'voice' in heterosexual marriage. However, Laura Sells offers an analysis of the film which suggests that it simultaneously criticizes the limited and limiting options for women. For her, this version of Andersen's tale is not only "more insidious because it sanitizes the costs of women's access to the 'male sphere' by vilifying women's strength and by erasing the pain that so often accompanies 'passing'," but also "more liberatory because it contains the means of its own undoing in the camp characters of Ursula the Sea Witch, and in Disney's compulsory happy ending, which bestows the mermaid with both access *and* voice" (176). That this later version of the tale retains the *potential* at least for subversion of cultural constraints on women's experience is significant for my reading of the figure of the mermaid and the allusions to "The Little Mermaid" in Woolf's writing.

The paradoxical figure of the mermaid is, then, a problematic one, speaking at once of a defiance of limiting gender definitions and of the dangerous potential of unrestrained female sexuality, but also of the powerful stigma of being perceived as monstrous, a stigma which goes hand in hand with women's rebellion and transgressions of hetero-patriarchal prescriptions. A figure of heterosexual male fantasy, the mermaid also more indirectly represents the idea of being an 'outsider' in constructions of lesbian and gay identities. In *The Voyage Out* and *Mrs. Dalloway* all of these paradoxes come into play. In these novels the mermaid figures and borderline spaces belie what seems at first to be a central concern with heterosexual relationships, suggesting instead an exploration of the more ambiguous margins of desire. The figure of the mermaid operates as a contradictory metaphor for the exploration of women-centred desires and seems to encapsulate the paradox of pleasure and danger that lesbian existence at the margins of heterocentric culture can entail. The negotiation of these margins as a strategy for survival in a homophobic world is not wholly positive for Rachel and Clarissa, however, and is synonymous with compromise and loss. Their loss is, not least, the sacrifice of the mermaid's voice in the silencing of any open expression of lesbian desires, which is the price necessary to gain acceptance into the heterosexual world. As her adoption of narrative strategies which *indirectly* represent lesbian desires confirms, Woolf was acutely aware of this price exacted for acceptance.

The Voyage Out tells the story of the sexual awakening, engagement and death of the central character, Rachel Vinrace, as she journeys from England to South America. On the surface, it is a tragic tale of thwarted heterosexual romance which mutinies from the conventional fairy tale marriage plot with the death of the heroine before she marries. Woolf's abandonment of the marriage plot seems to be symptomatic of a profound anxiety about the potentially limiting and damaging effects of conventional gender roles and sexuality in patriarchal culture. However, Rachel's dramatic abdication from the heterosexual romance script can also be read as a refusal of heterosexuality itself[10] and the

---

[10]Other critics read this novel in terms of its potential for a lesbian subversion of the heterosexual marriage plot. Jessica Tvordi and Patricia Juliana Smith offer readings which uncover/recover the homoerotic intimacy and lesbian possibilities submerged in Woolf's successive revisions of the novel. Tvordi reads the novel as Rachel's 'coming out' narrative through a focus on Rachel's relationship with Helen and on the lesbian subplots which "subvert the heterosexual plot and reveal the novel to be women-centred and lesbian" (227). Smith focuses her analysis on Helen's dissimulation about her own covert lesbian desires and reads the "undoing [of] the courtship plot" through a focus on the operation of "lesbian panic" in the novel (20). She defines "lesbian panic" as "the disruptive action or reaction that occurs when a character—or, conceivably, an author—is either unable or unwilling to confront or reveal her own lesbianism or lesbian desire" (2).

mermaid figures in this novel signal this refusal.

At first it seems as if Rachel and her fiancé, Terence Hewet, may be able to have a relationship based on equality. Given Rachel's perception of the potentially crippling effect that the heterosexual institutions of marriage, prostitution and the family can have on women, the promise of an equal relationship seems to be a crucial factor in the attraction she feels for Terence and in her decision to marry him. The setting and context in which they first realize their attraction for one another seems significant. The edge of the cliff to which they walk to see the spectacle of jelly-fish floating close to the shore is an unconventional borderline site from where the land and sea spaces are viewed paradoxically as both distinctly different and yet similar: the "infinite sun-dried earth" with its clearly defined "pinnacles" and "barriers" is likened to "the immense floor of the sea," "widening and spreading away and away" (*VO* 194). In their discussion, Terence is said to "instinctively" adopt "the feminine point of view" as he speaks to Rachel of his anger at the injustices and inequalities women face (*VO* 197).[11] Several critics remark that it is only when he and Rachel become engaged that the potential for an egalitarian marriage quickly erodes as cultural conventions and expectations about gender roles impose themselves and Terence increasingly conforms to the prescriptions of the marriage plot.[12] However, his feminist credentials are already in question in this pre-engagement cliff-top scene.

Although Terence's feminist discourse begins to raise Rachel's awareness about gender inequalities in her own experience, ironically, the pressure of his determined quest for knowledge about what women feel hampers Rachel.[13] Further, he objectifies Rachel as she lies staring into the sea, and his gaze constructs her as almost mermaid-like as she lies with her soft, deep blue dress clinging to the shape of her body and he stares, fascinated, like many a fisherman or sailor at her own rapt attention to the sea (*VO* 195). However, when Rachel begins to express her own views about the superiority of her own interests (music) over his occupation of writing novels, this spell and his seductive fantasy of her as an object of desire is broken. The tentative and implicit mermaid reference here begins to suggest a disruption of the conventional narrative of burgeoning heterosexual romance. Terence's objectifying gaze constructs Rachel as a sexually alluring mermaid, yet her own affinity with the sea and her defence of her own musical/siren voice suggests that for Rachel a mermaid identity is a

[11]As Marianne DeKoven also notes (107)

[12]For example, DeKoven (132-3) and Clare Hanson (38) note the radical reversal in Terence's earlier feminist views following his engagement to Rachel.

[13]As Rachel Blau DuPlessis remarks, "at no other point does the reader feel Rachel more talked at than in Terence's speeches to Rachel on women's potential and their anger" (51).

refusal of such fantasies. Already in the novel Rachel's affinity with the sea has marked her difference from and resistance to heterosexual imperatives.[14] Here, absorbed in her own gazing at the sea and experiencing "the exquisitely pleasant sensations which a little depth of the sea washing over rocks suggests," Rachel is indifferent to Terence's romantic and romanticizing gaze (*VO* 195).

These two positions—Terence's fantasy and Rachel's resistance to his fantasy and defiance of his assumed superiority—become increasingly apparent once Rachel and Terence are engaged. Their disagreement over whose creative voice should take precedence reaches a peak in a telling incident when Terence attempts to write in Rachel's workroom as she plays her piano. Rachel becomes irritated by his interruptions and he objects to her playing of difficult, challenging pieces of music because they disturb his concentration. However, it seems that it is not only the literal disturbance that Terence objects to, but also the disruptive influence Rachel's music (her creative, unconventional, siren voice) can have on the social order.[15] In this scene we see his fantasy of her as an object of desire change—Rachel's mermaid-siren allure turns into something unnatural and monstrous as her creative voice encroaches on Terence's male territory. His sense of her monstrous encroachment is revealed by his preference for "nice sim-

---

[14]For instance, at the point at which the *Euphrosyne* begins its journey Rachel's affinity with the sea and its creatures and her simultaneous difference and dissociation from conventional relationships (the married couple of the Ridleys, and her own relationship with her father) is signalled as, left alone, she gazes into the depths of the sea and dimly perceives the remains of wrecked ships and "the smooth green-sided monsters who came by flickering this way and that" (*VO* 20). Further, as St. John Hirst's teasing remark suggests, Rachel's reason for accompanying Terence to the cliff top may not be for the romantic possibilities of time alone with him, nor of seeing what he has seen (the breathtaking spectacle of "'about twenty jelly-fish, semi-transparent, pink, with long streamers, floating on the top of the waves'"), but it may be in the hope of seeing mermaids (*VO* 188). Later, Terence's recollection of his first impression of Rachel as resembling "a creature who'd lived all its life among pearls and old bones" is another instance of Rachel's affinity with the sea and her difference from others. Her wet hands also suggest her sexual elusiveness as she can slip away from Terence, out of his grasp (*VO* 277).

[15]Earlier in the novel Rachel's music/voice and her unconventional playing has the power to radically shake up hierarchies and categories of all kinds, as the revelry of the dances her music inspires demonstrates. Just as the mixture of styles of music she plays transgresses musical genres, so it inspires a transgression of conventional gender roles in the dancers (*VO* 152-3). Smith makes a similar point: "once the traditional dance music is discarded, so are gender-based dance traditions" (23). Rachel's experience of playing in this workroom scene similarly disrupts conventional gender notions as she plays with the vigor of physical exercise which would be considered unfeminine and which, as an earlier conversation with Helen reveals, gives Rachel a worryingly muscular body (*VO* 13).

ple tunes," and, more significantly, by his scornful criticism of her unconventional form of self-expression as implicitly unnatural in his allusion to Dr. Johnson's views on women who usurp male roles (*VO* 276).[16] Invoking Rachel's duties as a woman, Terence succeeds in silencing both her creative voice and her oppositions to his views as, with considerable resentment, she begins to respond to the letters of congratulation on their engagement. Their disagreement is thus seemingly diffused by Rachel's conforming to Terence's expectations and her apparent acquiescence in conventional roles for women. It seems as if, like Andersen's Little Mermaid, Rachel recognizes that her voice must be stifled in order to become fully human (for women this means becoming a 'proper' wife). However, the physical tussle that shortly ensues suggests something quite different.

Terence explains that what he finds attractive about Rachel is her potential to overpower him, to throw him from the rocks into the sea (*VO* 281). As earlier on the cliff top, his sense of her dangerous allure resonates with that of mermaids and sirens. That this is only a seductive fantasy for him, however, is demonstrated when, in the seemingly playful fight "for mastery" that they have, he overpowers Rachel (*VO* 281). She is flung to the floor, a space which is metaphorically the sea in this 'game,' and so into an appropriately feminine element. This looks like defeat for Rachel—she must give in to Terence's wishes and accept her role as subservient wife to his of 'master.' However, it is she who triumphantly escapes the binary logic of master/ servant, and implicitly the binary logic of the heterosexuality itself. Dishevelled and her dress torn, Rachel cries, "'I'm a mermaid! I can swim . . . so the game's up'" (*VO* 282).

Although critics have noted "Rachel's propensity to escape from normal sexual demands . . . by means of the sea" (Schlack 25), the significance of her embracing of a mermaid identity seems not to have been fully explored. Unlike Terence's version of Rachel as mermaid, which ultimately accords with conventional gender norms, Rachel's triumphant claiming of a mermaid identity here is a defiance and a disruption of the binary oppositions so fundamental to the structures of heterosexuality. With her torn dress metaphorically suggesting loss of virginity ('damaged goods'), this moment is also a defiance of the heterosexual value system in which women's virginity is so highly prized as a marketable commodity (as reference to Milton's *Comus* later makes apparent). Unlike Terence's fantasies which fix women as objects of male desire, the mermaid identity Rachel embraces keeps contradictions and paradoxes in play, maintaining a

[16]Hanson (38-9) and DeKoven (132) also note that the allusion to Johnson's dictum ("A woman's preaching is like a dog's walking on his hinder legs. It is not done well; but you are surprised to find it done at all," Darwin 275) is significant to the foregrounding of issues of women's creative expression in this novel.

disruptive refusal of categories and meanings. It is a defiant and empowered identity signalling a rejection of the Little Mermaid's self-sacrifice and speaking of something other than heterosexual romance.

In this tussle with Terence, being "flung into the sea" is not a losing position for Rachel and she finds the idea of being "washed hither and thither" to be "incoherently delightful" (*VO* 281). Rachel's affinity with the feminine body of the sea and with its creatures, which has marked both her difference and her distance from her heterocentric culture at a number of points in the novel, raises questions about her sexuality in this scene. Here, Terence interprets Rachel's powerful movement as if through an imaginary sea, "bending and thrusting aside the chairs and tables as if she were indeed striking through the waters," as a metaphorical clearing of the passage through life for them both (*VO* 281). However, the 'incoherence' of Rachel's 'delight,' the inexpressible source of her physical pleasure here, leaves this interpretation open to question and in fact recalls Rachel's sensations experienced in her tussle with Helen earlier in the novel. This scene in its physical intimacy and playful violence anticipates and parallels the scene of Rachel's tussle with Terence in a way which sheds much light on the nature of Rachel's 'delight' and her increasing awareness of her sexuality.

This erotically charged incident takes place during the expedition to the native village. Helen surprises Rachel and Terence and, as in the tussle with Terence, similarly flings Rachel to the ground, repeatedly rolling her over in the sea-like grass. The physicality of this contact leaves Rachel "speechless and almost without sense" (*VO* 268). Finally, finding herself pressed against Helen's "soft body" and embraced in her "strong and hospitable arms," Rachel, "panting," reaches a final peak of suggestively orgasmic pleasure, indicated by her feeling of "happiness swelling and breaking in one vast wave" (*VO* 268). As Jessica Tvordi and Patricia Juliana Smith also note, this moment of intensity is shot through with Rachel's realization of homoerotic possibility, signalled by imagery frequently associated with woman-centred sexual pleasure in Woolf's writing–the swelling and breaking wave.[17]

---

[17]For Tvordi this is a moment in which "Rachel realizes Helen–realizes the sexual power of a woman for the first time" and "is able, for a brief moment to give herself over to her fantasies" (234), and for Smith "the orgasmic images with which Woolf inscribes this embrace connote that what Rachel 'realises' is nothing less than the intent of Helen's lesbian desire" (25). However, for Smith Helen's behavior is completely out of character so that "the savage and erotic violence of Helen's actions" signals her lesbian panic born out of her "entangled desires" for Rachel's mother, her "quasi-incestuous" desires for Rachel, and her jealousy of Terence (25, 24). Whereas Tvordi and I read this scene as one

In contrast to this woman-centered pleasure experienced with Helen and in her movement in the imaginary sea after her tussle with Terence, Rachel finds the structures of heterosexuality to be increasingly claustrophobic and restrictive. As Rachel and Terence's engagement continues to fall into the conventional patterns modeled by the novel's other engaged couple, Susan Warrington and Arthur Venning, the tension begins to mount for Rachel and she falls ill. Her illness can be read as symptomatic of the social and sexual pressures and sense of entrapment she feels as she realizes the extent to which cultural expectations compel individuals to conform to a narrow set of behaviors. DeKoven draws attention to the problem of the narrow, culturally prescribed and severely limited structures through which desire can be experienced as key to Rachel's illness, and DuPlessis similarly suggests that Rachel's death is a consequence of the "cavalier and violent" way that Helen and Terence automatically 'write' Rachel "into the marriage plot" (52). Smith similarly suggests that Rachel's death can be attributed to a number of factors, including "the panic arising from the prospect of being permanently subsumed into institutional heterosexuality" (36). As for Clarissa in *Mrs. Dalloway*, marriage becomes synonymous with death for Rachel.[18] More important in Smith's analysis, however, is the operation of "lesbian panic," which she identifies as key to the development of the novel's narrative and which has its source in Rachel's uncertainty about her own sexuality. She attributes Rachel's death in part to her "very unwillingness or inability to attempt a resolution of her sexual dilemma" which makes her "an unviable, indeed, a non-narratable character" (36).

In addition to the 'causes of death' identified by DeKoven, DuPlessis and Smith, I want to suggest that Rachel's increasing awareness of the anxiety about lesbian sexuality in a hetero-patriarchal culture (which mounts in the novel after Rachel and Terence's engagement is announced) is an equally significant factor contributing to her death. Her panic and sense of claustrophobia are a result of her sense both of entrapment in marriage *and* of her awareness of the severely limited options for women's erotic fulfilment outside of marriage. Smith discusses the ambiguity around the two homoerotically charged meetings that Rachel has with Evelyn Murgatroyd and Miss Allan in their respective bedrooms. I agree that these two meetings are suggestive of homoerotic possibility, which is

---

which helps to bring the articulation of Rachel's emerging lesbian sexuality closer to the textual surface, Smith reads it as an explosion of tension and as a sign of lesbian panic on the part of Helen and also of Woolf herself (24).

[18]Christine Froula and Tvordi also note the equation of marriage and death/silence for female characters in *The Voyage Out*.

not fully realized in the narrative or spoken by the characters.[19] However, whereas Smith emphasizes the inability or reluctance of Evelyn, Miss Allan and Rachel to identify their desires as lesbian in order that they can remain "innocent of blame" (33), I read both of these meetings as compounding still further Rachel's growing awareness of the all-pervasive restrictions on and limited options for women's expression and fulfilment of desire in a hetero-patriarchal culture.[20]

She sees this restriction on women's expression of sexuality outside of marriage in evidence in the experience of the implicitly lesbian figures of Nurse McInnis and Miss Allan in the microcosm of British society at the hotel. In two key moments the virtual impossibility of lesbian fulfilment in Rachel's homophobic culture becomes starkly apparent and the severe restrictions on women's erotic expression and fulfilment are highlighted by reference to the decadent poet of Sapphic and homoerotic love, A. C. Swinburne. As in other lesbian modernist writing (such as that of H. D. and Renée Vivien), Swinburne functions as a symbol of 'alternative' desires[21] and his Sapphic associations generate a sense of

[19]More positively, Tvordi argues that Rachel's meeting with Evelyn "is as close to a seduction scene as *The Voyage Out* can offer" and sees it as "the scene of possible seduction" towards which the whole novel is moving (233, 231). She too reads this scene of failed seduction in terms of Rachel's "unsuccessful attempts to come to terms with her feelings for women" (234).

[20]I think this is particularly the case in the interaction between Rachel and Evelyn where Evelyn openly voices her own sense of repulsion from male sexuality as brutish and beastly in a way which resonates with Rachel's feelings expressed shortly after Richard Dalloway's kiss and in her nightmares. The description of Richard Dalloway's kiss, with "the roughness of his cheek printed on hers [Rachel's]," is echoed in Evelyn's complaint, "'I can still feel his nasty hairy face just there'," as she vigorously scrubs at her cheek (*VO* 66, 233). Both experience the sensation of being kissed by a hairy face and the imprinting on their skin of the assumed male right to act in this way similarly. More importantly to my reading here, though, is that Evelyn tells Rachel that one of her disgruntled suitors has called her "merely a siren" (*VO* 233). This term encapsulates both Rachel's woman-centred desires and defiance, but also her fears and anxieties about the way women's sexuality is made to function in hetero-patriarchal sexual economies. Evelyn's name and "siren" seem to demonstrate for Rachel the overwhelming containment of women's sexuality and desires within this system. Woman is simultaneously guilty of being the powerful temptress and corrupter of men, as well as the degraded prostitute/victim—as Evelyn's discussion of her plans to help prostitutes and to end this trade in women's sexuality further highlights for Rachel (*VO* 234-5).

[21]Cassandra Laity argues that the more fluid representation of gender identities and sexualities found in decadence writing enabled women modernists "to fashion a feminist poetic of female desire" (218). Beverly Ann Schlack also comments that Woolf's "coupling [of] Sappho and Swinburne" signals sexual and literary unconventionality (13).

sexual and social freedom which contrasts sharply with the reality of lesbian existence for the majority of women in Rachel's world.

The first moment juxtaposes St. John Hirst's reading of Sappho's "Ode to Aphrodite" and his reference to Swinburne's "Sapphics" with Rachel's observation of the spinster and religious devotee, Nurse McInnis, during a church service (*VO* 216-217). Sappho's and Swinburne's poems take for granted the primacy of women's desires for women and are replete with the bitter sweetness of lesbian love which Sappho's poems so frequently evoke. In stark contrast, Rachel is struck with horror at the devastating effects that her own homophobic culture can have on lesbians. Realizing the bitterness which motivates Nurse McInnis' religious devotion and conformity, and the denial of emotions, pleasures and sensations which underlies this devotion, Rachel characterizes her as "a limpet, with the sensitive side of her stuck to a rock, for ever dead to the rush of fresh and beautiful things past her" (*VO* 216). This realization marks a significant turning point for Rachel in terms of her rejection of "all that she had implicitly believed"—ostensibly her religious belief, but also her naïve and unquestioning acceptance of the homophobia inherent in her society (*VO* 216).

The second moment which highlights the restriction on lesbian expression is the coincidence of Miss Allan's congratulation of Rachel and Terence on their engagement with her announcement that she has cut short her primer of English Literature. Instead of ending her study with Swinburne, as she had planned, this implicitly lesbian spinster scholar has decided to end it with the overtly heterosexual poet Robert Browning, whose marriage to Elizabeth Barrett was one of the great romances of the late nineteenth century.[22] Her compromise signals the hard choices for single women and lesbians living on the margins of society and her reason for the change is overtly economic—she feels the alliteration of her title, "Beowulf to Browning," will be eye-catching for sale at railway station bookstalls (*VO* 299). However, her jettisoning of a potentially disruptive and threatening poet is also a forced complicity with the homophobic society in which the manly Miss Allan must survive. Her expression of her desire to include "everybody" in her primer highlights her exclusion of the homoerotic Swinburne and serves to emphasize her personal and intellectual compromise, as well as the public self-censorship and silencing of homoerotic desires that motivates this revision.

At the point at which Rachel does become ill, then, the options for her future in a heterocentric and homophobic culture have become blatantly clear, and the

---

[22]This was especially the case after the publication of their letters in 1899 which led to a wave of sentimental response to their heterosexual romance—a romance parodied by Woolf in her novel *Flush: A Biography* (1933).

pressure she feels is complex. She is faced with a terrifying choice of the life-denying institutions of heterosexuality (her ideas about marriage, maternity and prostitution are all conflated in her recurring nightmare of a dark, damp tunnel oozing slime),[23] or the self-censorship, compromise and equally life-denying and 'limpet–like' existence of the spinster/lesbian. In the face of such a choice, Rachel again makes a bid for freedom into the fantastical realm of the mermaid, here a more fully idealized and erotically charged woman-centered space than earlier in the novel, where her desires can find expression without fear of reprisal or censorship.

It is Milton's *Comus* which finally prompts Rachel's escape into fantasy, offering as it does yet another reminder of what it means to be a woman in a het-ero-patriarchal culture, and suggesting an escape route into a feminine space. In this poem, the virginal water-nymph, Sabrina, rescues a chaste Lady from the sexual threats posed by Comus and his magical spell. The Lady is 'saved' from the rapacious appetites of Comus and returned to her father's house with her highly prized chastity intact and her own desires unawakened. Since the poem is crucially concerned with women's chastity, it is easy to see that Rachel's illness could be read as psychosomatic and attributed to her general fear of her awaken-

---

[23]This nightmare, with its obvious vaginal/womb tunnel metaphor, readily suggests anxiety about heterosexual maturity and motherhood and, given Rachel's associations of the tunnel under the Thames with prostitutes, can be read as a stage in the process of her overcoming of a sense of sex as illicit or taboo. However, this nightmare, triggered by Richard Dalloway's kiss sprung upon the inexperienced Rachel earlier in the novel, suggests something more than a common anxiety about sexual awakening. Following the publication of "A Sketch of the Past," critics, notably Louise DeSalvo (*Impact*), have read this novel in relation to the long-term impact of Woolf's experience of sexual abuse on her life and writing. The implication that Rachel has been sexually abused by her father (raised in the text by the comment that Helen "suspected him of nameless atrocities with regard to his daughter" [*VO* 17]) and that Richard Dalloway's kiss is experienced as a fur-ther abuse might go some way to accounting for Rachel's fearful sense of the risk for women of violence and entrapment in heterosexual relationships. However, whilst in the novel Rachel's emerging homoeroticism coincides with her rejection of heterosexuality and its institutions, and with her perception of male sexuality as brutish, I think reading a direct causal link between the suggestion that she has been abused and her sexual orien-tation is too reductive. Rather, Rachel's emerging homoeroticism is part of a complex process bound up with her perception of the limited options for women's expression and erotic fulfilment in a heterocentric culture. Richard's kiss awakens Rachel to the existence of the "infinite possibilities" of her own desires, but simultaneously makes her aware of the restricted and claustrophobic lives women are forced to lead, lives of circumscribed actions, desires and emotions in which they are "hedged-in . . . made dull and crippled for ever" by men's desires and appropriations of women's bodies (*VO* 67, 72).

ing sexual appetites.[24] In a state of incipient fever, then, the overtly sexual threat that Comus poses for the Lady of Milton's poem—her initiation into heterosexuality–resonates quite forcibly with Rachel's own fears about sexuality which have surfaced earlier in the novel following her own 'initiation' into heterosexuality (experienced as a violation) by Richard Dalloway's kiss.

However, the poem also offers a lesson in the denial of women's desires in the operation of the heterosexual economy. Rachel understands that in this economy women are not perceived as actively desiring subjects, but as objects of exchange between men. This apparently proves overwhelming for Rachel and she must mutiny from the heterosexual script in which she is becoming trapped. Rachel's escape from the poem's narrative parallels her escape from her own marriage plot—she abandons both before all possibilities for women's expressions of desire are closed down. Rachel escapes, suggestively as a mermaid, into a fantasy of joining Sabrina beneath "[t]he glassy, cool, translucent wave" from which Sabrina emerges in Milton's poem (*VO* 311).

The presence and magical actions of the water-nymph in the poem are significant in more ways than one. The disruption of the conventional gender roles that "Sabrina fair" effects in usurping the traditionally male role of hero is positive for Rachel since Rachel experiences conventional gender roles as claustrophobic and restrictive.[25] Sabrina is also significant because of what an

[24]Several critics have explored the significance of Milton's poem to Rachel's feverish demise and connect her death with her anxiety about heterosexuality. For instance, Hanson connects Rachel's illness and death with "her repudiation of sexuality" (34), and Schlack suggests that Milton's poem acts as a "disguised, symbolic telegraph message to her unconscious," signalling to Rachel the danger of heterosexuality (23). Although they both offer different interpretations of what Woolf's allusion to this poem can mean in the context of Rachel's situation, their interpretations only operate within an assumed heterosexual paradigm for this novel. They identify Rachel's anxiety about the consequences of heterosexual sex (marriage and motherhood) and the personal loss of freedom that her loss of virginity signifies. However, although critical of the social and ideological structures which accord such importance and value to women's virginity, their interpretations seem to reinforce the idea that the moment of its loss in the heterosexual act is *the* defining moment for a woman's sense of self/identity. Given Rachel's lesbian tendencies, which become more suggestively apparent in this part of the novel, this virgin/non-virgin dichotomy may not have the same defining function for her.

[25]Belsey argues that although Milton's alteration of the original story of Sabrina lays greater emphasis on the moral duty of chaste women to control men's desires and so upholds conservative gender role stereotypes, Sabrina is the *real* hero of the poem. Belsey's suggestion that the allusions made to the heroic actions of other mythical female figures in the poem point to its potential for endorsing bonds between women as "special" and supportive adds yet greater significance to Rachel's response (52-3).

escape with, and implicitly as, an empowered and transgressive mermaid has come to mean for Rachel. Critical preoccupation with what Rachel is escaping from and an emphasis on the preservation of her chastity has left a gap in discussion about what she might be trying to escape *to*. This gap is partially filled by the idea of Rachel's imitation of Sabrina and her imagined future as a similarly immortal and virginal goddess (DeKoven 135, Schlack 27). However, the emphasis remains fixed on the denial of Rachel's sexual pleasure in these fantasies of her future.

Critical emphasis on what Rachel is escaping from is also suggested by the exploration of the associations of three words from Milton's description of Sabrina[26] which come to preoccupy Rachel. The words "curb," "Locrine" and "Brute" are read as significant to Rachel's perception of herself as being trapped in heterosexual structures, suggesting as they do restriction, confinement and fear of male sexuality.[27] However, in identifying with Sabrina, Rachel is not denying her sexual self, but is implicitly embracing the ambiguous, sexually transgressive, and paradoxical female sexuality associated with the figure of the mermaid and this can be explored by looking again at one of the words that preoccupy Rachel.[28]

As Rachel's headache develops, language itself has become unfixed and meanings more elusive—words not only "sounded strange," but had begun to slip their usual meanings (*VO* 308). It seems reasonable to suggest, then, that "curb" may not mean restriction, nor refer only to what Rachel is escaping from. For Rachel, then, the word "curb" has potential to slip its meanings in a radically erotic way, especially in the context of the "moist curb" that Sabrina uses to disrupt and sway "the smooth Severn stream" of Milton's poem. Already seman-

---

[26]There is a gentle nymph not far from hence,
    That with moist curb sways the smooth Severn stream;
    Sabrina is her name, a virgin pure;
    Whilom she was the daughter of Locrine,
    That had the sceptre from his father Brute (Milton, 92)

[27]For Hanson "[t]he *associations* of these words suggest coercion, force and also some sort of threshold or dividing line ('curbing' and 'locking')" (34-5, Hanson's emphasis); for Schlack the 'crin' (meaning 'hairy') of Locrine suggests brutish, threatening male sexuality, "*hair* has been an emblem of repellent masculinity in this novel" (22, Schlack's emphasis).

[28]My thanks to Alison Johnson for her helpful comments on earlier drafts of this analysis.

tically and phonetically a paradox, the construction "moist curb" could easily slip into the 'moist curve' or even the "curling" of Sabrina's wave that Rachel imagines at the end of her bed, the "refreshingly cool" sensation of which would afford her relief could she plunge into it (*VO* 311). So "curb" can suggest the more fluid, feminine erotic she is escaping to—the moist curb/curve/curling wave Sabrina represents to Rachel. Recalling the orgasmic "swelling and breaking" wave used to describe Rachel's realization of homoerotic possibility in her tussle with Helen, Sabrina's "moist curb" and the "curling" wave have suggestively erotic resonances. Rachel's desire to focus on such a curling wave may signal her now active lesbian desire. However, Rachel's imaginary escape with Sabrina remains highly equivocal and her fantasy of escape as a mermaid highly problematic, as is suggested by the heightened attention to the paradoxes of pleasure/danger, allure/elusiveness which come to prominence in this fantasy.

'Curb' can also, of course, mean edge and it is on the borderline or threshold of her imaginary ocean escape that Rachel seems to float in a blissful pre-Oedipal, semiotic state. Momentarily, she lingers on the edge of the Imaginary realm, where "all landmarks were obliterated" and where her connection to the cultural realm, to all referents beyond her body, "faded entirely" (*VO* 311). However, this escape is not wholly positive. In refusing her culturally endorsed identity Rachel risks dissolution. Instead of finding the release from the painful heat of her anxiety and the claustrophobia she associates with heterosexual relationships in the cool translucent wave, Rachel finally seems to drown in "a deep pool of sticky water," regressing to a fetal position at the bottom of a suggestively amniotic sea (*VO* 322).[29]

Rachel can not simply escape from the restrictive culture in which she exists into an idealized space where her desires can remain fluid. Although her earlier assertions of her mermaid identity presented a defiance of cultural regulations and heterosexual romance scripts, her metaphorical escape to the sea has tragic

---

[29]As Froula points out (158), the image of Rachel curled on the sand at the bottom of the sea recalls Mr Pepper's description, early in the novel, of "the white, hairless, blind monsters lying curled on the ridges of sand at the bottom of the sea, which would explode if you brought them to the surface" (*VO* 16). Froula reads this as part of the process of Rachel's female initiation into her culturally determined destiny, which is experienced by many women as a "symbolic death-in-life" (158). However, she also reads this association of Rachel with Pepper's deep-sea creatures as representing "the buried lives that women lead in male culture" and, referring to Cixous' ideas, with women's repressed and silenced lives (143). This 'hidden' part of women's experience associated with sea creatures recalls Woolf's fish metaphor for the female imagination and the submerged aspects of women's sexuality in "Professions for Women." The potential for explosion if the deep-sea creatures are brought to the surface in *The Voyage Out* resonates with the "smash" and "explosion," the "foam and confusion," Woolf imagines in her essay should the 'big fish'

consequences. Following the folkloric tradition of the mermaid, whose appearance, disappearance and revenge is frequently accompanied by a storm, Rachel's spirit seems to live on for a while in the charged atmosphere of Santa Marina. However, the novel ends with a sense of life going on and the waters metaphorically close over the potential disruption and threat that Rachel's overt awakening into same-sex desire would have meant.

Clarissa Dalloway's lesbian desire similarly does not overtly trouble the sexual structures and gender hierarchies in the world of *Mrs. Dalloway*. What Smith calls Clarissa's "self-closeting" (her repression of her erotic urges for women, which is driven by her lesbian panic, shame and desperation for respectability) appears to be a highly successful strategy (47). However, in *Mrs. Dalloway* the mermaid figure functions just as ambiguously as in *The Voyage Out* as a dangerous strategy for survival in a heterocentric culture.[30] Like Rachel, Clarissa is a border-crossing figure and has an affinity with the sea. Again it is a would-be male lover who envisages Clarissa as a mermaid in his own fantasy of her, but it is she who operates this border-crossing identity in her negotiation of the boundaries of permissible desire and social acceptability. Accepting a more compromised life than Rachel seems prepared to, Clarissa does not exclaim her triumph as a disruptive mermaid figure with her dress torn, but symbolically mends the tear in her "silver-green mermaid's dress" (*MD* 192). Like Rachel, Clarissa suffers an illness which symbolizes her resistance to heterosexual imperatives. However, this is not the feverish all-consuming illness which can be read as an abdication from a hetero-patriarchal system as in *The Voyage Out*, but is a more chronic heart condition which frees Clarissa from any sexual demands from her husband. Unlike Rachel, Clarissa does not die, but, as a number of critics have noted, accepts her marriage as a kind of metaphorical death.[31]

---

of women's hidden desires be brought to the surface of consciousness or the literary text (7). The association of Rachel with such sea creatures suggests both Rachel's repressed homoerotic desires, as well Woolf's acute awareness of the difficulty of bringing such desires to the surface of her novel. Rachel's death, then, might represent the limit of Woolf's risk-taking in bringing such 'fish' to light.

[30]Other critics offer readings of this novel which focus on the tensions between homoerotic pleasure and the cultural denial and repression of non-heterosexual desires, and also discuss the compromises Clarissa must make. See, for example, Elizabeth Abel, Tuzyline Jita Allan, Eileen Barrett, Lyndie Brimstone, Patricia Cramer, Suzette A. Henke and Emily Jensen in addition to critics already discussed.

[31]Jensen argues this point and Abel suggests that Clarissa's bed is grave-like and "links her adult sexuality with death" (105). Barrett (52) and Abel (100), amongst others, point out that Clarissa and Sally always regarded marriage as destructive, "a catastrophe" (*MD* 39).

With a room of her own she has a literal and emotional private space in which she can indulge her memories and fantasies.[32] However, this is a severely compromised life in many ways, and her weak heart suggests a lack of sufficient courage, passion or love to mount any overt challenge to the cultural structures which contain her. Thirty years into her marriage, her memories, fantasies and imagination reveal her same-sex desire in images similar to those in *The Voyage Out*, images (amongst others) of sea, waves and the physical exhilaration of 'plunging' and 'diving.' However, Clarissa is unable to act fully on her desires for women and lives on the metaphorical borders of land and sea, moving between heterosexual security and the pleasures and dangers of her desire for women.

From the outset of this novel, Clarissa's border-crossing strategy for survival is apparent and belies any sense of the identity of 'Mrs. Dalloway' being fixed and stable. As she walks through London, the morning of Clarissa's present time

---

[32]Critics have read the suggestions of chastity, silence and spirituality in the descriptions of Clarissa's cell-like attic room and of Clarissa as "[l]ike a nun withdrawing" both positively and negatively (*MD* 35). For instance, Henke interprets Clarissa's nun-like identity as a positive one which enables her to remain "spiritually aloof and emotionally inviolate," and she perceives Clarissa's room as "a refuge from the traditional female role of angel in the house" (131, 134). In contrast, although perceiving "a subplot that tingles with lesbian passion" in *Mrs. Dalloway*, Allan, interpreting the "'soul' as a code for lesbian love," reads Clarissa's room and nun identity as part of the process of "the deadening of Clarissa's soul" (108, 107). Barrett also reads the soul as a code for lesbian desire but, unlike Allan, sees it as representing a private space where Clarissa's homoerotic urges can find expression (158). Barrett suggests that "the repeated association of Clarissa's lesbian passion with the soul" (of lesbian desire as a spiritual experience) "helps Clarissa shield such erotic feelings from public scrutiny" (148). However, she argues that whilst the novel engages with the 'trapped soul' theory of inversion put forward by the sexologists, and in particular with Havelock Ellis' recommendation that inverts should "spiritualize the inverted impulse," Woolf also offers a critique of such discourses and the stereotypes they produce (148, 157). In response and at a tangent to Allan's and Barrett's readings of the soul in Woolf's writing, I would argue that the figure of the mermaid (a stealer of human souls in medieval Christian mythology [Benwell and Waugh 81, 130]) can also be read as a metaphor for the subversive seizing and laying claim to the discourses which aim to define women's homoeroticism and lesbian desire. Cutting across the theories and discourses operating in Woolf's contemporary culture, women's same-sex desire figured as a mermaid operates through contradictions and resists the reinforcement of gender binaries and the sexual denial implicit in early theories of homosexuality. However, as I argue throughout this essay, this metaphorical strategy for lesbian survival remains an ambiguous one.

is described as "fresh as if issued to children on a beach" and this image of the land/sea border leads directly to a crossing over into the past. She recalls a moment of literally stepping across a threshold as she 'plunges' out of the French windows at her family home at Bourton, into air which has a sensual, wave-like quality, "like the flap of a wave; the kiss of a wave" (*MD* 5). Such sensuality accords with her plunge into another space/time, a liminal phase of awakening desire and expectation (which is similar to that experienced by Rachel) when she is courted not only by Richard Dalloway and Peter Walsh, but also by Sally Seton. In fact, this period of her past is one in which she experienced the most important and "most exquisite moment of her whole life" when, standing by a fountain, she was kissed on the lips by her friend and would-be lover, Sally (*MD* 40).[33] Along with other memories and fantasies of erotic moments of intimacy with women, this memory of Sally's kiss remains vivid and troubles the apparently unproblematic nature of her public identity and role as Mrs. Dalloway. As Johanna X. K. Garvey suggests, the novel's title can be read as a "red herring that can misdirect the reader raised on or groomed for the traditional marriage plot" (60).

Clarissa enacts her border-crossing strategy for survival as she 'dives' and 'plunges' into her fantasies and memories. Her hybrid sexual identity is pointed out (but not fully recognized) by Peter Walsh in a number of passages in which Clarissa is suggestively associated with sirens/mermaids. The most fully developed and explicit is when he likens her to a mermaid at her party:

> She wore ear-rings, and a silver-green mermaid's dress. Lolloping on the waves and braiding her tresses she seemed, having that gift still; to be; to exist . . . all with the most perfect ease and air of a creature floating in its element. But age had brushed her; even as a mermaid might behold in her glass the setting sun on some very clear evening over the waves. There was a breath of tenderness; her severity, her prudery, her woodenness were all warmed through now, and she had about her . . . an inexpressible dignity; an exquisite cordiality; as if she wished the whole world well, and must now, being on the very verge and rim of things, take her leave. (*MD* 192)

[33]Other critics, including Brimstone and DuPlessis, remark on the importance of this moment. Abel reads it as the point of Clarissa's entry into the Oedipal complex (99) and Jensen reads it as the defining moment in Clarissa's life (162). Following Jensen, Smith argues that Clarissa's sense of lesbian panic sets in as a consequence of the male interruption of this moment of lesbian pleasure, and that her life is determined by her sense of the impropriety and shame of a lesbian union (46).

Like Rachel on the curb or edge of her watery escape from the marriage plot, Clarissa seems likely to make a similar retreat from her heterocentric world. However, this passage and vision of her as a mermaid raises many problems, given that it is offered from Peter's perspective. Firstly, it signals Peter's admiration for what he (mistakenly) perceives as Clarissa's success in embracing wholeheartedly her role as society hostess. It suggests his envy of the seeming social ease and security Clarissa exudes in this context, her being, he believes, "in her element." But it also signals his complex feelings for Clarissa. It suggests the powerful attraction she still holds for him—she is the alluring but unobtainable siren who is tempting but dangerous. However, this image of Clarissa as a mermaid at her party also signals his desire (like that of Terence in relation to Rachel) to contain this power she has over him, to tame and domesticate this dangerous mermaid figure. In fact he wants to contain her in her social role and identity as Mrs. Dalloway: she is ageing, stately, dignified and cordial rather than magically disruptive and empowered.[34] She is on the very verge or rim of things, but not beyond the social order this seems to imply.

However, his fantasies of her do not correlate fully with what we know of her. As in *The Voyage Out*, the mermaid as a male fantasy of seduction rings hollow against the potential for sexual transgression and lesbian desire the mermaid also represents in these novels. Peter's recognition of Clarissa "on the very verge and rim of things" is a clue to such subversive power and it is when we immediately slip into the consciousness of Clarissa herself that we get closer to what this position on the borderline can mean. For a moment she too feels the intoxication of her social success, but this moment quickly passes and she recognizes the "hollowness" of such social "triumphs" (*MD* 193). She catches sight of "the gilt rim" of a Sir Joshua Reynolds' painting of a middle-class girl (*MD* 193). This is suggestively an image of Clarissa herself, caught within the restrictive ideological frame of her social class and gender; caught, in fact, in a world in which lesbian desire is perceived as monstrous, hateful and is fiercely contained by a brutal homophobia.

At the sight of this frame, and her recognition of her metaphorical entrapment within it, she is consumed by an overwhelming feeling of anger which she directs at her daughter's teacher, Doris Kilman, the spinster/lesbian figure who

[34]Garvey offers a similar reading of Peter Walsh's fantasy of Clarissa in this passage, which she suggests "reveals [his] chauvinistic ways of assessing women, based on sex, age, looks" (69). However, although she mentions the mermaid as a potentially empowering image for women (later suggesting that Clarissa's identity as a diver and a mermaid allows her to maintain "her individuality and independence" in her marriage, 72), Garvey seems to accord with Peter's view of Clarissa as "provocative yet asexual," of her being in control in her hostess role, and able "to set aside her own more cosmic fears" (69).

haunts Clarissa.[35] The passion and danger of the mermaid figure–lost in Peter's fantasy of her–is restored to Clarissa as she gives vent to the profoundly ambivalent and heated emotions of love, hate, anger and envy that Miss Kilman rouses in her. The "satisfying" and "real" emotions she has for Doris are summed up in the paradox, "She hated her: she loved her" (*MD* 193). Her anger moves her beyond the socially acceptable feeling of wishing the world well, as Peter reads Clarissa's mermaid role. In fact, this borderline of the verge/rim is a space of fierce and disruptive emotions. In an earlier passage, going to "the farthest verge" signifies Clarissa's orgasmic, erotic woman-centred pleasure, a bodily and linguistic jouissance which confounds phallocentric binary logic:

> It was a sudden revelation, a tinge like a blush which one tried to check and then, as it spread, one yielded to its expansion, and rushed to the farthest verge and there quivered and felt the world come closer, swollen with some astonishing significance, some pressure of rapture, which split its thin skin and gushed and poured with an extraordinary alleviation over the cracks and sores. (*MD* 36)

Here the implied image of a "swelling and breaking" wave echoes the metaphor of woman-centred homoerotic desire in *The Voyage Out* and locates such desire at the margins of land and sea where waves swell and break, and boundaries are transgressed.

Thinking of Doris Kilman, Clarissa's excessive emotion similarly takes her beyond such binary logic as she feels both hate and love with equal intensity in a way which ruptures the oppositional structures of thought and disrupts the boundaries of classification of hetero-patriarchal culture. However, such disruption is not an unproblematic strike against oppressive cultural structures because Clarissa's anger is also physically painful to her. It reminds her constantly of her own hypocritical complicity in the violence of this homophobic world and also

---

[35]Barrett neatly sums up several important readings of Doris Kilman's significance in the novel (159). Critics discuss the way her character functions to expose the fears, contradictions and repression associated with Clarissa's own lesbian desires. The various explanations of why Clarissa feels so intensely about Doris demonstrate the entangled and contradictory nature of her thoughts and emotions. Clarissa feels envy because Doris is living an independent and lesbian life in defiance of the heterosexual conventions that constrain Clarissa, fear because Doris could expose Clarissa's lesbian sexuality and because she reminds Clarissa of the economic and emotional deprivations of lesbian experience (Cramer, Smith), revulsion because Doris seems to comply with sexologists' prescription about subsuming lesbian desire in spiritual devotion (Barrett), revulsion also because of the stigma of being poor and a spinster, and because her lesbian sexuality is considered to be monstrous in Clarissa's society (Brimstone, Smith). Finally, Clarissa's complex feelings for Doris are bound up with her guilt about her own complicity in the socio-economic and sexual systems which are the source of devastating homophobia.

signals the self-hatred her sense of hypocrisy causes. Her border-crossing, mermaid identity, then, is one fraught with complex and contradictory thoughts and emotions. Ultimately it is not one which liberates her or her desire, but is a compromise.

Although Clarissa can imagine moments in which her desire for women is satisfied, and can at one point allow a wave of positive feeling to lift her up and to surmount her self-hatred and anger at her own lesbian feelings (as in Miss Pym's florist shop where she buys the flowers for her party, *MD* 16),[36] ultimately her desire meets with obstruction and denial. Peter Walsh notes Clarissa's affinity with the types of people who don't seem to fit into her world–the artists and writers he refers to as "queer fish" (*MD* 86). But this "queer fish" identity, this being profoundly at odds with her world, is also Clarissa's identity. It is the secret identity that Peter never fully realizes and an identity which can never fully surface in this novel. In fact, Clarissa is less like the demonic, disruptive figures which pervaded Victorian cultural iconography, but more like Andersen's Little Mermaid, sacrificing her voice and glory for an immortal soul and the semblance of full humanity, a compromised position achieved only through 'passing' for heterosexual in her role as Mrs. Dalloway. Like the Little Mermaid, Clarissa experiences the pain of passing—her feet are not penetrated by phallic knives, but, as Jensen notes, the description of Clarissa 'staked' at the top of her stairs waiting to greet her guests is synonymous with the respectability she has craved. That her alter-ego, Septimus, is impaled on the rusty railings outside his window, however, signals that Clarissa too feels the constant threat of suffering this "classic punishment for social deviants" (Jensen 177). Sells' comment that the pain suffered by the mermaid in Andersen's tale "reflected his [Andersen's] discomfort and the price of his own integrity" in his attainment of respectability and financial security in aristocratic circles also resonates with Clarissa's sense of guilt and shame (180).

In these two novels the mermaid is an ambiguous, problematic metaphor for lesbian sexuality and subjectivity. On the one hand, it seems to speak of women's mobility, powerful allure and freedom from dominant cultural structures. It offers a possible strategy for survival—a means of negotiating the culturally prescribed boundaries of desire and sexuality. Rachel escapes the restrictions of marriage in a fantasy of becoming a defiant mermaid and Clarissa plays the marriage card for all it is worth, successfully negotiating the margins between her lesbian desire and social acceptance. Simultaneously, however, this identity carries the risk of being caught in the scripts of heterosexual male fantasies and/or being forced

[36]Smith reads this as a key moment in Clarissa's experience of lesbian bliss which acts as a parallel scene to that experienced earlier by the urn with Sally (43).

into a dangerous position on the margins of hetero-patriarchal culture where being perceived as monstrous and not fully human is always a danger. A mermaid escape beyond patriarchal 'territories' to the feminine or pre-Oedipal space of the sea carries the risk of dissolution and death—literally for Rachel. On one level, this death represents a failure to escape the constraints of the heterocentric and homophobic worlds the characters inhabit. On another level, it can be read as a critique of these constraints and the values that underlie them via a radical revision of heterosexual romance narratives. Refusing to see heterosexual marriage as a happy ending for these heroines, the novels question and contest the inscription of hetero-patriarchal gender roles and structures of desire embedded in such narrative closure.

The complex and compromised mermaid negotiations which signal the pleasures and dangers of woman-centred desire in Woolf's fiction may also speak of the difficulties that a woman writer representing such desires must face. Other critics, for instance Allan, have remarked on the difficulties of representing lesbian desire. Allan argues that Woolf was "aware of the prohibitive nature of sexual imperialism and the caution required to express transgressive sexuality" and that she, like Nella Larsen, was "[c]aught between silence and censorship" so that she "resorted to subterfuge to inscribe lesbian desire" (109, 112). However, whereas I read the contradictions and ambivalences in Woolf's writing as a positive strategy for negotiating the constraints of heterocentric structures and sexual imperatives, Allan equates "the contradictory impulse to express and rein in female desire" in *Mrs. Dalloway* with "killing the possibility of a lesbian love life" for the characters and "stifling authorial expression of lesbian desire" (106, 107). Whereas Allan reads Woolf's "evoking male-centred heterosexual desire" as "part of a narrative strategy of containment that frustrates the author's subversive intent" (109), I read Woolf's evoking of heterosexual male fantasies in the form of the mermaid as a highly subversive strategy which enables her to explore the possibilities for representing lesbian desire. At risk of being perceived as a "queer fish" herself, then, Woolf's use of the highly ambiguous figure of the mermaid may also be a strategy for her own survival as woman writing of desire between women. With its multiple associations the mermaid both screens and reveals the lesbian possibilities in her texts and, as such, may represent the negotiations and manipulations of the literary text necessary to get such material into print. In "Professions for Women" she claims not to have solved the problem of writing openly, "telling the truth," about women's bodily passions unimpeded by the many intangible "phantoms and obstacles" which block her path (8). The multiple associations of the mermaid offer scope for negotiating the social, literary, external and internal prohibitions which surround the writing of passions between women. In *A Room of One's Own*, Mary Carmichael's novel similarly explores women's same-sex desires indirectly, and Woolf may be modelling her own writing of lesbian desire when she reveals that the implicit significance of Mary's writing is coaxed out in a suggestively mermaid-like fashion—with the "beckoning and summoning" of hidden meanings to the surface of the text and the reader's awareness (89).

The slippery figure of the mermaid also operates as a productive metaphor in Woolf's writing for representing desires between women whilst resisting recuperation into a system of classification. The contradictions and paradoxes, and the hesitations and indeterminacies of content and form that such a metaphor implies keep possibilities in play by refusing to comply with any neat categorization of either/or, heterosexual/homosexual. It is via such ambiguities and uncertainties that usually inexpressible desires, those which mutiny from the heterosexual script, can be so tantalizingly explored. In embodying woman-centered eroticism, whilst refusing to explicitly name or define this desire, Woolf's writing of desire between women maintains a radically queer evasion of precise definition as, like a "queer fish" itself, it remains on the borderlines and refuses binary oppositions or categorization.

Works Cited

Abel, Elizabeth. "Narrative Structure(s) and Female Development: The Case of *Mrs. Dalloway.*" *Virginia Woolf: A Collection of Critical Essays.* Ed. Margaret Homans. New Jersey: Prentice Hall, 1993. 93-114.

Allan, Tuzyline Jita. "The Death of Sex and the Soul in *Mrs. Dalloway* and Nella Larsen's *Passing.*" *Virginia Woolf: Lesbian Readings.* Ed. Eileen Barrett and Patricia Cramer. New York and London: New York U P, 1997. 95-113.

Andersen, Hans Christian. "The Little Mermaid." *Hans Andersen's Fairy Tales: A Selection.* Oxford: Oxford World's Classics, 1984. 76-106.

Auerbach, Nina. *Woman and the Demon: The Life of a Victorian Myth.* Massachusetts and London: Harvard UP, 1982.

Barrett, Eileen. "Unmasking Lesbian Passion: The Inverted World of *Mrs.. Dalloway.*" *Virginia Woolf: Lesbian Readings.* Ed. Eileen Barrett and Patricia Cramer. New York and London: New York UP, 1997. 146-164.

Belsey, Catherine. *John Milton: Language, Gender, Power.* Oxford: Basil Blackwell, 1988.

Benwell, Gwen and Arthur Waugh. *Sea Enchantress: The Tale of the Mermaid and Her Kin.* London: Hutchinson and Co. Ltd. 1961.

Brimstone, Lyndie. "Towards a New Cartography: Radclyffe Hall, Virginia Woolf and the Working of Common Land." *What Lesbians Do in Books.* Ed. Elaine Hobby and Chris White. London: The Women's Press, 1991. 86-108.

Cramer, Patricia. "Notes from Underground: Lesbian Ritual in the Writings of Virginia Woolf." *Virginia Woolf Miscellanies: Proceedings from the First Annual Conference on Virginia Woolf.* Ed. Mark Hussey and Vara Neverow-Turk. New York: Pace UP, 1992.177-188.

Darwin, Bernard (Intro.). *The Oxford Dictionary of Quotations, Third Edition.* Oxford: Oxford UP, 1986.

DeKoven, Marianne. *Rich and Strange: Gender, History, Modernism.* New Jersey: Princeton UP, 1991.

DeSalvo, Louise A. *Virginia Woolf's First Voyage: A Novel in the Making.* London and Basingstoke: Macmillan, 1980.

——, *Virginia Woolf: The Impact of Childhood Sexual Abuse on her Life and Work.* London: The Women's Press, 1989.

DuPlessis, Rachel Blau. *Writing Beyond the Ending: Narrative Strategies of Twentieth-Century Women Writers.* Bloomington: Indiana U P. 1985.

Froula, Christine. "Out of the Chrysalis: Female Initiation and Female Authority in Virginia Woolf's *The Voyage Out.*" *Virginia Woolf: A Collection of Critical Essays.* Ed. Margaret Homans. New Jersey: Prentice Hall, 1993. 136-161.

Garvey, Johanna X. K. "Difference and Continuity: the Voices of *Mrs. Dalloway.*" *College English*, Volume 3, Number 53, 1991. 59-76.

Goldman, Jane. *The Feminist Aesthetics of Virginia Woolf: Modernism,Post-Impressionism and the Politics of the Visual.* Cambridge: Cambridge UP, 1998.

Hanson, Clare. *Virginia Woolf.* Basingstoke and London: Macmillan, 1994.

Henke, Suzette A. "*Mrs. Dalloway*: The Communion of Saints." *New Feminist Essays on Virginia Woolf.* Ed. Jane Marcus. London and Basingstoke: Macmillan, 1981. 125-147.

Jensen, Emily. "Clarissa Dalloway's Respectable Suicide." *Virginia Woolf: A Feminist Slant.* Ed. Jane Marcus. Lincoln and London: U of Nebraska P, 1983. 161-179.

Laity, Cassandra. "H.D. and A.C. Swinburne: Decadence and Sapphic Modernism." *Lesbian Texts and Contexts: Radical Revisions.* Ed. Karla Jay and Joanne Glasgow. New York: New York UP, 1990. 217-240.

Marcus, Jane. *Virginia Woolf and the Languages of Patriarchy.* Bloomington and Indianapolis: Indiana UP, 1987.

Milton, John. *Comus: A Masque.* 1637. *Milton: Poems.* Selected Laurence D. Lerner. London: Penguin, 1985.

Nead, Lynda. "Woman as Temptress: The Siren and the Mermaid in Victorian Painting." *Leeds Art Calendar*, no. 91, 1982. 5-20.

Rosenman, Ellen. "A Fish on the Line: Desire, Repression, and the Law of the Father in *A Room of One's Own.*" *Virginia Woolf: Emerging Perspectives.* Ed. Mark Hussey and Vara Neverow. New York: Pace UP, 1994. 272-277.

Russo, Mary. *The Female Grotesque: Risk, Excess and Modernity*. London: Routledge, 1995.

Schlack, Beverly Ann. *Continuing Presences: Virginia Woolf's Use of Literary Allusion*. University Park and London: The Pennsylvania State UP, 1979.

Sells, Laura. "'Where Do the Mermaids Stand?': Voice and Body *in The Little Mermaid*." *From Mouse to Mermaid: The Politics of Film, Gender and Culture*. Ed. Elizabeth Bell, Lynda Haas, and Laura Sells. Bloomington and Indianapolis: Indiana UP, 1995. 175-192.

Smith, Patricia Juliana. *Lesbian Panic: Homoeroticism in Modern British Women's Fiction*. New York: Columbia UP, 1997.

Tvordi, Jessica. "*The Voyage Out*: Virginia Woolf's First Lesbian Novel." *Virginia Woolf: Themes and Variations: Selected Papers from the Second Annual Conference on Virginia Woolf*. Ed. Vara Neverow-Turk and Mark Hussey. New York: Pace UP, 1993. 226-237.

Vanita, Ruth. *Sappho and the Virgin Mary: Same-sex Love and the English Literary Imagination*. New York: Columbia UP, 1996.

Vlasopolos, Anca. "Staking Claims for No Territory: The Sea as Woman's Space." *Reconsidered Spheres: Feminist Explorations of Literary Space*. Ed. Margaret R. Higonnet and Joan Templeton. Amherst: University of Massachusetts Press, 1994. 72-88.

Wilson, Deborah. "Fishing for Woolf's Submerged Lesbian Text." *Re: Reading, Re: Writing, Re: Teaching Virginia Woolf. Selected Papers from the Fourth Annual Conference on Virginia Woolf*. Ed. Eileen Barrett and Patricia Cramer. New York: Pace UP, 1995. 121-128.

Woolf, Virginia. *The Voyage Out*. 1915. London: Penguin, 1992.

——. *Mrs. Dalloway*. 1925. London: Penguin, 1974.

——. *Orlando: A Biography*. 1928. London: Grafton, 1989.

——. *A Room of One's Own*. 1929. London: Grafton, 1989.

——. *The Diary of Virginia Woolf, Volume 3 1925-30*. Ed. Anne Olivier Bell, assisted by Andrew McNellie. London: Penguin, 1982.

——. *Flush: A Biography*. 1933. London: The Hogarth Press, 1991.

____. "Professions for Women." 1942. *Killing the Angel in the House: Seven Essays*. London: Penguin, 1995.

——. "A Sketch of the Past." 1976. *Virginia Woolf Moments of Being*. Ed. Jeanne Schulkind. London: Grafton, 1990. 69-173.

Zipes, Jack. "Breaking the Disney Spell." *From Mouse to Mermaid: The Politics of Film, Gender and Culture*. Ed. Elizabeth Bell, Lynda Haas, and Laura Sells. Bloomington and Indianapolis: Indiana UP, 1995. 21-42.

Virginia Woolf and Literary History
Part I

**Edited by Jane Lilienfeld, Jeffrey Oxford
and Lisa Low**

In May 1999, Jeffrey Oxford and I became the co-editors of a project initiated and conceptualized by Lisa Low. The original volume, entitled "Virginia Woolf and the Politics of Literary History," was to have contained sixteen essays, considering Woolf's theories of literary history, pairing Woolf with writers from the Early Modern period to the present. The project did not take the shape the original editor envisioned, and in September 1998, the project as originally intended was shelved. Five essays of the original project are included among the ten that will appear in "Virginia Woolf and Literary History," to be published in volumes 9 and 10 of Woolf Studies Annual. *Jeffrey Oxford and I thank Lisa Low for allowing us to take on and reshape the project, which reflects the views of all three editors. I thank Jeffrey Oxford for his expert handling of all the technical requirements of readying the manuscript for publication.*

Jane Lilienfeld
Lincoln University
Jefferson City, MO

Introduction: Virginia Woolf and Literary History

Jane Lilienfeld

During the past twenty years, scholarship on Virginia Woolf has flourished, and her place at the center of twentieth-century literary history has been firmly established. *Virginia Woolf and Literary History* comprises eleven essays to be included in Volumes 9 and 10 of *Woolf Studies Annual*. These essays theorize new contexts and methods with which to reconsider Woolf's historical analyses. Moreover, the debates among the essays' authors illustrate how contested and dynamic the understanding of literary history can be, an assumption central to Woolf's re/vision of the terms "literature" and "history."

The essays converse with divergent views of Virginia Woolf as subject and object of literary her/history, international and postcolonial feminism, as feminist, as lesbian, as politically astute artist, and as artistic political theorist. Laura Marcus dryly notes that "[a]nalysis of [Woolf's] reception, feminist and otherwise, in other national and cultural contexts would reveal rather different histories of reception and response" (241 n1). Although many of the essays in *Virginia Woolf and Literary History* are situated theoretically in the North American tradition of feminist academic scholarship, all intersect with the increasingly international conversations about Virginia Woolf, drawing on and responding to a wide range of references and scholarly debates.

"I want to claim the Virginia Woolf of *A Room of One's Own* and *Three Guineas*, the Woolf of the literary and critical essays and of the letters, as worthy of a world scale interest as a social thinker" Jane Marcus declared in 1997 ("Wrapped" 18). Although Anna Snaith can confidently remark that "it is by now well established that Woolf was a political being,"[1] her confidence is not shared by all Woolf scholars. Jane Marcus was reacting to what she saw as the "denigration," the "scapegoat[ing]," the "ignor[ing]" of Woolf by those who insist on Woolf's apolitical stance in the 1930s "as a lady, a straw woman, or an anti Semite [. . .]" ("Wrapped" 19). Merry Pawlowski, writing in 2001, agrees, pointing out that many still regard

> Woolf as an apolitical, lyrical modern novelist so carefully cultivated by generations of New Critics and fueled by Woolf's own nephew's assessment of her during the 1930s as a "distressed gentlewoman caught in a tempest and making little effort either to fight against it or to sail before it." (3-4)

---

[1]Snaith cites one reference for this assertion, Hermione Lee's biography of Woolf, which presents a view of Woolf that those espousing more radical political interpretations find insufficient.

A central tenet of the essays in *Virginia Woolf and Literary History* is that Virginia Woolf was a feminist writer, embedded and writing within what Chapman and Manson's recent anthology delineates as "a milieu" of men and women engaged in active local, national, and international political campaigns and grass roots organizing. Gender considerations were a central organizing principle of Woolf's aesthetic experiments and philosophical disputations.

As Elena Gualtieri has recently reminded scholars, Virginia Woolf wanted to be an historian before she sought to be a novelist (*Sketching* 32). As an apprentice historian, Woolf began formulating questions which remain current today: What is the discipline of history? Who are its subjects, and what are the materials which constitute and grant access to the constructed past? Increasingly as she studied the texts and contexts of European and international history, Woolf gradually came to interpret systems of organization—familial, social, cultural—as constructing and reproducing gendered subjects who complexly enacted and resisted the imperial ethos on which British culture rested.

Claiming Virginia Woolf as a political radical, scholars such as Berenice Carroll, Blanche Wiesen Cook, Jane Marcus, Sara Ruddick, and Alice Fox further argued that Woolf's textual reconfiguration of historical narratives was inseparable from her gendered exclusion from the professionalized, "Oxbridge" trajectory written by university educators of elite British males.[2]

Numerous scholars have reconstructed the figure of Virginia Woolf, feminist historian. Natania Rosenfeld's *Outsiders Together,* in which the essays, novels, and political analyses of Leonard and Virginia Woolf are placed in fruitful dialogue, and Helen Wussow's *The Nightmare of History,* in which the works of D. H. Lawrence and Virginia Woolf interrogate one another and their authors, both re-examine Woolf's understanding of the discipline and documents of history within a discourse conversant with philosophical inquiry, in which gendered considerations are one aspect, rather than the main focus (Rosenfeld 178). Merry Pawlowski's *Virginia Woolf and Fascism*, Wayne Chapman and Janet Manson's *Women in the Milieu of Leonard and Virginia Woolf,* and Gualtieri's *Sketching the Past* remind readers of the nuanced, intricately interconnected conversations within which Woolf's historical interrogations and investigations took place, conversations, to Woolf's view, in which gender was foundational.

The essays in *Virginia Woolf and Literary History* interrogate the term "historian," and for that reason, Melba Cuddy-Keane's "Virginia Woolf and the Varieties of Historicist Experience," previously published and so not included here, provides important theoretical articulation of the interconnected issues addressed by the essays that follow. Cuddy-Keane situates Woolf's historical

---

[2]Alex Zwerdling, Naomi Black, and Pamela J. Transue, who also view Woolf as a political thinker, question so radical an interpretation.

practices in the context of Victorian and twentieth-century historical methodologies and disputes. Cuddy-Keane is careful not to make totalizing claims for Woolf as a precursor of historical modes of constructing postmodern subjectivities as a foundational basis of contemporary historical analysis (61-2).[3]

Nevertheless, Cuddy-Keane's careful scrutiny of Woolf's methodologies demonstrates that Woolf's historical analyses were both ahead of and part of Woolf's time (62). For Woolf, the "various, multiple, dynamic" and interconnected documents of history include, but are not limited to, "unpublished and noncanonical works," "literary, social, and economic history," and "historical questions rather than historical patterns [. . .]" (Cuddy-Keane 61). Further, Woolf "directs attention to the silent or silenced voices that an inclusive history must be attuned to hear" (61).[4]

Cuddy-Keane contextualizes Woolf's methodology within earlier theoretical debates among Thomas Carlyle, T. B. Macaulay, Jane Harrison, and Leslie Stephen (63), suggesting that some of these Victorian historians whose works Woolf studied were themselves rebels against the grand view of linear, human (read "male") progress often said to have been espoused by Victorian historians (63-4). Cuddy-Keane situates Woolf's work among her own contemporaries, particularly Eileen Power, whose *Medieval People* appeared in the same year as Virginia Woolf's essay "Lives of the Obscure" (65). Both Eileen Power and Virginia Woolf reexamined issues about anonymity, obscurity, social class, and gender that feminist historians continue to debate today.[5]

This depiction of Woolf has some philosophical points of agreement with scholars such as Pamela Caughie, who views Woolf as a dispersed subject constituted through a range of discourses which themselves fracture and reassemble

[3]This essay thereby engages with such critics as Leila Brosnan and Elena Gualtieri, who oppose what might be called the hagiographical valorization of Virginia Woolf, which they see as animating much North American feminist scholarship (Gualtieri 28-9).

[4]A fascinating scholarly debate concerns Woolf's insistence in *A Room of One's Own* (47-8) that there were no easily available records about women's achievements and lives, that they had been excised and must be reconstructed. Margaret Ezell and Alison Booth ("Well-Lit") have attacked Woolf as deliberately excluding numerous easily-available documents about historical women in her exaggerated statements that all women's lives had been obliterated from the historical record. Melba Cuddy-Keane answers this attack by reminding such critics that "as essentialist history, Woolf's texts may be limiting today, but contextualized in history, its rhetorical power is very clear" ("Varieties" 71). Elena Gualtieri contextualizes this debate by placing it within the genre of the European essay (36-48 and 122-28).

[5]Current work by Elena Gualtieri, Anna Snaith, and Natania Rosenfeld looks at these issues from varied perspectives, differently defining "history," "obscure lives," and Woolf's methodologies in researching and theorizing "history."

traditional genres and the human subject.[6] As such, Cuddy-Keane's analyses speak to such contemporary feminist historians as Joan W. Scott and Denise Riley who ask if there is no female subject, can there be a history of "women"? Although Cuddy-Keane keeps many terms of discourse and interrogation circulating simultaneously, for her Woolf is a subject writing multiple modes of discourse.

Explaining Woolf's techniques for establishing the impact of cultural situatedness on the construction of the reader, the writers, and the subjects of history, Cuddy-Keane engages with the not dissimilar arguments advanced by Dusinberre, Snaith, and Gualtieri and those scholars contributing to Sally Greene's *Virginia Woolf: Reading the Renaissance*. Modeling how Woolf read, Cuddy-Keane suggests that Virginia Woolf's historical methodologies are relevant to contemporary cultural and literary constructions of the postmodern methods of historical disputation and exploration:

> My point is not simply that Woolf articulates these multiple and complex perspectives; it is having these different perspectives—and indeed experiencing the shifts among them—that for her is the nature of the reading process, a process that she further historicizes as her own reading in her own time and as therefore differing from the various historical readings that have preceded and will follow her (Cuddy-Keane 74).[7]

Melba Cuddy-Keane's analyses of Woolf's materials and methods provide much of the foundational underpinnings of the ten essays that comprise *Virginia Woolf and Literary History*.

I Theorizing History

1. Merry Pawlowski, "Exposing Masculine Spectacle: Virginia Woolf's Newspaper Clippings for *Three Guineas* as Contemporary Cultural History"

Pawlowski's essay[8] argues that Woolf's work is "embedded in and actively engaged in making the history of her time." The essay troubles Cuddy-Keane's challenge to Woolf's prescience as a methodological foremother.

[6]Patricia Waugh (98-118) and Makiko Minow-Pinkney also articulate a postmodern view of Woolf's works.

[7]Laura Doyle extends Cuddy-Keane's theoretical formulations about Woolf's complicated "shifts" (138). Karen Levenback's *Virginia Woolf and the Great War*, for example, takes into account contemporary disputes in historical methodology.

[8]In 1998 Patricia Laurence examined the "the principle of verbal and visual juxtaposition" in Woolf's *Notebooks*, analyzing this material in the context of Leonard Woolf's *Quack, Quack* ("Couple" 136). Although Patricia Laurence, like Merry Pawlowski, credits Woolf with constructing what might be termed a multimedia narrative, Laurence's reading of Woolf's political interpretation differs markedly from that of Pawlowski. See also Elena Gualtieri's "*Three Guineas* and the Photograph" and Julia Duffy and Lloyd Davis' essay and Chapman and Manson's "Carte and Tierce."

In writing *Three Guineas*,[9] Woolf assembled three scrapbooks of media materials that compose a coherent narrative of written and photographic evidence, incorporating gesture, costume, rituals of hierarchical and bureaucratic "manhood," unspoken but physically enacted records of power. Synthesizing Guy Debord's interrogation of cultural spectacle and Laura Mulvey's methodological deconstruction of the male gaze, Pawlowski's argument participates in important current debates about Woolf's multilayered, multimedia stylistic discourses. Virginia Woolf's complicated reading of the visual materials[10] current in her time has impelled scholars to ask: "Does Woolf [. . .] make visible the process of producing history [and] thus raise her readers to the level of metahistorical awareness or plunge them deeper into the contemplation of spectacle?" (Barnaby 312)

Pawlowski's essay demonstrates Woolf's metahistorical practice. Virginia Woolf's scrapbooks of newspaper and pamphlet materials create a montage of visual artifacts, a narrative making visible how Woolf came to understand the causal connection between the exclusion of British women from male occupations and the cultural engendering of war. By reading Woolf's reading of the artifacts of mass-culture, Pawlowski makes a case for Woolf as an historian of the inception of those unconscious attitudes and behaviors which are crucial to the formation and critique of dominant cultural assumptions.

[9]The now infamous denunciation of *Three Guineas* by Q. D. Leavis, which appeared in *Scrutiny* in September, 1938, has been analyzed by numerous critics, among them, Alex Zwerdling (233), Jane Marcus in "No More Horses," and Marion Shaw. Brenda Silver discusses "the Leavisite attitude" against Woolf (*Icon* 154-6). For a history of *Three Guineas*'s critical reception in America and Europe, see Hussey, *Z* 294-300. Studying the works of Leonard and Virginia Woolf in conjunction, Natania Rosenfeld has recently hypothesized that "Woolf's resentment toward the men of such groups seems misdirected" (178). Rosenfeld's is a not unusual argument among those who, like Herbert Marder (calling it "a neurotic book"), for example, find that *Three Guineas* undercuts its case by strident hyperbolic vitriol (*Feminism* 174). Vara Neverow disputes the often-repeated view that *A Room of One's Own* is charming, while *Three Guineas* is aggressive by a thorough analysis of the satirical punch of the former ("Freudian").

[10]Looking at Woolf's reading of an increasingly visual popular culture, scholars interrogate Woolf's texts using film theory, a method pioneered and exemplified by the work of Leslie Hankins. Through divergent theoretical positions, essays by Humm, Wollaeger, Luckhurst, and Hotchkiss examine Woolf as a participant in the production of visual culture and visual commentary. See also Diane Gillespie's "Kodak" and *Muses*.

2. Jeanette McVicker, "'Six Essays on London Life': A History of Dispersal"

McVicker's essay, published in two parts, unsettles Cuddy-Keane's reading, while also expanding that of Pawlowski. McVicker locates a series of popular articles for *Good Housekeeping* entitled "Six Essays on London Life" within the continuum of Woolf's writing of the early 1930s (including the materials, first discussed in Woolf's 1931 speech to the London and National Society for Women's Service, that Woolf laboriously transformed into *The Pargiters, The Years, Three Guineas*). She establishes these essays as in/sites, methodologies of reading contemporary culture, arguing that in these essays Woolf crafted a literary form that could display the transformations occurring in British culture from 1870 through 1931.

This essay demonstrates Woolf's argument that the physicality of London—its roads, buildings, wharves, monuments—has for centuries been recreated as symbolic currency. Woolf interrogates Britain's "monumentalized past" through deconstructing the sites of British commerce and culture. Woolf's verbal tours of London reveal the hidden interconnections between the periphery of the Empire and the metropolitan center, between the rise of fascist ideologies and the dynamics of mass culture.

Woolf directed these literary walking tours to the women entering the professions, women targeted as sites of mass-market consumer capitalism. The vexed question of Woolf and class in this essay intersects with the conscription of the female subject into consumerism.[11] The gendered consumer, recently a site of critical analysis in Woolf studies, is, according to many critics, urged to consume not just commodities but the cultural situatedness of those commodities, thus herself becoming commodified.[12] McVicker's essay intervenes in this debate, speculating about how Woolf came to understand and then to represent this multicausal, multisituated process. McVicker convincingly argues that the

[11]Marion Shaw's analysis of the complex British reception and mystification of Woolf's views on class is foundational to any discussion of Woolf's complicated thinking about class and gender. See also Susan Stanford Friedman (" Uncommon" 31). Christine Sandbach-Dahlström, Mary Childers, and Michael Tratner analyze Woolf's patronizing, separating, and appropriating behaviors. Recently, however, there has been a critical movement to recognize Woolf's methods of reading gendered social class as respectful rather than appropriating. Laurie Quinn, for example, notes that "Instead of representing that which she did not experience, namely, an easy solidarity across class lines, Woolf chooses to show that women of distinct classes might use writing differently toward the same progressive political ends" (325). In a similar theoretical move, Shiela Pardee contextualizes James Frazer's (an influence on Jane Ellen Harrison) anthropological method for observing "the other," problematizing Woolf's view of "the primitive" (291-8).

[12]For an excellent analysis of the discourse of consumerism in Woolf studies, see Jennifer Wicke's and Elizabeth Outka's essays.

visual imagery and ironic tone of Woolf's walking tours replace the male "Englishness" of received culture with a radical view of how the working man and woman are made to bear the burdens of the metropole and the imperial periphery.

In this work of uncovering, Woolf creates a critical discourse that makes visible the hidden connection between the patriarchal elites and institutions, resonating with the argument of Pawlowski's essay. McVicker thus convincingly argues that Woolf's methods and topics establish her as a precursor, whose work predates Heidegger's work of "unconcealing" and Foucault's studies of the disciplined bodies of power and knowledge. Pawlowski's and McVicker's participation in "feminizing" male philosophical debate, bringing it into dialogue with feminist materialist practices, is part of a tradition that is both contested and ongoing in literary theory and in Woolf studies.[13] Virginia Woolf, as many essays within and beyond *Virginia Woolf and Literary History* argue, herself refused to accept as given the practices and the discoveries of male-authored theories and texts without rigorous debate.

3. Evelyn Haller, "Alexandria as Envisioned by Virginia Woolf and E. M. Forster: An Essay in Gendered History"

E. M. Forster's "misogyny" (Furbank 56, 175, 182) interfered with his friendship with Virginia Woolf, biasing his view toward the importance of her work, especially *Three Guineas*, and is clear in his dismissal of her feminism as "spots," or acne, disfiguring her novels (Forster 32-3). Recent feminist analyses of the women's lives within "the Bloomsbury Group"[14] have complicated what had heretofore been naturalized as an empowering intellectual interconnectedness.

---

[13]For example, the work of Jane Flax, Susan Wolfe and Julia Penelope, and Diamond and Quinby's edited collection, *Feminism and Foucault,* rigorously question the phallocentric theorizing that underpins much postmodern theory.

[14]For representative memoirs of this group, see Quentin Bell, *Bloomsbury.* Less partisan descriptions can be found in S. P. Rosenbaum and Stansky and Abrahams. Hermione Lee does not add new material (258-73). Contesting the positive assessment is Jane Marcus's feminist analysis of the male homosocial elite, and the impact of their attitudes and alliances on the women in the Bloomsbury Group (for example, *Languages* 75-95). See also, D. A. Boxwell's "In the Urinal." Brenda Silver's analysis of Woolf as an icon illuminates the cultural representation of Bloomsbury (for example, *Icon* 108-16). Mark Hussey's elegant summary provides an important context for situating the friendship of Forster and Woolf: "'Bloomsbury' as a cultural signifier, a shorthand for a set of attitudes to art and culture, has been in circulation for more than eighty years now, and the problems of determining who was or was not in the Bloomsbury Group have long since given

Evelyn Haller analyses the historical practices of Virginia Woolf, E. M. Forster, and their teachers[15] by asking "how sexually determined or slanted cultural training affects what and how one perceives?" Woolf enjoyed the craft of history for its own sake, but such study was a recompense. Woolf had been deprived of a university and preparatory school education by her father, Sir Leslie Stephen, whose refusal to allow Woolf to go to school was, as Haller points out, offset by his allowing his daughter uncensored access to his extensive library, and by modeling a tradition of hard-working historical scholarship. That Woolf was both hampered and freed by such limitation is a crucial point of Haller's essay, for Haller makes clear that Woolf's excavations into the history of Isis formed part of a conscious competition with her colleague and friend, E. M. Forster. Haller contrasts Forster's Hellenic, misogynist views of Egyptology and the city of Alexandria with Woolf's more accurate representation of the female tradition which underpinned worship of Isis.

For Virginia Woolf the search for the materials by which to forge a reconstructed Alexandria expanded Woolf's use of numerous feminist images and allusions throughout her fiction. Haller suggests that Woolf's methods for discovering the buried female traditions in mythology was not a separate endeavor from the writing of fiction. Haller locates the powerful imagery of Isis in Woolf's works *To the Lighthouse*, *The Waves*, *Between the Acts*, and segments of *Three Guineas* and *A Room of One's Own*.

---

way to arguments with more serious implications for the relations between aesthetics and politics, art and society" (*Z* 38). Hussey analyzes entries in Woolf's diaries (*D* 4: 297-8 and *D* 5: 337) and notes her painful rejection by Forster on the library steps, pointing out Forster's rage at *Three Guineas* (*Z* 92). Recently Troy Gordon argued that politically, the alliances forged between politically active gay men, feminists and lesbians will open up avenues of activism and discourse that perhaps were unavailable to Forster and Woolf (108-9).

[15]Haller carries forward a long tradition in biographical analyses of Virginia Woolf, noting the plusses and minuses of her father's preventing her enrollment at university, while modeling for her the role of an intellectual historian. Woolf herself, as Haller points out, considered her exclusion as detrimental, yet Katherine Hill asked whether such lack of "Oxbridge" training freed Woolf for her more daring experiments in thought (See also Hussey, *Z* 270-1). Haller valorizes Woolf's home schooling as "woman instructed learning" (4). Clara Pater tutored Woolf in Latin and Greek beginning in 1899, and Janet Case tutored her in Greek from 1902-3 (Jane Marcus, *Languages* 48; *D* 5: 103). Stephen J. Ramsay contests the wide-spread view that Woolf was insufficiently educated in the Classics, demonstrating Woolf's excellent command of Greek language and culture. Emily Dalgarno's second chapter in *Virginia Woolf and the Visible World*, entitled "On the far side of language: Greek studies and *Jacob's Room*," deepens scholarly understanding of the excellent tutelage of Woolf by Pater and Case, and, like Evelyn Haller's essay, delineates the gendered importance of such education for Woolf's critical and fictional work.

Haller's essay substantiates one of the most important aspects of the North American feminist, academic interpretive methods used to study Virginia Woolf in the past thirty years.   Starting with Harvena Richter (201), Alice Fox ("Literary") and Jane Marcus (*Languages* 36-74), North American scholarship first established a consistent counter-narrative in all of Woolf's writings, from novels to polemics. This narrative was of imagery and allusion, presented without overt narrative intervention. As feminist scholars mined these images, they became aware that the images referred to much more than individual memory. Instead, the images formed a thicket of historical and cultural allusion.[16] Examined as a whole, the imagery established an alternative world-view through which Woolf interrogated and defamiliarized militarism, patriarchal hierarchy, violence, and misogyny. Haller's essay anchors this submerged literary narrative in Woolf's conscious historical practice. Haller thus sketches the trajectory of one pathway by which Woolf sought sites of feminist historical imagination, and the imagery by which to make apparent that which had been obscured and silenced by patriarchal practices of remembering, preserving, and teaching the materials of the past.

II Storming the Library: Taking Back the Texts

Most readers of Virginia Woolf are familiar with the scene in *A Room of One's Own* in which the narrator is chased away from the male-domain of the Oxbridge library (7-8), her gender proving an insurmountable barrier to her admission to what Harold Bloom, Lionel Trilling, or F. R. Leavis would call "the great tradition." Less dramatic, perhaps, but no less painful, is Woolf's description in *Three Guineas* of "Arthur's Education Fund" (4-6). The "funds" that paid for middle-class British brothers' education were accrued by the exclusion of their sisters from preparatory school and university. Blocked from access to the university curricula of literary texts and standard interpretations, Virginia Woolf transformed literary tradition, interrogating it and constructing alternate, often competing trajectories of "literary history."

1. Miriam Wallace, "Thinking Back Through Our Others: Rereading Sterne and Resisting Joyce in *The Waves*"

"Western feminist literary productions have long roots, and those roots are neither exclusively modern, nor restricted to female authored texts," argues Wallace in her rereading of Woolf's male predecessors and contemporaries. Expanding the work of Evelyn Haller's essay contrasting Woolf and Forster, both Miriam Wallace and Lisa Low scrutinize the accouterments of male, elite educa-

---

[16]For examples, see, in addition to Jane Marcus, Fox, "Literary," Schlack, Zeck, Haller, Lipking, Phillips, *Empire*.

tion—Low in *Lycidas*, Wallace in *Tristram Shandy*—from which Woolf was excluded due to gender. Woolf studied the tropes of the pastoral elegy—with its insistence on male bonding and male mourning—and the purposeful narrative digressions of *Tristram Shandy*—a lexicon of allusions to elite, classical culture--not at University, but through private tutoring and rigorous writing and reading, as evidenced in Brenda Silver's edition of *Virginia Woolf's Reading Notebooks*.

Using the varied interpretive strategies of feminist historicism, close textual analysis, and Woolf's own efforts to create an intertextual historical body of texts, Miriam Wallace demonstrates how Woolf participated in what Wallace terms "an inter-literary conversation." Wallace argues that the constructed figure of Laurence Sterne served for Woolf as a harbinger of the formal experiments of *The Waves*. Both *Tristram Shandy* and *The Waves* evade traditional plot and trouble, if not contravene, generic boundaries, melding poetry with prose, literary criticism with fiction.[17] Sterne's didactic, invasive narrator created a gendered reader who could understand his text, an important model for Woolf who sought in her fiction and essays to construct a feminist reader able to negotiate narrative experimentation. Wallace argues that *Tristram Shandy* demonstrates the use of textual shape as a container for the dispersed selves of the reader, the interpolated narrator, and the textualized consciousnesses.

James Joyce enters Wallace's essay as a barrier to Woolf's absorption of and entry into literary history. Wallace ingeniously renegotiates Joyce's misogyny by suggesting that Joyce's often-remarked continuation of Sterne's narrative experiments in *Ulysses* enabled Woolf to use Sterne for her purposes as a literary historian, thus circumventing Joyce's imperious shadow. Wallace argues that Woolf rejected many of Joyce's methods due to gender rather than social class issues.[18] Rereading Joyce through Sterne as read by Woolf, Wallace reviews literary history, imitating by example those transgressive actions by which Woolf enunciated an/other tradition.

---

[17] Melba Cuddy-Keane's essay "The Rhetoric of Feminist Conversation" further interrogates the interconnections between Woolf's sudden shifts of tone and Woolf's blurring of generic boundaries.

[18] This mock literary epic—the so-called rivalry between Woolf and Joyce—is played out in Woolf's *Diaries* (for example, *D* 3: 16, 67-8, 199, 207) and in the works of numerous critics. Representative of the work of Joyce scholars is that of Richard Pearce and Christine Froula, "Gender". Jane Lilienfeld's comparison of *To the Lighthouse* and *A Portrait of the Artist as a Young Man* questions the scholarly insistence on privileging Joyce's work over that of Woolf ("Flesh"). Henke (626-7) reframes both the writers' and critics' views.

2. Lisa Low, "Feminist Elegy/Feminist Prophecy: *Lycidas, The Waves*, Kristeva, Cixous"

That Woolf complexly interpolated her own readings of male authored philosophy and fiction into her methods and constructions of literary history is a central argument of much current critical thinking. Lisa Low's essay expands the scope of this assessment of Woolf's contestations of the male literary tradition by examining poetry, the genre that Woolf famously claimed as dominant (*AROO* 13-17, 64-5, 69-70).

To examine Woolf's views of poetry, Lisa Low interrogates Woolf's passionate relation to the figure of John Milton. Low's essay applies Kristevan views of pre-Oedipal language[19] to Milton[20] through the agency of Woolf, explaining the cross-gender appeal of *Lycidas*[21] and transforming approaches to Milton's poetry by applying French Feminist theory to Woolf's syntax and systems of metaphor.

Low's essay deconstructs *Lycidas* by using varied theories and techniques suggested in Woolf's polemics in *A Room of One's Own* and *The Waves*. Having dismantled the major male form of pastoral elegy, Low's argument then re-establishes *The Waves* as a foundational transformation of male elegy tradition into female chora, "the new language" posited by Kristeva and Cixous and partly enunciated by Woolf's texts. For Low, in writing *The Waves*, Virginia Woolf becomes a Cromwellian, a revolutionary force, "turning the poem's furniture upside-down, smashing its laws, breaking its truths with laughter." Through Low's interrogations, *The Waves* emerges as a tribute, a commentary on, and a rewriting of *Lycidas*.

(The second part of *Virginia Woolf and Literary History* will appear in *Woolf Studies Annual* 10 [2004].)

---

[19] "Writing the body" discourse, an important topic in earlier Woolf studies, is well represented in the essay by Carpentier, and supplies one theoretical approach in Lisa Low's essay in this special issue. This approach is now contested by theories of performative genderization, such as those of Judith Butler, an argument extended to Woolf's works, for example, in essays by de Gay, Haines-Wright and Kyle and Carstens.

[20] Lisa Low's essay draws on the pre-existing critical analysis of Woolf's complicated relation to John Milton, to which she has added in several other essays ("'Listen'," "Reconciling," "Two"). In addition to Low's previous work on this topic, Mark Hussey (Z 160-1) examines the iconography of the representation of Milton in Woolf's works, discussing Milton as a figure in Leslie Stephen's emotional and intellectual life (160). See also Jane Marcus *Art and Anger* (201-3).

[21] "Lycidas" is the manuscript that Woolf seeks to read when she is refused admission to the library in *A Room of One's Own* (7-8).

III Emerging Narratives of Gender

Just as Virginia Woolf questioned the methods and materials that make up history, so she challenged the heretofore limited means by which to represent gender in narrative. Woolf's questions remain relevant: Can gender be theorized as an opportunity rather than an obstacle? If so, should it be so theorized? Can—and should—gender be perceived as fluid, as embodying a narrative that interrogates the constraints of one's immersion in one's family, society, culture?

The figure of the lesbian in Woolf's life and works has been heatedly contested by several generations of scholars.[22]   Patricia Cramer's and Vara Neverow's essays argue for a literary history of the woman-centered figure, both as a biographical reality for Virginia Woolf,[23] and as a central thematic and stylistic presence in her essays, fiction, letters, diaries, and polemics. But these essays do more than reconfigure the occluded narratives of the lesbian in Woolf's life and work.

Woolf's dialogics of gender trouble rigid gender demarcations and inscriptions.[24] Satirizing gender, Woolf enlarged the ways that language could represent and reconceptualize the embodied, loving presence of the human. Her practices

[22]See, for example, Patricia Juliana Smith's analysis of Woolf's lesbian situatedness or the diverse perspectives offered in Barrett and Cramer's *Virginia Woolf: Lesbian Readings*. Useful also are Judith Roof's essay "Hocus Crocus" and the vigorous challenges to it by Eileen Barrett and Patricia Cramer, theorizing how and in what ways Woolf might be seen from a lesbian rather than postmodernist interpretive perspective. At stake in such theoretical disputes are several issues, many of them a staple of years of Woolf studies. Is the theoretical postmodern a useful way to understand Woolf's narratives? Will such study move Woolf's works further into theoretical discourse in such a way as to further the impact of her varied generic productions? Does such incorporation and exploration, however, occlude, if not erase, the ongoing practical contribution that Woolf's works can make to political struggles for peace, justice, gender and racial parity? This debate was brilliantly staged at the Ninth Annual Conference on Virginia Woolf by the interconnected presentations of Judith Roof, Troy Gordon, Eileen Barrett, and Patricia Cramer. Expanded beyond Woolf Studies, this crucial debate about the negative impact of postmodern theory on feminist political activism is well presented by Jane Flax's now classic texts, Wolfe and Penelope's *Sexual Practice/Textual Theory*, and Marilyn Boxer's history of Women's Studies in the U.S.A.

[23]This issue, too, is deeply contested. The erasure of the lesbian in Woolf's life is an intrinsic part of biographical narrative on Woolf. For the erasure, see Nicolson (185, 204-7), Q. Bell (Vol. 2 115-20), and Hermione Lee (479-504), as representative. Patricia Cramer's "Plain" vigorously refutes the denial of Woolf's lesbian sexuality. See also essays by Olano, Risolo, and Cramer, "'Pearls.'"

[24]Representative essays include those by Carstens, for example, or Allen, "Constructing," or Haines-Wright and Kyle's essay.

thus gain depth and resonance when studied in conjunction with the work of those who came after her, offering a means of viewing her as an historical fore-bear and as a contemporary writer.

1. Patricia Cramer, "*Vita Nuova*: Courtly Love and Lesbian Romance in *The Years*"

Methodologically, Cramer's essay is connected to those of Pawlowski, McVicker, and Haller. Those three essays hypothesize the methods by which Woolf reshaped into cultural history her subversive undermining of "the official story" as reported in contemporary media. Similarly, Cramer's essay suggests that Woolf's rereading of literary history enabled Woolf to apply the great male-authored texts of the past to her experience, and to transform these through and into literature. Hence, like Miriam Wallace and Lisa Low, Patricia Cramer demonstrates Woolf's impassioned interventions into literary history.

Reading Virginia Woolf through the unlikely lens of Dante, Cramer propos-es that *The Years* is "a retrospective elegy to [Woolf's] beloved Vita [Sackville-West] and a reassessment of the impact of lesbian desire on her self-development and her vocation as an artist."[25] Such a reading redefines the political texture of *The Years*, which remains one focus of critical discourse on the novel.

Placing those passages from Woolf's diaries and letters that address the loss to another woman of Vita Sackville-West next to passages from *The Years*, Cramer creates a method by which she can read *The Years* as, in part, a fiction-alized lesbian autobiography. Writing the lesbian subtext of *The Years*, Woolf engages with romance traditions in her private life as well as fiction, just as in *Vita Nuova* Dante repeats and revises the courtly love conventions he inherited.

Cramer's revolutionary conclusion is that Woolf has left behind in *The Years* a record of what lesbian love felt like to her. Woolf created, "through metaphor and fantasy, a lesbian romance classic potentially as influential as the 'revolu-tionary ideology' [. . .] and 'new cult of emotion' [. . .] inaugurated, respectively, by Dante and courtly love." This radical political action in narrative form recon-

[25]Extensive discussion of the politics of *The Years*—in its creation and its representa-tion—has been led by Grace Radin's *The Years* and Mitchell Leaska's *The Pargiters*. This view is expanded by Jane Marcus's early readings of the novel as integral to Woolf's proj-ect in *Three Guineas* ("Gotterdammerung" and "Pargetting," reprinted in *Languages* 36-74). Mark Hussey provides an excellent history of the novel's reception in literary studies and its impact on Woolf's biography (Z 387-89, 390-94). Cramer's study of *The Years* as an autobiographical exploration of the lesbian links the novel back to *Orlando* and thus joins current critical explorations of blurred generic boundaries as one means to expand analyses of the representation of gender in Woolf's fiction.

nects the "novel" and the "essay" portions of *The Years*, demonstrating seamless interconnections between home/state, country/empire, sexuality/political choice.

2. Vara Neverow, "The Return of the Great Goddess: Immortal Virginity, Sexual Autonomy and Lesbian Possibility in *Jacob's Room*"

Current studies of *Jacob's Room* often view the novel as foundational to Woolf's pacifist stance, readings exemplified by Christine Froula's "War" and Alison Booth's "Architecture." The political texture of *Jacob's Room* however, encourages additional interpretive strategies. Both Patricia Cramer in studying *The Years* and Vara Neverow writing about *Jacob's Room* hypothesize how the hidden histories of women's erotic connections might be recovered and narrated.[26]

Like Cramer's experiments in methodologies of reading, Neverow's essay postulates that the well-known admiration Woolf felt for the work of the classicist Jane Ellen Harrison took the form of an homage via allusion in the novel *Jacob's Room*. Neverow's reading of the goddess in a pre-Hellenic world of women as suggested by Harrison's scholarship[27] is similar to Haller's study of Isis and Alexandria.[28] In Neverow's essay "the spectral presence of the female goddesses" returns, "creating lesbian narrative possibility." The symbols of the twinned goddess—mother and maid, Demeter and Persephone, and of Artemis, Aphrodite, Hera, her other manifestations—reappear in allusions in *Jacob's Room* to the goddesses' activities, her sacred creatures, and her beloved companions.

Reading the pre-Hellenic subtext to the patriarchal story of the first world war in *Jacob's Room*, Neverow explicitly voices that which tropes and allusions in the novel suggest. For example, tracing out the ways in which the narrative connects Clara Durrant to Artemis reveals another Clara, with a life other than the one usually attributed to her by literary critics. Following the theoretical example set by Harvena Richter and Jane Marcus, Neverow pieces these allusions together, a method that proves the allusions form a coherent story about a Clara who is woman-centered, not a woman whose life ends with the death of Jacob Flanders. Similarly, when Jacob's mother, Betty Flanders' subversive female friendship with Mrs. Jarvis is analyzed through the insistent narrative

[26]Diana Swanson's essay on *Jacob's Room* from a sister's point of view offers another means by which to discover a hidden history.

[27]This classical scholar is invoked in *A Room of One's Own* (17), and her influence on Woolf, who admired her greatly, has long been acknowledged by Woolf scholars (See, for example, Shattuck). Scholarship on "the great mother" has been a recurring motif in Woolf studies, discussed in conjunction with Harrison in Eileen Barrett's "Matriarchal Myth," Jane Lilienfeld's "Mother Love and Mother Hate," and Mark Hussey's "Reading and Ritual."

[28]See also Haller's articles "The Anti-Madonna" and"Isis Unveiled."

allusions to the twinned Goddess, their friendship glows with lesbian suggestion. Voicing that which the novel suggests through a narrative of imagery, Neverow models a methodology by which Virginia Woolf may be read as a lesbian writer: "a collage of hints, allusions and glancing remarks [may] cumulatively suggest but never specifically state that the relations between two women are erotically charged or romantic."

Exploring images, allusions, metaphors, Patricia Cramer and Vara Neverow bring to the surface those overlooked narratives implicit and explicit in the novels under consideration that express the political implications of gender, an intersection that the essays that follow theirs investigate and expand.

IV Virginia Woolf, Our Contemporary

In *Virginia Woolf Icon*, Brenda Silver suggests that Virginia Woolf's living presence assumes an iconic significance, that Woolf, like Elvis, can be sited/sighted in popular and elite culture. Certainly the essays in this section will demonstrate Woolf's impact on diverse living writers. Woolf's works, not just her constructed persona, have "a life of their own" that current writers explore, rewrite, and continue.

1. Meena Alexander, "'The Shock of Sensation': On Reading *The Waves* as a Girl in India, and as a Woman in America"

From the start of the annual conferences on Virginia Woolf, Woolf's vexed relation to issues of class, race,[29] and empire has been an integral part of scholarly argument.[30]

---

[29]In 1993 at the Third Annual Conference on Virginia Woolf, Barbara Christian, Michelle Cliff, Elizabeth Abel, Eileen Barrett, and Ann Harris-Williams contributed to this on-going debate in Woolf Studies. Worth noting in this regard is Tuzyline Jita Allan's essay, "The Death of Sex and the Soul in *Mrs. Dalloway* and Nella Larsen's *Passing*." There Allan suggests that "Their arm linking across the deep racial and cultural divide that separated them is a signpost that will guide contemporary Black and white feminists through a loose alliance into a cohesive feminist ferment" (112). Using an approach similar to that suggested by Susan Stanford Friedman (*Mappings*), Lisa Williams' comparative analysis of Virginia Woolf and Toni Morrison grows out of and extends a rich, conflicted scholarly discourse.

[30]For example, Kathy J. Phillips and Jeanette McVicker presented two important essays on Woolf and Empire at the First Annual Conference on Virginia Woolf. McVicker's continued work on this topic can be seen in her essay in this anthology, while Phillips' essay was incorporated into her important book reading Woolf within context of postcolonial theory. Essays by Chene Heady, Steven Putzel, and Genevieve Abravanel from the Tenth Annual Conference on Virginia Woolf, for example, are highly sophisticated, densely intertextual incorporations into Woolf studies of much current Diaspora and postcolonial theory.

Meena Alexander is a contemporary poet and novelist who first read Virginia Woolf's *The Waves* when she was a pre-teen, visiting her paternal grandmother in Kozencheri, Kerala, India. For Alexander, as for many readers, Woolf was a site fraught with painful ambiguities. Depicting her movement toward and away from Virginia Woolf as writer and persona, Alexander reveals the pull of Woolf's achievements, "that words could do that," piercingly evoking the sensual world—but in the language of the oppressor of India. For as Alexander came to realize, Virginia Woolf was one against whom Ghandi struggled to free India from colonial bondage.

But as Alexander charts her own journeys, she interweaves these with her growing sense of Woolf's fragmented identities. Rereading Woolf as an adult, living in Manhattan (an exile from her paternal grandmother's garden), Alexander can see the Woolf of dislocation, absence, of voices muffled and silenced. Grasping the ambiance of exile in Woolf's narratives through her own experiences of loss and change, Alexander's recognition defamiliarizes Virginia Woolf's narrative stances. The gendered, racialized, de/colonized subjectivity that Alexander's essay voices thus illuminates the layered, multivocal presences in Woolf's language, "humanizing" the claims of the postmodern theorists about Woolf's narrative strategies of multiple embodiment.

Meena Alexander's essay is a contemporary example of the discourse about India in Woolf studies. Alexander's freighted, complicated re/view of Woolf's place in her imagination has some similarities to the novelist Chitra Banerjee Divakaruni's playful, complicated use of the fictional figure of Woolf in her novel *Sister of My Heart*. There, Woolf's works are used as a means by which a handsome young man flirts with one of the two heroines of the text, as a prelude to the possibility of romance within the confines of an arranged marriage (Knowles 69-72). Like Alexander, Banerjee interrogates Woolf's status as an icon of British upper-class hegemony.

As Alexander and Banerjee recognize Woolf's complexity, so Leonard Woolf and Virginia Woolf appreciated Indian history and politics as more than footnotes to British imperial domination. Leonard Woolf's *Growing*, the second volume of his autobiography, discusses his work as a member of the British Imperial government in Ceylon, an experience that made him passionately anti-Empire, a view reflected in his discussion of his work in the Labor Party on behalf of India's independence (Woolf, *Downhill* 223-232).[31] Critical interpretation of Virginia Woolf's anti-imperialism, however, is by no means unanimous.

[31]As several essays in this anthology make clear, there is no scholarly consensus on Virginia Woolf's biographical and literary response to the British exercise of imperial domination. Leonard Woolf's excoriates his own work as an Imperialist in his multi-volume autobiography. He had been sent to Ceylon, which became the basis for his novel

Virginia Woolf subtly undermines the official representation of the British Raj in *The Waves*, as Jane Marcus's now-classic article "Britannia Rules The Waves" establishes. In contrast, Hanif Kureishi's representation of Woolf as Imperial icon in his screenplay for the film *Sammy and Rosie Get Laid* (Silver, *Icon* 161-172) reflects the more widespread interpretation of Virginia Woolf that Meena Alexander ultimately rejected.

2. Monica Ayuso, "The Unlikely Other: Borges and Woolf"
Recent scholarly work indicates a growing recognition of the place of Woolf in Spanish letters. Alberto Lazaro, in "An Early Spanish translation of 'Time Passes,'" (2) has contributed a recent brief essay about the Spanish reception of Virginia Woolf, and Antonio Bivar has published "As if Virginia Woolf were a Great Brazilian Writer . . ." (2). Monica Ayuso's ground-breaking essay expands her previous analyses of Woolf's influence on literature written in Spanish.

Nevertheless, Diane Gillespie has rightly argued that Spain "remains the neglected geographical sister in Bloomsbury and Woolf studies" ("'Rain'" 271), a fact seemingly borne out by the absence of Spain as a locus of Woolf studies in the 1997 Virginia Woolf Special Edition of the *South Carolina Review*, "Virginia Woolf International." Gillespie's article reminds readers that Woolf traveled to Spain at three important junctures in her life: "after her father's death; [at the] the beginnings of her married life with Leonard Woolf; and, [on] having turned forty" ("'Rain'" 272).[32]

Spanish literature and geography are an integral part of several of Woolf's essays and *The Waves*. Biographically, Gillespie notes the importance of Gerald Brenan, a peripheral member of the Bloomsbury Group, who had moved to Yegen in Spain. Visiting him in this remote area in 1923, Woolf described the experience as "moving not just horizontally across European geographical space, but vertically and diagonally to a high vantage-point" (Gillespie, "'Rain'" 274). The geography of Yegen, Gillespie argues, is inseparable from the characterization of Rhoda in *The Waves* ("'Rain'" 275-6). Further, the literary importance of Spain for Woolf's works is seen in the repeated appearance of Cervantes in

---

The Village in the Jungle, now often read in conjunction with Woolf's *Melymbrosia* and *The Voyage Out* (Thompson). Leonard Woolf's letters to Lytton Strachey offer a detailed record of his time in Ceylon, for example (Spotts), an aspect of his experience discussed in detail in the excellent biography by Sir Duncan Wilson. Leonard Woolf also published the diaries that he kept when in Ceylon, where the growth of his anti-imperial views can be clearly traced. See also Rosenfeld, 39-54. Yuko Ito disputes the generally-accepted view of Leonard Woolf's anti-imperialism.

[32]See also Virginia Woolf's *PA* 246, 257, *L*1 184-6, 187, *D*1 192, *L*3 157-8, *L*2 8, *D* 2 55-6, *D*3 203.

Woolf's reading and writing (Gillespie "'Rain'" 273-4).

Virginia Woolf's complicated recognitions of her judgments and observations of those Spaniards whom she met (Gillespie, "'Rain'" 272) mark her growth in recognizing issues of her own "othering." This nexus of seeing and being seen is part of the ongoing debate in Woolf studies about Woolf's appropriation of those whom she perceived as different in class or geography, an issue still heatedly argued in discussions of Woolf's conceptualization of the colonizing process.

Spain was also for Woolf a marker of gender issues. One of the most important Spanish feminist writers, Victoria Ocampo, avidly pursued Woolf throughout the 1930s, a campaign that amused and interested Woolf who, nevertheless, resisted such intimacy.[33] One can see Woolf's charming refusal in her letters to Ocampo, which are both playful and reticent. These letters differ greatly in tone, imagery and allusion from letters to Woolf's women lovers, such as those to Violet Dickinson (for example, *L*1 73-6) and Vita Sackville-West (for example, *L*3 231-3). Typical is the letter by which Woolf tried to calm Ocampo's passionate concern over Woolf's delay in responding to Ocampo's letter (*L*5 364-5).

Diane Gillespie and Monica Ayuso's essays suggest that although the importance of France and Germany to Virginia Woolf's intellectual and artistic development has been amply documented,[34] that of Woolf's response to Spain and Spanish culture needs additional attention.

It was through Victoria Ocampo that Borges began his literary relationship to Virginia Woolf. During his affiliation with *Sur*, published in Argentina under the leadership of Victoria O'Campo between 1931 and 1970, Jorge Luis Borges's numerous contributions to the literary magazine helped fulfill the mission of making European culture accessible to a wide Latin American readership. Along with the works of many contemporary prose writers like Kafka and Faulkner,

---

[33]Ocampo's passion for Woolf is traced in Woolf's diaries, *D*4 263; *D*5 219-220n.

[34]For a discussion of the French reception of Woolf's works, see Villeneuve. For the importance of France to painters Duncan Grant and Vanessa Bell, see Frances Spalding (211-39) and Hussey (*Z* 23). The conflicted relationship between Virginia Woolf and Vanessa Bell is pertinent to the sisters' excellence in what they considered one another's territories of words and visuals (Gillespie, *Sisters' Arts*). See as well Caws and Wright on the importance of France to the painters. Gillespie notes the importance to Carrington of the Yegen landscape ("'Rain'" 274). For an extensive analysis of Woolf's reception in German belles lettres, see the Nünnings' essay. See also Leonard Woolf (*Downhill* (185-194) on the Woolfs' pre-World War Two trip to Germany, a trip analyzed by Hermione Lee (667-69).

Borges was also asked by Ocampo to translate the works of Virginia Woolf. Borges's translation of *Orlando*, published in 1937, and of *A Room of One's Own*, published from December 1935 to March 1936, became the standard texts from which Virginia Woolf was read in Latin America well into the twentieth century.

Monica Ayuso's article incorporates gendered translation studies, an emerging field, into scholarly study of Virginia Woolf. Ayuso argues that Borges seems an unlikely choice to read and to recreate—as he thought translators did—the work of Virginia Woolf. His disparagement of the modern psychological novel would seem to put him at odds with Woolf's themes and methodologies. Further, Borges's renowned postmodern denial of individual agency opposed the relational, socially-developed self that Ayuso sees as exemplified in Woolf's works. However, Borges proved to be a perfect match for Woolf. As a brilliant stylist, he had knowledge of Spanish, the language into which he translated Woolf's works. He also regarded translation and exercises related to it as literary practices worthwhile in their own right.

Ayuso's essay focuses on Borges's translations of *Orlando* and *A Room of One's Own*, speculating about the literality of Borges's translations, noting which passages of Woolf's he elides or expands. Since he is a man translating two of the most outspoken of Woolf's feminist works, Ayuso explores how Borges's translations expand and comment on Woolf's *A Room* and *Orlando* as aesthetic formulations and as feminist statements. Interrogating gendered readings of Woolf, Ayuso's essay becomes part of the trajectory of such insights as presented by the essays of Low, Wallace, and Cramer.

3. Jane Lilienfeld, "Shirking the Imperial Shadow: Virginia Woolf and Alice Munro"

Virginia Woolf's ambiguous relation to the privileges rendered by serving the empire connects her to those whose lands Britain once claimed to own. Just as Meena Alexander recognized Woolf as someone whose privileged Imperial position impeded Alexander's national independence, so too did Alice Munro claim to reject Virginia Woolf. In an interview in the early 1980s, Munro extolled James Joyce's insistence on speaking the truth of the male body, while depicting Woolf as a lesser writer, the disembodied, suicidal Bloomsbury writer of privilege (Rasporich 21). Lilienfeld's essay argues that despite Munro's claims, Woolf served as the [m]other country for several of Munro's narrative strategies.

Almost as if "Modern Fiction" had served as a guide-book on how to structure her narratives, Alice Munro implemented Woolf's instructions in her two short stories "How I Met My Husband" and "Accident." Each of these stories

flouts traditional plot devices by deploying a series of seemingly fortuitous inci-
dents that the protagonists manipulate to their economic and sexual advantage.
Such narrative strategies enact Woolf's suggestions for how to plot "Modern
Fiction." Further, "Modern Fiction" suggests that the interweaving of layered
time and space in memory and consciousness might provide both the focus of
and the method of narration. These two Munro stories under discussion are narrated through multiple sites of speech, for Munro's subtle use of free indirect
discourse is fully the equal of Woolf's in the manipulation of narrative focaliza-
tion.

As Woolf is not free of white privilege, neither is Munro, whose paternal
forebears emigrated to "crown lands" in the Ontario, Canadian bush in the 1850s.
Munro maps the time/space coordinates of personal and cultural memory
(Howells 4-7, 10-12) onto the captured territory of expelled Canadian natives.
Just as Woolf recognized her descent from those who reaped the profits of colo-
nization, so, too, does Munro unveil the usurped lands of the expelled other, their
haunting invisibility a powerful presence in Munro's fiction, which, through its
manipulation of a technique of which Woolf, too, was a master—indirect interi-
or discourse—can make present that which is not seen. Viewing Munro through
the lens of Woolf suggests the continuing power of Woolf's theory and practice
of fiction to influence the writing of Munro, who has been called the heir to
Chekhov (Ozick, qtd. in McCulloch and Simpson 229) and one of the greatest
living short story writers in the English language.

V Virginia Woolf, Teacher

Beth Daugherty, "Teaching Woolf/Woolf Teaching"

One of the most important legacies that Virginia Woolf left is realized daily
as "Virginia Woolf" is invoked in the North American college classroom. The
range of courses in which Woolf's works are used is as varied as the settings in
which such teaching takes place. Virginia Woolf's works are taught in high
schools (Shay, Pettigrew), in community colleges (Gilmore), to non-traditional
students in elite institutions (Lazare) and in urban university settings (Hussey,
"For," Laurence, "'Some'," Folsom). Woolf's works are taught in colleges and
universities in gender studies courses (Farris, Backus, MacMaster), in Women's
Studies courses (McNaron, Bazin, Oxindine), in courses on Modernism
(McVicker, "Reading"), in Nineteenth- and Twentieth-Century literature courses
(McGill, Pinkerton, Braendlin, Currier), and in sophomore, junior, and senior lit-
erature courses (Murphy and McNett, Yunis, Levenback, "Teaching," Paul,
Davis).

As one would expect, Virginia Woolf's works are used extensively by teachers of freshman composition. Presentations and publications by Krista Ratcliffe,
Lisa Williams ("'Legacy'"), Deborah Malmud, Vara Neverow ("Model"), and

Annis Pratt, to cite only a few such examples, explore how these teachers have used the works of Virginia Woolf to help their writing students.   Woolf's acknowledgment that putting thoughts into words was labor-intensive, can sometimes evoke a grudging recognition in the struggling writer that his or her efforts are part of a task shared by "the famous." Particularly relevant to freshman writers is the idea that writing is a process of discovery, and that multiple revisions of a written text bring the writer closer to his or her argument. Woolf wrote by successive revisions, and revising is one of the most important aspects of teaching freshman writers to find and to clarify their ideas.

This essay by Beth Daugherty has many similarities to the plethora of excellent pedagogical, theoretical, and practical applications of Woolf's work. However, this essay breaks new ground, for its detailed observations of Virginia Woolf as a young educator can be found only in Daugherty's work.

Intriguingly, the essay moves back and forth from Virginia Woolf as a teacher in Morley College, the University of London, and Beth Daugherty, teacher at Otterbein College, Columbus, Ohio, between Woolf's educational and cultural context and that of Daugherty, between Woolf's students and those of Daugherty. What methods helped Woolf teach? Are these useful to a contemporary literature teacher?   Did Woolf's multiple revisions of texts help Daugherty's students in their struggle to verbalize their insights? How? This essay asks from what positions can contemporary students and teachers learn? What can a writer and reader of literature such as Woolf teach today's writers and readers of literature? Methodologically, the essay's movement between the pedagogical and the scholarly, the personal and the political, the exploratory and the expository carries forward a now-established discourse about Woolf in the classroom, exploring the practical uses of literary history in the lives of students.

Closing *Virginia Woolf and Literary History* with an essay about teaching grounds Woolf's works in that which almost all readers of her texts have experienced. Literary history is not something fashioned only for and within the physical or theoretical library. It comes alive every day as "the common reader" (Dubino) and the struggling writer look to the works of others to help him or her to make sense of experience. "Virginia Woolf" has been constructed by her numerous readers, thus, as an access to the creation of their own texts and their own meanings.

Virginia Woolf wrote literary history and herself became the subject of literary history, as numerous twentieth-century writers experienced her impact on their imaginations and looked to her for inspiration. *Virginia Woolf and Literary History* demonstrates the diversity of ways in which Woolf constructed history and its trajectory. These essays illuminate the many on-going conversations that Woolf's works generate.

I thank Marcia Deihl, Staff Assistant at Tozzer Library, Harvard University, and David Eberly, Director of Resource Development, John F. Kennedy School of Government, Harvard University, for their assistance with library materials and interlibrary loans.

Works Cited

Abel, Elizabeth. "Matrilineage and the Racial 'Other': Woolf and Her Literary Daughters of the Second Wave." The Third Annual Conference on Virginia Woolf. Jefferson City, MO. 13 June 1993.

Abravanel, Genevieve. "Woolf in Blackface: Identification across *The Waves*." Berman and Goldman: 113-19.

Allan, Tuzyline Jita. "The Death of Sex and the Soul in *Mrs. Dalloway* and Nella Larsen's *Passing*." Barrett and Cramer, *Lesbian*: 95-113.

Allen, Judith. "Those Soul Mates: Virginia Woolf and Michel de Montaigne." Neverow-Turk and Hussey: 190-99.

Ardis, Ann and Bonnie Kime Scott, eds., *Virginia Woolf: Turning the Centuries, Selected Papers from the Ninth Annual Conference on Virginia Woolf*. New York: Pace UP, 2000.

Ayuso, Monica. "Remote Inscriptions: *To the Lighthouse* and *The Waves* in Julieta Campos' Caribbean." Ardis and Scott: 86-92.

——. "Thinking Back through Our Mothers: Virginia Woolf in the Spanish-American Female Imagination." McVicker and Davis: 97-102.

Backus, Margot Gayle. "Exploring The Ethical Implications of Narrative in a Sophomore-level Course on Same-Sex Love: *Mrs. Dalloway* and *The Last September*." Barrett and Cramer, *Re: Reading*: 102-5.

Barnaby, Edward. "Visualizing the Spectacle: Virginia Woolf's Metahistory Lesson in *Between the Acts*." Ardis and Scott: 311-17.

Barrett, Eileen. "Matriarchal Myth on a Patriarchal Stage: Virginia Woolf's *Between the Acts*." *Twentieth-Century Literature* 33 (1987): 18-37.

——. "Response." Ardis and Scott: 111-16.

——. "Septimus and Shadrack: Woolf and Morrison Envision the Madness of War." Hussey and Neverow: 26-32.

Barrett, Eileen and Patricia Cramer, eds. *Re: Reading, Re: Writing, Re: Teaching Virginia Woolf, Selected Papers from the Fourth Annual Conference on Virginia Woolf*. New York: Pace UP, 1995.

——, eds. *Virginia Woolf: Lesbian Readings*. New York: New York UP, 1997.

Bazin, Nancy T. "Articulating the Questions, Searching for Answers: How *To the Lighthouse* Can Help." Daugherty and Pringle 107-113.

Bell, Quentin. *Bloomsbury*. London: Futura Publications, 1974.

——. *Virginia Woolf: A Biography*. 2 Vols. New York: Harcourt Brace Jovanovich, 1972.

Berman, Jessica and Jane Goldman, eds. *Virginia Woolf Out of Bounds: Selected*

Papers from the Tenth Annual Conference on Virginia Woolf. New York: Pace UP, 2001.

Bivar, Antonio. "As if Virginia Woolf Were a Great Brazilian Writer . . . ." *Virginia Woolf Miscellany* 54 (Fall 1999): 2.

Black, Naomi. "Virginia Woolf and the Women's Movement." Jane Marcus, *Slant*: 180-97.

Booth, Alison. "The Architecture of Loss: Teaching *Jacob's Room* as a War Novel." Barrett and Cramer, *Re: Reading*: 65-72.

——. "The Well-Lit Corridors of History." Ardis and Scott: 24-34.

Boxer, Marilyn. *When Women Ask the Questions: Creating Women's Studies in America.* Baltimore: Johns Hopkins UP, 1998.

Boxwell, D. A. "In the Urinal: Virginia Woolf Around Gay Men." McVicker and Davis: 173-8.

Braendlin, Bonnie. "'I Have Had My Vision': Teaching *To the Lighthouse* as *Kunstleroman*." Daugherty and Pringle: 148-153.

Brosnan, Leila. *Reading Virginia Woolf's Essays and Journalism: Breaking the Surface of Silence.* Edinburgh: Edinburgh UP, 1997.

Butler, Judith. *Gender Trouble: Feminism and the Subversion of Identity.* New York: RKP, 1990.

Carpentier, Martha C. "Why an Old Shoe? Teaching *Jacob's Room* as *l'écriture feminine*." Barrett and Cramer, *Re: Reading*: 142-8.

Carroll, Berenice A. "'To Crush Him in Our Own Country': The Political Thought of Virginia Woolf." *Feminist Studies* 4 (1978): 99-131.

Carstens, Lisa. "The Science of Sex and the Art of Self-Materializing in *Orlando*." Berman and Goldman: 39-46.

Caughie, Pamela. *Virginia Woolf and Postmodernism: Literature in Quest and Question of Itself.* Urbana: U of Illinois P, 1991.

Caws, Mary Ann and Sarah Bird Wright. *Bloomsbury and France: Art and Friends.* New York: Oxford UP, 2000.

Chapman, Wayne K. and Janet M. Manson, "Carte and Tierce: Leonard, Virginia Woolf, and War for Peace." Hussey, *War*: 58-78.

——, eds. *Women in the Milieu of Leonard and Virginia Woolf: Peace, Politics, and Education.* New York: Pace UP, 1998.

Childers, Mary. "Virginia Woolf on the Outside Looking Down: Reflections on the Class of Women." *Modern Fiction Studies* 38 (1992): 61-79.

Christian, Barbara. "Layered Rhythms: Virginia Woolf and Toni Morrison." Hussey and Neverow: 164-77.

Cliff, Michelle. "Virginia Woolf and the Imperial Gaze: A Glance Askance." Hussey and Neverow: 91-102.

Cook, Blanche Wiesen. "'Women Alone Stir My Imagination': Lesbianism and the Cultural Tradition." *Signs* 4.4 (Summer 1979): 718-39.

Cramer, Patricia. "'Pearls and the Porpoise': *The Years*—A Lesbian Memoir." Barrett and Cramer, *Lesbian*: 222-40.

——. "Plain as a Pike's Staff: A Response to Recent Biographers." The Ninth Annual Conference on Virginia Woolf. Newark, Delaware. 12 June 1999.

——. "Response." Ardis and Scott: 116-26.

Cuddy-Keane, Melba. "Brow-Beating, Wool-Gathering, and the Brain of the Common Reader." Berman and Goldman: 58-66.

——. "The Rhetoric of Feminist Conversation: Virginia Woolf and the Trope of the Twist." *Ambiguous Discourse: Feminist Narratology and British Women Writers.* Ed. Kathy Mezei. Chapel Hill: U of No. Carolina P, 1996. 137-61.

——. "Virginia Woolf and the Varieties of Historicist Experience." Rosenberg and Dubino: 59-77.

Currier, Susan. "Portraits of Artists by Woolf and Joyce." Daugherty and Pringle: 157-62.

Dalgarno, Emily. *Virginia Woolf and the Visible World.* New York: Cambridge UP, 2001.

Daugherty, Beth and Eileen Barrett, eds., *Virginia Woolf: Texts and Contexts, Selected Papers from the Fifth Annual Conference on Virginia Woolf.* New York: Pace UP, 1996.

Daugherty, Beth and Mary Beth Pringle, eds. *Approaches to Teaching Woolf's* To the Lighthouse. New York: Modern Language Association, 2001.

Davis, Laura. "Reading and Writing: Helping Students Discover Meaning in *To the Lighthouse*." Daugherty and Pringle: 79-84.

De Gay, Jane. "' . . . though the fashion of the time did something to disguise it': Staging Gender in Woolf's *Orlando*." Ardis and Scott: 25-31.

Diamond, Irene and Lee Quinby, eds. *Feminism and Foucault: Reflections on Resistance.* Boston: Northeastern UP, 1988.

Doyle, Laura. "The Body Unbound: A Phenomenological Reading of the Political in *A Room of One's Own*." Berman and Goldman: 129-40.

Dubino, Jeanne. "Creating 'the Conditions of Life': Virginia Woolf and the Common Reader." Barrett and Cramer, *Re: Reading:* 129-37.

Duffy, Julia and Lloyd Davis. "Demythologizing Facts and Photographs in *Three Guineas*." *Photo-Textualities: Reading Photographs and Literature.* Ed. Marsha Bryant. Newark: U of Delaware P, 1995. 128-40.

Dusinberre, Juliet. *Virginia Woolf's Renaissance: Woman Reader or Common Reader?* Iowa City: U of Iowa P, 1997.

Ezell, Margaret J. M. *Writing Women's Literary History.* Baltimore: Johns Hopkins UP, 1993.

Farris, Christine. "What's Gender Got to Do With It?: Introducing Non-English Majors to Gendered Textuality." Hussey and Neverow: 52-8.

Flax, Jane. *Disputed Subjects: Essays on Psychoanalysis, Politics and Philosophy.* New York: RKP, 1993.

——. *Thinking Fragments: Psychoanalysis, Feminism, & Postmodernism in the Contemporary West.* Berkeley: U of California P, 1990.

Folsom, Marcia McClintock. "Transformations: Teaching *To the Lighthouse* with

Autobiographies and Family Chronicles." Daugherty and Pringle: 119-125.

Forster, E. M. *Virginia Woolf.* New York: Harcourt, Brace and Co.,1942.

Fox, Alice. "Literary Allusion as Feminist Criticism in *A Room of One's Own.*" *Philological Quarterly* (Spring 1984): 145-61.

——. *Virginia Woolf and the Literature of the English Renaissance.* Oxford: Clarendon, 1990.

Friedman, Susan Stanford. *Mappings: Feminism and the Cultural Geographies of Encounter.* Princeton: Princeton UP, 1998.

——. "Uncommon Readings: Seeking the Geopolitical Woolf." *South Carolina Review* 29.1 (Fall 1996): 24-44.

Froula, Christine. "Gender and the Law of Genre: Joyce, Woolf, and the Autobiographical Artist-Novel." Bonnie Kime Scott, *New*: 155-64.

——."War, Civilization, and the Conscience of Modernity: Views from *Jacob's Room.*" Daugherty and Barrett: 280-95.

Furbank, P. N. *E. M. Forster: A Life.* New York: Harcourt Brace Jovanovich, 1978.

Gillespie, Diane Filby. "Her Kodak Pointed at His Head: Virginia Woolf and Photography." Gillespie: 113-147.

——, ed. *The Multiple Muses of Virginia Woolf.* Columbia, MO: U of Missouri P, 1993.

——. "'The Rain in Spain': Woolf, Cervantes, Andalusia, and *The Waves.*" Berman and Goldman: 271-8.

——. *The Sisters' Arts: The Writing and Painting of Virginia Woolf and Vanessa Bell.* Syracuse: Syracuse UP, 1988.

Gilmore, Lois J. "'She speaks to me': Virginia Woolf in the Community College Classroom." Berman and Goldman: 165-70.

Ginsburg, Elaine and Laura Gottlieb, eds., *Virginia Woolf: Centennial Essays.* Troy, NY: Whitston, 1983.

Gordon, Troy. "The Place of Cross-Sex Friendship in Woolf Studies." Ardis and Scott: 102-11.

Greene, Sally. *Virginia Woolf: Reading the Renaissance.* Athens: Ohio UP, 1999.

Gualtieri, Elena. "*Three Guineas* and Photography: The Art of Propaganda." *Women Writers of the 1930s.* Ed. Maroula Joannou. Edinburgh: Edinburgh UP, 1999. 165-78.

——. *Virginia Woolf's Essays: Sketching the Past.* New York: Palgrave, 2000.

Haines-Wright, Lisa and Traci Lynn Kyle. "From He and She to You and Me: Grounding Fluidity, Woolf's *Orlando* to Winterson's *Written on the Body.*" Daughtery and Barrett:77-83

Haller, Evelyn. "Isis Unveiled: Virginia Woolf's Use of Egyptian Myth." Marcus, *Slant*: 109-31.

——. "The Anti-Madonna in the Work and Thought of Virginia Woolf." Ginsburg and Gottlieb: 93-109.

Hankins, Leslie. "'Across the Screen of My Brain': Virginia Woolf's 'The Cinema' and Film Forums of the Twenties." Gillespie: 148-79.

——. "The Doctor and the Woolf: Reel Challenges—*The Cabinet of Dr. Caligari* and *Mrs. Dalloway*." Hussey and Neverow: 40-51.

——. "Virginia Woolf, Literary Tourism and Cultural Site-Seeing." Hussey and Neverow-Turk: 71-86.

Harris-Williams, Ann. "Woolf and Toni Morrison: Moments from the Critical Dialogue." Hussey and Neverow: 32-37.

Heady, Chene. "'Accidents of Political Life': Satire and Edwardian Anti-Colonial Politics in *The Voyage Out*." Berman and Goldman: 97-104.

Henke, Suzette. "Virginia Woolf: The Modern Tradition." Bonnie Kime Scott, *Gender*: 622-57.

Hill, Katherine C. "Virginia Woolf and Leslie Stephen: History and Literary Revolution." *PMLA* 96 (1981): 351-62.

Hotchkiss, Lia M. "Writing the Jump Cut: *Mrs. Dalloway* and the Context of Cinema." Daugherty and Barrett: 134-9.

Howells, Coral Ann. *Alice Munro*. Manchester: Manchester UP, 1998.

Humm, Maggie. "Matrixial Memories in Virginia Woolf's Photographs." Berman and Goldman: 206-13.

Hussey, Mark. "'For Nothing Is Simply One Thing': Knowing the World in *To the Lighthouse*." Daugherty and Pringle: 41-6.

——. "Reading and Ritual in Between the Acts." *Anima* 15.2 (Spring 1989): 88-99.

——. *Virginia Woolf A to Z: A Comprehensive Reference for Students, Teachers and Common Readers to Her Life, Work and Critical Reception*. New York: Facts on File, 1995.

——. ed., *Virginia Woolf and War: Fiction, Reality and Myth*. Syracuse: Syracuse UP, 1991.

Hussey, Mark and Vara Neverow, eds., *Virginia Woolf: Emerging Perspectives, Selected Papers from the Third Annual Conference on Virginia Woolf*. New York: Pace UP, 1984.

Hussey, Mark and Vara Neverow-Turk, eds., *Virginia Woolf Miscellanies: Proceedings of the First Annual Conference on Virginia Woolf*. NY: Pace UP, 1992.

Ito, Yuko. "The Masked Reality in Leonard Woolf's Writings." McVicker and Davis: 136-41.

Knowles, Nancy. "Dissolving Stereotypical Cultural Boundaries: Allusions to Virginia Woolf in Chitra Banerjee Divakaruni's *Sister of My Heart*." Berman and Goldman: 67-73.

Laurence, Patricia. "A Writing Couple: Shared Ideology in Virginia Woolf's *Three Guineas* and Leonard Woolf's *Quack, Quack!*" Chapman and Manson: 125-43.

——. "'Some Rope to Throw to the Reader': Teaching the Diverse Rhythms of *To the Lighthouse*." Daugherty and Pringle: 66-71.

Lazaro, Alberto. "An Early Spanish Version of 'Time Passes.'" *Virginia Woolf Miscellany*. 55 (Spring 2000): 2.

Lazarre, Jane. "Structures of Common Experience: Learning from Virginia Woolf." Hussey and Neverow: 57-61.

Leaska, Mitchell. *Virginia Woolf, The Pargiters: The Novel-Essay Portion of The Years*. New York: New York Public Library, 1977.

Lee, Hermione. *Virginia Woolf*. New York: Knopf, 1997.

Levenback, Karen. "Teaching *To the Lighthouse* as a Civilian War Novel." Daugherty and Pringle: 142-47.

——. *Virginia Woolf and the Great War*. Syracuse: Syracuse UP, 1999.

Lilienfeld, Jane. "Flesh and Blood and Love and Words: Lily Briscoe, Stephen Dedalus, and the Aesthetics of Emotional Quest." Bonnie Kime Scott, *New*: 165-78.

——. "'The Deceptiveness of Beauty': Mother Love and Mother Hate in *To the Lighthouse*." *Twentieth Century Literature* 23 (October 1977): 345-76.

Lipking, Joanna. "60/70's Woolf Scholars." Fifth Annual Conference on Virginia Woolf. Westerville, Ohio. 17 June 1995.

Low, Lisa. "'Listen and save': Woolf's Allusions to *Comus* in her Revolutionary First Novel." Greene: 117-35.

——. "Reconciling the Sexes: Milton and Woolf in the Women's Studies and English Literature Classroom." Barrett and Cramer, *Re: Reading*: 92-5.

——. "Two Figures Standing in Dense Violet Light: John Milton, Virginia Woolf, and the Epic Vision of Marriage." Hussey and Neverow-Turk: 144-5.

Luckhurst, Nicola. "Photoportraits: Gisele Freund and Virginia Woolf." Berman and Goldman: 197-206.

MacMaster, Anne. "Anguished Love for the Angel in the House: *To the Lighthouse* and the Women's Studies Generations Paper." Barrett and Cramer, *Re: Reading*: 269-72.

Malmud, A. Deborah. "Virginia Woolf Meets Audre Lorde at 125th Street and Adam Clayton Powell Blvd." Hussey and Neverow: 121-26.

Marcus, Jane. "Britannia Rules *The Waves*." *Decolonizing Tradition: The Cultural Politics of Modern Literary Canons*. Ed. Karen Lawrence. Urbana: U of Illinois P, 1991: 136-62.

——, ed. *New Feminist Essays on Virginia Woolf*. Ed. Jane Marcus. Lincoln: U of Nebraska P, 1981.

——. "No More Horses." *Art and Anger: Reading Like a Woman*. Columbus: Ohio State UP, 1988.

——. "Pargetting *The Pargiters*." Marcus, *Languages*: 57-74.

——. "Quentin's Bogey." *Art and Anger: Reading Like a Woman*. Columbus: Ohio UP, 1988. 201-214.

——, "*The Years* as Götterdämmerung, Greek Play, and Domestic Novel." Marcus, *Languages*: 36-56.

——, ed. *Virginia Woolf: A Feminist Slant*. Lincoln: U of Nebraska P, 1981.

——, ed. *Virginia Woolf and Bloomsbury: A Centenary Celebration.* Bloomington: Indiana UP, 1987.

——. *Virginia Woolf and the Languages of Patriarchy.* Bloomington: Indiana UP, 1987.

——. "Wrapped in the Stars and Stripes: Virginia Woolf in the U.S.A." *South Carolina Review* 29.1 (Fall 1996): 17-23.

Marcus, Laura. "Woolf's Feminism and Feminism's Woolf." *The Cambridge Companion to Virginia Woolf.* Ed. Sue Roe and Susan Sellers. New York: Cambridge UP, 2000. 209-44.

Marder, Herbert. *Feminism and Art: A Study of Virginia Woolf.* Chicago: U of Chicago P, 1968.

McCulloch, Jeanne and Mona Simpson. "The Art of Fiction CXXXVII [An Interview with Alice Munro]." *Paris Review* 131 (1994): 226-64.

McGill, Allyson F. "Living Voices: Virginia Woolf's *A Room of One's Own* and Vera Brittain's *Testament of Youth* in the Classroom." Barrett and Cramer, *Re: Reading*: 259-65.

McNaron, Toni A. H. "Look Again: Reading *To the Lighthouse* from an Aesthetic of Likeness." Daugherty and Pringle: 85-90.

McVicker, Jeannette. "Reading *To the Lighthouse* as a Critique of the Imperial." Daugherty and Pringle: 97-104.

——. "Vast Nests of Chinese Boxes, or Getting from Q to R: Critiquing Empire in 'Kew Gardens' and *To the Lighthouse*." Hussey and Neverow-Turk: 40-42.

McVicker, Jeanette and Laura Davis, eds. *Virginia Woolf and Communities: Selected Papers from the Eighth Annual Conference on Virginia Woolf.* New York: Pace UP, 1999.

Minow-Pinkney, Makiko. *Virginia Woolf and the Problem of the Subject.* New Brunswick: Rutgers UP, 1987.

Munro, Alice. "Accident." *The Moons of Jupiter.* New York: Vintage, 1982. 77-109.

——. "How I Met My Husband." *Something I've Been Meaning To Tell You: Thirteen Stories.* New York: Plume, 1984. 45-66.

Murphy, Ann and Jeanne McNett. "Women's Learning, Women's Work." Ardis and Scott: 317-24.

Neverow, Vara. "*A Room of One's Own* as a Model of Composition Theory." Hussey and Neverow: 58-65.

——. "Freudian Seduction and the Fallacies of Dictatorship." Pawlowski, *Fascism*: 56-72.

Neverow-Turk, Vara and Mark Hussey, eds., *Virginia Woolf: Themes and Variations, Selected Papers from the Second Annual Conference on Virginia Woolf.* New York: Pace UP, 1993.

Nicolson, Nigel. *Portrait of a Marriage: V. Sackville-West and Harold Nicolson.* New York: Atheneum, 1973.

Nünning, Vera and Ansgar Nünning. "From Thematics and Formalism to Aesthetics and History: Phrases and Trends of Virginia Woolf Criticism in Germany, 1946-1996." *South Carolina Review* 29.1 (Fall 1996): 90-108.

Olano, Pam. "'Women Alone Stir My Imagination': Reading Virginia Woolf as a Lesbian." Neverow-Turk and Hussey: 158-71.

Outka, Elizabeth. "'The Shop Windows Were Full of Sparkling Chains': Consumer Desire and Woolf's *Night and Day*." Berman and Goldman: 229-35.

Oxindine, Annette. "Pear Trees Beyond Eden: Women's Knowing Reconfigured in Woolf's *To the Lighthouse* and Hurston's *Their Eyes Were Watching God*." Daugherty and Pringle: 163-8.

Pardee, Shiela. "Assuming Psyche's Task: Virginia Woolf Responds to James Frazer." Ardis and Scott: 291-8.

Paul, Janis. "Teaching *To the Lighthouse* as a Traditional Novel." Daugherty and Pringle: 35-40.

Pawlowski, Merry M., ed., *Virginia Woolf and Fascism: Resisting the Dictators' Seduction*. New York: Palgrave, 2001.

Pearce, Richard. "Who Comes First, Joyce or Woolf?" Neverow-Turk and Hussey: 59-67.

Pettigrew, Nita (with Julia Gray and Rebecca Weisser). "First Encounters: Student Responses to Woolf." McVicker and Davis: 276-82.

Phillips, Kathy. *Virginia Woolf Against Empire*. Knoxville: U of Tennessee P, 1994.

——."Woolf's Criticism of the British Empire in *The Years*." Hussey and Neverow-Turk: 30-31.

Pinkerton, Mary. "Reading Personally: Narrative Theory and *To the Lighthouse*." Daugherty and Pringle: 60-5.

Pratt, Annis. "Lupine Pedagogies: Teaching Woolf to Terrified Undergraduates." Hussey and Neverow-Turk: 90-97.

Putzel, Steven. "Virginia Woolf and British 'Orientalism.'" Berman and Goldman: 105-13.

Quinn, Laurie. "A Woolf with Political Teeth: Classing Virginia Woolf Now and in the Twenty-First Century." Ardis and Scott: 325-30.

Radin, Grace. *Virginia Woolf's* The Years: *The Evolution of a Novel*. Knoxville: U of Tennessee P, 1981.

Ramsay, Stephen J. "'On Not Knowing Greek:' Virginia Woolf and the New Ancient Greece." Ardis and Scott: 6-11.

Rasporich, Beverly. *Dance of the Sexes: Art and Gender in the Fiction of Alice Munro*. Edmonton, Alberta: U of Alberta P, 1990.

Ratcliffe, Krista. "Educating Bathsheba: Reading Woolf to Construct a Feminist Reading/Writing Pedagogy." Third Annual Conference on Virginia Woolf. Jefferson City, MO. 10 June 1993.

Richter, Harvena. *Virginia Woolf: The Inward Voyage*. Princeton: Princeton UP, 1970.

Riley, Denise. *"Am I That Name?" Feminism and the Category of "Women" in History.* Minneapolis: U of Minnesota P, 1989.

Risolo, Donna. "Outing Mrs. Ramsay: Reading the Lesbian Subtext in Virginia Woolf's *To the Lighthouse.*" Neverow-Turk and Hussey: 238-48.

Roof, Judith. "Hocus Crocus." Ardis and Scott: 93-102.

Rosenbaum, S. P., ed. *The Bloomsbury Group: A Collection of Memoirs, Commentary and Criticism.* Toronto: U of Toronto P, 1975.

Rosenberg, Beth Carole and Jeanne Dubino, eds., *Virginia Woolf and the Essay.* New York: St. Martin's P, 1997.

Rosenfeld, Natania. *Outsiders Together: Virginia and Leonard Woolf.* Princeton: Princeton UP, 2000.

Ruddick, Sara. *Maternal Thinking: Towards a Politics of Peace.* New York: Ballantine, 1989.

——. "Private Brother, Public World." Jane Marcus, *New*: 185-215.

Sandbach-Dahlström, Catherine. "Virginia Woolf With and Without State Feminism." *South Carolina Review* 29.1 (Fall 1996): 78-89.

Schlack, Beverly Ann. *Continuing Presences: Virginia Woolf's Use of Literary Allusion.* University Park: Penn State UP, 1979.

Scott, Bonnie Kime, ed. *New Alliances in Joyce Studies.* Newark: U of Delaware P, 1988.

——, ed. *The Gender of Modernism.* Bloomington: Indiana UP, 1990.

Scott, Joan Wallach, ed. *Feminism and History.* New York: Oxford UP, 1996.

Shattuck, Sandra D. "The Stage of Scholarship: Crossing the Bridge from Harrison to Woolf." Jane Marcus, *Centenary* 278-298.

Shaw, Marion. "*A Room of One's Own* to A Literature of Their Own." *South Carolina Review* 29.1 (Fall 1996): 58-66.

Shay, Nancy S. "'I'm Not a Feminist or Anything, But . . .': Teaching *A Room of One's Own* in High School." Berman and Goldman: 180-5.

Silver, Brenda. *Virginia Woolf Icon.* Chicago: U of Chicago P, 1999.

——, ed. *Virginia Woolf's Reading Notebooks.* Princeton: Princeton UP, 1983.

Smith, Patricia Juliana. *Lesbian Panic: The Homoerotics of Narrative in Modern British Women's Fiction.* New York: Columbia UP, 1997.

Snaith, Anna. *Virginia Woolf: Public and Private Negotiations.* New York: Palgrave, 2000.

Spalding, Frances. *Vanessa Bell.* New Haven: Ticknor and Fields, 1983.

Spotts, Frederick, ed., *Letters of Leonard Woolf.* San Diego: Harcourt, Brace, Jovanovich, 1989.

Stansky, Peter and William Abrahams. *Journey to the Frontier: Two Roads to the Spanish Civil War.* Boston: Little, Brown, & Co., 1966.

Swanson, Diana. "With Clear-Eyed Scrutiny: Gender, Authority, and the Narrator as Sister in *Jacob's Room.*" Berman and Goldman: 46-51.

Thompson, Theresa M. "Confronting Modernist Racism in the Post-Colonial Classroom: Teaching Virginia Woolf's *The Voyage Out* and Leonard Woolf's *The Village in the Jungle*." Barrett and Cramer, *Re: Reading*: 241-50.

Transue, Pamela J. *Virginia Woolf and the Politics of Style*. Albany: SUNY, 1986.

Tratner, Michael. *Modernism and Mass Politics: Joyce, Woolf, Eliot, Yeats*. Stanford: Stanford UP, 1995.

Trombley, Stephen. *All That Summer She was Mad: Virginia Woolf, Female Victim of Male Medicine*. New York: Continuum, 1982.

Villeneuve, Pierre-Eric. "Virginia Woolf and the French Reader: An Overview." *South Carolina Review* 29.1 (Fall 1996): 109-21.

Waugh, Patricia. *Practicing Postmodernism, Reading Modernism*. London: Edward Arnold, 1992.

Wicke, Jennifer. "Frock Consciousness: Virginia Woolf's Dialectical Materialism." Berman and Goldman: 221-9.

Williams, Lisa. "Teaching 'The Legacy' in a Freshman Writing Course." Barrett and Cramer, *Re: Reading*: 12-15.

——. *The Artist as Outsider in the Novels of Toni Morrison and Virginia Woolf*. Westport, CT: Greenwood P, 2000.

Wilson, Duncan, assisted by J. Eisenberg. *Leonard Woolf: A Political Biography*. London: Hogarth Press, 1978.

Wolfe, Susan and Julia Penelope. *Sexual Practice, Textual Theory: Lesbian Cultural Criticism*. Cambridge: Blackwell, 1993.

Wollaeger, Mark. "Woolf, Picture Postcards, Memory." Berman and Goldman: 213-21.

Woolf, Leonard, ed., *Diaries in Ceylon, 1908-1911: Records of a Colonial Administrator [. . .] and Stories from the East by Leonard Woolf*. London: Hogarth Press, 1963.

——. *Downhill All The Way: An Autobiography of the Years 1919-1939*. London: Hogarth Press, 1970.

——. *Growing: An Autobiography of the Years 1904 to 1911*. London: Hogarth Press, 1970.

Woolf, Virginia. *A Room of One's Own*. New York: Harcourt, Brace & World, 1957.

——. *The Diaries of Virginia Woolf*. 5 Volumes. Ed. Anne Olivier Bell, (Vols. 2-5 assisted by Andrew McNeillie). New York: Harcourt Brace Jovanovich, 1977-84.

——. *The Letters of Virginia Woolf*. Ed. Nigel Nicolson and Joanne Trautmann. 6 vols. New York: Harcourt Brace Jovanovich, 1975-80.

——. *Three Guineas*. New York: Harcourt, Brace & World, 1963.

Wussow, Helen. *The Nightmare of History: The Fictions of Virginia Woolf and D. H. Lawrence*. Bethlehem, PA.: Lehigh UP, 1998.

Exposing Masculine Spectacle: Virginia Woolf's Newspaper Clippings for *Three Guineas* as Contemporary Cultural History

Merry Pawlowski

Virginia Woolf discovered, as she accumulated the underlying documentary and historical research for *Three Guineas,* a compelling insight into the gendering of her contemporary culture: that the tables could be turned on "Man," lord of the public domain and its spectacle, by allowing women, from within the walls of their private sphere, to gaze upon a masculine, imperialist, and fascist iconography inherently linked to war. In three scrapbooks of newspaper clippings and

It is the figure of a man; some say, others deny, that he is Man himself, the quintessence of virility—Virginia Woolf, *Three Guineas* [1]

[1]The man in the photograph is identified by the subtitle "Count Ciano in flying kit." Woolf clipped only this photograph and left no identifying remarks, including it on page 20 of her scrapbooks, *Monks House Papers* B16.f, Vol. 2. The photo is found on a page with two other newspaper clippings, both reporting on Hitler and the Nazis and dated by Woolf 12th August, 1935. In fact, Count Galeazzo Ciano was Mussolini's son-in-law, marrying his 19-year-old daughter, Edda, in 1930. Ciano, the son of an admiral, became a journalist and diplomat as well as an airman, serving as a bomber pilot in the Abyssinian war. Politically, he was connected with Mussolini's offices for propaganda and became Foreign Minister in 1936. In this capacity, he negotiated the Axis agreements with Germany and favored Italian expansion into the Balkans. After Italian defeats in North Africa, he was dismissed from the Foreign Ministry and sent to the Vatican as ambassador. In July, 1943, he voted for the overthrow of Mussolini and left Italy for Germany, where he was blamed by Hitler for Mussolini's downfall and sent back to Verona to face execution on January 11, 1944. His image serves, in my view, as an emblem of Woolf's "Man himself, the quintessence of virility."

other printed materials (*Monks House Papers* B 16.f, Vols. 1, 2, and 3) collected from 1927–1937 for documentation to write *Three Guineas,* Woolf's discovery is evidenced through the selection and combination of cuttings included.[2] In addition, Woolf would make a striking departure in this research activity from her previous practices in writing the literary essay. Here, Woolf was concerned with a critique of contemporary culture expanded to embrace all segments of a society preparing for war, a society already deeply flawed, in her view, by nature of its segregation of genders; and the history of her scrapbooks reveals the search for an altered methodology to accomplish this larger aim.

Little within the pages of the scrapbooks, Woolf's own alternative cultural history, is taken from "standard" versions of contemporary or past history; Woolf took notes only once, for example, in the 3-volume scrapbooks from Macaulay's *History of England.*[3] The contemporary news account rather than literary or historical sources evolved in these pages as a major current of investigation, where Woolf would use mainstream, conservative newspapers, *The Times* and *The Daily Telegraph,* for example, against themselves by frequently selecting letters to the editor, back page and offbeat articles to collect rather than "front page" news. Woolf, while amply provided with the discourse of patriarchal ideology in the major papers, could find means to resist these standard versions of contemporary history, by constructing contextual messages in the contiguous placement of articles and by clipping tiny articles that most other readers might have missed to demonstrate a point. To enhance her points, she focused on the visual image, the news photograph collected alone or as part of accompanying text, as an icon of the spectacle of masculine social organization of the public sphere, a sphere in which women were largely absent.

Three Guineas was conceptualized very early by Woolf as the "child" of *A Room of One's Own* (1929), her trenchant investigation into literary and cultural history in search of the footprints of women. We know this from her diaries,[4] and, indeed, she clipped two reviews of *A Room* and placed them early in the first volume of her scrapbooks, suggesting equally strong evidence of her desire to

---

[2]For an online publication of these important manuscripts in the University of Sussex collection, please see the website I have developed with Vara Neverow: <http://www.csub.edu/woolf_center>.

[3]See *Monks House Papers* B16.f, Vol 2, p. 54.

[4]On Tuesday, January 20, 1931, Woolf wrote in her diary that she had "conceived an entire new book—a sequel to *A Room of One's Own...*" This moment is identified by Olivier Bell, editor of the diaries, as the moment of conception of *Three Guineas* and *The Years*, first drafted together and then split into two separate works. *The Diary of Virginia Woolf, Volume IV. 1931–1935* (Penguin Books, 1987) p. 6.

extend the arguments of the earlier book.[5] But the work of *Three Guineas* would expand the parameters of literary history explored in *A Room* to a searing analysis of the culture at large during the 30s. Evidence of this observation exists in the choices Woolf made for the scrapbooks; notes and cuttings on technically literary subjects are the greatest in number in Volume 1—a total of eleven—but they decrease to three in Volume 2 and to two in Volume 3. In sharp contrast to these numbers are the numbers of clippings on broadly cultural matters concerning gender which grow from twenty-five in Volume 1 to forty-eight in Volume 2 and fifty-four in Volume 3, more than double the amount in the first volume. Although the status of women is clearly a major track of the "charming" argument of *A Room of One's Own*, Woolf's groundbreaking insights about the masculine ego grow as her discoveries grow through the progress of the scrapbook volumes, coupled with her ongoing concern about the gendered segregation of social space.

While the scrapbooks contain a variety of materials—116 news articles, reading notes from eighty-five books, letters of solicitation, clippings of journal and magazine articles, manifestoes, and a pamphlet eyewitness account of the fall of Madrid—the newspaper and journal clippings form the major avenue of exploration for my argument. The clippings suggest not only Woolf's passion for the history of the present moment captured in the immediacy of newsprint but also her conscious formation of the fragments of news into cultural history. There are, however, so many clippings in the three-volume scrapbooks that I have chosen for discussion those which provide, in my view, greatest evidence of Woolf's processes as a feminist cultural historian as well as those which are the strongest links to *Three Guineas*. What will spring full-blown into the pages of *Three Guineas* exists in embryonic theoretical clusters in its scrapbooks: the gendering of social and cultural space; the construction of masculine, public space as a visual spectacle; and the deconstruction of the power of the masculine gaze objectifying Woman as icon.

Feminist scholars have recently made extensive investigations into the division of the social world in the West into public and private spheres, linking it with industrialization in the 19th century.[6] Woolf's awareness of the masculinization of the public sector, both economic and cultural, predates these by at least

[5]See *Monks House Papers* B16.f, Vol. 1, pp 16 and 26.

[6]See as examples: Judith Newton, *Women, Power, and Subversion: Social Strategies in British Fiction 1778–1860* (Athen: U of Georgia P, 1981); Catherine Belsey and Jane Moore, eds., *The Feminist Reader: Essays in Gender and the Politics of Literary Criticism* (New York: Basil Blackwell, 1989); Jean Bethke Elshstain, *Public Man, Private Woman: Women in Social and Political Thought* (Brighton, UK: Harvester, 1982); and Elizabeth Janeway, *Man's World, Woman's Place: A Study in Social Mythology* (New York: Dell, 1971).

forty years and is evident in *Three Guineas* through her continual invocation of "man" as master of a public world upon which women, locked within the private house, can only gaze:

> Let us then by way of a very elementary beginning lay before you a photograph—a crudely colored photograph—of your world as it appears to us who see it from the threshold of the private house; through the veil that St. Paul still lays upon our eyes; from the bridge which connects the private house with the world of public life (*TG* 18).

Woolf substantiates these insights about the separation of public, masculine space from private, feminine space in numerous articles clipped and pasted in the scrapbooks.

But, while consciously clipping articles which take up the issue of women's place (or lack thereof) in public space, Woolf was encountering evidence of masculine society as "spectacle," suggesting what Guy Debord's *The Society of the Spectacle* would later explore. Debord does not gender the spectacle as does Woolf, but his pronouncements on the spectacle replicate in large part what Woolf observes and tracks in her scrapbooks. Debord's first thesis characterizes Woolf's earlier assumptions about British empire and spectacle:

> The whole life of those societies in which modern conditions of production prevail presents itself as an immense accumulation of *spectacles*. All that once was directly lived has become mere representation.[7]

Debord goes further as he describes a situation which Woolf predicts in her use of the photograph as icon in *Three Guineas*:

> Understood on its own terms, the spectacle proclaims the predominance of appearances and asserts that all human life, which is to say all social life, is mere appearance. But any critique capable of apprehending the spectacle's essential character must expose it as a visible negation of life—and as a negation of life that has *invented a visual form for itself* (Thesis 10).

For Woolf, too, the spectacle negates; specifically, the masculine spectacle of empire to which she is witness has a direct link to war: "Obviously the connection between dress and war is not far to seek; your finest clothes are those you wear as soldiers" (*TG* 39).

As she gathered proof of masculine spectacle and its dominance of the public, social sector, Woolf was utilizing the photograph as an icon, referring

---

[7]Thesis 1. This and other citations will be listed by the thesis number found in the online version of Debord's work. *The Society of the Spectacle* is readily available as e-text at a number of websites, but the one I used is the online version of the 1994 Zone Books edition translated by Donald Nicholson-Smith: <hhtp://www.situationist.cjb.net/>

repeatedly in *Three Guineas* to photographs both visible and invisible to deconstruct the power of the masculine gaze.[8] Laura Mulvey's work in feminist film
criticism and classic Hollywood cinema offers an important conclusion about
man as the bearer of the look and woman as image or object to be gazed upon.
The masculine gaze, Mulvey argues, controls the image of woman as "spectacle," for the bearer of the look has power over the object looked upon and
cannot be sexually objectified. [9] Woolf anticipates Mulvey while accomplishing
a stunning reversal of the gender of gazer and gazed upon. Woolf suggests
instead that women have the power to look upon the spectacle of "Man" as icon
in *Three Guineas*, a spectacle which offers, however, no scopophilic pleasure to
the woman gazer:

> It is the figure of a man . . . His eyes are glazed; his eyes glare. His body, which
> is braced in an unnatural position, is tightly cased in a uniform. Upon the breast
> of that uniform are sewn several medals and other mystic symbols. His hand is
> upon a sword. He is called in German and Italian *Fuhrer* or *Duce*; in our own
> language Tyrant or Dictator. And behind him lie ruined houses and dead bod-
> ies—men, women and children (*TG* 142).

The scrapbooks for *Three Guineas* serve as the forge in which Woolf makes these
two important discoveries: that the power of a dominant society has gendered
public space as masculine domain and private space as the only "natural" abode
for women, while women within that private space can refuse to be "gazed

---

[8]In "Demythologizing Facts and Photographs in *Three Guineas*" by Julia Duffy and
Lloyd Davis (ed. Marsha Bryant, *Photo-Textualities: Reading Photographs and
Literature*, Newark, DE: U of Delaware P, 1996, 129-140), the authors assert in footnote
10 that certain news clippings which they saw referenced in Brenda Silver's *Virginia
Woolf's Reading Notebooks* were linked to the photographs in the first editions of *Three
Guineas*. However, they never make clear how they are linked nor do they provide information about the contents of the clippings beyond their titles. Such a claim indicates to
me that the authors, while familiar with Silver's wonderful guide, are not familiar with the
scrapbooks themselves, Monks House Papers B16f. Additionally, Maggie Humm, in a
very fine article "Memory, Photography, and Modernism: The 'dead bodies and ruined
houses' of Virginia Woolf's *Three Guineas*," *Signs* 28.2 (2002): 645-663, claims that "the
published photographs [in *Three Guineas*] are copies of some of the newspaper photographs that Woolf collected together with press cuttings, quotations, and letters in three
scrapbooks [Monks House Papers B16f] dating from the early 1930s" (648); but that is
just not so. Nowhere in these scrapbooks does one find the photographs from the first editions of *Three Guineas*. The photographs are found in the Hogarth Press archives for
Three Guineas with brief additional information about their subjects but no information
about their source.

[9]"Visual Pleasure and Narrative Cinema," in *Feminisms,* eds. Robyn R. Warhol and
Diane Price Herndl (New Brunswick, New Jersey: Rutgers UP, 1991) 438–48.

upon," acting rather as "voyeurs" themselves upon a scene of masculine spectacle directly linked to war.

In Volume I of her *Reading Notes* scrapbooks, Woolf's attention rests primarily on her investigation of the presence of women in public space, and she chooses articles which examine variations of this major theme. I will begin by discussing five clippings which, predictably, track masculine resistance to the presence of women in the public sector. "Whitehall Storm Over a Woman," from the *Evening Standard*, April 8, 1932, records a mounting protest to the appointment of a woman, K. M. Walls, to the management of the Shoreditch Labour Exchange. R. D. Cook, secretary to the Ministry of Labour Staff Association, told the *Evening Standard*, "We believe that she [Miss Walls] is fully competent, but we do not think it desirable that a woman should be appointed to the charge of a Labour Exchange which deals with a bigger percentage of men than women" (I: 15; LVIII, B.22).[10] On the same page with this clipping Woolf pasted another in a related vein, "Woman Appointed Librarian: Eleven Committee Members Resign." Claiming that, despite the full qualification and experience of a woman appointed as branch librarian, "they wished a male librarian to occupy the office," eleven members of the Wolverhampton Art Gallery and Public Library Committee resigned in protest. A few pages away, a third article, "Coveted Post Won by Woman" (May 16, 1932), purports that women are "making good" after having been admitted to higher appointments in the Civil Service only within the last few years (I: 19; LVIII, B.28). The "women making good," though, is really only one woman, N. F. E. Cracknell, the first woman "appointed to assist in dealing with economic subjects," promoted to private secretary to the chief economic adviser to the government, a sure stepping-stone to high appointment. One can't help but wonder if Ms. Cracknell ever received that higher appointment.

However, an undated article "Civil Service Women: Preferences and Dislikes" (I: 57; LVIII, B.63) insists that women in government services, nearly 80,000 of them, prefer male superiors. The author, T. J. Curtin, neglects to give details of how statistics were obtained to substantiate this apparent evidence of female preference for male domination in "every branch of the Civil Service where women are employed." Men, he suggests, do not return the favor; "the male official would consider it humiliating to give obedience to a woman and take his orders from her."

It's preferable, according to this logic, that if women must work, they drudge in factories or offices, operating machines, where the machines can appreciate

---

[10]All quotations from the clippings scrapbooks will be cited by indicating the volume and item number in the scrapbooks as well as the volume and item number assigned to it in Brenda Silver's invaluable guide *Virginia Woolf's Reading Notebooks* (Princeton: Princeton UP, 1983).

them. In "'Machines Prefer Girls': More Accurate Than Men," Sir Herbert Austin reports that "In the new accountancy women have a capacity for concentration which makes them far more accurate than men" (I: 18; LVIII, B.26). The machines "prefer girls," Sir Austin continues, "I do not know whether they prefer blondes, but, at any rate, they are worked better by girls." The girls, Sir Austin finds, are more attentive to their work when it is of "a monotonous character;" but women are prevented under the Factory Acts, he laments, from working the night shift. In sum, Woolf has collected a set of clippings here which cannot fail to acknowledge women's competence in the workforce while mounting evidence of the extreme difficulty, despite their qualifications, that women face in countering sexism in public space.

As a contrast to the issue of women in public space, Woolf is concerned as well to track the attitudes in her contemporary society toward women in private space. "Fifty Years: Society and the Season, The Chaperoned Age" (*The Times,* March 9, 1932, p. 13), by Mary, Countess of Lovelace, is an example of this concern. In it, Lovelace reminisces about a society fifty years before when upper-class women without chaperones were denied access to public space (I: 29; LVIII, B.36). As Lovelace remembers the past, she acknowledges the protection of chaperonage but laments, "Our social restrictions were often irksome." Woolf uses Lovelace's own words as an occasion to attack the jailing of women in the private house, lifting a phrase about the shortage of unattached males as "the price we pay for our splendid Empire, and the price is paid mainly by the women," to write in *Three Guineas*: "Thus consciously she desired 'our splendid Empire'; unconsciously she desired our splendid war" (39). While echoing the phrase, Woolf completely reverses Lovelace's lament about the shortage of husbands to insist upon the way in which the gendering of public and private space in Victorian society has encouraged women's complicity with war.[11]

Once we open Volume II of the scrapbooks, we find that Woolf takes up once more the issue of women in public space. Many of the articles Woolf collected

[11]In "A Preliminary Bibliographic Guide to the Footnotes of *Three Guineas*," *Woolf Studies Annual* 3 (1997): 175, Vara Neverow and I indicate where two different segments of Countess Lovelace's article are cited by Woolf. See *Three Guineas,* footnotes 1 and 33 of Chapter One. It appears from Woolf's page number citations, though, that she is referring to a book edition of this and other articles in a series published by *The Times* entitled *Fifty Years: Memories and Contrasts* (1932). A reprint of Countess Lovelace's article is found on pages 24–31. The quotation Woolf cites in footnote 1, p. 264 of *Three Guineas* (London: Hogarth P, 1938, 1st edition) is found on page 27 of the article and not page 37 as Woolf indicates. The second time Woolf cites Countess Lovelace, in footnote 33, page 283 of *Three Guineas,* she gives the correct page number, 29.

in this volume form the data and evidence for *Three Guineas*. Interestingly, a significant number of the clippings found here are letters to the editor, most frequently penned by men reacting against women's apparent freedom, status, or presence in the workforce; hence, Woolf appears to be taking the pulse of a masculine backlash. The earliest dated letter to appear, "one from a great number to the same effect provided by the daily papers" (*TG* 73) is "Woman's Handicap," dated February 13, 1935, by Woolf. Signed by Cyril Chaventre, the letter complains that women face an invisible barrier against them in the public world because they are "essentially dependent, not creative" (II: 14; LIX, B.19). Woolf uses his piece in *Three Guineas* as emblematic of many such letters to the editor, quoting Chaventre:

> "A woman's sense of values," he writes, "is indisputably different from that of a man. Obviously therefore a woman is at a disadvantage and under suspicion when in competition in a man-created sphere of activity. More than ever today women have the opportunity to build a new and better world, but in this slavish imitation of men they are wasting their chance" (*TG* 73).

Chaventre neglects to explain how, if women are essentially dependent, they are to stop their slavish imitation of men; but his message remains all too clear—women don't belong in public space.

A second letter to the editor from another man, Wm. H. Collin, appears several pages earlier but is dated almost a year later. Entitled "Should Women Work?" and annotated January 20, 1936, *The Daily Telegraph*, the clipping is quoted almost in its entirety in *Three Guineas* (II: 6; LIX, B.8). Choosing this piece as an example of the repugnant odor attached to "Miss" in Whitehall, i.e., the undesirability of women in the public sphere, Woolf quotes:

> "I think your correspondent . . correctly sums up this discussion in the observation that woman has too much liberty. It is probable that this so-called liberty came with the war, when women assumed responsibilities so far unknown to them. They did splendid service during those days. Unfortunately, they were praised and petted out of all proportion to the value of their performances" (*TG* 51).

A third letter to the editor, this one entitled "Women and Clerical Unemployment," adds to Woolf's growing portrait of misogyny (II: 15; LIX, B.20). This unsigned piece expresses very overtly its author's attitude toward women working. Women, the author argues, should leave clerical service and enter domestic service, for which there is great demand and, of course, for which they are better suited: "'I am of the opinion that a considerable amount of the distress which is prevalent in this section of the community (the clerical) could be relieved by the policy of employing men instead of women, wherever possible'" (quoted in *Three Guineas* 51). The clincher, though, is a letter in *The Daily Telegraph*, January 22, 1936:[12]

> "I am certain I voice the opinion of thousands of young men when I say that if men were doing the work that thousands of young women are now doing the men would be able to keep those same women in decent homes. Homes are the real places of the women who are now compelling men to be idle. It is time the Government insisted upon employers giving work to more men, thus enabling them to marry the women they cannot now approach" (II: 5, *TG* 51).[13]

Woolf uses this capstone quote in *Three Guineas* to underscore misogyny and adds: "There! There can be no doubt of the odour now. The cat is out of the bag; and it is a Tom" (*TG* 52). Indeed, "Tom" is Woolf's icon of male ego—the perpetrator of the spectacle which keeps women enslaved in private space while men bask in the glory of public recognition.

How much difference is there, Woolf seems to ask, between the opinions of these authors of letters to the editor and those more easily recognizable fascist views of Hitler. "Praise for Women: Their Part in the Nazi Triumph," a clipping from the September 13, 1936, issue of the *Sunday Times* (II: 22; LIX, B.31), records a speech by Hitler to Nazi women instructing them about their proper place in the Nazi "nation of men." "'So long as we have a strong male sex in Germany—and we Nazis will see to it that we have,' Hitler told the women, 'we will have no female hand-grenade-throwing squads in our country.'" Hitler's famous quote regarding women's sphere, one Woolf herself cites in *Three Guineas* (53), emerges in this report: "'There are two worlds in the life of the nation, the world of men and the world of women. Nature has done well to entrust the man with the care of his family and the nation. The woman's world is, if she is happy in her family, her husband, her children, and her home.'" Hitler's closing comments were sure to inflame Woolf's sense of the complexity of women's complicity in their own oppression: "'While our enemies assert that women are tyrannically oppressed in Germany, I may reveal that without the devoted and steady collaboration of German women the Nazi movement would never have triumphed.'"

---

[12]See *Three Guineas,* fn13, 161, for Woolf's identification of newspaper source and date.

[13]This letter to the editor signed "Out of Work," only appears in part at the bottom of Woolf's clipping. In it, the writer states that "thousands of young women are now doing" the work that thousands of young men should be doing to support them. Woolf cites the entire clipping in *Three Guineas*, p. 51; yet, interestingly, she didn't include the entire clipping on her scrapbook page, cutting it off at the fifth of 12 lines.

Five pages before the report of Hitler's speech to Nazi women, Woolf pasted in "Women of To-Day and To-Morrow" by C. E. M. Joad, that appeared in the January 12, 1934, issue of *Everyman* (II: 17; LIX, B.22). Aligning himself with fascist ideology, Joad keynotes his article with three citations from Nazis on women—Goebbels on women's task of bearing children, Goering on women's place in the home, and Hitler on women's duty to children, church, and kitchen—and is highly complimentary of the Nazi movement, commending it as the "most modern in the contemporary world." Joad insists that higher education for women "is from the utilitarian point of view a monster of false promise, giving women tastes and equipping them with capacities which there is no reasonable prospect that the world will permit them to use." Joad is careful not to make a claim about women's innate inferiority but rather about the world's unwillingness to allow women to advance. In the face of such overwhelming obstacles, Joad concludes with his Nazi counterparts, "It may be better to be boss of one's own home, however small, than to be everybody's drudge in office or factory, better to look after a man's comforts than to look after his correspondence, better to attend to children than to a card-index." As a fitting accompaniment to the message, the article bears in its center a photograph of an aproned woman looking into and stirring her pot.

By far, the greatest number of articles (approximately 26) in Volume 3 of the scrapbooks continues this conflicted theme of women in the public and private sectors. The fourth entry in the volume, "Women Divided on 'More Babies' Campaign" (Friday, March 5th, 1937), suggests the presence of a current of women's resistance to providing "cannon fodder" for the next war (III: 4; LX, B.10). The article reports the disagreement among women delegates at the National Council for Equal Citizenship over a resolution to check the declining population. Helena Normanton, a woman barrister, argued rigorously that the resolution was in line with what Hitler and Mussolini wanted. Normanton insisted that: "'The only thing that women in any country can do to prevent war is to stop the supply of cannon fodder.'" Despite this and other objections, the resolution carried.

Woolf takes up the issue in a footnote to *Three Guineas* writing, "And one method by which she (the educated woman) can help to prevent war is to refuse to bear children" (*TG* 147). Woolf quotes Normanton and adds reference to another, allied clipping from *The Daily Telegraph* (September 6, 1937), a letter to the editor from Edith Maturin-Porch, who writes, "I can tell Mr. Harry Campbell why women refuse to bear children in these times. When men have learnt how to run the lands they govern so that wars shall hit only those who make the quarrels, instead of mowing down those who do not, then women may again feel like having larger families. Why should women bring children into such a world as this one is to-day?" (III: 17; LX, B.30).

A large segment of clippings in Volume III counter the masculine attacks on women in public space that Woolf found in the daily newspapers. She found and included articles which report on the complications, successes, and failures of women in an array of professions and jobs: veterinarians, M.P.s, doctors, women clergy. The first set of clippings addresses the issue of women's education and preparation for the professions as well as their acceptance into them. "Poor Prospects for Women 'Vets'," annotated by Woolf October 1st, 1937, from *The Daily Telegraph*, reports that the numbers of women interested in becoming veterinarians had increased so that space in the colleges had to be limited since prospects for employment were not good; women were not wanted on the farms working on large animals (III: 22; LX, B.35). Woolf cites this article in a footnote to *Three Guineas* (184) as support for her argument about women's limited access to education and the professions and includes in the same footnote reference to another clipping, "Girl Medi[ ]: Demand for More Schools," *Evening News*, March, 1937 (III: 44; LX, B.60).[14] Women doctors and medical students, the article claims, are demanding better training facilities and are challenging "why almost all the medical schools attached to great London hospitals are barred to them, in spite of the fact that opportunities for women in the medical profession have increased steadily and there is a big demand for their services to-day." Woolf included another article on this theme, "Middlesex Hospital

[14]Woolf has torn or cut this article to include the full column but not the entire banner headline which extends beyond the column.

School," annotated *The Times*, August 17, 1935, a book review of the history of the school indicating that since the exclusion of women acting as midwives at the hospital, the school has maintained a policy of women's exclusion, to the point of declining the offer of a scholarship for women students from a woman doctor, Garrett Anderson (III: 13; LX, B.24).

Women medical students were not the only ones experiencing difficulty of access to a quality education. "Three Church Colleges to Close: Women Teachers' Training," (III: 12; LX, B.23) an undated, unidentified article, suggests that prospective women teachers will find it harder to get an education as well; three of their training colleges must close due to financial difficulties. Men's colleges are experiencing no such hardships, though, as Woolf notes in the following observation from *Three Guineas*:

> As for poverty, *The Times* newspaper supplies us with figures; any ironmonger will provide us with a foot-rule; if we measure the money available for scholarships at the men's colleges with the money available for their sisters at the women's colleges, we shall save ourselves the trouble of adding up; and come to the conclusion that the colleges for the sisters of educated men are, compared with their brother's colleges, unbelievably and shamefully poor (30).

In her footnote to this passage, Woolf adds "The men's scholarship list at Cambridge printed in *The Times* of December 20, 1937, measures roughly thirty-one inches; the women's scholarship list at Cambridge measures roughly five inches" (*TG* 154). In her clippings scrapbook, Woolf has placed the short, single-column announcement of women's scholarships next to the multi-columned men's announcements as graphic demonstration to herself and some future reader of her point (III: 64-65; LX, B.86).

Granted that women's access to higher, quality education was severely limited in the late 1930s, how do women fare in the professions and the working world at large? "Motor Learner Drivers: Men and Women Testers" makes quite clear from a Parliamentary debate that men are unwilling to be tested on their driving by women (III: 8; LX, B.16). Nor did women M.P.s find themselves well accepted in the House of Commons. In "Women M.P.s have missed their chance," *Evening Standard* (March 20, 1936), Robert Bernays complains that women have made no impact on steering the course of government toward peace. Indeed, he blames the very fact that there are only eight women among 600 men on women who have failed to vote more women into Parliament (III: 27; LX, B.42). Woolf counters this misogyny with "Call for More Women M.P.s," The *Daily Telegraph* (October 23, 1937), in which women at a conference of the Women's Freedom League present the facts of massive masculine resistance to women entering politics or the professions at every level (III: 43; LX, B.58). What Mr. Bernays has obviously ignored is carefully pointed out by women at the conference; legislators, the women claim, "seem incapable of visualising the vast mass of business and professional women who have nothing to do either with babies or machines." Further, the women feel that many men consider it an offense for women to have well-paid jobs, and women legislators are needed who will dispel the misconception that women should work only for "pin money." While women may be the majority voters, men still control who gets nominated; as A. Munro argues, "most of the chairmen and officials of our political parties are men, and when there is a safe seat there are a great many men who want to get into the House and Commons and who are prepared to see that they do." Helena Normanton, the barrister against women producing babies for cannon fodder, aptly points out in this article that, given the atmosphere of corruption in Parliamentary elections, it's difficult for men and women of moderate means to get elected. Woolf knew that lack of money eliminated most women from running for office.

Woolf includes an acknowledgment of working class wives by citing "Cleaning 5 Miles of Floor: The Average Wife's Annual Work," in a footnote to *Three Guineas.* She intends to support a budding argument about class differences and women's place in that debate; and also, I believe, makes, for her time, a daring, implicit suggestion that wives are working women (III: 21; LX, B.34).[15] Arguably, the vast majority of women would be just those who in the space of a year, as the article reports, "Washed an acre of dirty dishes, a mile of glass and three miles of clothes: and scrubbed five miles of floor." And, for the unluckiest of women, all this in three million homes where there was no hot water system.

Two articles, placed one after another, offer women's voices in response to the culture's open, and apparently accepted, misogyny. In "Are Women So Hateful?" from *Everyman* (February 1, 1935), H. Pearl Adam examines the presence of a backlash against women's advances in public life as she reviews two particularly obnoxious examples, *Men Dislike Women* by Michael Arlen and *The Dominant Sex* by Michael Egan (III: 38; LX, B.55). Adam recalls the struggles of suffragism and the enormous contributions of women in World War I which almost automatically won them the vote. So Adam must question what has called this recent "ill-humour" into being, quoting as example from Egan who told an interviewer:

> . . . women have got no ethics and no morality, they would make of life, if they could, a sort of erotic holiday. I don't mean only in the physical sense, but emotionally. Women have no biological urge—though they create the children.

[15]Support for this view can be found in notes Woolf took from a talk by Linda P. Littlejohn on the BBC, October 7, 1937, and reported in the November 10, 1937 issue of *The Listener.* Littlejohn argued that the status of homemaker should be raised legally to that of a profession.

They have no direction. They are not interested in objectives. They have no general ambition, as apart from a personal ambition. And also there are none who resent being dominated by a man of real character.

What makes Egan an authority Adam does not offer, but she does question sadly, "Is it possible too that it needs a war to bring the sexes into real comradeship?"

"Votes for Women" by Flora Drummond in the August 25, 1937, issue of *The Listener* revisits the history of the suffragist movement from the memories of one of its founders (III: 39; LX, B.56). "To see a woman speaking on a street corner on a soap box," Drummond writes, "made her fair game for any sort of rough house, and to be told to 'Go home and darn socks' was the mildest form of abuse." Drummond recounts the arrest in 1905 of Christabel Pankhurst and Annie Kenney for simply asking Sir Edward Grey and Winston Churchill at a Liberal Party meeting what they would do to give women the vote. Drummond reminds her readers of the great acts of courage on the part of large numbers of women who were arrested and imprisoned for demanding equality and concludes: "Whether we won the vote by our agitation, as I believe, or whether we got it for other reasons, as some people say, I think many of the younger generation will find it hard to believe the fury and brutality aroused by our claim for votes for women less than thirty years ago." In line with Woolf's interest in the visual image, the article includes photos of women demonstrating for the vote and one suffragette chained to the fence of Buckingham Palace to demand the vote.

Citing the masculine proclivity for making war, Woolf adds a footnote to *Three Guineas* which includes this closing quote from Drummond's article and adds:

> The fight for the vote is still generally referred to in terms of sour depre-
> cation . . . The younger generation therefore can be excused if they believe that
> there was nothing heroic about a campaign in which only a few windows were
> smashed, shins broken, and Sargent's portrait of Henry James damaged, but not
> irreparably, with a knife. Burning, whipping, and picture-slashing it would seem
> become heroic when carried out on a large scale by men with machine-guns (*TG*
> 163).

Companion to this major theme of women's uneasy inhabitance in public and private space, Woolf worked to deconstruct a lengthy tradition of women's vanity and the aesthetic of Woman as icon by insisting upon masculine vanity, display, and love of public spectacle as a direct avenue to war. As an early example, one clipping left untitled and undated by Woolf in Volume I of her scrapbooks is identified only by a subtitle, "Sex Allurement." The article is significant for it contains the seed of an idea that Woolf would enlarge in *Three Guineas*—the deconstruction of Woman as visual icon. The article contains standard pronouncements of masculine ideology—the natural decree, for example, that men will lead in physical strength and intellectual achievement and women must compensate through self-decoration, i.e., an instinct for dress. "A reasonable indulgence in dress is needed to counterbalance what I may call the inferiority complex of women . . . In matters of dress women often remain children to the end" (I: 12; LVIII, B.19). The fragment contains clues that we are reading quoted speech, the findings of a judge, identified by Woolf in her index to the volume as MacCardie, who has presided over a case involving the extravagant expenditures of "Mrs. Frankau." MacCardie uses his bench to characterize all women as marked by "a constant and insuperable physical handicap." We know, of course, what that handicap is—the lack of a phallus. Woolf fills in even more details about the clipping in her footnote reference to it in *Three Guineas*. Quoting the "late Mr. Justice MacCardie," Woolf is fully aware of the irony of the situation where a judge, "wearing a scarlet robe, an ermine cape, and a vast wig of artificial curls . . . was able to lecture the lady without any consciousness of sharing her weakness" (*TG* 150). Despite the apparent early date of this clipping (possibly 1932–33), Woolf uses it to point to male vanity relatively late in the text of *Three Guineas,* suggesting that this may indeed have been a catalyst for Woolf's recognition of the connections among the iconography of Woman, the necessity of dress to cover so-called irrevocable inferiority, and the irony of unself-aware masculine display. Woolf cuts through the subterfuge of a masculine ideology which insists upon women's vanity for dress and appearance to expose that very same "flaw" at the core of male power. Once having made this extraordinary discovery, Woolf's search for articles in the next two volumes seems largely driven by the need to expose the spectacle of society to her female audience who, in Mulvey's terms, take on power as bearers of the gaze.

The articles chosen by Woolf for Volume II of the scrapbooks work toward the reversal from Woman as spectacle to Man as spectacle by beginning to develop Woolf's key insight into the spectacular nature of empire. Woolf appears increasingly taken with the notion of the visual image, specifically the photographic image, as the external and "real" sign of empire, fascism, public space, and all the trappings associated with these interrelated phenomena. Indeed, the second volume includes four clippings that are purely photographs and one article including two photographs.

First is a photograph of a German officer, captioned "Major Fey" with no further description or explanation (II: 5; LIX, B.6), which Woolf has annotated Oct. 18th, 1935, and indexed as "head dresses for men." Then, Woolf follows up on this theme by clipping three sets of news photos and pasting them on consecutive pages of her scrapbook. She begins this series with a photo of the Pope on his throne at St. Peter's on the occasion of his 79th birthday (II: 44; LIX, B.72). The pope, of course is decked out in full papal regalia against the backdrop of the twisted columns of Bernini's altar.

The second consists of four photos of women, consecutively arranged in horizontal fashion, in their fashions for the Ascot races—Woolf indicates in her index that there are "Different fashions for heralds and Ascot."

Accordingly, the next page of her scrapbook includes four consecutive photos of heralds, taken from the same issue of *The Daily Telegraph*, May 30, 1936, proclaiming the coronation of King Edward (II: 45, 46; LIX, B.73, 74). Certainly the women's dress seems tame, almost drab, compared to the elaborateness of

heraldic splendour. Extending her insights further, Woolf clipped a page from an article by Julian Huxley, "The Colours of Animals," in *The Listener* (June 10, 1936), which includes two photographs of male animals in full mating display— the mandrill and peacock (II: 21; LIX B.29). Woolf has indexed this article "Huxley and the Mandrill. The advertising sex," making her intention for including it overt.

The male mandrill advertises his fighting qualities by his coloring, and so too off rivals.—*J. Huxley*

The significance of these photos relates directly to Woolf's intentions in including five photos in the early editions of *Three Guineas*: those of the general, the heralds, the university procession, the judge, and the archbishop. Woolf has chronicled, with her photographs, five major patriarchal, institutional areas where not only has history been synonymous with the exclusion of women from public space but also a social order has been constructed as spectacle, mere representation: the army, empire and sovereignty, the university, the law court, and the church.

Additionally, the impetus toward this chronicling continues amply apparent in her scrapbook clippings; for not only does Woolf collect photographs, she collects and clips articles that point to the spectacle of masculine dress and pageantry as emblems of empire. One such article among several is a tiny clipping, one that anyone could easily have missed and part of a larger, now lost article, subtitled "Decorations Will Not Be Worn" (II: 25; LIX, B.34). Annotated by Woolf April 21st 1936, this fragment describes a new decoration in Germany for scientists and other distinguished civilians—a Silver Shield which is not to be worn but placed upon the writing desk. Woolf footnotes the article in *Three Guineas* (179, fn 19) and argues in the text that women must refuse pleasure in gazing at such spectacle: "With the example then, that they [men] give us of the power of medals, symbols, orders and even, it would seem, of decorated ink-pots [Woolf's comic description of the new Silver Shield award] to hypnotize the human mind it must be our [women's] aim not to submit ourselves to such hypnotism" (*TG* 114).

Masculine spectacle continues to be for Woolf a very suggestive theme in the third volume of the scrapbooks, but seems to serve here as backdrop to her foregrounded concern with women in public space. Typed notes Woolf copied from an untitled article in *The Times* (June 11, 1937), for example, indicate the writer's belief that the British Army's function is to withstand and prevent war, now a universal affliction, and that the tattoo in "masque and symbol" demonstrates "the ultimate nobilities of human valour defying the powers of darkness" (III: 1; LX, B.1). Woolf's argument in *Three Guineas* is just the opposite; she insists that such markings, emblems, and symbols are explicitly connected to war and the potential glory of conquest.

In "Mr. Baldwin's Last Speech as Prime Minister," Woolf read from *The Daily Telegraph* of May 25, 1937, that Baldwin made his last speech "[b]efore one of the most brilliant and distinguished gatherings of Empire representatives ever assembled" (III: 7; LX, B.14). So her attention would have been captured by the imaginary image of that spectacle, but she could not have failed to notice the last section, subtitled "Never Guided by Logic," where Baldwin claims, "One reason why our people are flourishing and alive is because we have never been guided by logic in anything we have done." Surely Woolf's funny bone must have been struck by such a ridiculous conclusion to a speech which upholds the splendor of the Commonwealth as "the greatest political experiment yet tried in the world—an experiment which may mean much to mankind, the failure of which may mean disaster."

Woolf was uninterested in the photo of Baldwin at No. 10 Downing Street which accompanied the article about his last speech, tearing through its middle; but another article, "The Lord Mayor's Show" from *The Times*, annotated November 10, 1937, may have interested Woolf most for its photograph. The photo depicts an aerial shot of the Lord Mayor's coach passing through Moorgate and certainly suggests a connection to Woolf's photo of the heralds and their regalia included in *Three Guineas*. The text of the article, too, supports the pageantry, what it calls the "tableaux" of empire to welcome in the new Lord Mayor of London with "all the pomp, humour, and honest commercial symbolism of the Lord Mayor's Show" (Ill: 61; LX, B.80).

The procession described seems to have included representatives from cavalry, infantry, and artillery, as well as exhibits of trade and produce and representatives from the dominions. The article clearly suggests a conclusion later argued by Debord about social spectacle:

> The growth of the dictatorship of modem economic production is both exten-
> sive and intensive in character. In the least industrialized regions its presence is
> already felt in the form of imperialist domination by those areas that lead the
> world in productivity (Thesis 42).

Indeed, a section of the article entitled "Empire Exhibits" reports that the African possessions provided the most impressive exhibits for the festivities and offers a view of British Empire that shocks us today with its callousness: "Southern Rhodesia provided a miniature field dotted symbolically with tobacco plants and worked by cheerful natives under a white overseer."

There is, however, a comic side to Woolf's perception of spectacle as "Postmen Want To Be Smarter," dated February 27, 1937, indicates in its report on the demands from the postal union for smarter cut uniforms (III: 4; LX, B.9). "New Uniforms for Army: Smarter 'Walking Out' Dress," though, reminds the reader of the darker side of masculine vanity and spectacle, the powerful con-nection to war: "The authorities," the article reports, "have come to the

conclusion that smartness in dress and bearing, which are bound up with tradition, influence greatly the potential recruit" (Ill: 47; LX. B.63).

War is the subject to which a number of the clippings in the third volume
attend, and we know from *Three Guineas* that the masculine spectacle Woolf
invites women to gaze upon is inextricably linked to militarism. "Smarter dress"
for soldiers is the theme of another portion of an article, untitled and dated March
17, 1937, which reports the state of the army's anti-aircraft and territorial divisions and the efforts being made to increase Britain's readiness for defense from
the Minister of Defense, Duff Cooper (III: 3; LX, B.8). The article moves from
the issue of "Ground Defence" to appealing to recruits for the regular army and
makes the unbelievable suggestion that dress would be an appropriate entice-
ment: "It has often been suggested that a more attractive uniform would prove a
strong inducement, and it has now been arranged that men on parade at the
Coronation shall wear the blue uniform which has hitherto been an option dress."

Woolf takes up the theme of Spain and its place in impending war a few
pages later by including in her scrapbook an article entitled "First Full Account
of Almeria Havoc," from *The Daily Telegraph,* June 5, 1937 (III: 9–10; LX.
B.17). The image of Spain loomed in Woolf's mind as her nephew Julian Bell
was scheduled to depart for Spain within two days to offer his services as an
ambulance driver to the Republican forces. The article describes the devastation
of the town of Almeria, on the Spanish coast, by a German squadron of warships
while, some distance away, a British destroyer watched. Thousands of people
were rendered homeless, and buildings suffered thousands of pounds sterling in
damage. The *Telegraph*'s correspondent, Henry Buckley, writes: "I have seen
Madrid and other Spanish towns bombed from the air again and again, but never
have I seen anything to equal this bombardment, judged by the amount of damage done in such a short period." Within six weeks of his arrival, Julian Bell was
killed in Spain, July 18, 1937; but Woolf memorializes him in *Three Guineas*,
resurrecting the specter and spectacle of Spanish devastation in photographs of
dead bodies and ruined houses which the reader never sees but to which she
refers as a recurring refrain.

By October 5, 1937, members of Parliament were again concerned with the
state of the empire's defense. In "Chairman's Address: 'Our Country Must be
Powerfully Armed'," Hugh Dalton, M.P., chairman of the Labour party, recognizes the threat of a grim world situation and calls for the removal of the present
government and a change in foreign policy (III: 26; LX, B.41). "'Tremendous
dangers overshadow us,' the article quotes Dalton. 'Nothing is to be gained by
playing ostrich. The peace of the world to-day is not merely in peril. It is being
brutally broken without declaration of war both in China and in Spain, as yes-
terday in Abyssinia.'" On the 22nd of October, Woolf clipped out a very brief

column consisting of two single paragraphs: "The War Office and Women's Corps" and "More Army Recruits" (III: 43; LX, B.59). The British army is enlisting more recruits, the bottom piece relates; but, as the top paragraph indicates, women won't be among them. This should make it easy, Woolf insists in *Three Guineas*, for women to take an oath not to fight with arms as their first step to preventing war (106).

On November 10, 1937, *The Listener* printed the text of a BBC address by George Bernard Shaw, "As I See It" (III: 60; LX, B.79). Woolf pasted only the first page of the two-page article in her scrapbook, enough to indicate it as the lead piece in the issue and to firmly establish Shaw's pacifist stance. Shaw suggests that the appropriate way to stop war is for all people to become conscientious objectors, and continues: "I dislike war not only for its dangers and inconveniences but because of the loss of so many young men any of whom may be a Newton or an Einstein, a Beethoven, a Michelangelo, a Shakespeare, or even a Shaw." Woolf cites Shaw liberally in a footnote to *Three Guineas*, especially noting Shaw's reference to "civilized" women, who, at the outbreak of war, hand out white feathers as a sign of cowardice to men who are not in uniform (*TG* 182). Shaw's speech is laced with his usual ironic touch but there is throughout an unmistakably serious message about a socialist leveling of class structures and a redistribution of the causes of breakdowns in civilizations, "a silly misdistribution of wealth, labour and leisure." Yet, Shaw concludes, "it is the one history lesson that is never taught in our schools, thus confirming the saying of the German philosopher Hegel. 'We learn from history that men never learn anything from history'. Think it over. So long."[16]

A month later, on December 16,1937, Woolf clipped "Life in Modern Germany: Dr. Woermann on the State's Aims, Status of Women," annotated it "*Times*," and added it to the page with "New Uniforms for Army" to provide the serious contrast of German propaganda to the comic concern with masculine dress for battle (III: 47; LX. B.64). Woermann, Counselor of the German Embassy, delivered a lecture to the Royal United Service Institution on December 15, 1937, which upheld Germany's nationalism while denying its lack of international cooperation and its status as a dictatorship and arguing that instead of re-arming, Germany was putting its people back to work. What must have held Woolf's attention most closely, though, is the final section of the arti-

---

[16]This quote and the one in the sentence before come from the second page of the article, which is not included in Woolf's third volume of her scrapbook. Bernard Shaw, "As I See It: Broadcast to the Empire on November 2," *The Listener*, Wednesday, 10 November 1937 (XVIII, No. 461): 998.

cle where Woermann denies women's inequality in Germany; for Woolf had read widely to the contrary. Woermann's speech averred:

> In some foreign countries fantastic ideas were current about the position of women in Germany to-day. Nothing could be more ridiculous and stupid than the assertion that National Socialism looked on women only as breeding machines. There were millions of German women working in all kinds of professions . . . To believe that a woman's principal work was family life and bringing up the young generation was simply to return to natural and eternal law.

In a further demonstration of his lack of candor, Woermann insisted, when asked about concentration camps, that they were only for criminals and political offenders whose treatment there was "reasonable."

As an indication that not all women blindly accepted fascist ideology, Woolf chose a clipping which returns to her major theme of women's status and position in public space and links it to the second major theme of masculine spectacle and its relation to the growing threat of global war. "Mayoress Would Not Darn Socks for War" (*Evening Standard*, December 20, 1937) details a storm of disapproval in Woolwich over remarks made by the new mayoress, Kathleen Rance (III: 63; LX, B.84). Rance claimed, "So far as my husband and I are concerned, we shall do all we can for peace during our year of office. We are both members of the Peace Pledge Union, and neither of us would take part in a war. I myself would not even do as much as darn a sock to help in a war." Rance's sentiments were those of Woolf herself, who writes of Rance as an example of her "Outsiders' Society" in *Three Guineas*: "At any rate, we shall agree that the Mayoress of Woolwich, Mrs. Kathleen Rance, has made a courageous and effective experiment in the prevention of war by not knitting socks" (116).

About a third of the way through the last volume of her scrapbooks, Woolf seems to pose the question of how much "culture" can do to save civilization from a devastating war. She clipped a banner headline from a French news source, undated and unidentified, which reads: "Seule la culture désintéressée peut garder le Monde de sa ruine" (III: 24; LX, B.37, "Only disinterested culture can guard the world from its ruin").[17] In *Three Guineas,* without attributing it, Woolf cites the headline: ". . . you say that war is imminent; and you go on to say

[17]On the same scrapbook page with this headline banner, Woolf includes a printed pamphlet asking for a donation from the International Peace Campaign. Two additional documents that I don't discuss here since they are not news or journal clippings include a manifesto entitled "War and Writers" sent to Woolf for her signature from the International Peace Campaign and a circular about their activities from the International Association of Writers for the Defence of Culture. I am not aware if Woolf signed the manifesto of the first group or attended any activities of the second.

in more languages than one—here is the French version: *Seule la culture désintéressée peut garder le monde de sa ruine*—you go on to say that by protecting
intellectual liberty and our inheritance of culture we can help you to prevent war"
(*TG* 87). Woolf is insistent that "disinterested culture" has excluded women;
women have been largely segregated out of the public space where culture exists
and forced to gaze upon the spectacle of empire from the window of the private
house. Woolf recognized women's double bind, caught between private and public space:

> Behind us lies the patriarchal system; the private house, with its nullity, its
> immorality, its hypocrisy, its servility. Before us lies the public world, the pro-
> fessional system, with its possessiveness, its jealousy, its pugnacity, its greed.
> The one shuts us up like slaves in a harem; the other forces us to circle, like
> caterpillars head to tail, round and round the mulberry tree, the sacred tree, of
> property (TG 74).

Despite what appears to be a kind of despair, though, Woolf signed a statement
of public support for the Spanish government and its people in 1936. Entitled
"Democracy at Stake," published as a letter to the editor, and signed by Woolf
and 32 others, the clipping is included in the second volume of Woolf's scrapbooks (II: 34; LIX, B.44). The weight of evidence Woolf collected strongly
suggests, though, that culture as masculine spectacle, may not be worth saving.
The last clippings Woolf pasted in her scrapbooks are dated December 20, 1937;
the scrapbooks were finished, their purpose complete. From late 1936 throughout 1937, Woolf was at work on *Three Guineas*, substantially finishing it in
October of 1937, but continuing to revise it in late 1937 and early 1938 to substantiate her claims by adding citations from the clippings. By June, 1938, *Three
Guineas* was in print; what it had to say was unpopular and largely unheeded. But
Woolf never relinquished her hold on the discovery she had laid bare, writing in
her diary of *Three Guineas* (and by extension of the clippings scrapbooks which
fed it) that: "the book which was like a spine to me all last summer . . . remains,
morally, a spine: the thing I wished to say, though futile"(*D5* 130).[18]

---

[18]*The Diary of Virginia Woolf,* Vol. V, 1936-1941, ed. Anne Olivier Bell (San Diego:
Harcourt Brace Jovanovich, 1984) 130.

Works Cited

Belsey, Catherine and Jane Moore, eds. *The Feminist Reader: Essays in Gender and the Politics of Literary Criticism.* New York: Basil Blackwell, 1989.

Debord, Guy. *The Society of the Spectacle.* Trans. Donald Nicholson-Smith. New York: Zone Books, 1994. <hhtp://www.situationist.cjb.net/>

Elshstain, Jean Bethke. *Public Man, Private Woman: Women in Social and Political Thought.* Brighton: Harvester, 1982.

Janeway, Elizabeth. *Man's World, Woman's Place: A Study of Social Mythology.* New York: Dell, 1971.

Macaulay, Thomas Babington. *The History of England: From the Accession of James The Second.* 5 vols. London: Longman, 1849–1861.

Mulvey, Laura. "Visual Pleasure and Narrative Cinema." *Feminisms.* Eds. Robyn R. Warhol and Diane Price Herndl. New Brunswick, NJ: Rutgers UP, 1991, 438–48.

Neverow, Vara and Merry Pawlowski. "A Preliminary Bibliographic Guide to the Footnotes of *Three Guineas.*" *Woolf Studies Annual* 3 (1997) : 170–210.

Newton, Judith. *Women, Power, and Subversion: Social Strategies in British Fiction 1778–1860.* Athens, GA: U of Georgia P, 1981.

Pawlowski, Merry and Vara Neverow. *Reading Notes for* Three Guineas*: An Edition and an Archive.* <http://www.csub.edu/woolf_center>.

Shaw, George Bernard. "As I see It: Broadcast to the Empire on November 2." *The Listener* 18 (November 10, 1937): 997–98.

Silver, Brenda. *Virginia Woolf's Reading Notebooks.* Princeton, NJ: Princeton UP, 1983.

Twenty-seven Contributors to *The Times. Fifty Years: Memories and Contrasts, A Composite Picture of the Period 1882–1932.* Foreword by George Macaulay Trevelyan. London: Thomas Butterworth, 1932.

Woolf, Virginia. *The Diary of Virginia Woolf.* 5 vols. Ed. Anne Olivier Bell and Andrew McNeillie. NY: Harcourt Brace Jovanich, 1997-84.

——. *Monks House Papers* B16.f, Volumes 1, 2, and 3. U of Sussex Manuscript Collection.

——. *Three Guineas.* 1938. San Diego: Harcourt Brace Jovanovich, 1966.

——. *Three Guineas.* London: Hogarth P, 1938.

"Six Essays on London Life": A History of Dispersal Part I

Jeanette McVicker

> Is it possible to coordinate what is dispersed, to make incoherence coherent, to reduce what is erratic to a unified whole?
> —Maurice Blanchot, "Outwitting the Demon—A Vocation," *The Siren's Song* (1982)

> A total description [of history] draws all phenomena around a single centre—a principle, a meaning, a spirit, a world-view, an overall shape; a general history, on the contrary, would deploy the space of a dispersion.
> —Michel Foucault, *The Archaeology of Knowledge* (1972)

Virginia Woolf's six-part series on London for British *Good Housekeeping* in 1931-32 is worth considering in some detail, in my view, and not simply because this magazine seems such an unlikely place of publication for this novelist.[1] Together with the speech Woolf delivered to the National Society for Women's Service only weeks prior to their composition,[2] "Six Essays on London

---

[1]"Six Essays on London Life" appeared in British *Good Housekeeping* from December 1931 to December 1932 in the following order: "The Docks of London," December 1931; "Oxford Street Tide," January 1932; "Great Men's Houses," March 1932; "Abbeys and Cathedrals," May 1932; "'This is the House of Commons,'" October 1932; "Portrait of a Londoner," December 1932. The 3rd edition of B. J. Kirkpatrick's bibliography does not mention the last essay and neither does the *Letters of Virginia Woolf*, ed. Nigel Nicolson and Joanne Trautmann. However, *The Diary of Virginia Woolf*, ed. Anne Olivier Bell does mention all six.

The publisher Frank Hallman, with permission from Angelica Garnett and Quentin Bell, published the first five essays in a book entitled *The London Scene* (1975), reprinted by Random House (1982). I will use this source in quoting the first five because it is the most widely accessible and will thus use the parenthetical citation in text of (*LS*). When quoting from "Portrait of a Londoner," I will use the parenthetical citation in text of (*GH*) for *Good Housekeeping*. I am grateful to the assistance of Ms. Susanna Van Langenberg, of the Library and Syndication office at The National Magazine Co., London (publisher of British *Good Housekeeping*) for her assistance in obtaining the sixth essay.

Woolf contributed several pieces to British and American *Vogue* as well; see Jane Garrity's essay in *Virginia Woolf in the Age of Mechanical Reproduction*, ed. Pamela Caughie (New York: Garland, 2000) and in *Modernism/Modernity* 6.2.

[2]The speech was delivered to the London/National Society for Women's Service, a group of "mainly professional women who were struggling to increase the presence of women in higher education and in the professions," according to Morag Shiach, editor of the Oxford edition of *A Room of One's Own* and *Three Guineas* (xviii). Philippa Strachey

Life" can be read as Woolf's preliminary reflection on the transformation from a Victorian social order to a modern one that would find its most explicit expression in her major project of the decade, *The Pargiters*. Woolf's work from the late 1920s through the 1930s highlights this transformative moment, tracing the imperial center that governed relations from the patriarchal Victorian household to the farthest reaches of the empire through a network of powerful institutions--including the cultural apparatuses that monumentalized its history—to its displacement by a neo-imperialist[3] commodity capitalism, one which has its center "elsewhere," to borrow a phrase from Jacques Derrida.[4] I suggest in this paper that the *Good Housekeeping* series and the Women's Service speech func-

---

(one of Lytton's sisters) served as secretary to the Society from 1914-1951; she had invited Woolf and composer Ethel Smyth to address the members in January 1931. Woolf was an ardent supporter of the Society's library, according to Mark Hussey *(Virginia Woolf A-Z* [NY: Facts on File, 1995: 278]). Pippa Strachey, long active in the cause of women's suffrage and professional activity, organized the first major march in London for women's suffrage on 9 February 1907 (Hussey, *A-Z* 278). Anna Snaith provided a lively and lucid discussion of the Society's library in the paper she delivered to the 10th Annual Conference on Virginia Woolf, "'Stray Guineas': Woolf, Women Readers and the Marsham Street Library," *Virginia Woolf Out of Bounds: Selected Papers from the Tenth Annual Conference on Virginia Woolf,* ed. Jessica Berman and Jane Goldman (Pace UP, 2001). The Fawcett Library correspondence, with an informative contextualizing essay by Merry Pawlowki, has been published in *Woolf Studies Annual* 8 (2002): 3-62.

[3]There are many ways one can define "imperialism" and "neoimperialism"; as Ania Loomba notes in *Colonialism/Postcolonialism*, it is important to differentiate "imperialism" from "colonialism" as well. I will follow her definitions, knowing that others (such as Sonita Sarker) use these terms differently. Loomba states, "One useful way of distinguishing between [imperialism and colonialism] might be to not separate them in temporal but in spatial terms and to think of imperialism or neo-imperialism as the phenomenon that originates in the metropolis, the process which leads to domination and control. Its result, or what happens in the colonies as a consequence of imperial domination is colonialism or neo-colonialism. . . . Imperialism can function without formal colonies (as in United States imperialism today) but colonialism cannot" (6-7). See Loomba, *Colonialism/Postcolonialism*, part of Routledge's *New Critical Idiom* series (1998).

[4]See Derrida's "Structure, Sign and Play in the Discourse of the Human Sciences." "The concept of a centered structure is in fact the concept of a play based on a fundamental ground, a play constituted on the basis of a fundamental immobility and a reassuring certitude, which itself is beyond the reach of play. And on the basis of this certitude anxiety can be mastered . . . Successively, and in a regulated fashion, the center receives different forms or names. The history of metaphysics, like the history of the West, is the history of these metaphors and metonymies. Its matrix . . . is the determination of Being as *presence* in all senses of this word" (279).

tion together—a kind of dual analysis—marking an important bridge between *The Waves* and *The Pargiters.* Written only three years after British women over 21 obtained the vote, these parallel texts offer a glimpse into Woolf's thinking process between two major phases of her writing, the former phase (culminating in *The Waves)* foregrounding the aesthetic and visionary, the latter phase (culminating in *Three Guineas* and *The Years)* foregrounding the political, social and economic. Both Molly Hite and Herbert Marder have recently commented, in their distinctive ways, on a major transition in Woolf's project (*The Waves* a significant pivot for each), and I am indebted to them both.[5] My interest lies in a vague but significant in-between moment of a transition in Woolf's focus, one that for me is manifest in both the series and the speech, texts which are linked together by the death in each of an Angel in the House, the symbolic monitor of the old imperial order that has not only contributed to women's exclusion from the professions but has censored "the truth about women's bodies" from multiple discourses, literature among them.[6] I think Woolf genuinely believed that with the end of the imperial formation—represented by the death of this symbolic angel—would come middle class women's freedom of expression, so that (white) women could find their voices in the public sphere of the professions as

---

[5] I have benefited tremendously from Herbert Marder's insightful *The Measure of Life: Virginia Woolf's Last Years* as well as Molly Hite's provocative essay, "Virginia Woolf's Two Bodies," which I read in its online version. Both critics discuss the transition from Woolf's "aesthetic" work to the more "political" work, though the way each conceptualizes this is quite different; both note the importance of *The Waves* as a transitional marker. Marder specifically notes the role of the death of the Angel in the House: "Three years later, looking ahead to a new decade after completing *The Waves* . . . Virginia announced with some confidence that the Angel was dead at last. She would now enter a phase in which she created chronicles without nostalgia—juxtaposing Victorian and modern times, observing that the domestic tyranny of the former led to the political fanaticism of the latter" (6).

Hite calls *The Waves* the apotheosis of Woolf's "visionary" period, a period that is not strictly chronological. For Hite, the distinction entails a careful analysis of the ways in which women's bodies figure in Woolf's writings; the "visionary body" "was fundamentally new to modernist representation although arguably always an element of experience. One of Woolf's signal contributions to a distinctively female modernism was this female modernist body," in contrast to "the body for others, the body cast in social roles and bound by the laws of social interaction."

[6] One might argue that the death of Mrs. Ramsay in *To the Lighthouse* marked the beginning of this transition, if one reads Mrs. Ramsay as an early version of the angel in the house, a reading given credibility by the biographical references to Woolf's mother, Julia Stephen, who clearly *did* function as a Victorian angel. Hite makes great use of this in her thesis in her recent *Genders* essay.

well as through their literary pens. What I find most fascinating about these parallel texts, however, are their indications that Woolf is simultaneously becoming aware that power is much more densely layered, that killing the angel—i.e., that the end of Victorian imperialism—may not bring about this desired freedom for women because "something else" is getting in the way. In 1931, I don't think Woolf could fully articulate this "something else"; with the hindsight provided by 70 years, however, one might call it, utilizing the work of Michel Foucault, the refinement, via consumer capitalism, of what the latter called the "disciplinary society." I will return to a full exploration of this concept shortly.

My essay thus foregrounds the discursive connections between imperialism and consumerism (and gives passing glances toward fascism), each of which operates according to a grid of power relations that constitutes the individual body in order to gain control over the collective body. All three discourses of power are dependent upon a "center" that controls and regulates both discourses and bodies, yet that center is in the process of transformation and operates differently in each. Both imperialism and fascism function by means of a visible and definable center; both of these formations seek to maintain traditional mechanisms of power grounded in the "old" concept of sovereignty. Woolf's parallel texts of 1931 highlight the transformation to a center which is "invisible": the multivalent operations of power, truth and knowledge that are the condition for the possibility of a liberal, democratic consumerist capitalism. Woolf seems keenly aware that women's entrance into higher education and the professions is symptomatic of this transformative moment; at the same time she is beginning to glimpse that these new economic and political freedoms are in danger of being coopted in ways that will have significant repercussions on women's lives at every level. What Woolf couldn't articulate was that liberal democracy would establish itself by means of what Foucault called a "regime of truth" that would redefine the "truth of women's bodies" through a process of normalization. I hope to articulate how prescient Woolf nevertheless was in observing the kinds of changes in discourse and power that would mark the modern era.

Just as the Romans insisted that "all roads lead to Rome," so Woolf—mindful, like Conrad, of Britain's imperial project—suggests that all ships "in time" come to anchor in the Port of London. The scattered lands of the British Empire come together here as the ships come up the Thames River and into the heart of London. The *Good Housekeeping* series begins with a gritty Dickensian description of the docks, a scene of warehouses, garbage, and tenements; in its focus on the corrosive effects of the utilitarian initiative, it describes a London remote from the green and pleasant land of the pastoral, romantic tradition so intrinsic to the representation of the British colonial project. As one proceeds further upriver toward the city-center, one eventually comes to "the knot, the clue, the hub of all those scattered miles of skeleton desolation and ant-like activity. Here growls and grumbles that rough city song that has called the ships from the sea and brought them to lie captive beneath its warehouses" (*LS* 10).[7] The series concludes with the return of "travellers absent for years, battered and sun-dried men just landed from India or Africa, from remote travels and adventures among savages and tigers" whose final destination is the tea-table of the modern siren Mrs. Crowe. They "would come straight to the little house in the quiet street to be taken back into the heart of civilisation at one stride" (*GH* 132). With biting sarcasm, Woolf writes that it is in Mrs. Crowe's drawing room "that the innumerable fragments of the vast metropolis seemed to come together into one lively, comprehensible, amusing and agreeable whole" (*GH* 132). In this series of six essays written for the presumably white middle-class women readers of *Good Housekeeping*, Woolf implies that the heart of darkness of British imperialism is in the London that has been constructed and maintained at Mrs. Crowe's insular tea-table, where the life and death struggles of the imperial project are reduced to "talk" of the most general kind. *This* imperial London is coming to its end, Woolf implies, as Mrs. Crowe—an angel in the house—dies at the end of the article which concludes the whole set of six articles. Woolf suggests throughout the *Good Housekeeping* series, however, that even as the empire fades, society's emerging normalizing apparatuses are already at work catering to "our" desires (*LS* 14): "we" are the "necessary animals" of commodity capitalism while simultaneously being accommodated to a monumentalized tradition celebrating British imperialism, art and culture. And yet, there are other social, political and economic formations vying for the authority to satisfy "our" desires, most ominously an emergent fascism. All of the ideologies contending for dominance as the imperial center is dismantled seek regulation of the new masses by means of particularized constructions of the individual body. As the imperial center comes to its "end," so too do the metaphorics making it visible, such as the center and periphery image so crucial to conceptualizing the spatial relations inherent in imperialism. Woolf's walking tour through London offers glimpses of this process through a series of historical juxtapositions and contrasts at specific locations of power, from the hub of commerce (the docks and Oxford Street) to cultural and political iconographic centers ("great men's houses," the House of Commons, abbeys and cathedrals). Reconciling the final essay, which

[7]I find it quite interesting that Woolf invokes Homer's *Odyssey* here in describing the gritty industrialism of the docks. In *The Dialectic of Enlightenment,* Adorno reads the myth of the sirens as a facade for the development of capitalism. See especially "Excursus I" in *The Dialectic of Enlightenment*, Theodor Adorno and Max Horkheimer (New York: Continuum, 1990; orig. pub. 1944).

takes place in the Victorian home of a Cockney hostess, is the point of departure for my analysis.

Readers should not overvalue Woolf's journalistic writing (of this series in particular she said, "I'm being bored to death by my London articles—pure brilliant description—six of them—and not a thought for fear of clouding the brilliancy. . . ." [*L4* 301]). On the other hand, within the constellation of work undertaken between May 1930 (the date of her preface to *Life As We Have Known It,* the collection of writings by working class women edited by Margaret Llewelyn Davies), and October 1932 (the date she began writing *The Pargiters*), these essays take on interest and, I would argue, significance as a window into Woolf's thinking during the transition from finishing *The Waves* to beginning the complex project that would consume the next six to seven years of her life and eventually produce both *The Years* and *Three Guineas*. In the first four months of 1931, Woolf has her "bathtub epiphany" for a sequel to *A Room of One's Own* (20 January),[8] gives her speech to the London and National Society for Women's Service (21 January), finishes *The Waves* (7 February), writes a review of *Aurora Leigh"* for the *TLS* (early April; in it she contemplates the need for new forms of literature[9]) and composes these six articles (Feb-April), among other projects. Taken together, these writings represent a deepening of Woolf's engagement with the social structures of women's oppression, her understanding of the connections between imperialism and the rise of commodity capitalism and of the fascist or totalitarian dynamics of mass culture,[10] and her search for new literary forms that might be adequate to the representation of this transformative period

[8]Woolf records the conception of this new work in her diary for Tuesday, 20 January 1931: "I have this moment, while having my bath, conceived an entire new book—a sequel to A Room of Ones Own—about the sexual life of women: to be called Professions for Women perhaps—Lord how exciting! This sprang out of my paper to be read on Wednesday to Pippa's society. Now for The Waves. Thank God—but I'm very much excited" (*D4* 6).

[9]The search for new forms that might more adequately represent the political, economic, social, and cultural transformations taking place is significant for Woolf in this period; clearly the revisionary projects of *A Room of One's Own* and *Orlando* were early precursors. But *The Waves* and *The Pargiters* are the boldest of these; *Flush* is part of this moment as well and one of the most politically engaged (see Anna Snaith's recent work, read at the 11th Annual Conference on Virginia Woolf in Bangor, Wales, "Of Fanciers, Footnotes and Fascism: *Flush* and the 1930s"). Woolf admired Browning's experiment in *Aurora Leigh*, calling it an "essay-poem." Woolf understands that representation itself must change if it is to be relevant in such a transformative moment, even if she is ultimately unable to keep the "novel-essay" intact.

[10]Michael Tratner explores in great depth the role of totalitarian politics and the masses on modernist writing, including Woolf's, in his exceptionally interesting book, *Modernism and Mass Politics: Joyce, Woolf, Eliot, Yeats*. I have found his thinking about

in British (and European) history.[11]

The period between May 1930 and October 1932 provides an explosive historical context for Woolf's work in political, economic, and social terms, a context which manifests itself, I would argue, significantly in the *Good Housekeeping* series. Five years after the General Strike of 1926—an event that marked a turning point in the relation of workers to both the state and to capitalism[12]—1931 marked a watershed year in the economic and political crisis Britain

---

the politics of the era, especially in regard to Bloomsbury, to be very helpful for my thinking about Woolf's work in the early 1930s. His comments in the Epilogue regarding how/why modernism lost its "edge" against capitalism are relevant to cite here: "Modernism became separated from its anticapitalist politics because capitalism changed, giving up its individualist, liberal core in the development of the welfare state; the modernist period was mostly a period of such adjustment. The sense that the masses—as folk or as proletariat—represented an alternative to capitalism disappeared because yet another image of the masses emerged: as consumers. The women's, workers', nationalist, and aristocratic movements did not then lead to revolution at all, because they could all be satisfied as 'market segments': the discovery of alternative mentalities and the demise of the universal individual translated not into the demise of capitalism but into alternative sets of objects to buy" (242). What I am attempting to do in the present essay is demonstrate how cannily Woolf perceived the double-edge of this transformation as it was taking place, from imperialism to liberal capitalist democracy, and in its reconstruction of the individual *vis à vis* the collective or mass.

[11]Pamela Caughie provides a highly insightful discussion of the first two essays of the *Good Housekeeping* series in her landmark book, *Virginia Woolf & Postmodernism*; see especially pp. 119-37. I find her reading more compelling than that of Susan Squier, though like many others who have commented on these essays at all, she takes up the first two to the exclusion of the other four.

[12]According to historian David Thomson, "the General Strike of 1926 is one of the most controversial and significant events of the inter-war years. To the making of the situation which produced it converged most of the industrial dilemmas, political party feuds, and social schisms of post-war Britain. From it flowed many of the constituent elements in the industrial and parliamentary history of the following decade" (108). The strike originated in the coal mining industry, beginning on 26 April. The Trades Union Congress called a "partial" national stoppage, Thomson explains, to support the miners' cause, though such action was intended to be a selective sympathetic strike rather than a general one. "It extended, however, to all forms of transport, the main heavy industries, the building and printing trades, gas and electricity workers" (111), according to Thomson. When all was said and done, the "general" strike lasted nine days though the miners continued to strike for another six months. "When at last their strike was ended they forfeited everything they had fought for," Thomson says, including previously won agreements, shorter hours, better wages, 60 million British pounds in lost wages, and the bankruptcy of the union's support funds (115). Moreover, in 1927 the Trade Disputes and Trade Union Act made all sympathetic strikes illegal and attacked the political use of union funds.

was undergoing. The number of those officially unemployed in 1931 was 3.25 million; it would rise to 3.75 by September 1932 (Thomson 131). In May 1930 Sir Oswald Mosley, a former Labour M.P., resigned his seat in government and formed the "New Party," the immediate precursor to the British Union of Fascists.[13] By 1932, the British Union of Fascists was already mirroring Mussolini's Blackshirts by committing open violence in the streets. In March 1931, both the Labour Party and the Conservative Party were each undergoing crucial internal power struggles; by August 1931 the Labour Government led by Ramsay MacDonald collapsed, leading directly to the formation of a "National Government," an event that Labour supporters (which included most of Bloomsbury) saw as betrayal and what contemporary economists and historians claim as the most significant event in the interwar years (Thomson 129-41). Ireland and India were in the process of demanding full "Dominion" status, a series of events and transitions that would permanently change the nature of the British Empire. Woolf marked the release of Gandhi from prison in her diary on 26 January 1931; he had been jailed for civil disobedience since May 1930.[14]

The *Six Essays on London Life* were written between February and early April 1931, apparently commissioned by the magazine as a series. Woolf undertook visits to each of the sites (the docks, the House of Commons, etc.) as she

---

The greatest legacy of the General Strike of 1926, according to Thomson, was the death of "the myth of syndicalist revolution as the road to better times. . . . What gained new life, though again nobody noticed, was parliamentary socialism and the prospect of building a democratic Welfare State" (115-16).

[13]For a very general discussion of Mosley and the New Party, which would eventually become the British Union of Fascists, see Thomson 132-60. Much more helpful and specific for my reading have been Martin Durham, *Women and Fascism*, esp. Ch. 2 on "Women in the Greater Britain" (pp. 27-48) (Routledge, 1998), and, especially, David Bradshaw's extremely interesting and insightful essays in *Woolf Studies Annual* 3 and 4: "British Writers and Anti-Fascism in the 1930s, Parts I and II": 1997 (pp. 3-27) and 1998 (pp. 41-66).

See also Woolf *D*4 38n7 re: Harold Nicolson, who had joined the New Party (Mosley's party) in March 1931. Woolf, in fact, toured the London docks for the first *Good Housekeeping* article, "The Docks of London," in a "Port of London Authority launch with a party which included Leonard, Vita Sackville-West, and the Persian Ambassador; she returned with Harold Nicolson" (*D*4 15n8). By August 1931, Nicolson had left the *Evening Standard* to edit the New Party journal, *Action*. He would give up that journal by December.

[14]See Thomson 101-108 and 148-50 on the issue of Dominion status. See *D*4 7-8 for Woolf's comment on Gandhi's release.

drafted the articles. The sixth essay, "Portrait of a Londoner," represents a radical departure from focus on a British landmark to concentration on the drawing
room of an elderly hostess, and perhaps not surprisingly, it was deleted from the
reprint of the series undertaken in 1975 entitled *The London Scene* authorized by
Quentin Bell and Angelica Garnett (of which more will be said at the end of this
essay). The significance of the series nevertheless lies precisely in reading them
together *as a whole* and through the lens offered by the Women's Service speech
written only weeks earlier; only in this way does the final strangeness of "Portrait
of a Londoner" make sense. While several critics have commented on the *Good
Housekeeping* series, including Susan Squier, Pamela Caughie, Reginald Abbott,
Sonita Sarker, Molly Hite and Jocelyn Bartkevicius,[15] attention has focused primarily on the first two essays, "The Docks of London" and "Oxford Street Tide,"
and it's easy to see why, since these lend themselves most overtly to discussions
of class, consumerism and women's economic status. My purpose in this essay
is to suggest that the *Good Housekeeping* essays *collectively* constitute a pre-
meditation, not simply on the implications of modernity, but on cultural,
political, economic and social citizenship, particularly as these pertain for white
women moving into the middle class; a pre-meditation that, together with the
speech, paves the way for Woolf's thinking in *The Years* and, perhaps especially, *Three Guineas*. The symbolic death of the angel in the house, which Woolf
describes in both the speech and in "Portrait of a Londoner," must be accom-

[15]Susan Merrill Squier, *Virginia Woolf and London: The Sexual Politics of the City*
(University of North Carolina Press, 1985). Squier brought these essays to the attention of
Woolf scholars in the most sustained way up to that point; all who write on the essays are
indebted to that initial work, however much we might disagree with her reading. See also:
Pamela L. Caughie, *Virginia Woolf & Postmodernism: Literature in Quest and Question
of Itself* (University of Illinois Press, 1991); Reginald Abbott, "What Miss Kilman's
Petticoat Means: Virginia Woolf, Shopping and Spectacle" *Modern Fiction Studies* 38.1,
Spring 1992: 193-216.
Jocelyn Bartkevicius focused on these essays in her paper for the Third Annual
Conference on Virginia Woolf (1993, Lincoln University), "A Form of One's Own:
Reclaiming Virginia Woolf's London Essays," which as far as I am aware has not been
published. I thank Beth Rigel Daugherty for providing a copy of this paper. Molly Hite
made reference to the essays in her 1999 MLA paper "Anon. As Poacher: Virginia Woolf
and the Practice of Everyday Life" for the IVWS panel, "Virginia Woolf and the
Everyday," organized by Lisa Ruddick; Sonita Sarker also gave a paper entirely devoted
to these essays at the 1999 MLA, "Siting Englishness in Virginia Woolf's *The London
Scene*." My apologies if I have left out other people's work on these essays.

plished before such thinking can take place, yet even as early as 1931, Woolf seems to intuit that this death—heralding the end of Victorian imperialism—by itself will not finally allow "the truth about women's bodies" to be heard.

I The Women's Service Speech and the Repressive Hypothesis

Nearly all the work that follows *A Room of One's Own* (1929) deals thematically in some way with the connection between "the sexual life of women," "the truth of women's bodies," and the entrance of women into the professions. The theme, which one can trace back to the mythical Judith Shakespeare, becomes much more overt in the Women's Service speech and *The Pargiters,* where it is tied directly to the passing of imperialism and the rise of the middle classes. What makes it such a subversive topic that it will take at least another 50 years "until men have become so civilised that they are not shocked when a woman speaks the truth about her body" (*Pargiters* xl)? In a fictional dialogue between the woman writer and the imagination, Woolf says in the speech:

> We have only got to wait fifty years or so. In fifty years I shall be able to use all this very queer knowledge that you are ready to bring me. But not now. You see I go on, trying to calm her [the imagination], I cannot make use of what you tell me—about womens bodies for instance—their passions—and so on, because the conventions are still very strong. If I were to overcome the conventions I should need the courage of a hero, and I am not a hero (*Pargiters* xxxviii-xxxix).

"The future of fiction," she says a few paragraphs later, "depends very much upon what extent men can be educated to stand free speech in women" (*Pargiters* xl). Literature, as one of the institutions regulated by the imperial center, has *not* told the truth about women's bodies, thereby contributing to women's exclusion from the professions. What changes must take place in order for fiction to tell the truth, and what will be the effect on women entering the professions? Are these changes simply dependent on the dismantling of imperialism? The struggle for women's suffrage, to which Woolf contributed, asserted that women's greater political role would have dramatic effects on women's participation in other aspects of the public sphere, and no one would doubt that the vote did alter women's access to the public sphere in important ways. On the other hand, other ideologies competing to fill the void precipitated by imperialism's demise also promised varying degrees of greater visibility for women within the public sphere while continuing to construct them as particularized subjects.

Foucault's formulation of the disciplinary society as a polyvalent "regime of truth" that works together with an instrumentalized version of power relations assists readers of Woolf's essays to recognize the relatedness of the discourses she renders visible in the Women's Service speech and the London essays written in its wake.[16] Foucault locates a transformation in the relations of what he calls "power/knowledge" in the post-Enlightenment: the monarchical relation had located power in the sovereign (the king but also the State), was focused generally on the extraction of wealth and commodities from the earth and its products, and was generally exercised by arbitrary force and repression—i.e.,

[16]I consider the potentialities for thinking offered by poststructuralist theorists such as Michel Foucault and Jacques Derrida (among others) enabling in sharpening a contemporary context for reading Woolf's insightful pacifist feminism, while also recognizing the limitations of these theorists' work for feminism. Woolf critics Maria DiBattista, Michèle Barrett and many others have utilized the insights provided by poststructuralist critics, including Foucault, for the past two decades. Irene Diamond and Lee Quinby's introduction to their useful anthology, *Feminism and Foucault: Reflections on Resistance*, succinctly suggests why I find Foucault useful for feminist practice and by extension, for reading Woolf's cultural criticism:

> Four convergences of feminism and Foucault are especially striking. Both identify the body as the site of power, that is, as the locus of domination through which docility is accomplished and subjectivity constituted. Both point to the local and intimate operations of power rather than focusing exclusively on the supreme power of the state. Both bring to the fore the crucial role of discourse in its capacity to produce and sustain hegemonic power and emphasize the challenges contained within marginalized and/or unrecognized discourses. And both criticize the ways in which Western humanism has privileged the experience of the Western masculine elite as it proclaims universals about truth, freedom, and human nature. Despite their seemingly different objectives, then, feminist and Foucauldian analyses come together in the ways they have attempted to dismantle existing but heretofore unrecognized modes of domination. In short, these convergences comprise some of the most powerful forms of resistance available to us. . . . Certainly one of Foucault's most notable contributions to contemporary social criticism generally and feminist concerns specifically is his explication of power/knowledge. . . . (x).

My quotations from Foucault in this essay come primarily from two essays/interviews, "Two Lectures" (78-108) and "Truth and Power" (109-33) in *Power/Knowledge: Selected Interviews and Other Writings 1972-1977,* ed. Colin Gordon, trans. Gordon, Leo Marshall, John Mepham and Kate Soper (New York: Pantheon Books, 1980). My in-text citations are made parenthetically as (*P/K*) and page number. Other quotations from Foucault's texts will be noted separately.

power was *visible*. A new formation, what he calls "the disciplinary," shifted that relation of power in two important ways, one by means of surveillance of bodies, the other by means of knowledge-production: *"This new mechanism of power is more dependent upon bodies and what they do,"* Foucault writes, "than upon the Earth and its products. *It is a mechanism of power which permits time and labour . . . to be extracted from human bodies."* This new mechanism of power is "constantly exercised by means of surveillance . . . and presumes a tightly knit grid of material coercion. . . ." (*P/K* 104; my italics). Disciplinary power works, above all, through the creation of knowledge that makes bodies *useful*; it works by means of invisibility, by establishing norms.

This disciplinary power, according to Foucault, is "one of the great inventions of bourgeois society. *It has been a fundamental instrument in the constitution of capitalism and of the type of society that is its accompaniment"* (*P/K* 105; my italics). But the disciplinary society did not simply supplant the earlier relations of power located within the sovereign. Instead, "the theory of sovereignty has continued not only to exist as an ideology of right, but also to provide the organizing principle of the legal codes which Europe acquired in the 19th century" (105). This shift in the mechanism of power/knowledge has taken place "in such a way as to conceal its actual procedures, the element of domination inherent in its techniques, and to guarantee to everyone, by virtue of the sovereignty of the State, the exercise of his [or her] sovereign rights" (105). This concealment of the way power/knowledge comes to function is what Foucault calls "the repressive hypothesis"—it is, in other words, a *false* hypothesis perpetrated by the liberal bourgeoisie to rationalize what they claimed to be the disassociation of "power" (overt measures of force) from its bases in discourses of truth and the production of knowledge ("enlightenment") as power underwent the transformation from monarchical to "democratic." Understood in terms of the repressive hypothesis, truth takes on a highly specific role in the disciplinary society:

> 'Truth' is to be understood as a system of ordered procedures for the production, regulation, distribution, circulation, and operation of statements.
> 'Truth' is linked in a circular relation with systems of power which produce and sustain it, and to effects of power which it induces and which extend it. A 'regime of truth.'
> This regime is not merely ideological or superstructural; it was a condition of the formation and development of capitalism (*P/K* 133).

Understood in this context, one might say that in the 1930s, Woolf was challenging the regime of truth by focusing on how it silenced women's bodies in regard to their expression of sexuality, passion, and pain, and by extension, on how this silence was linked to women's exclusion from the professions.[17] Even in the case of art and literature, "disciplinary" measures—norms—were inscribed; the Angel in the House functions as a general normalizing metaphor for the idealization of Victorian womanhood as well as a particular normalizing metaphor for monitoring women writers and reviewers. In other words, the modern "regime of truth" was *already operating* in the Victorian era: disciplinary power is a modern, post-Enlightenment phenomenon. The "end" of the visible imperial center is the transformation to an invisible "center elsewhere" of the technological, liberal democratic regime of truth. Woolf intuits the network of discourses when she overtly establishes a connection in the Women's Service speech between women's bodies, the professions, and imperialism. The Angel as emblem

> was created by the imaginations of men and women at a certain stage of their pilgrimage to lure them across a very dusty stretch <of the journey>. They agreed to accept this ideal, because for reasons I cannot now go into—they have to do with the British Empire, our colonies, Queen Victoria, Lord Tennyson, the growth of the middle class and so on . . . (*Pargiters* xxx).

Woolf renders visible another discursive component of the regime of truth, one indissolubly linked to all the above and most important: she calls it, in that list of references to Empire, "the growth of the middle class" (*Pargiters* xxx). Though it is undeveloped in the speech, the relay of sites accommodated to an

---

[17]Michèle Barrett's recent book of essays, *Imagination in Theory: Culture, Writing, Words and Things,* contains as a final chapter an "encounter" between Woolf and Foucault, primarily focusing on issues dealing with reason and unreason, and primarily reading Foucault's *Madness and Civilization* and his interview "The Minimalist Self" in conjunction with *Mrs. Dalloway.* She writes, "What ... did Virginia Woolf and Foucault understand by 'truth'? It is not clear, despite the comparisons I have made and the resonances I have drawn out, that the meaning of 'truth' was comparable for them. Woolf's conception of truth is more immanent and mystical than that of Foucault, who goes to considerable trouble to insist repeatedly that 'truth' always appears in a 'regime of truth' which secures our perception of it as truth" (203); she goes on to claim that Foucault then is "not entirely consistent" with his own statements.

I find this way of bringing Woolf and Foucault together fairly unhelpful, though I respect Barrett's work tremendously. Rather than try to compare what each means by "truth," I would argue that Foucault's insistence that the process of how statements become true is consistent with Woolf's growing understanding of how fascism takes hold in people's minds, of how women have been excluded from the public sphere, etc. To bring them into a one-to-one correspondence, especially on a concept as difficult and complex as truth, is to miss the insights that each brings to our understanding of how truth works in the social, political, economic, cultural world.

imperial center extends from the Angel in the House, through the cultural apparatus of literature, to the Victorian era generally and the expansion of the middle
class. The class aspect of that relay manifests itself again in the speech, first in
her angry critique of Maynard Keynes's review in *The Nation* of a book on the
history of Clare College, Cambridge and what it signifies about the lack of
endowments for women's colleges. It is then made more personal by her admission that she eventually "grew ambitious" and "desired not merely a cat but a
motor car" (*Pargiters* xxxvi), and thus had to evolve from a book reviewer to a
novelist, for which she would be paid more money. What was no doubt intended as rhetorical gesture reveals a connection between commodity capitalism and
the "truth of women's bodies," for they are both regulated within a disciplinary
framework. Whereas one aspect of the body is made docile and silenced, the
other can only be "satisfied" through the pleasures of consumption. Foucault's
work on truth and power stresses that the regime of truth operating from the 19th
century into modernity is produced by this dual focus of silencing, on the one
hand, and the satisfaction of desire, on the other:

> In defining the effects of power as repression, one adopts a purely juridi-
> cal conception of such power, one identifies power with a law that says no . . .
> [but] what makes power hold good, what makes it accepted, is simply the fact
> that it doesn't only weigh on us as a force that says no, but that it traverses and
> produces things, it induces pleasure, forms knowledge, produces discourse. It
> needs to be considered as a productive network which runs through the whole
> social body. . . . (*P/K* 119).

Highlighting the discursive threads of class, gender and cultural production
that combine in Woolf's speech to signify imperialism, one gains a sharper
appreciation of the cultural work accomplished by the Women's Service speech
in its unconcealment[18] of the different but related discourses of power operating
in the transformation of late Victorian to modern society; one could characterize
the speech as a critique of a regime of truth that is reconstructing the

---

[18]I'm using the word "unconcealing" to invoke Heidegger's discussion of truth as
aletheia, as the process of concealing and unconcealing that he found practiced by the
Greeks, especially the pre-Socratics, and which he separates from the imperial Roman
translation of *aletheia* into *veritas*, which necessitated a one-to-one correspondence
between "word" and "thing." See "On the Essence of Truth" in the collection *Basic
Writings*, ed. David Farrell Krell (Harper & Row, 1977) as well as the lectures published
as *Parmenides*, trans. Andre Schuwer and Richard Rojcewicz (Indiana University Press,
1992). See William V. Spanos's discussion of this important distinction for the poststructuralist critique of the politics of humanism in *Heidegger and Criticism: Retrieving
the Cultural Politics of Destruction* (University of Minnesota Press, 1993).

power/knowledge framework of imperialism. It also provides a multi-faceted critical strategy for reading the rich metaphor of the Angel in the House. Since critics have analyzed this metaphor extensively, I will limit discussion here to a sketch to orient readers toward the unexamined relation between this figure and the character of Mrs. Crowe, the revelatory symbolic figure of the sixth *Good Housekeeping* essay, "Portrait of a Londoner."[19]

The Angel in the House is, above all, "pure" (*Pargiters* xxx); she represents the ideal of Victorian womanhood. Her representation, formed by consensus between British men and women unable to attain a "real" relationship, traces a connection extending from the Victorian house to the colonies. Literature functions as one discursive but crucial site through which this connection is legitimized and naturalized as norm.[20] It "pulls down the blinds" on the scenes characterizing the house—and by extension, the Empire. It is complicit in this network, though it works not through overt repression or force, but in alignment with the repressive hypothesis, i.e., as a normalizing apparatus that conceals its repressiveness. The modern writers, Woolf implies, have begun to write literature that "raises the blinds," i.e., that *discloses* and, however unevenly, challenges that norm and what it legitimates.

The transformation of society that Woolf envisions, in which women would enter the professions and therefore begin to tell the truth about their bodies, can only begin with the death of the Angel, a process Woolf believes she has begun.[21] When Woolf recounts her narrative act of "murder," we again encounter multiple effects of the regime of truth. "I now record the one act for which I take some

[19]"Speech before the London/National Society for Women's Service," January 21, 1931, reprinted in *The Pargiters: The Novel-Essay Portion of* The Years, ed. Mitchell A. Leaska (HBJ, 1977), xxvii-xliv. The original speech differs substantially from its much revised and more widely read version, "Professions for Women."

[20]Edward W. Said's work is especially relevant here, by way of his extension of Foucault's thinking for his originative postcolonial criticism. His landmark book *Orientalism* (Vintage, 1978) is certainly an important point of departure, but his most trenchant critique of the imperial project and the use it makes of cultural production, particularly literature, is *Culture and Imperialism* (Knopf, 1993). Said also praised *A Room of One's Own* in the BBC Reith Lectures, collected as *Representations of the Intellectual* (Vintage, 1994); see pp. 33-35.

[21]The speech reads: "In short I was forced to attack many of the most sacred objects in the house, and that the Angel did not like. Therefore I did my best to kill her. Whenever I felt the shadow of her wings or the radiance of her halo upon the page I took up the inkpot and flung it at her. But though I flatter myself that I did kill her in the end, the struggle was severe; it took up much time that had better have been spent in learning Greek grammar or in roaming the world in search of adventures. Well, that is one professional experience—killing the Angel in the house" (*Pargiters* xxxii-xxxiii).

credit," she says, "though the credit belongs rather to my income than to me—if one has 500 a year there is no need to tell lies. . ." (*Pargiters* xxxi). The fantasy scene near the end of the speech in which the working-class women servants in the master's house "contrived, by practising their silly little accomplishments"— such as reading Plato, writing a mass in B minor, doing a mathematical problem—"to have saved enough money to hire rooms of their own" (*Pargiters* xliii), shows them moving out of the house altogether, dashing the master's "deepest instincts" and "most cherished traditions." The connection between ideal womanhood and British imperialism is thus riven by the entrance of working class women into the professions, along with a certain group of "men of . . . civilization . . . with whom a woman can live in perfect freedom, without any fear" (*Pargiters* xliv).

Ironically, however, this scene describes the inauguration of modern mass culture and its even greater definition in terms of disciplinary power/knowledge. The list of professions opening for women that Woolf mentions is, with few exceptions, a survey of professions that regulate, measure, define and ultimately subject the body (and the earth) to what Foucault calls "bio-power": "doctors, civil servants, meteorologists, dental surgeons . . . agricultural workers, analytical chemists, investigators of industrial psychology . . . hospital dietitians . . . makers of scientific models . . ." and so forth (*Pargiters* xliii). While there are no soldiers, judges, university dons, prime ministers, or colonial governors—i.e. none of the servants of the old imperial center—there are instead all the technicians constitutive of disciplinary formation. "Whereas the juridical systems define juridical subjects according to universal norms, the disciplines characterize, classify, specialize; they distribute along a scale, around a norm, hierarchize individuals in relation to one another, and if necessary, disqualify and invalidate," Foucault says in *Discipline and Punish* (223)

The various discursive components of modern relations of power are unevenly developed in the Women's Service speech, but one can nevertheless see quite clearly how the social-collective body is linked to the individual body through networks of power operating polyvalently. It thus makes sense that Woolf's thinking regarding all these discourses has its point of departure in her bathtub epiphany about "the sexual lives of women." In this, she anticipates Foucault, who observes that "the political significance of the problem of sex is due to the fact that sex is located at the point of intersection of the discipline of the body and the control of the population" (*P/K* 125). The women to whom Woolf addressed her speech in January 1931 were those entering the disciplinary professions referred to above. These same women were also the targets of the new consumer culture symbolized, above all, by women's magazines such as *Good Housekeeping*. One should not forget that the very name of this magazine founded by William Randolph Hearst and its famous "seal of approval" mark another symptom of the transformation in western society that I've been outlining with the help of Foucault's work. Obviously the name of this periodical invokes the old private sphere of the Victorian house, together with its ideal of womanhood and family and its dependence for entertainment on exotic fictional locales of the imperialist project. But it is definitely a house in the process of transformation into one befitting the emerging disciplinary society. This process included celebrating the rise of technology and a focus on "modern conveniences," scientific management theory—especially features by the new authorities, doctors and nutritionists, on health and hygiene—and, above all, the advertising industry, all of which produce normalization—*good* housekeeping— as well as the pleasures of conspicuous consumption.

II Undermining the Imperial Center

The epigraph from Foucault's *The Archaeology of Knowledge* orients the approach I am taking in this paper and helps align both his and my project with Woolf's own rewriting of "totalizing history" in her work extending from *Orlando* (1928), *A Room of One's Own* (1929), and *The Waves* (1931) to the end of her life.[22] Foucault's description of "total history" as that which seeks to inscribe everything around a center links it fundamentally to imperialist ideology. Woolf, I am suggesting, turns the imperial metaphorics of center/periphery on its head in this series of texts, demonstrating with mocking irony that the imperial center is filled with garbage, tombs and carrion. But what happens when the center collapses upon itself? What replaces the imperial logic? At the end of the 1920s and early 1930s, a new social order based on collectivism, cooperative economics, social democracy and the League of Nations seemed perhaps genuinely possible, though not everyone understood the League as a positive force for peace.[23] By 1931, such optimism, even among Liberals, was already being tempered. A detailed exploration of the thematics of the six *Good Housekeeping*

[22]One way of thinking the connections linking the texts produced between 1928 and 1941 is to read them as rewritings of official—patriarchal, imperial, mass, i.e. totalizing— history. According to the reading I'm suggesting, the *Good Housekeeping* essays would serve as bridge pieces between Woolf's foregrounding of the role of patriarchy (*Orlando* and *A Room of One's Own*) to a foregrounding of the relay from domestic private sphere to the imperial public sphere (*The Waves*) and the transformation of the imperial to democratic consumer/mass culture (*The Years, Three Guineas, Between the Acts* and the final essays on literary history and the role of the reader).

[23]Ho Chi Minh, in a speech founding the Communist Party of Indochina in 1930, offered a very different view of the struggles endemic to the time: "Imperialist contradictions were the cause of the 1914-18 World War. After this horrible slaughter, the world

essays, read especially as companions to the Women's Service speech, enables Woolf's 21st century readers to interpret this work as an aspect of her effort to write a "general history" that, in Foucault's words, "would deploy the space of a dispersion," i.e., would demystify the logic of the center, imperial and otherwise.

As I noted earlier, Woolf begins and ends the *Good Housekeeping* essays with parallel images of the center/periphery metaphor: in the first, ships come into the Port of London from the far-flung reaches of the world, supplying goods for the great metropolis and the rest of England. As the ships proceed *up* the river, they meet coming *down* the river all of London's garbage: "Barges heaped with old buckets, razor blades, fish tails, newspapers and ashes—whatever *we* leave on *our* plates and throw into *our* dustbins—are discharging their cargoes upon the most desolate land in the world" (*LS* 9; my emphasis). In the last essay, the "sun-dried men" from India and Africa come into the hub of the city, straight to Mrs. Crowe's tea-table, to be "taken back into the heart of civilization at one stride" (*GH* 132). This "heart of civilization," however, is filled with empty gossip, meant solely for entertainment. In the perpetual present of Mrs. Crowe's drawing-room, "there must be talk, and it must be general, and it must be about everything. It must not go too deep, and it must not be too clever. . ." (*GH* 29). Mrs. Crowe no longer goes out, relying instead on those who come to her to bring with them the required bits of gossip which admitted them to her "club." Mrs. Crowe and her "cronies" reduce lived experience to "idle talk";[24] they reduce the predatory actions perpetrated in the name of the imperial project—the "civilizing mission" to pacify the colonial "other" which from the beginning had its roots in the domestic patriarchal family and the primary institutions of British society—into a social occasion. Mrs. Crowe's "great gift consisted in making the vast metropolis seem as small as a village with one church, one manor house and twenty-five cottages" (*GH* 29). The "heart of civilization" symbolized by Mrs. Crowe's drawing-room is revealed as an illusion, a perpetual present (like the Empire) having its origin in the unifying metaphor of the feudal sovereign, to

was divided into two camps: one is the revolutionary camp including the oppressed colonies and the exploited working class throughout the world. The vanguard force of this camp is the Soviet Union. The other is the counter-revolutionary camp of international capitalism and imperialism whose general staff is the League of Nations." Quoted in Gettleman et al., 22.

[24] I take this phrase from Heidegger's *Being and Time*. "The groundlessness of idle talk is no obstacle to its becoming public; instead it encourages this. Idle talk is the possibility of understanding everything without previously making the thing one's own. . . . Idle talk is something which anyone can rake up; it not only releases one from the task of genuinely understanding, but develops an undifferentiated kind of intelligibility, for which nothing is closed off any longer" (213). Above all, it is a means of flight from the existential occasion—the anxiety that has 'nothing' as its object: see especially pp. 211-24.

whom everyone is "known" and to which everything is made useful through relations of fealty. Mrs. Crowe herself is a symbol for but also a legitimation of the various institutional practices of British imperialism, which domesticates those at home and colonizes those beyond the pale of British "civilization." She is what sustains these practices and they are ostensibly all for "her" benefit. Gender is the ironic means by which class, race and nation work to construct, legitimize and maintain modern imperial society. At the "heart of civilization," Mrs. Crowe and the other "corbies" feed on the body of England and its colonized others, sending the refuse "down the dustbin," down the Thames on barges, to be dumped into "the long mounds" lining the Port of London which "have been fuming and smoking and harbouring innumerable rats and growing a rank coarse grass and giving off a gritty, acrid air for fifty years" (*LS* 9).[25]

Mrs. Crowe, as I have noted, dies at the end of the last essay in the series, entitled "Portrait of a Londoner." Woolf begins her announcement of this death through a series of negative constructions, which have the effect of turning Mrs. Crowe and her drawing-room into an absent center.[26] For the "new women" readers of *Good Housekeeping* in 1931-32, this may have seemed a fitting yet disturbing end to a series which on the surface served as a kind of tour book of London, particularly for those women (and men) from the provinces who flocked to the city as a consequence of the economic depression.[27] As newly migrated women moving into society and taking on greater responsibilities in the public sphere, these readers would likely have seen themselves as quite different from the insulated, gossiping, old-fashioned Mrs. Crowe. These readers were the women whom Woolf was, ostensibly, addressing in her speech to the Society for

[25]William Spanos alerted me to the interesting parallel between Woolf's description of Mrs. Crowe and her "cronies" and a famous ballad in the English ballad collection by Francis J. Child called "The Twa Corbies," in which two "corbies" or crows sit on a fence waiting for new carrion to feed on and come upon the body of a newly slain knight, whom they proceed to devour. Given that Woolf knew her English tradition, I'm convinced she was invoking this popular ballad here, even though I cannot offer proof. One can download the text, its variants and midi recording from a website listing all the Child Ballads. See www.contemplator.com/child/twacorbies.html for this particular ballad. The site is devoted to "Folk Music of England, Scotland, Ireland, Wales and America."

[26]"But even London itself could not keep Mrs. Crowe alive for ever. It is a fact that one day Mrs. Crowe was not sitting in the armchair by the fire as the clock struck five; Maria did not open the door; Mr. Graham had detached himself from the cabinet. Mrs. Crowe is dead, and London—no, though London still exists, London will never be the same again" (*GH* 132).

[27]See, for example, Thomson 120-21 on the explosive population growth of the London/Home counties in 1931.

Women's Service in January 1931; they might have included the working-class women in Margaret Llewelyn Davies's Co-operative Guild. The magazine's readers would probably not be likely to identify themselves with the same impulses for which Woolf mocks the old Angel, Mrs. Crowe—wasting one's day waiting for friends to bring gossip; turning social, political and economic issues into "entertainment." On the contrary, *Good Housekeeping* was committed to the new modern, scientific principles that were transforming the private Victorian home into the modern consumer house. Woolf's negative imagery equating the garbage floating down the Thames with the idle chatter floating from the dark, old-fashioned drawing room of Mrs. Crowe condemns her and the imperialism she sustained, together with the Angel whom Woolf killed by means of inkpot in the Women's Service speech. The magazine series concludes with the disappearance of Mrs. Crowe related by the narrator: her death, though "unseen," is obviously necessary in order for magazines such as *Good Housekeeping* to exist, yet the preceding stops along the tour of London which comprise the other five articles make it very clear that the London of Mrs. Crowe is a London still very much intact. *This* modern London is, indeed, a London "that will never be the same"—and yet, the more things change, the more things *do* stay the same. For example, the parties to which Woolf herself was often invited and about which she was terribly ambivalent form one of those connections linking the old imperial center to the new consumerist one. Whether the hostess is a Mrs. Crowe or a Lady Rosebery, the London party set thrives on gossip, reducing art and ideas to entertaining party talk, and perpetrating, in effect, the violence that is committed on the bodies of the working classes, on women under patriarchy, on the "others" domesticated by the imperial hegemonic order.[28] By careful reading of the first five articles together with this last, we can appreciate Woolf's sarcastic skepticism about what the "new" modern London was in the process of becoming, and savor the subversiveness of the message in

---

[28]I am certain that the point of departure for this last article, so different in tone and format from its predecessors, was Woolf's violent reaction to a party given by Lady Rosebery on 24 February in honor of the opening of *The Prison*, Ethel Smyth's latest work. Woolf records that she felt "dragged" to both events, just as she was completing revisions to *The Waves*, an arduous task that had jangled her nerves in the extreme. In a letter to Ethel dated 11 March, she tried to explain her reaction:

> It was the party. I dont know when I have suffered more; and yet why did I suffer? and what did I suffer? Humiliation: that I had been dragged to that awful Exhibition of insincerity and inanity against my will (I used to be dragged by my half-brothers against my will—hence perhaps some latent sense of outrage).

this particular medium. But only through the death of that normalizing agent (the angel of *Good Housekeeping*, Mrs. Crowe) can Woolf use this magazine to point to and subvert the slippage from the Victorian imperial center to the "center else-where" of a disciplinary formation with its accompanying techno-scientific, consumerist ethos. Whereas the imperial order turned domestic and foreign bodies into fodder for the perpetuation of Empire, the disciplinary order turns these bodies into fodder for the market by means of another kind of normalization and surveillance. Killing the Angel in the House allows Woolf to begin raising the

---

> . . . And I felt betrayed . . . I to whom this chatter and clatter on top of any art, music, pictures, which I dont understand,—is an abomination. Oh then, the eld-erly butlers, peers, champagne and sugared cakes! It seemed to me that you wantonly inflicted this indignity upon me for no reason, and that I was pinioned there and betrayed and made to smile at our damnation—I who was reeling and shocked, as I see now, (to excuse myself,) by my own struggle with the Waves . . . (*L4* 297-98).

The party not only represented a negative turning point in Woolf's relation to Smyth; it produced such a violent reaction that she apparently contemplated suicide. In a letter to Smyth dated 29 March, Woolf wrote: "Why did I feel violent, after the party? It would be amusing to see how far you can make out, with your insight, the various states of mind which led me, on coming home, to say to L:–'If you weren't here, I should kill myself—so much do I suffer.'..." (*L4* 302). Readers will recall that Gerald and George Duckworth, her half-brothers, introduced Virginia and Vanessa into the social world after the death of Leslie Stephen. Virginia often felt "dragged" by them to parties, but it is clear that the memory of another kind of "dragging against my will" is operative here; Woolf acknowl-edges it as "latent." The fact that she links it to a feeling of being "exhibited," recalling not only the molestation at Hyde Park Gate but the mirror scene at Talland House as well as a sense of "outrage," "humiliation" and "betrayal," seem sufficient evidence for her violent emotional reaction.

I believe that this occasion took on deeply personal overtones for Woolf, merging her sense of alienation from Ethel Smyth and her disgust at the London party circuit with her devastating critique of the Angel in the House and the relay of power from the Victorian drawing-room (with its "curtains pulled down") to the colonial brutality being revealed in India and elsewhere. For more on Woolf's sexual molestation, see "A Sketch of the Past," *Moments of Being*, ed. Jeanne Schulkind (Harvest, 1985) and, especially, Louise DeSalvo, *The Impact of Childhood Sexual Abuse On Her Life and Work* (Ballantine, 1989).

In responding to my essay, Jane Lilienfeld noted that in light of this revealing letter, Mrs. Crowe is "more than an Angel in the House": she "is the introjected female censor who will not permit the disclosure of incest, because the truth of women's bodies is the truth of incest" (personal correspondence, 6.2.2000). While pursuing this line of thinking is beyond the scope of this essay as I have framed it, I appreciate such an insight and hope that Professor Lilienfeld or someone with greater expertise in this subject will develop it.

blinds of the house, a first step toward enabling her to rethink literary form as a site for the possibility of creating new kinds of emancipatory meaning in an increasingly disciplinary world. The "truth about women's bodies" monitored by the Angel, however, is already being accommodated to a different discursive formation, a truth-discourse in which women's bodies will be made increasingly docile even as women believe themselves to be increasingly free.

[Part II of this essay will be published in *Woolf Studies Annual* 10 (2004)]

Works Cited

Barrett, Michèle. *Imagination in Theory: Culture, Writing, Words and Things.* New York: New York UP, 1999.

Blanchot, Maurice. *The Siren's Song: Selected Essays.* Trans. Sacha Rabinovitch. Ed. Gabriel Josipovici. Bloomington: Indiana UP, 1982.

Child, Francis J., ed. "The Twa Corbies." Online: www.contemplator/com/child/twacorbies.html.

Derrida, Jacques. "Structure, Sign and Play in the Discourse of the Human Sciences," *Writing and Difference.* Trans. Alan Bass. Chicago: U of Chicago P, 1978. 278-293.

Diamond, Irene and Lee Quinby, "Introduction," *Feminism and Foucault: Reflections on Resistance.* Ed. Diamond and Quinby. Boston, MA: Northeastern UP, 1988.

Foucault, Michel. *Discipline and Punish: The Birth of the Prison.* Trans. Alan Sheridan. New York: Vintage, 1977.

——. *The Archaeology of Knowledge.* Trans. A.M. Sheridan Smith. New York: Pantheon, 1971.

——. "Truth and Power." Trans. Alessandro Fontana and Pasquale Pasquino. *Power/Knowledge: Selected Interviews and Other Writings, 1972-1977.* Ed. Colin Gordon. New York: Pantheon, 1980. 109-33.

——. "Two Lectures." Trans. Alessandro Fontana and Pasquale Pasquino. *Power/Knowledge: Selected Interviews and Other Writings, 1972-1977.* Ed. Colin Gordon. New York: Pantheon, 1980. 78-108.

Gettleman, Marvin E., Jane Franklin, Marilyn Young and H. Bruce Franklin, Eds. *Vietnam and America: A Documentary History.* New York: Grove Press, 1985.

Heidegger, Martin. *Being and Time.* Trans. John Macquarrie and Edward Robinson. New York: Harper and Row, 1962.

Hite, Molly. "Virginia Woolf's Two Bodies." *Genders* 31 (2000). Online:

www.Genders.org/g31/g31_hite.txt

Lilienfeld, Jane. Personal correspondence. 2 June 2000.

Loomba, Ania. *Colonialism/Postcolonialism.* New York: Routledge, 1998.

Marder, Herbert. *The Measure of Life: Virginia Woolf's Last Years.* Ithaca, NY: Cornell UP, 2000.

Shiach, Morag, "Introduction." *A Room of One's Own/Three Guineas* by Virginia Woolf. Ed. Morag Shiach. London: Oxford UP, 1992. xii-xxviii.

Thomson, David. *England in the Twentieth Century*, 2nd ed. Ed. Geoffrey Warner. London: Penguin, 1991.

Tratner, Michael. *Modernism and Mass Politics: Joyce, Woolf, Eliot, Yeats.* Stanford, CA: Stanford UP, 1995.

Woolf, Virginia. *The Diary of Virginia Woolf.* Ed. Anne Olivier Bell and Andrew McNeillie. 5 vols. New York: Harvest/Harcourt, 1980.

——. *Letters of Virginia Woolf.* Ed. Nigel Nicolson and Joanne Trautmann. 6 vols. New York: Harvest/Harcourt, 1978.

——. *The London Scene: Five Essays by Virginia Woolf.* New York: Random House, 1982.

——. "Six Essays on London Life," *Good Housekeeping* (December 1931-December 1932). The National Magazine Company, London.

——. "Speech Before the London/National Society for Women's Service." *The Pargiters*: *The Novel-Essay Portion of* The Years. Ed. Mitchell A. Leaska. New York: Harcourt, 1977. xxvii-xliv.

Alexandria as Envisioned by Virginia Woolf and E. M. Forster: An Essay in Gendered History[1]

Evelyn Haller

> "To any vision must be brought an eye adapted to what is to be seen."
>
> Plotinus
> Epigraph to Forster's *Alexandria: A History and a Guide*

I propose to analyze the responses of two modernists to the city founded by Alexander the Great in Egypt, for this city focuses differences in the perceptions of Virginia Woolf and E. M. Forster that were initially determined by their classical educations: Woolf's through women tutors—Clara Pater and Janet Case—after she had started the study of Greek in a class at King's College in London; Forster's through Athenian-minded dons at Cambridge—Goldsworthy Lowes Dickinson and Nathaniel Wedd. For both writers the idea—hers and his— of Alexandria fulfilled a need.

While Forster had lived in Alexandria for over three years while volunteering for the Red Cross during the First World War, Woolf knew it as a city of her mind assembled through her reading, her knowledge of art, and her predilections. Alexandria as Forster presented it in his history and guide as well as in essays was seen through the lens of a misogynous education. The misogyny[2] of Forster's view is apparent when it is compared and contrasted with Woolf's despite her Alexandria having to be excavated from sub-texts. Literary history, as any other, is often determined by the eye of the beholder. "Herstory," by its construction as a word, invites a reinterpretation of materials already chosen and interpreted by male historians with agenda that often focus on the lives of great men as well as domination and subjugation of various kinds, including that of women.

---

[1]Earlier versions of this essay were presented at "Virginia Woolf and the Life of a Woman: A Conference for Common Readers and Scholars," at the College of St. Catherine, St. Paul, Minnesota, October 22–23, 1982 and at the Third Annual Conference on Virginia Woolf at Lincoln University in Jefferson City, Missouri, June 14–16, 1993. A portion of this essay was also presented at the International Virginia Woolf Conference at the University of Wales, Bangor in June, 2001: "Virginia Woolf, E. M. Forster, and Alexandria: An Essay in Gendered Criticism."

[2]P. N. Furbank, whom Forster asked to write his biography, makes frequent reference to the writer's misogyny. *E. M. Forster: A Life*, 2 vols. (London: Secker & Warburg, 1977) I, 98, 104, 180; II, 56, 175, 182.

The idea of Alexandria contributed to Woolf's inner landscape and seascape as well as giving her symbols to express it while she considered Alexandria's Egyptian siting and Egyptian Isis. Woolf had seen numerous statues of Isis in the British Museum. Moreover, she declared a "passion for Marius the Epicurean" while she was still in her adolescent years. This novel, written by Clara Pater's brother, Walter, and dedicated to his sisters, has a lengthy description of Isiac ritual as well as the loving and devoted homage that continued to be accorded the goddess far into the Christian era. Among further significant literary accounts were E. M. Forster's *Alexandria: A History and a Guide* (1922; 1938)[3] and *Pharos and Pharillon*,[4] which the Woolfs published under the Hogarth imprint in 1923. The most immediate associations with Alexandria in Woolf's work—the Lighthouse, the Mouseion or House of the Muses, and the Library as well as a pageant—owed substantially to Forster's accounts.

But Forster's eye was not Woolf's eye, and what each was adapted to see induced quite different visions and hence versions. Woolf, as I believe and intend to demonstrate, came closer to the spirit of Alexandria than Forster ever could, for she was captured by Egyptian Isis, while he persisted in looking through eyes trained by a Cambridge-toned Hellenism. Woolf understood, as Forster could not, that in Isis' world "Science and religious belief went hand in hand and ... all spheres of human inquiry were held to be interrelated ..."[5]

Forster's view or angle of perception was Hellenic or "classical" according to his Athenian-centered training; it was a straitened view of pre-history and antiquity. As an ideal if not as a spiritual city, the Periclean Athens of G. Lowes Dickinson would have been more to Forster's taste than Greco-Egyptian Alexandria. Evidence suggests that the two ancient cities represented a dichotomy to Forster's mentors and contemporaries. Nathaniel Wedd, who taught Forster classics at King's, had "opposed the 'researching don' and ardently backed the idea that King's should be an Athens and not an Alexandria." Wedd's standing in Forster's mental pantheon was high: "It is to him," Forster wrote, "rather than to Dickinson—indeed to him more than to anyone—that I owe such

[3]E. M. Forster, *Alexandria: A History and a Guide* (London: Messrs. Whitehead Morris of Towerhill, 1922; rev. ed., 1938; rpt. New York: Doubleday, Anchor Books, 1961). Hereafter cited in the text as *AHG*. "The guide [first edition] was obtainable in England at Francis Birrell and David Garnett's bookshop . . ." B. J. Kirkpatrick, *A Bibliography of E. M. Forster*, 2nd rev. ed., The Soho Bibliographies (London: Rupert Hart-Davis, 1968), 39.

[4]E. M. Forster, *Pharos and Pharillon* (London: The Hogarth Press, 1923). Hereafter cited in the text as *PP*.

[5]E. Witt, *Isis in the Greco-Roman World* (Ithaca: Cornell UP, 1971) 49–50.

awakening as has befallen me."[6] Nonetheless, Dickinson was "the man above all others whose esteem Forster treasured."[7] A written version of the King's College vision of Periclean Athens (since Wedd's had been oral) was made by Dickinson in *The Greek View of Life* published in 1896. Of this book, for which Forster wrote a preface to the twenty-third edition, Wilfred Stone observes: "The book is neither history nor criticism but a new myth of the Golden Age. ... Dickinson belonged to that considerable band of Victorian Hellenists—sons of Jowett ... who saw in Periclean Athens a happy balance of virtues (aristocracy and democracy, authoritarianism and freedom, heroism and sensitivity, more strength and sexual latitude) corresponding to their own hopes for the human condition."[8] In his preface to Dickinson's book written in 1956, Forster writes that Dickinson's "discovery" was that "The Ancients are modern ... because many of their problems are ours, and have been expressed, particularly in Athens, with a lucidity beyond our power."[9] A key paragraph from Forster's loving biography of his friend and guide suggests the cause of both their limited visions: the elder's toward "the revelations of archaeology" and the younger's toward evidence of the importance of Isis to the ancient world, especially to Alexandria and to those places Isis influenced during Alexandria's centuries of maritime importance. In a paragraph that begins "His [Dickinson's] other university activities are not important," the third cited example of unimportant university activities concerns women:

> And he assisted in the unchaining of women, but without enthusiasm. His suicidal sense of fairness left him no alternative here. If women wanted a degree or vote or anything else which men monopolized, it was his duty to help them get it, even if they overwhelmed him afterwards. There were a few women to whom he was devoted and a few to whom he would have confidently entrusted the destiny of mankind, but he was not a really creditable feminist. He did think that men on the whole are superior.[10]

These statements suggest that, like Dickinson, Forster found the idea of distributive justice to women threatening as well as emotionally abhorrent.

[6]E. M. Forster, *Goldsworthy Lowes Dickinson and Related Writings*, Abinger Edition, Vol. 13 (1934; rpt. London: Edward Arnold, 1973) 61.

[7]Oliver Stallybrass, "Introduction," E. M. Forster, *The Life to Come and Other Short Stories* (New York: W. W. Norton, 1972) xii.

[8]Wilfred Stone, *The Cave and the Mountain: A Study of E. M. Forster* (Stanford: Stanford UP, 1966) 79–80.

[9]Forster, "Forster's Preface to *The Greek View of Life*," Appendix C, *Dickinson*, 213–14.

[10]Forster, *Dickinson*, 88.

Woolf's view or angle of perception, on the other hand, grew out of her auto-didactic and woman-instructed learning. Woolf's Isis vision (the organic and integral oneness of experience and knowledge) had, however, a more fundamental source: it arose from her insights as a woman. Her sensitivity to Isis and Forster's lack of it reflected fundamentally different viewpoints which were genetically (in Freud's sense) rooted in sexual differences: sexually determined differences in cultural perception. Obviously, this is not bio-determinism: sexual differences involve different cultural holisms. My theme is perception: what we see and why we see it. By contrasting two modernists who saw differently while being contemporaries more or less in sympathy with one another,[11] I can suggest how sexually determined or slanted cultural training influences what and how one perceives. The question of who was closer to historical Alexandria is not at issue here, but rather what this ancient city came to mean to each of them. For E. M. Forster, who lived there, a conflation of modern Egypt with the past was inevitable. For Woolf, who like the fictional Marius the Epicurean to whom she was passionately drawn as one who lived in his "sensations and ideas," Alexandria was a city of the mind, or, if you will, a spiritual home.

This essay emphasizes Woolf's aesthetic achievement in turning Forster's books on Alexandria to her own use not only by attacking his misogynous biases through satire, that weapon of refined and intensified anger, but also by taking his Greco-Egyptian gold to reinforce and decorate—if not to construct—a city of the mind not only for herself but for those with eyes to see her vision. Thanks in part to E. M. Forster, Virginia Woolf came to have a city of the mind, one that grew out of her construction of necropolis after necropolis to elegize[12] her beloved dead, but one that, ironically, became for her a biopolis, a city of life.[13]

[11] As early as the publication of *Night and Day* in 1919 Woolf had written of Forster: "I felt happier and easier on account of his blame than on account of the others' praise—as if one were in the human atmosphere again, after a blissful roll among elastic clouds and cushiony downs." Again, "Morgan has the artist's mind; he says the simple things that clever people don't say; I find him the best of critics for that reason. Suddenly out comes the obvious thing that one has overlooked" (*D*1 308). See also *D*2 209, *D*3 24, *D*4 52. For Forster's attitude toward Woolf's work, see Wilfred Stone's commentary on his "deeply critical assessment" in *Cave*, 371–73. Stone had talked with Forster at length.

[12] "I have an idea that I will invent a new name for my books to supplant 'novel' . . . Elegy?" (*D*3 34).

[13] Woolf's motives for building both necropolises and a biopolis are congruent with A. H. Gardiner's statement that a belief existed in Ancient Egypt that "the primary purpose of literary composition was to maintain life, whether that of the gods, of the king, or of mankind generally" ("The House of Life," *Journal of Egyptian Archaeology* 24 [1938] 157–79).

For personal as well as political reasons Woolf chose early in life to become a woman of letters and in her craft to eschew male-dominated systems of thought for one informed by the oldest, most enduring, and most coherent female myth: that of Isis. Woolf was, however, to build upon received myth by emphasizing Isiac roles of artist, intellectual, and peace-gatherer. Moreover, she developed this bent with increasing literary and political sophistication. Thus, mythic figures, especially that of Isis, enabled Woolf to make aesthetic war on patriarchy, imperialism,[14] and Christianity, as I have argued earlier.[15]

In Lemprière, an eighteenth century classical dictionary named in the text of *Between the Acts*, we read that Alexandria was "a grand and extensive city built, 332 B.C. by Alexander, on the western side of the Delta. The illustrious founder intended it not only for the capital of Egypt, but of his immense conquests, and the commercial advantages which its situation commanded continued to improve from the time of Alexander till the invasion of the Saracens in the seventh century."

Isis, the dominant religious force in Alexandria, took her origin from the Egyptian cow-goddess Hathor—the horns of both the cow and the moon survive in her representations—and she became a central figure in Egyptian political culture, for "every Pharaoh was the incarnation of the youthful Horus, and therefore was the son of Isis." The consort and brother of Isis was Osiris, at whose loss the tears of Isis caused the rising of the Nile.[16] Isis, therefore, was the stable, life-

---

[14]It should be noted that Forster was not in sympathy with the imperial imperative. His years in India as well as his time in Alexandria working for the Red Cross among the war-wounded revealed much to him. In his "Egypt," the introduction to a long pamphlet entitled *The Government of Egypt, Recommendations by a Committee of the International Section of the Labour Research Department* (1920) he gives "a brief history of Egypt's domination and exploitation by foreigners, and a criticism of British stewardship. He points out that even though as early as 1883 Gladstone's government had indicated a desire to end the British occupation as soon as possible, the British were still there in 1920, on the pretext of giving 'advice' to the Egyptians." Forster agrees with the committee's recommendation that Britain should withdraw and recognize Egypt as an independent state. "His main criticism is that the colonial bureaucracy is hypocritical and inept—especially in its failure to treat the Egyptians as individuals." For more information on Forster's attitudes and experiences in the colonial world, see Stone, *Cave*, 286ff.

[15]See my "Isis Unveiled: Virginia Woolf's Use of Egyptian Myth." *Virginia Woolf: A Feminist Slant*, ed. Jane Marcus (Lincoln: U of Nebraska P, 1983) 109–131.

[16] "The river that seemed dead as Osiris was reborn as the living water, Horus, emerging to rejuvenate the whole land: and the Lord, the human embodiment in control of it all was the Pharaoh . . . At death the King of Egypt sped away like the spent Nile. Henceforth as Osiris he held sway over female principles in Egyptian thought is most graphic in that

giving female factor—the horizontal line of the triangle, as Plutarch[17] termed her. While Pharaohs came and went, and her brother and consort died each year to be reborn as Horus with the flooding of the Nile, Isis remained constant, the source of life.

Were it simply an Egyptian city, Alexandria's aptness as the psychic home of Virginia Woolf would suffice, for her work is permeated with the matter of Egypt, including early references to Mr. Ramsay's predecessor, Ridley Ambrose, as a figure of Thoth, the god of writers, in *The Voyage Out*. In addition, Alexandria was the city founded by the Greek (Macedonian)[18] conqueror Alexander, student of Aristotle, who succumbed to the ways of cultures older and perhaps wiser than his own, and who in Egypt proclaimed himself a god when he was saluted as a son of Jupiter-Ammon by the priests at his temple in the desert. Forster, a Hellenist, says of this event which, as a Woolfian, I am tempted to call Alexander's "moment of being": "He was never—despite the tuition of Aristotle—a balanced young man, and his friends complained that in the latter period he sometimes killed them. But to us, who cannot have the perilous honor of his acquaintance, he grows more lovable than before. He has caught, by the unintellectual way, a glimpse of something great, if dangerous, and that glimpse came to him first in the recesses of the Siwan Oasis" (*PP* 27). But, to Forster's amazement, thereafter Alexander's "Greek sympathies declined. He became an Oriental, a cosmopolitan almost, and though he fought Persia again, it was in a new spirit. He wanted to harmonize the world now, not to Hellenise it" (*AHG* 9).

Our knowledge of Alexandria is enlarged through Forster's *Alexandria: A History and a Guide*. What does not become enlarged either in Forster's history and guide or in his other tribute to the city entitled after its lighthouses, *Pharos and Pharillon*, is our knowledge of the goddess Isis. In the former, Forster barely mentions three temple sites, several coins, and her maternal image transferred to the Virgin Mary, while in the latter not only does he avoid mentioning Isis by

---

Osiris from this aspect was the deity of vanished life, whereas his consort Isis, like his Hellenic successor Sarapis, was a force which produced living things and therefore enjoyed immortality in the land of the Nile where every year her son Horus was reborn under the name of 'fresh water'" (Witt 15-18).

[17]Plutarch, according to the *Oxford Classical Dictionary*, 2nd ed., lived from before A.D. 50 to after A.D. 120. For the last thirty years of his life he was a priest at Delphi where he was a devout believer in its ancient pieties and a profound student of its antiquities. He played a notable part in the revival of the shrine in Trajanic and Hadrianic times. R. E. Witt writes, "For Plutarch, 'wise and wisdom-loving' Isis was a 'philosophic' divinity, sharing in the love of the Good and Beautiful and imbued with the purest principles. She taught her followers to pursue penitence, pardon, and peace" (22).

[18]As Forster notes, "a Balkan barbarian by birth" (*PP* 24).

name but makes his only reference to her from the sidelong perspective of a Christian monk, considering the syncretic god Serapis: "a devil worse than any ... who ... had summoned his wife and child and established them on a cliff to the north, within sound of the sea. The child never spoke. The wife wore the moon" (*PP* 54). Moreover, in *Alexandria: A History and a Guide,* Forster had flown in the face of received opinion—Gibbon, Frazer, numerous handbooks and sourcebooks, even classical writers—by claiming for a syncretism of male gods (Osiris-Apis-Dionysius-Zeus-Aesculapius-Pluto)—"the last stronghold of paganism against Christianity" (*AHG* 21).

What, then, did appeal to Forster about Alexandria, given his evident distaste for a dominant and, from the evidence, a strongly attractive goddess? There was the literature that had grown up in the Mouseion whose "vast areas" included "lecture halls, laboratories, observatories, a library, a dining hall, a park, and a zoo." Forster tells us that it was a literature "disillusioned" but "not embittered" which "had strength of a kind, for it saw that out of the wreck of traditional hopes three good things remained—namely, the decorative surface of the universe, the delights of study, and the delights of love. ..." (*AHG* 19, 32). (This description sounds like G. E. Moore's *Principia Ethica.*)[19] For Forster, these remnants justified a continuing if muted and valedictory enthusiasm, but for Woolf Alexandria was all as the Isiac myth in its fullness expressed the feminism, the individualism, the pacifism she had taken as her own. That the Isis myth was not only aesthetically rewarding but evidently irritated misogynists like Morgan Forster and his fellow Apostle Lowes Dickinson was—given her malicious streak—all to the good.

In *To the Lighthouse* and *Between the Acts*, Woolf reinstated an Isis dethroned from Alexandria by E. M. Forster as she had earlier challenged Lowes Dickinson's misrepresentation of Mozart's Isis.[20] By using what T. S. Eliot called "the mythic method ... a step toward making the modern world possible for art," Woolf had already set right, and continued to set right, what she considered the

[19]For a discussion of G. E. Moore's influence on Virginia Woolf as an epistemological novelist, see S. P. Rosenbaum, "The Philosophical Realism of Virginia Woolf," *English Literature and British Philosophy*, Ed. S. P. Rosenbaum (Chicago: U of Chicago P, 1971) 316–56.

[20]The work in question is Lowes Dickinson's *The Magic Flute: A Fantasia.* Jane Marcus argues that Woolf shaped *Night and Day* "around the initiation, quest, and journey myths of *The Magic Flute*" (Marcus 97).

misappropriation of the classics by Cambridge educated Apostles.[21]

To understand the degree to which Forster refused to see what was to be seen about Isis, we should consider what Forster wrote about the presiding deities of Alexandria in the context of authoritative opinion. First, Forster agrees with others on the henotheistic nature of Egyptian and Greek religion:

> The idea that one religion is false and another true is essentially Christian, and had not occurred to the Egyptians and Greeks who were living together in Alexandria. Each worshipped his own gods just as he spoke his own language, but he never thought that the gods of his neighbor had no existence, and he was willing to believe that they might be his own gods under another name.... So when Ptolemy Soter decided to compound a god for his new city, he was only taking advantage of this tendency, and giving a local habitation and a name and a statue to sentiments that already existed (*AHG* 20).

Secondly, Forster's explanation of the compounding of Osiris with the bull-god Apis of Memphis to form "Serapis" (which is also spelled with an "a" as in "Sarapis") is conventional enough, though one might take issue with his assertion that Osiris was "the most celebrated of the Egyptian deities" (*AHG* 21). In this context Forster mentions Isis as "wife of Osiris" who "was equally united to his successor Serapis" (*AHG* 162). I dwell on Forster's assessments of the relative positions accorded Isis and Osiris in the Alexandrian world because of a curious discrepancy in his account: while Forster takes scrupulous care to distinguish among shades of theological nuance within Trinitarian controversy in a section entitled "The Spiritual City," he gives Isis short shrift in the first two sections: those of the "Greco-Egyptian period" and the "Christian period." In the former the city was in her glory, and in the latter the Isiac cult posed a serious threat to the eventually triumphant Church. As Sarah Pomeroy writes: "The worshippers of Isis were everywhere, of all ages and sexes. The only segment of society where Isis did not attract devotees was the Roman army, for whom the masculine god Mithras held more appeal" (Pomeroy 219). Or, as we read in Seltman's *Women in Antiquity*, a work Forster would later come to know, there is a speculation that the cult of Isis "might have been the best of the three alter-

---

[21]T. S. Eliot, "Ulysses, Order, and Myth," *The Dial* 75 (1923), 480–83. Indeed, Louise DeSalvo has argued that in *Melymbrosia*, her first extended fiction, Woolf was engaged in "writing a female version of the *Odyssey*, a female reinterpretation of the hero's voyage of initiation." DeSalvo also suggests a connection with Forster when she writes that Woolf had been moved to establish "A View of One's Own" in part through writing her review of his *A Room with a View*, engaged as it is with the travels of a young Englishwoman (xxxix).

natives [Christianity[22] and Mithraism being the other two], since it would have elevated womanhood, instead of ignoring it as in the military homosexual world of the Mithraists, or despising it for its terrible temptation as in the virginal penitential world of the monastic Religious" (Seltman 62, 70, 130 ff. 137, 134).

Forster's reference to representations of the Egyptian god and goddess are scarce. Colossal green granite statues discovered at Nouzha where Callimachus the poet lived are barely mentioned, though one is of Antony as Osiris and the other of Cleopatra as Isis (*AHG* 132, 173). But Forster gives a detailed description of the statue attributed to the Greek sculptor Bryaxis wherein Serapis is shown:

> seated in Greek garments upon a classic throne, his features were those of the bearded Zeus, but softened and benign, indeed he more closely resembled Aesculapius, god of Healing, to whom in a civilised age men naturally turned. The basket on his head showed that he was a harvest god, the three-headed Cerberus stood by his side to show that he represented Pluto, god of the underworld (*AHG* 21).

Gibbon, however, was not so indulgent toward Serapis: "His attributes ... were so imperfectly understood, that it became a subject of dispute, whether he represented the bright orb of day, or the gloomy monarch of the subterranean regions....an honorable and domestic genealogy was provided; and this fortunate usurper was introduced into the throne and bed of Osiris, the husband of Isis..."

Moreover, Gibbon's note emphasizes the greater importance of the position of Isis:

> At Rome Isis and Serapis were united in the same temple. The precedency which the queen assumed, may seem to betray her unequal alliance with the stranger of Pontus [Serapis]. But the superiority of the female sex was established in Egypt as a civil and religious institution, and the same order is observed in Plutarch's *Treatise of Isis and Osiris*; whom he identifies with Serapis (Gibbon II, 603 n39).

---

[22]That Forster held no brief for "the virginal penitential world" himself is demonstrated in his story "The Torque" which Oliver Stallybrass thinks he wrote no later than 1958 ("Introduction," E. M. Forster, *The Life To Come* [New York: W. W. Norton, 1972] xii). This work is biased by misogyny crudely exhibited in the characterization of the consecrated virgin Perpetua who lives on the North African family estate in the late Roman Empire where she makes life uneasy if not unbearable for all around her. In addition to a caricature of antipathy to married sex in the early Church, there is a homosexual fantasy preceded by the fortunate rape by a Goth of Perpetua's younger brother (he interposes his body), whose African heredity is evinced by his thick lips (151–65).

There are no descriptions of statues of Isis. This is a pity, given Forster's sensitive treatment of the Demeter of Cnidus in a 1904 essay[23] and his use of her photograph in his novel *The Longest Journey* (1907). Still, the Ptolemaic coin displays at the modest Greco-Roman museum should have suggested that an important element in Forster's history and guide was missing: the centrality of Isis. Thus a coin of Trajan (no. 750) shows "a temple of Isis in Alexandria, with pylons between which the goddess stands" and, more importantly: no. 1450: "Isis as guardian of the Pharos" (*AHG* 119–20). Additionally, Forster does recognize the site of "a temple to Isis Pharia who watched over the lighthouse" now crossed over by a road leading to the most considerable square in Turkish Town where Nationalist demonstrations take place" (*AHG* 136–37).

In contrast, R. E. Witt, drawing on ancient and recent historians besides the evidence of coin, wall, ruin, and tomb, writes:

> At Alexandria the Sarapeum [the temple complex of Serapis] was hers by obvious divine right, and to her as Isis Pelagia was dedicated the lighthouse on the island of Pharos, one of the Seven Wonders of the World. Such in Alexandrian times was the position of Isis in Egypt. During the same period Isis gained much power over Greek lands, both along the coast of Asia Minor, on the islands of the Archipelago, and on the mainland itself (65).

Isis Denied becomes a powerful aspect of Modernist art—negative space—and that is how she dominates the structure of *Forster's Alexandria: A History and a Guide*. By repressed force she becomes an element as central to Forster's book as the line in the center to Lily Briscoe's painting. Ironically, Isis Denied not only gives form to Forster's vision; but in spite of himself, makes for him "a golden crown, set with pearls, perfumed with musk and camphor, and shining from the East to the West" for Morgan Forster fell in love with Isis's lighthouse, the Pharos. Of it he writes ecstatically:

> to the imagination of contemporaries, the Pharos became Alexandria and Alexandria became the Pharos. Never in the history of architecture, has a secular building been thus worshipped and taken on a spiritual life of its own. It

---

[23]Forster writes of the statue now in the British Museum: "And if, as I believe she is alive, she must know that she had come among people who love her, for all they are so weak-chested and anaemic and feeble-kneed, and who pay her such prosaic homage as they can. Demeter alone among the gods has true immortality. The others continue, perchance, their existence, but are forgotten, because the time came when they could not be loved. But to her, all over the world, rise prayers of idolatry from suffering men as well as suffering women, for she has transcended sex. And Poets too, generation after generation, have sung in passionate incompetence of . . . the wanderings of the Goddess, and her gift to us of corn and tears . . ." ("Cnidus" 176).

beaconed to the imagination, not only to ships at sea, and long after its light was extinguished memories of it glowed in the minds of men (*AHG* 145).[24]

His enthrallment is shown more graphically by his having used the pseudonym "Pharos" to sign the twenty-one essays he wrote for *The Egyptian Mail* from 26 August 1917 to 26 January 1919 (Kirkpatrick 114–17). When Forster gives the reader of his history and guide an imagined vantage point from the heights of Pharos into ancient Alexandria, he, in effect, stands upon the shoulders of Isis Pharia but snubs her along with her numerous adherents—both men and women. As he wrote in "The Consolations of History": "We can recover self-confidence by snubbing the dead" (167).

Putting Forster's conscious[25] and unconscious intentions aside, he had exalted the Pharos.[26] Thereupon Woolf took her cue, making the Pharos and, by extension, Isis Pharia a symbol of the ordering and comforting of art. To see the connection between Forster's exaltation of Pharos from a summarizing description of the Ptolemaic lighthouse of Taposiris, "the first of a chain that stretched from the Pharos of Alexandria all down the African coast to Cyrene":

> It has, like the Pharos, three stages: a square basement, an octagonal central stage and a cylindrical top. On the north, where the octagonal wall of the octagon has fallen, one can see the marks of the staircase by which the wood was carried to the top—a simpler version of the double spiral that ascended the huge Alexandrian building. There can be no doubt that the Taposiris lighthouse was modelled on its gigantic contemporary—scale about 1/10—and it is thus of great importance to archaeologists and historians (*AHG* 207–09).

[24]"A golden crown" as promised by Ibn Dukmak to the man who makes a pilgrimage around Alexandria in the morning, in the second epigraph of Forster's history and guide.

[25]"Never, in the history of architecture, has a secular building been thus worshipped and taken on a spiritual life of its own" (*PP*17).

[26]See, however, "The Obelisk" (probably written in 1939), another of Forster's posthumously published stories wherein a walk to phallic monumental column provides an occasion and excuse for sexual activity a pair of sailors engage in with a vacationing husband and wife previously unknown to them. Only the wife realizes that her spouse was similarly engaged when a vendor says of a picture postcard of the obelisk "It's fallen right over to the landslip upside-down, the tip of it's gone in ever so far, rather laughable" ("The Obelisk," *The Life to Come*" [128]). Despite the sometimes pornographic tone of "The Obelisk," Forster provides literary and mythological references, for the two sailors recall the Dioscuri, the Saviour Gods, who are also known as Castor and Pollux. As Forster describes the inscription on the ancient Pharos: "in great letters of lead was a Greek inscription mentioning the architect, 'Sostratus of Cnidus, son of Dexiphanes, to the Saviour Gods: for sailors.'" Consider also Oliver Stallybrass's observation concerning the stories in this collection: "'a muscle thickened up out of gold' is perhaps the most explicit sexual statement in the book" (xv).

Not only Forster's description of the prototypical Pharos but also the drawing accompanying the text[27] resembles Rhoda's formulation of how Percival's death has adapted her eye to what can be seen through music:

> There is a square; there is an oblong. The players take the square and place it upon the oblong. They place it very accurately; they make a perfect dwelling place. Very little is left outside. The structure is now visible; what is inchoate is here stated; we are not so various or so mean; we have made oblongs and stood them upon squares. This is our triumph; this is our consolation.
>
> The sweetness of this content overflowing runs down the walls of my mind, and liberates understanding. Wander no more, I say; this is the end. The oblong has been set upon the square; the spiral is on the top. We have been hauled over the shingle, down to the sea (*TW* 163).

Recalling Forster's statement that after Alexander's experience at the Siwan Oasis, he no longer wanted to Hellenise the world but to harmonise it, the shape of the beaconing lighthouse of art has harmonised Rhoda's perceptions even in the midst of grief so that, for a while, she is not infected by "the world's slow stain":

> As we lurch down Regent Street, and I am flung upon this woman, upon this man, I am not injured, I am not outraged by this collision. A square stands upon an oblong. Here are mean streets where chaffering goes on in street markets, and every sort of iron rod, bolt and screw is laid out, and people swarm off the pavement, pinching raw meat with thick fingers. The structure is visible. We have made a dwelling place (*TW* 163–64).

Rhoda's soliloquies are reeded with allusions to the matter of Egypt, especially to Isis. Rhoda's name resembles "Rhodes," a well known Isiac cult center (Witt 319 n3). Before the string music which evokes Isis Pharia begins, "the sea-green woman comes to our rescue" (*TW* 162) or, more prosaically, a singer wearing green satin. This figure evokes Isis under the title of Pelagia or Ruler of the Sea, the Egyptians having called the Mediterranean the Great Green. The "rescue" refers to the somnolent state of the audience following lunch, a condition akin to that of devotees who underwent the rite of incubation, a healing process performed within the temple precincts.[28] The metaphor of the singer's hitting the note shifts from that of an arrow shot from a bow (suggestive of Artemis often conflated with Isis) to a curious passage: "An axe has split a tree to the core; the core is warm; sound quivers within the bark" which parallels the penultimate

---

[27]See *AHG*, Fig. 1, 148.

[28]For a discussion of Lucy Swithin's "healing" William Dodge in this context, see my "The Anti-Madonna in the Work and Thought of Virginia Woolf" 103.

item in the appendices of Forster's history and guide: passages from "The Uncanonical Gospels of Egypt." One "From Uncertain Sources (about 200 A.D.)" reads: "Jesus saith: '... Raise the stone and there thou shalt find me; cleave the wood, and there I am'" (*AHG* 236). Rhoda then thinks of a woman in maritime Venice crying "Ah" to her lover while leaning from a window. On a first level the reference wittily suggests the tuning of stringed instruments; on another level of the palimpsest, the window itself refers to the first portion of *To the Lighthouse* entitled "The Window" wherein Mrs. Ramsay, a figure of Isis Pharia, sits enthroned. The concluding image in the paragraph following reference to "the beetle-shaped" violinists (associations with the morning sun and the concept of "becoming" among the Egyptians) harkens back to Mr. Ramsay's springing "lightly, like a young man ... on to the rock" of the lighthouse in the third portion entitled "The Lighthouse" (*TTL* 308). Thus, as Rhoda hears the opening bars she thinks of the sound of the "myriad-tongued grey leaves" of olive trees "when a seafarer, biting a twig between his lips where the many-backed steep hills come down, leaps on the shore."

The next paragraph asks what is beyond simile: "what is the thing that lies beneath the semblance of the thing?" Rhoda will see "the thing," for her eye has been adapted to what is to be seen by the central event of the novel: the death of the hero: "Now that lightning has gashed the tree and the flowering branch has fallen and Percival, by his death, has made me this gift, let me see the thing." The implied Pharos description quoted above is "the thing," or, more precisely, the Pharos is the significant form of art itself, abstracted,[29] whole, and perfect: "The structure is visible. We have made a dwelling place."

In the concluding paragraph of Part Five, Rhoda takes her violets to offer Percival. The choice of verb evokes the most frequently depicted scenes on the walls of Egyptian temples: offerings, often of flowers, made to gods. On the tram

---

[29]An analogous reason for Woolf's choice of the geometrical structure of the Pharos to be significant form is congruent with T. E. Hulme's commentary on why persons and cultures are drawn to "geometric" rather than "vital" art. Consider Rhoda's inability to cross a puddle (*TW* 285), which is related to an incident in Woolf's childhood as an instance of what Worringer calls "space shyness," the inability to cross open spaces being a sign of excessive emotional pain at "the varied confusion and arbitrariness of existence." "In art," writes Hulme, "this state of mind results in a desire to create a certain abstract geometrical shape, which, being durable and permanent shall be a refuge from the flux and impermanence of outside nature." For these reasons Rhoda finds temporary rest by envisioning a geometrical construction while listening to music. For similar reasons Woolf herself may have been attracted by the geometrical art of the Egyptians because "The geometrical line is something absolutely distinct from the messiness, the confusion, and the accidental details of existing things" (Hulme 86–87).

she takes to the river, leading to the sea, Rhoda looks at masts, obelisk-like chimneys, and ships that sail to India where Osiris journeyed and where Percival died. As she walks by the river, she watches "the ships bowling down the tide." With evocations of Isis Sothis (Isis of the Dog Star) soon to follow, the reference to a rapidly rising tide suggests the "solemn inundation festival that was celebrated on the banks of the Nile by priests of Isis with rites that must have existed even in prehistoric days" as well as its Alexandrian version when "Ptolemy III ordained a pan-Egyptian festival on the day when the star of Isis rises, New Year's Day, for the sacred scribes." Isis, "who arises in the star Sothis," is the goddess who "has invented the hieroglyphics and given them their esoteric value." Representations of Isis Sothis or Isis of the Dog Star often show her in the company of the Sothis dog. (Fourth century Roman *vota publica* coins provide examples [Witt, 15; 284 n12; 101; pls. 63, 64].) Woolf conflates this image with the wind-blown image of Isis Pelagia (Isis Ruler of the Sea) and Isis Pharia as Rhoda observes a woman walking "on deck, with a dog barking round her. Her skirts are blown." Before making her offering to Percival, she expresses her desire "to be spent, to be consumed" in imagery of the self-willed metamorphosis of Isis into swallow to search for and revive Osiris (Shelley's "Adonais" is a form of Osiris[30]) with the beating of her wings: "We will gallop together over desert hills where the swallow dips her wings in dark pools and the pillars stand entire" (*TW* 164). The image of pillars standing entire takes us to a Plotinian world, "where for Plato's doctrine that Art 'imitates' natural objects he [Plotinus] substitutes the view that Art and Nature alike impose a structure on Matter in accordance with an inward vision of archetypal Forms."[31]

In *To the Lighthouse* Mrs. Ramsay is a figure of Isis Pharia. Again, Forster's commentary on the Pharos sheds light on Woolf's writing. There was, according to tradition, a mirror at the top of Pharos: "Was it a polished steel reflector for the fire at night or for heliography by day?" (*AHG* 146) Pharos was covered with marble and was between 400 and 500 feet high. Similarly, the lighthouse for James Ramsay as a child was "A silvery, misty-looking tower with a yellow eye"

[30]"Adonis is often taken for Osiris, because the festivals of both were generally begun with mournful lamentations, and finished with a revival of joy as if they were returning to life again" ("Adonis" in *Lemprière*). The Fifteenth Idyll of Theocritus has an example.

[31]Plotinus studied philosophy eleven years in Alexandria under Ammonius Saccas. Although Woolf stated her intention to read Plotinus in 1934 (*D4* 257), I suspect that she was already familiar with his work, given how well he fits with her epistemology. "Plotinus also made important contributions to psychology, particularly in his discussion of problems of perception, consciousness, and memory" as well as to aesthetics as quoted above in the text ("Plotinus," *Oxford Classical Dictionary*, 2nd ed.).

(*TTL* 186). As Mrs. Ramsay finds rest during her moment of being, her moment of identification with the third stroke of the lighthouse beam, so Pharos had associations with refreshment, light, and peace. This can be seen, for example, in Apuleius' *Metamorphoses*. Witt observes of the central character Lucius who had been turned into an ass, an animal abhorrent to Isis:

> After all his tribulations Lucius begs the Queen of Heaven to grant him "rest" (*pausa*) and peace. Here we are involved in the symbolism of the Isiac faith, an extension of earlier ideas, that human life is a pilgrimage or voyage over the sea of life and a return, after pausing at many mansions [abodes of men and women in this life according to the detailed account of Egyptian religion given by Diodorus of Sicily], to the haven of final rest [the tomb which is "the eternal home"], typified by Alexandria with its Sarapeum and its Lighthouse. The Isis of the Pyramid Texts who stands on sentinel duty at the tomb has become the Isis who guides the sailor throughout his travels by land and sea and after all the vicissitudes of life and all its storms brings him safely to his rest at home (Witt 183).

Mr. Ramsay's springing "like a young man" (*TTL* 207) onto the rock of the lighthouse as Lily draws a line in the center of her picture also signifies a rest for them both under the aegis of Mrs. Ramsay as Isis Pharia as I have argued elsewhere.[32] To establish further the Egyptian connection, consider the eponym Rameses, a prominent name for pharaohs and most notably borne by Rameses II. His long reign of 67 years was essentially a peaceful one, but like his namesake, Mr. Ramsay, he was gravely concerned with his own reputation both in his own time and in time to come. Mr. Ramsay's ego is, by implication, of a size with that of Rameses II, who had built on a larger scale than any other pharaoh and had colossi with idealized representations of himself set up throughout Egypt incised with hieroglyphs two inches deep. Repeated inscription has him single-handedly taking on Hittites with greater success than the six hundred cavalry of the Light Brigade had with their relatively impossible odds.[33] Mr. Ramsay's anxiety is not unlike that of Rameses II: the philosopher knows that while his light will be absorbed and then lost in the light of stars of greater magnitude, his fame rests essentially on one small book. Moreover, he lacks the comfort of tangibly inscribed stone—not that that is any guarantee of immortality either, for the shattered colossus now lying near the funerary temple of Rameses II (once having

[32]See my "Anti-Madonna" 100.

[33]See Amelia Edwards' account in *One Thousand Miles up the Nile*. Edwards was a novelist who had founded the Egypt Exploration Fund (Later the Egypt Exploration Society) in 1882, with which James Russell Lowell, Virginia Woolf's quasi-godfather was deeply involved.

stood nearly 60 feet high and having been nearly 1000 tons in weight) probably inspired Shelley's poem, for, once again, Ozymandias was the name of Rameses II in Greek. The metaphoric implications are simply that while Mr. Ramsay is a shattered colossus, Mrs. Ramsay is the lighthouse, a Wonder of the World, as I have argued elsewhere.[34]

Forster's inclusion in both *Alexandria: A History and a Guide* and *Pharos and Pharillon* of Cavafy's poem "The God Abandons Antony"[35] anticipates Mr. Ramsay's desperation as he goes to Mrs. Ramsay for comfort: "Do not lament your fortune that at last subsides, your life's work that has failed, your schemes that have proved illusions." The entire poem provides a parallel to the scene, especially in the notion of "bid[ding] farewell to her, to Alexandria, who is departing." "Go to the window firmly," the persona continues, "and listen with emotion ... listen to the notes ... and bid farewell to her, to Alexandria whom you are losing." Mr. Ramsay, it will be remembered, is in fact about to lose Mrs. Ramsay before whom he "does homage to the beauty of the world" (*TTL* 36) in

[34]See my "Anti-Madonna" 101.

[35]C. P. Cavafy's poem "The God Abandons Antony," trans. George Valassopoulo (*AHG* 104 and *PP* 56).

> "The God Abandons Antony"
>
> When at the hour of midnight
> an invisible choir is suddenly heard passing
> with exquisite music, with voices—
> Do not lament your fortune that at last subsides,
> your life's work that has failed, your schemes that
>   have proved illusions.
> But like a man prepared, like a brave man, bid farewell to her, to Alexandria
> who is departing.
> Above all, do not delude yourself, do not say that
>   it is a dream,
> that your ear was mistaken.
> Do not condescend to such empty hopes.
> Like a man for long prepared, like a brave man,
> like the man who was worthy of such a city.
> go to the window firmly,
> and listen with emotion
> but not with the prayers and complaints of the coward
> (Ah! supreme rapture!)
> listen to the notes, to the exquisite instruments of
>   the mystic choir,
> and bid farewell to her, to Alexandria whom you
>   are losing.
>   C. P. Cavafy

the first section of the novel entitled "The Window."

One might also consider Forster's explanation of his title *Pharos and Pharillon*: "Pharos, the vast and heroic lighthouse that dominated the first city ... Pharillon, the obscure successor of Pharos, which clung for a time to the low rock of Silsileh and then slid unobserved into the Mediterranean" (*PP* 10). Again, Mrs. Ramsay is Isis Pharia, the protector of the lighthouse; not only does she identify herself with the third beam of the lighthouse, but with her green shawl she resembles the Isis Pharia of Alexandrian coinage holding a sail beside Pharos. Mr. Ramsay is, however, of ultimately smaller dimension like Pharillon:

> It was his fate, his peculiarity, whether he wished it or not, to come out thus on a spit of land which the sea is slowly eating away, and there to stand ... alone ... and so to stand on his little ledge facing the dark of human ignorance, how we know nothing and the sea eats away the ground we stand on—that was his fate, his gift (*TTL* 43-44).

A specifically elegiac voice in the novel is that of Lily Briscoe, whose name signifies lotus or water-lily. When she desires "intimacy itself," which is "knowledge" she sits on the floor with her arms around Mrs. Ramsay's knees (a classical position of the suppliant). While Mr. Ramsay is cast in the role of the god-abandoned Antony when he goes to the window where Mrs. Ramsay is seated, the goddess abandons neither Mr. Ramsay nor Lily, for Mrs. Ramsay, in effect, "appears" in the window to Lily enabling her to finish her painting: "I have had my vision" (*TTL* 209) has a double meaning, given the instance of theophany.

While many Isis figures are in Woolf's posthumously published novel, *Between the Acts*, an important Alexandrian correspondence is the paratactic structure of its thirty-three panels with their resemblance to "The Idylls" or "little pictures" of Theocritus. Moreover, like other works of Alexandrian literature such as Appolonius' "epic" of the golden fleece, the panels of Woolf's novel "might be illustrated by terra cotta statues and [carvings on] gems" (*AHG* 35). "History is too much an affair of armies and kings" (*AHG* 37) Forster wrote in praise of Theocritus' Fifteenth Idyll as a corrective; *Between the Acts* leaves out the British Army and concentrates on the queens with a rapid reference to the abdicated Edward VIII as the Duke of Windsor.

Theocritus is known to us in various translations and editions as well as in the original Greek because of libraries. The fact that the most divisive encounter between Woolf and Forster—at least for Woolf—had taken place at a library is unfortunate; but it has symbolic import since, as Woolf tells us, not only was women's access to education limited but also to libraries—collections as well as governing boards. Woolf recounts having "flown into a passion" after meeting Morgan at the London Library where he had told her that the possibility of seat-ing "ladies" on the Library Committee had been considered and rejected while leading her to think that her name might have been involved. The encounter with Forster also recalled a further instance of such prejudice—this time on the part of her father, Sir Leslie Stephen, who, despite having spent otherwise lonely evenings with the one woman who had sat on the Committee, the Widow Green, said of his generous hostess in response to inviting other women to share that honor: "never again. She was too troublesome" (D4 297).

Woolf thereupon channeled her anger by composing a conversation with a hypothetical friend who had turned down a token offer, for which Woolf wrote: "The veil of the temple—which, whether university or cathedral, academic or ecclesiastical, I forget—was to be raised and as an exception she was to be allowed to enter in. But what about my civilisation? for 2,000 years we have done things without being paid for doing them. You can't bribe me now" (D4 298). This work, then entitled "On Being Despised," probably flowed into *Three Guineas*. Woolf's civilization is to be found, I believe, in Alexandria as a city of her mind as well as in what it represented for her—a civilisation most emphatically having libraries open to women as profitably as her father's had been to her.

Given their values, both Woolf and Forster would have ranked the libraries of Alexandria with the Wonders of the Ancient World. The Mother and Daughter (the Great) Libraries are often conflated into one, though the first had been destroyed in Julius Caesar's war; the successor, begun by Cleopatra with help from Antony, exceeded it in holdings as the Ptolomies paid generously for Greek manuscripts considering that the fame of the Library would redound to them. "Here," wrote Forster, "for four hundred years was the most learned spot on the earth" (*AHG* 160).

"'The Library's always the nicest room in the house'" (*BTA* 19), Isa misquotes a guest to arrive at a sentiment apposite to Alexandrian influence. The titles Isa sees on the shelves of the library at Pointz Hall are relevant to a variety of issues, those on antiquities and archaeology, for example, not to mention Keats and *Lemprière's Classical Dictionary* which he knew well. There in the fifth panel of *Between the Acts,* a function of Isis of which she speaks to Lucius (Meta. XI, 6) is attributed to Isa: extending the life of her follower.[36] In this instance Isa's father-in-law, Bart Oliver, is the beneficiary. Woolf deftly alludes to crucifixion, a form of violence the Romans probably borrowed from Carthage, through Lucy Swithin's entering the library carrying a hammer and in her closed

---

[36]Apuleius, *The Golden Ass, Being the Metamorphoses of Lucius Apuleius*, trans. W. Adlington (1566) in the Loeb Classical Library (London: William Heinemann, 1922) 546–47. This translation of the second century A.D. novel was among the Woolfs' books, though Virginia's Latin would have been equal to it.

fist nails. Lucy's entrance merges with Isa's reading a newspaper account of a group rape. These interweavings of historical and contemporary violence are appositely placed in the library at Pointz Hall because of the violence to art and learning committed against the libraries at Alexandria. The seventh panel returns to the library with conversation about Ancient Egypt. It is here that Lemprière is named as an authority.

It is difficult to read scholarly as opposed to propagandistic accounts of the origins of Christianity and not encounter Isis. When Woolf, for example, looked in "the seven volumes of Renan" to illuminate "that dark spot" in her reading: "What happened in Rome?" (*D*4 271), she would have found references to Isis in the context of the journeys of St. Paul and in an extended comparison of Christian worship to Isiac ritual (Renan III, 219; VII, 257ff.). Yet, when the eye is not adapted to what is to be seen, one does not see it. Forster's eye, most notably was not adapted to see Isis, nor because of where his emphasis falls, was his eye adapted to see Cleopatra except as a literary creation. As for the historical Hypatia rather than Hypatia as a symbol of the end of Greek culture in Alexandria, there his vision fails utterly. In view, again, of received opinion and contemporary response to it, Forster's treatment of Hypatia is a misogynist element in his history and guide, though he does recognize the significance of her martyrdom in 415 A.D.

The Mouseion, or the House of the Muses, can with justice be called the first university, and in its ambience Hypatia was head of the Plato Academy in the city that was the center of Neoplatonism as propounded by Plotinus. As Marina Warner points out, "Hypatia represented the highest learning flourishing in direct opposition to Christianity" (Warner 302 n58). Lemprière describes Hypatia as "celebrated for her beauty, her virtues, for great erudition, and her writings on algebra."[37] In a contemporary classical dictionary (Oxford, 2nd ed.), G. J. Toomer describes her as "learned in mathematics, astronomy, and philosophy ... she revised the third book of her father Theon's *Commentary on the Almagest*. Commentaries by her on Diophantus and Apollonius are lost." Gibbon observes that "her article in the Lexicon of Suida is curious and original." His comment that "In the bloom of beauty and in the maturity of wisdom, the modest maid refused her lovers and instructed her disciples" invites comparison with Jane Harrison's preference for a mode of living that enables a woman to think and write in spacious surroundings of libraries and gardens, that is, to lead a joyous

---

[37]Woolf might have chosen the given name of Katharine Hilbery in *Night and Day* in view of Hypatia's connection with algebra and astronomy. The legend of St. Catherine of Alexandria, which might simply have absorbed material from Hypatia's biography, emphasizes her learning and her ability to refute error.

life of the mind (Harrison 88–89). Gibbon attributes her murder to the jealousy of Cyril, patriarch of Alexandria. "The title of *saint*," he observes, "is a mark that his opinions and his party have finally prevailed." Thus Cyril "prompted or accepted, the sacrifice of a virgin" as he beheld "with jealous eye, the gorgeous train of horses and slaves [of those persons most illustrious of rank or merit] who crowded the door of her academy."

Although Gibbon declared that "The murder of Hypatia has imprinted an indelible stain on the character and religion of Cyril of Alexandria," the Reverend Charles Kingsley not only chose her for the subject of a novel,[38] but probably based his account of her death on Gibbon's: "Hypatia was torn from her chariot, stripped naked, dragged to the church, and inhumanly butchered by the hands of Peter the reader and a troop of savage and merciless fanatics; her flesh was scraped from her bones with sharp oyster shells." To the last point he adds a footnote: "I am ignorant, and the assassins were probably regardless, whether their victim was yet alive" (Gibbon IV, 117–20 [Ch. 47]). Kingsley expanded upon Gibbon's "oyster shells ... plentifully strewed on the sea beach before the Caesareum": "Why did the mob ... pour down upon the beach, and return brandishing flints, shells, fragments of pottery?" (Kingsley 414). Forster lets the murder weapons be simply "tiles," though Gibbon disputed that idea in the eighteenth century. Moreover, he ignores the tradition that she was killed in a Christian church (*AHG* 56). The mode of Hypatia's death resembles the aftermath of Osiris' death when he was torn into pieces that Isis would search for, find, and reassemble. It is possible that the Christian fanatics chose such a death for a feared leader whom they regarded as an enemy as a further attack on "pagan" ideas. Marina Warner summarizes the convincing case that is made for the migration of features of Hypatia's biography to the legend of St. Catherine of Alexandria, citing Sylvester Houédard's suggestion that the "whirring blades on the Catherine wheel are the transmuted images of the oyster shells that killed Hypatia" (Warner 302 n58).

Still, Hypatia's death signified the end of what Forster valued most. He prefaces his brief tribute—a tribute not to her but to what the time of her death represented to him as a Hellenist—with an unfortunate disclaimer: "She is not a great figure. But with her the Greece that is a spirit expired—the Greece that tried to discover truth and create beauty and that had created Alexandria." More tellingly, Forster must diminish her by suggesting that all she did was *teach* mathematics, by denying her the fleeting charm of youth at the distance of 1500 years, and finally by calling into question her gifts as a philosopher by citing the

---

[38]Charles Kingsley, *Hypatia: New Foes with an Old Face* (1853; rpt. New York: A. L. Burt Company, n.d.).

lack of received texts. He writes: "The achievements of Hypatia, like her youth-fulness, have been exaggerated; she was a middle-aged lady who taught mathematics at the Mouseion and though she was a philosopher too we have no record of her doctrines" (*AHG* 41, 55–56).

Although Forster preferred to think of Hypatia as middle-aged, it is not unlikely in view of her accomplishments and established reputation. An irony lies in the intensification of Woolf's anger at misogyny that came with age,[39] given that Forster had already felt uneasy around the young Virginia. This angu-larity—that of a magnifying glass held to catch the rays of the sun—influenced the cluster of mature women that form the motif of Isa in *Between the Acts*—Isa, Lucy Swithin, Mrs. Manresa, Mrs. Sands, and Miss LaTrobe—a motif which is anticipated in fifty-year-old Mrs. Ramsay in *To the Lighthouse*. Mrs. Ramsay's son James was born in her middle years even if we are to take "fifty" as an approximation. Mrs. Ramsay's eighth maternity at forty-four is of a pattern with Isa's recent delivery of the baby[40] in the perambulator and her possible impreg-nation immediately beyond the open ending of the novel. While it is true that Woolf herself was writing in her middle years—forty-three when she began *To the Lighthouse*; fifty-six when she began *Between the Acts*—other factors are likely to have contributed to the ages, roles, and positions of women under the aegis of Isis in her last novel.

One, I suggest, is Forster's condescending treatment of Cleopatra in his his-tory and guide ("Cleopatra is of course a meaner figure than Alexander the Great."), especially in his assumption that women lose what charm they have with passing years:

> She was captured and taken to Octavian, with whom even in Antony's life-time she had been intriguing, for the courtesan in her persisted. She appeared this time not in a carpet nor yet a barge, but upon a sofa, in the seductive negli-gence of grief. The good young man was shocked. Realising that he intended to lead her in his triumph in Rome, realising too that she was now thirty-nine years old, she killed herself (*AHG* 29-30).

[39]See Marcus, "Art and Anger" for an insightful discussion of Woolf's "growth into an angry old woman."

[40]As the name of Isa's son George is evocative of recent English kings, so the infant daughter's name Caro (Caroline) evokes English queens during the earlier Georgian period. That Egyptian monarchs were thought to derive life and power from Isis is graph-ically represented in temple iconography by adult pharaohs suckling at her breast.

Isa, we are told, is the age of the century, which makes her thirty-nine, but unlike Cleopatra she neither shocks a "good young man,"[41] nor does she kill herself. Instead Isa, as a manifestation of Isis—in company with Mrs. Manresa, Lucy, Miss LaTrobe and Sands, the cook—is that of the "force which produced living things and therefore enjoys immortality" (Witt 18).

Isis, through Woolf, is triumphant in matters both great and small. While E. M. Forster displayed a consistent bias against women and the idea of women, his friend and peer Virginia Woolf took matters in hand. Not only did she recognize the pullings to the side in his work, but she enriched the weaving of her own texts through the inclusion of Alexandrian threads.

But there is more to be addressed: the exoskeleton or exterior structure of *Between the Acts*. Thus, the method of Forster's *Alexandria*—its division into a history and guide, especially since his history "attempts (after the fashion of a pageant)[42] to marshal the activities of Alexandria during the two thousand two hundred fifty years of her existence" including the career of the last of the Ptolomies, Cleopatra (*AHG* xix)—bears comparison with Woolf's last novel wherein she not only provides a pageant of English history and literature but also makes use of an external guide named Figgis who, despite his having written in 1833, would have found little change either in topography or in constituency on the day of the Pointz Hall pageant in June of 1939 (*BTA* 52). In 1935 Woolf wrote: "We suggest a comic guide to Bloomsbury by Morgan & he nibbles" (*D4* 289). *The Waves*, *To the Lighthouse*, and *Between the Acts* are surreptitious guides to Alexandrian elements in E. M. Forster's work as well as to the misogyny of E. M. Forster himself, as I have shown.

A further connection between Forster and Woolf is the pageant at the center of *Between the Acts*, related as it is to two village pageants he had written: "The Abinger Pageant,"[43] first performed on July 14, 1934 in aid of the Abinger Church Preservation Fund with music by Woolf's cousin Ralph Vaughan

[41]Voltaire called Octavius-Augustus "that debauched murderer and coward," *Philosophical Dictionary*, trans. Peter Gay, 2 vols. (New York: Basic Books, 1962), 1, 78–79.

[42]Forster suggests the same pattern for "A serious history of Alexandria" that "has yet to be written . . " In this prognostication, however, he places "After the fashion of a pageant first" in his "Conclusion" to *Pharos and Pharillon* (98) which was published in 1923, the year following the publication of *AHG*. Forster's pattern was astute, for it echoes the visual drama of the celebration of the construction of the Pharos: "For the building of the lighthouse (279 B.C.) was connected with an elaborate dynastic program known as the 'As-good-as Olympic Games,' and with a mammoth pageant which passed through the streets of Alexandria, regardless of imagination and expense" (*PP* 18).

[43]E. M. Forster, "The Abinger Pageant," *Abinger Harvest*, 349–63.

Williams, and "England's Pleasant Land," originally produced at Milton Court, Westcott, Surrey July 10, 1938, published by the Hogarth Press in 1940. The latter "play was written for the Dorking and Leith Hill District Preservation Society, and its Programme included an account of the various Acts which Parliament has passed for the preservation of the countryside, and a list of the various preservation societies."[44] Again, Vaughan Williams had composed the music.

The emphasis in each instance is on preservation of the countryside, especially provision for trees as synechdochical of care for the land. In "Abinger Pageant" this nurturance is expressed through "The Woodman" who is the narrator. Although Forster had been presented with a scenario—"he was to write the speeches and program notes"—he was taken with the idea put forward by the producer Tom Harrison, to whom the Hogarth Press edition is dedicated, "that the pageant should stress the theme of woods and trees." Indeed Forster thought of the work as a "Pageant of Trees." This theme was to have special poignance for Forster who was removed from his aunt's house, West Hackhurst at Abinger, by order of the landowning gentry for the convenience of a relative of theirs. He also turned Piney Copse over to the National Trust to outwit his "enemies." Piney Copse was a wood he had bought and commemorated in the essay "My Wood." Forster moved out at seventy-eight angrily and bitterly, especially because another plan to return to Stevenage, the site of his childhood home of happiest memory, the house he commemorates in *Howards End*, was thwarted by the Labour Government's recently having declared it the site of a "new town." He then saw himself as victim to "feudalism" and "socialism" (Furbank 2: 198, 264). The well-being, indeed the happiness, of his old age was made possible by a hypothetical return to Ancient Alexandria—if not the House of the Muses, the next best thing and what, mercifully, reality had to offer was his becoming a resident Honorary Fellow in King's College, Cambridge in rooms that had been occupied by Nathaniel Wedd, the teacher of Athenian persuasion, who had encouraged him to become a writer. In retrospect it was Wedd who had directed him to his course in life.

The other pageant, "England's Pleasant Land," entirely of Forster's own devising, is more universal though it is tied to fairly specific historic events such as the settling effects of the Domesday Book, disruptions caused by the enforcement of the Enclosure Acts in 1760, the labourers' revolt in 1830, and the imposition of death duties. The latter take effect in the play in 1899 causing the hereditary gentry to lose the estate. The worst time depicted is when the lands are sold to a developer whose "fully established" chaos is taken over by officials planning regional development. The narrator is a "Recorder." As Forster wrote,

[44]E. M. Forster, *England's Green and Pleasant Land: A Pageant Play* (London: The Hogarth Press, 1940) 11.

"The play is not about any particular person. It is about the land ..." In an introductory note Forster refers to rain during the performance and "aeroplanes" which "messed about overhead and anticipated the final desolation."[45] In *Between the Acts* Woolf was to make rain serve a mythic purpose during the pageant as it ran down Isa's cheeks evoking the tears of Isis over her loss of Osiris. These tears symbolically cause the river to overflow and bring an end to a wasteland desolation of drought. And during Woolf's pageant airplanes also signaled the incipient Second World War.

Incantatory use of local names is common to both Forster's pageant and Woolf's novel. While Forster frequently names trees in "Abinger Pageant" to give a sense of chronology, Woolf uses trees to suggest architecture echoing the style of the Greco-Egyptian city; for example, "The other trees were magnificently straight. They were not too regular; but regular enough to suggest columns in a church; in a church without a roof; in an open-air cathedral ..." (*BTA* 64–65). Compare this passage with Forster's statement that the Pharos "stood in a colonnaded court" (*AHG* 145). Trees, as we have seen, focussed the movement of "Abinger Pageant." One might discuss *Between the Acts* as an arboreal pageant given the climactic focus on the starling-pelted tree which Miss LaTrobe stands by which becomes a whirring buzzing Isiac sistrum as she conceives her new play, a play that sings of the beginning.

Woolf's achievement in transforming Forster's Greco-Egyptian gold into the structures and decorations of Alexandria as a city of her mind would not have been possible unless she had respected Forster as a fellow artist and fit contender. That he represented what she was always to feel as a lack and painful loss in her own artistic development—a university education—strengthened her desire to contend with him on his own ground but in her own contrasting mode.

[45]Forster, *England's Green and Pleasant Land* 15, 14.

Works Cited

Apuleius. *The Golden Ass, Being the Metamorphoses of Lucius Apuleius.* Trans. W. Adlington. 1566. Loeb Classical Library. London: William Heinemann.

DeSalvo, Louise. "'A View of One's Own': Virginia Woolf and the Making of *Melymbrosia.*" In Louise A. DeSalvo, ed. *Melymbrosia by Virginia Woolf. An Early Version of The Voyage Out.* New York: New York Public Library, 1982.

Dodds, Erik Robertson. "Plotinus." *Oxford Classical Dictionary,* 2nd ed.

Eliot, T. S. "Ulysses, Order, and Myth." *The Dial* 75 (1923): 480-83.

Forster, E. M. *Alexandria: A History and A Guide.* 1922. New York: Doubleday, Anchor, 1961.

——. "Cnidus." *Abinger Harvest.* New York: Harcourt, Brace, 1936.

——. "The Consolations of History." *Abinger Harvest.*

——. "Egypt." *The Government of Egypt, Recommendations by a Committee of the International Section of Labour Research Department.* 1920.

——. *England's Green and Pleasant Land: A Pageant Play.* London: Hogarth P, 1940.

——. Preface to *The Greek View of Life, Goldsworthy Lowes Dickinson and Related Writings.* Appendix C. 213-14.

——. *Goldsworthy Lowes Dickinson and Related Writings.* 1934. Ed. Oliver Stallybrass. Abinger Edition. Vol. 13. London: Edward Arnold, 1973.

——. *The Life to Come and Other Short Stories.* Ed. Oliver Stallybrass. New York: W. W. Norton, 1972.

——."The Obelisk." *The Life to Come.*

——. *Pharos and Pharillon.* 1923. 3rd Ed. London: Hogarth P, 1926.

——. "The Torque." *The Life to Come and Other Stories.* Ed. Oliver Stallybrass. London: Edward Arnold, 1972. 151-65.

Edwards, Amelia. *A Thousand Miles up the Nile.* 1877. London: Century, 1982.

Furbank, P. N. *E. M. Forster: A Life.* 2 vols. London: Secker & Warburg, 1977.

Gardiner, A. H. "The House of Life." *Journal of Egyptian Archaeology* 24 (1938): 157-79.

Gibbon, Edward. *The History of the Decline and Fall of the Roman Empire.* Ed. J. B. Bury. London: Methuen, 1900-1913.

Haller, Evelyn. "The Anti-Madonna in the Work and Thought of Virginia Woolf." *Virginia Woolf: Centennial Essays.* Eds. Elaine Ginsberg and Laura Gottlieb. Troy, New York: Whitston, 1983. 93-109.

——. "Isis Unveiled: Virginia Woolf's Use of Egyptian Myth." *Virginia Woolf: A Feminist Slant.* Ed. Jane Marcus. Lincoln: U of Nebraska P, 1983. 109-31.

Harrison, Jane. *Reminiscences of a Student's Life.* London: Hogarth P, 1925.

Hulme, T. E. *Speculations: Essays on Humanism and the Philosophy of Art.* 1924. Ed. Herbert Read. London: 1924; rpt., New York: Harvest Books, n.d.

Kingsley, Charles. *Hypatia: New Foes with an Old Face.* 1853. New York: A. L. Burt, n.d.

Kirkpatrick, B. J. *A Bibliography of E. M. Forster.* 2nd ed. The Soho Bibliographies. London: Rupert Hart-Davies, 1968.

Lemprière's Classical Dictionary of Proper Names Mentioned in Ancient Authors with a Chronological Table, new ed. 1788. London: Routledge & Kegan Paul Ltd, 1972.

Marcus, Jane. "Enchanted Organs, Magic Bells: *Night and Day* as Comic Opera." *Virginia Woolf: Revaluation and Continuity.* Ed. Ralph Freedman. Berkeley: U of California P, 1980. 97-122.

——. "Art and Anger," *Feminist Studies* 4.1 (1978): 69-98.

Pomeroy, Sarah B. *Goddesses, Whores, Wives, and Slaves: Women in Classical Antiquity.* New York: Schocken Books, 1975.

Renan, Ernest. *The History of the Origins of Christianity.* 7 vols. London: Mathieson, n.d.

Rosenbaum, S. P. "The Philosophical Realism of Virginia Woolf." *English Literature and British Philosophy.* Ed. S. P. Rosenbaum Chicago: U of Chicago P, 1971. 316-56.

Seltman, Charles. *Women in Antiquity.* New York: St. Martin's P, 1956.

Stallybrass, Oliver. Introduction. *Goldsworthy Lowes Dickinson and Related Writings.* By E. M. Forster. New York: W. W. Norton, 1972. xi-xix.

Stone, Wilfred. *The Cave and the Mountain: A Study of E. M. Forster.* Stanford: Stanford UP, 1966.

Toomer, G. J. "Hypatia." *Oxford Classical Dictionary.* 2nd ed.

Voltaire. *Philosophical Dictionary.* Trans. Peter Gay. 2 vols. New York: Basic Books, 1962.

Warner, Marina. *Joan of Arc: The Image of Female Heroism.* New York: Knopf, 1981.

Witt, R. E. *Isis in the Greco-Roman World.* Ithaca: Cornell UP, 1971.

Woolf, Virginia. *Between the Acts.* 1941. San Diego: Harcourt Brace Jovanovich, n.d.

——. *The Diary of Virginia Woolf.* Ed. Anne Olivier Bell. 5 vols. New York: Harcourt Brace Jovanovich, 1977-1984.

——. *To the Lighthouse.* 1927. San Diego: Harcourt Brace Jovanovich, 1989.

——. *The Voyage Out.* New York: Harcourt, Brace, & World, n.d.

Thinking Back Through Our Others: Rereading Sterne and Resisting Joyce in *The Waves*

Miriam L. Wallace

Much has been written since the 1970s about Virginia Woolf's legacy for feminist writers, critics, and activists.[1] Her famous injunction in *A Room of One's Own*, that a woman who writes "thinks back through her mothers," tells part of the story of Woolf's own writing processes and literary lineage, but not the whole story (*AROO* 97). Feminist critics have traced Woolf's imaginative debt to female antecedents, from neglected women writers to ancestral figures; however, this is only part of the heritage of Woolf's work.[2] Feminist critics need also to explore and explain Woolf's relation to her male predecessors, especially since much of Woolf's writing engages with her literary antecedents and male contemporaries as important sources of inspiration and/or difference. Juliet Dusinberre has made an important effort to trace Woolf's own rendering of and creation of the "Renaissance" as a period for her own inspiration, while critics such as Beth Rosenberg, Jeanne Dubino, Elena Gualtieri, and Hermione Lee have begun to trace Woolf's debt to and experiments with the essay genre.[3] Much

---

[1] See for example Elaine Showalter, *A Literature of Their Own: British Women Novelists from Brontë to Lessing*; Jane Marcus, *Virginia Woolf and the Languages of Patriarchy* and "Thinking Back Through Our Mothers" in *New Feminist Essays*, 1-30; Michèle Barrett, "Introduction" to *Virginia Woolf: Women and Writing*, 1-35; Madeline Moore, *The Short Season Between Two Silences: The Mystical and the Political in the Novels of Virginia Woolf*; Brenda Silver's Introduction to *Virginia Woolf's Reading Notebooks* and "Cultural Critique" in *The Gender of Modernism*, 646-58; Hermione Lee, *The Novels of Virginia Woolf*; Pamela Caughie, *Virginia Woolf and Postmodernism*; and Juliet Dusinberre, *Virginia Woolf's Renaissance*. An excellent overview of key feminist approaches to Woolf's work and life is given in Laura Marcus's "Woolf's Feminism and Feminism's Woolf," in *The Cambridge Companion to Virginia Woolf*, 209-44.

[2] See Jane Marcus, "The Niece of a Nun: Virginia Woolf, Caroline Stephen, and the Cloistered Imagination," 7-36, and "Thinking Back Through Our Mothers." See also Ellen Hawkes, "Woolf's 'Magical Garden of Women,'" 31-60. Juliet Dusinberre argues that "Woolf believed, as did T. S. Eliot, that writers need a tradition and that tradition nourishes the individual talent. But what was for him ... a lucid interaction between the voices of the past and the individual voice of the poet in the present, for Woolf was complicated by the fact that the voices of the past were predominantly male voices" (5).

[3] See Jeanne Dubino's "Rambling Through *A Room of One's Own* vs. Marching Through I. A. Richards' *Practical Criticism*," Dubino and Beth Carole Rosenberg's edited collection *Virginia Woolf and the Essay*, Elena Gualtieri's *Virginia Woolf's Essays: Sketching the Past*, and Hermione Lee, "Virginia Woolf's Essays," 91-108.

yet remains to be done in exploring how Woolf both borrowed from earlier literary "masters" for her own work and revised those master texts and literary
history in so doing.[4] As Hermione Lee argues, until quite recently, "her stylish,
formal, and at first sight conventional-looking appreciations of male authors—
Gibbon, Montaigne, Boswell, Hardy, James—were harder for her feminist
admirers to deal with, and great tracts of her essay writing fell into 'benign neglect'" ("Essays" 94). This essay is particularly interested in the ways in which
Woolf borrowed from and revised her formidable literary antecedent Laurence
Sterne in her essays and her novels. Rather than simply a matter of tracing
Sterne's or his period's influence and arguing that feminist critics need to pay
greater attention to this problematic but complex figure, I argue that Woolf's
revisioning of Sterne's significance is an important window into her own efforts
to create herself as a significant figure in English letters, and reveals her technique of oblique quoting as an implicitly feminist strategy of reading.

The range of Virginia Woolf's writing—fiction, diaries, letters, and literary
criticism—echoes eighteenth-century literary production not only in its generic
breadth, but in the conjunction of personal impressions with public statements
about the value and quality of art. Both Woolf's critical work and her fiction
explore the tensions between social concerns and individual artistry, political
change and artistic style. As writer and critic she asks how is human experience
most effectively and most truthfully represented through art, and to what ends?
The authority of personal experience is granted in Woolf's own diaries and letters, but as she frequently notes, is notoriously difficult to share. This is a
problem at the center of many of her statements about the value of art; it was also
a pressing concern inherited from eighteenth-century British thought.
Eighteenth-century British literature after about 1740 developed "sensibility" as
a mode for exploring and representing personal connection, social critique and
psychological interiority.[5] An emphasis on personal feeling and narrating indi-

[4]There has been some recent work on Woolf's relation to earlier, canonical male writ-
ers, including Dusinberre's 1999 *Virginia Woolf's Renaissance* and Rosenberg's 1995
Virginia Woolf and Samuel Johnson: Common Readers. In "Virginia Woolf's Postmodern
Literary History" Rosenberg argues that "there has been remarkably little work done on
Virginia Woolf's relationship to literary history" (1113), citing Alison Booth's *Greatness
Engendered: George Eliot and Virginia Woolf*, Dusinberre's *Virginia Woolf's Renaissance*,
Alice Fox's *Virginia Woolf and the Literature of the English Renaissance*, Beverly Ann
Schlack's *Continuing Presences: Virginia Woolf's Use of Literary Allusion*, Perry Meisel's
The Absent Father: Virginia Woolf and Walter Pater, and her own *Virginia Woolf and
Samuel Johnson*.

[5]See Janet Todd, *Sensibility: An Introduction* and G. J. Barker-Benfield, *The Culture
of Sensibility: Sex and Society in Eighteenth-Century Britain* for good introductory discussions of the problems and possibilities of eighteenth-century sensibility.

vidual experience marked this rise in the popularity of sensibility, along with a diminishing emphasis on the elite educated wit privileged by the Augustans. Moreover, the possibilities and limitations of literary sensibility are closely tied to late eighteenth-century British political radicalism, marked by sympathy with the principles of the French Revolution, emerging abolitionist and anti-imperialist sentiment, and not incidentally, the emergence of early feminism. Early British feminists such as Mary Wollstonecraft and Mary Hays struggled with the radical power of sensibility to recognize emotional knowledge and personal experience as socially meaningful and the concomitant problem that feminine "sensibilities" could be used as a rationale for dismissing women's capacity for reason and political agency. Likewise, Woolf struggled with the tensions between feminist attention to the specificity of women's experiences and emotional knowledge and feminism's historical commitment to the Enlightenment individual and its "rights." Because feminine sensibility became so problematic from the late eighteenth-century and was transmuted into Victorian sentimental femininity, Woolf needed another location from which to imagine the conjunction of aesthetics and politics. Curiously, Laurence Sterne's *The Life and Opinions of Tristram Shandy, Gentleman* (1759-67) became one such location.

Eighteenth-century writing's historical distance from Woolf's own period also enabled her writerly insertion of herself into literary history. By associating her work with eighteenth-century novelistic inclusiveness, Woolf could mine nineteenth-century critical judgements about these literary periods without being subservient to the moral imperatives under which nineteenth-century critics such as her father, Leslie Stephen, had worked. This allowed Woolf-as-critic to use what came before her without subscribing to its ideological judgements. Woolf's relation as a writer to her modernist male colleagues was also fraught, as her essays and diary entries on the works of E. M. Forster, T. S. Eliot, and James Joyce reveal. Eighteenth-century and Elizabethan writers often served her as critical predecessors with whom she could engage both critically and responsively; "[Woolf] stated that she used the past for a purpose, as an empowering model for herself as a woman writer, and particularly as a writer ... of criticism and literary history" (Dusinberre 1).[6] This kind of inter-literary conversation is the model for Woolf's critical and literary work more generally, and is at heart a feminist model of inclusive digression. As Adrienne Rich puts it, "re-vision—the act of

[6]See also Beth C. Schwartz, "Thinking Back Through Our Mothers: Virginia Woolf Reads Shakespeare," 721-46.

looking back, of seeing with fresh eyes, of entering an old text from a new critical direction—is for women more than a chapter in a cultural history: it is an act
of survival" (35). Reading Woolf's own oeuvre is an exercise in following
echoes and repeated metaphors, much as she herself read across literary periods
for shared concerns of style and form. The reader of Woolf is well paid by noting the recurrence of images (the wild goose, a flapping curtain), colors
(amethystine purple, a black shape), and "orts, scaps and fragments" of citations
throughout her works ("fear no more the heat o' the sun," "we perished each
alone") in ways which accrete significance as the reader reads and rereads among
her novels and other writings. Finally, her fiction's extraordinarily complex dia-
logic relation to literary history argues for a more embedded reading and critical
assessment of Woolf's own oeuvre than restricting her to the canon of "modernist" British writers or to the counter-canon of "women" writers alone can
offer.

Sterne and Woolf

    Woolf's work, both critical and fictional, was deeply in conversation with
the eighteenth century generally: the "Common Reader" is borrowed from
Samuel Johnson, and Woolf's essays for the series invoke key figures of the
1700s including, but not limited to, Oliver Goldsmith, Eliza Haywood, Frances
Burney, Edward Gibbon, Aphra Behn, Daniel Defoe, William Addison, Jane
Austen, Jonathan Swift, Horace Walpole, Samuel Johnson, and Hester Lynch
Thrale Piozzi. The figure of Laurence Sterne recurs particularly frequently in
Woolf's essays; Sterne functions as a central figure in an early essay, "Sterne"
(1909) and a late essay, "The *Sentimental Journey*" (1932); and as a transitional
figure in important essays on the state of fiction generally, "Modern Fiction"
(1919), "The Narrow Bridge of Art" (1927), "Art of Fiction" (1927), and
"Phases of Fiction" (1929). Several later essays also focus on more obscure figures surrounding Sterne: "Eliza and Sterne" (1922) focuses on the object of
Sterne's late romantic obsession, Eliza Fowler, while "Sterne's Ghost" (1925)
tells the story of nineteenth-century Eliza Mathews and the room in which she
wrote herself to death (Woolf, "Eliza and Sterne," *E*3 100-4, and "Sterne's
Ghost," *E*3 94-9). Seemingly an unlikely source of inspiration for a modernist
feminist writer, *Tristram Shandy* bears a special relationship to Woolf's writing
and to her project to create an active feminist reader. In fact, the essays suggest
that *Tristram* stood as a central touchstone for Woolf as a writer in its stylistic
innovations and its attention to the practices of reading and writing.
    Many of the concerns Woolf represented as Sterne's were also central con-
cerns of her own work. The complex interaction with literary history which
informs all of Woolf's writing bears a particular debt to the problems and partial

solutions worked out in *Tristram*; *The Waves* is a specific site for intertextual conversation with both the history of the novel and with Woolf's oeuvre itself. Woolf's project in *The Waves*, to net "the fin" of her vision, is allied with what she had represented elsewhere as Sterne's project, to capture life and the mind through artistic form (*D4* 10; *D3* 113).[7] The novel, she argues, is the literary form which will become the site of artistry, balancing material reality (prose) with spirit (poetry). In her essay of 1927, "The Narrow Bridge of Art," Woolf described a new form of writing, imagined as deriving from the novel but filling the place formerly restricted to poetry. Seeing prose as the direction of the future, she argues that the novel, as a cannibalistic form, will be the site for new modern literary form:

> We shall be forced to invent new names for the different books which masquerade under this one heading. And it is possible that there will be among the so-called novels one which we shall scarcely know how to christen. It will be written in prose, but in prose which has many of the characteristics of poetry. It will have something of the exaltation of poetry, but much of the ordinariness of prose. It will be dramatic, and yet not a play. It will be read, not acted. By what name we are to call it is not a matter of very great importance. What is important is that this book which we see on the horizon may serve to express some of those feelings which seem at the moment to be balked by poetry pure and simple and to find the drama equally inhospitable to them. ("Narrow Bridge," 224)

Woolf's vision here of a new literary form "on the horizon," a new "book," echoes both her own project in *The Waves* and her assessment of *Tristram* as midway between prose and poetry in "Phases of Fiction."[8] This project is both indebted to Sterne's model and moves beyond it, as Woolf imagines a form which will enable her to construct feminine subjectivity which is both grounded in material conditions and attentive to the poetic excess of the human mind. Representing her own project and the central project of literature as the conjunction of prose and poetry, the material and the psychological/spiritual, Woolf negotiates the tensions between a materialist politics and an allegiance to formal

[7]On September 30, 1926, Woolf first records the image of the fin as the emblem of a new book: "One sees a fin passing far out." (*D3* 113), and later on February 7, 1931, she records the capture of that idea with the completion of *The Waves*: "I have netted that fin in the waste of water which appeared to me over the marshes out of my window at Rodmell when I was coming to an end of *To the Lighthouse*" (*D4* 10).

[8]See for an important discussion of "Phases of Fiction" and its strategy of reading for pleasure Anne E. Fernald's "Pleasure and Belief in 'Phases of Fiction.'"

artistry. Her efforts to conjoin the two in her fiction and her criticism is a mark of a specifically feminist project, to attend to the fluidity of the internal psychological self without erasing the material conditions which impinge upon that self. Woolf called her effort in *The Waves* "a play-poem," and recorded her plan to write a new book which is not a novel, but rather a combination of poetry and drama in the shape of prose fiction(*D*3 128). This conjoining of narrative and poetic forms replicates formally her continuing concern with attending to the double demands of human, particularly women's, lives and experience. Sterne's success in balancing the crass and the poetic, sentimentality and bawdiness, sensibility and Augustan wit, serves as a formal model for her project, despite his novel's overtly misogynistic content.

Woolf argues for a "poetic play" which can provide a larger frame than "personal relationships" offer: "We long for some more impersonal relationships. We long for ideas, for dreams, for imagination, for poetry" ("Narrow Bridge" 224-5). The focus of prose fiction on individual and private emotions and on chronological events is not fully adequate to the task of great literature both to record and to guide the self-construction of subjects in the world. Engaged art must combine the individual-personal with the larger-than-personal, the figurative with the formal and the political. This is at bottom a critique of the individualist focus of liberal politics and a perceptive recognition of the limitations of the Victorian novel's allegiance to formal realism for effecting cultural change. Without a larger view, fiction loses some of its power to inspire and create ideals, hence to theorize its concerns rather than merely to replicate the conditions of its own creation. Woolf-the-critic seeks a form which combines psychological inspiration with a larger view of the condition of humankind, connecting the interior self (the personal) with the exterior world (the political):

> [T]he variety of novel which will be written in time to come will take on some of the attributes of poetry. It will give the relations of man to nature, to fate; his imagination; his dreams. But it will also give the sneer, the contrast, the question, the closeness and complexity of life. It will take the mould of that queer conglomeration of incongruous things—the modern mind. Therefore it will clasp to its breast the precious perogatives of the democratic art of prose; its freedom, its fearlessness, its flexibility. ("Narrow Bridge" 225-6)

Woolf cautions that prose, however, cannot "say the simple things which are so tremendous" nor "leap at one spring at the heart of its subject as the poet does" ("Narrow Bridge" 226). She calls the poetic moment within works of prose a "purple patch," arguing that it is not the mere presence of the poetic which is disjunctive, but the patchiness of it ("Narrow Bridge" 226). This tension between prose and poetry stands as the great challenge to modern literature in Woolf's argument, and she solves it by turning to Sterne and the eighteenth-century.

Woolf's model of successful poetry in prose is Sterne's *Tristram Shandy*: She writes that "It [*Tristram Shandy*] is a book full of poetry, but we never notice it; it is a book stained deep purple, which is yet never patchy. Here though the mood is changing always, there is no jerk, no jolt in that change to waken us from the depth of consent and belief" ("Narrow Bridge" 227). Sterne's novel functions for Woolf as an example of artistry balancing two different impulses effectively. Twentieth-century critics have also debated whether to read *Tristram* as more properly part of an Augustan tradition of satire and learned wit with sentiment functioning primarily ironically, or as part of the mid-century novel tradition with a strong component of sentimentality.[9] Woolf's version of this debate situates *Tristram* as an example of formal style which contains the more general impulses of poetry and puts them into dialogue with the earthiness of everyday prose. She recognizes that to choose either reading exclusively is to lose the essence of the work itself. The delicate balance which art can achieve is a power which Woolf clearly valued, and which sheds light on her own insistence throughout her writing both that artistic style matters deeply and that material reality impinges upon art's possibilities. In "The Narrow Bridge" Woolf comments:

> In the same breath Sterne laughs, sneers, cuts some indecent ribaldry, and passes on to a passage like this:
>
> > Time wastes too fast: every letter I trace tells me with what rapidity life follows my pen; the days and hours of it more precious—my dear Jenny—than the rubies about thy neck, are flying over our heads like light clouds of a windy day, never to return more....
> >
> > Chap. IX
>
> > Now, for what the world thinks of that ejaculation—I would not give a groat.
>
> ... There, one sees, is poetry changing easily and naturally into prose, prose into poetry. Standing a little aloof, Sterne lays his hands lightly upon imagination, wit, fantasy; and reaching high up among the branches where these things grow, naturally and no doubt willingly forfeits his right to the more substantial vegetables that grow upon the ground. For, unfortunately, it seems true that some

---

[9] See for example: Martin Battesin's "Sterne: The Poetics of Sensibility," Frank Brady's "*Tristram Shandy*: Sexuality, Morality, and Sensibility," D. W. Jefferson's "Tristram Shandy and the Tradition of Learned Wit," Helene Moglen's *The Philosophical Irony of Laurence Sterne*, James Rodgers's "Sensibility, Sympathy, Benevolence: Physiology and Moral Philosophy in *Tristram Shandy*," and John Mullan's *Sentiment and Sociability: The Language of Feeling in the Eighteenth Century*.

> renunciation is inevitable. You cannot cross the narrow bridge of art carrying all
> of its tools in your hands. ("Narrow Bridge" 227)

Sterne's novel stands here as an exemplar of the possibilities and limitations of prose which moves towards poetic abstraction and back again to prose-realism. The fluidity of the model is appealing, but part of the material grounding of more solidly realist fiction, the "substantial vegetables that grow upon the ground," is relinquished. *Tristram Shandy* explores the difficulty of creating art out of baser material, poetry out of the subject matter of prose. Tristram's doomed effort to capture and relate his life in the process of living it is a problem Woolf also set herself in her novels. Sterne's elegiac invocation of the fleeting nature of time and human experience, and his recognition of the gross materiality of language and writing echo Woolf's own reformations of language into the "little language such as lovers use" and her stylistic experimentation. However, while Woolf admires the fluidity which this style makes possible, she recognizes that the solidity of the material everyday tends to get lost in the move to more overtly poetic abstraction and form. Sterne's writer-author is distanced and aloof; while Tristram occasionally descends into bawdy jokes about physical sensations this works as a counterpoint to the elegiac poetic moments according to Woolf, rather than marking a deep engagement with the details of daily life. While this is a serious critique, we should also remember Woolf's dismissal of the "Edwardian" over-emphasis on material details in "Modern Fiction" (103-10). As Woolf succinctly and dryly puts it, "Life is not a series of gig-lamps symmetrically arranged; life is a luminous halo, a semi-transparent envelope surrounding us from the beginning of consciousness to the end" ("Modern Fiction" 106).

Woolf herself struggled with the problems of balancing prosaic materiality and poetic abstraction most specifically in *The Waves*, placing the writer-figure in the background as the "woman writing" seen through the window at several points in the novel. The unlocated "she" and the poetic interludes are Woolf's solution to and echo of Sterne's "aloofness," rather than his gendered and historically contingent strategy of alternating bawdiness and poetic sentiment. A woman writer living and writing in a different time, Woolf's strategies are not Sterne's, although she can adapt his work as a model for combining formal experiment with psychological concerns. Woolf's strategy in *The Waves* is to focus on poetic meta-vocalization in order to explore the difficult and continuous construction of subjectivity. By contrast, *Tristram* alternates between bawdiness and sensibility, thereby keeping its representations of (male) subjectivity fluid. Sterne's focus on the male body's excesses, its permeability and leakage, subverts the emerging binary gender structure in which masculinity is defined by its phallic exclusion of feminine openness and multiplicity. Within an exclusively male homosocial world, Sterne's representations of masculinity are both fluid and varied, open to the sympathetic look and the penetration of wit.[10] But, for Woolf, the insistently present male body of Sterne's narratives is not a site for gender fluidity, at least for women. By the nineteenth century, the female body has become either the site of women's reduction to mere materiality or must be excluded to produce the "angel in the house." Instead of Sterne's strategy of excessive embodiment, Woolf borrows Sterne's formal solution, interweaving the poetic within a prose-narrative form.

Woolf's reading notes on *Tristram* further clarify the explicit appeal of Sterne's formal structure and stylistic play: "The relief of reading a book which is really composed—words have stuck to the magnet instead of lying strewn.... There is a design in it all" (Holograph Reading Notes). The emphasis on design, formal structure as the tool for combining the material and the poetic, is a strategy she uses herself in *The Waves*. The meta-voices of that novel also come to consider artistic form as a solution to their difficulties in defining a self: Bernard tells stories, Neville writes poetry, Louis reads poetry, and Rhoda has a vision of the history of Western art as an oblong set upon a square, and so is able to take a bus alone. *The Waves* is constantly playing out the difficult problems of human communication in language, thought, and art. *The Waves* argues in part for the curative powers of art to contain and remake the raw material of human life through artistic form.[11] Rhoda's ritual gesture with the violets and the music she hears as "a square set upon an oblong," Bernard's airy floating words, and Neville's escaped poem mark the respect which formal art garners within the novel.

Woolf's effort to create herself as a writer and to write herself into literary history is enacted by presenting processes of reading as the appropriate ground of literary history. "Woolf's insistence on the active, participatory nature of reading," as Brenda Silver notes, reverberates through her extensive oeuvre (*Reading Notebooks*, 11).[12] Her essays in the *Common Reader* series bear witness to the concern and attention with which she investigated and sought to guide readerly response. Woolf, not unlike women writers before her, combined artistry and criticism in her writing.[13] In Woolf's work and thought, these two functions are

[10]See Miriam L. Wallace, "Gender Bending and Corporeal Limitations" for extended discussion of *Tristram*'s homosocial and homoerotic male corporeality.

[11]See Wallace, "Theorizing Relational Subjects: Metonymic Narrative in *The Waves*" for an extended discussion of constructions of subjectivity in *The Waves*.

[12]See also Rosenberg, "Virginia Woolf's Postmodern Literary History," and Fernald.

[13]Eighteenth-century British women authors whose work importantly spans criticism and literature include notably, Mary Wollstonecraft, Mary Hays, Clara Reeve, and even Elizabeth Inchbald, whose novels, plays, and critical introductions combined a similar interest in how people ought to read and interpret their reading matter. As Laura Marcus

intrinsically connected rather than in opposition. This comprehensive, inclusive view of fiction and critical thought is part of her feminist politics, and oxymoronically is also a central tenet of Sterne's *Tristram Shandy* as Woolf reads and recasts it.

Sterne's novel figures explicitly as a central text in much of Woolf's critical thinking about literary form and history. In "Phases of Fiction," the essay which developed out of her effort to construct her own theory of fiction in December of 1925, Sterne's novel occupies a central and transitional place.[14] Woolf's diary entry provides the earliest record of her distinction between two poles of literary art, realist fiction and poetic fiction:

> I think I will find some theory about fiction. I shall read six novels, & start some hares. The one I have in view, is about *perspective*. But I do not know . . .
> I don't think it is a matter of "development" but something to do with prose & poetry, in novels. For instance Defoe at one end: E. Brontë at the other. Reality something they put at different distances. (*D3* 50)

In the essay itself, Woolf distances herself from the Victorian and early Modernist understanding of literary fiction as a continual development from flawed beginnings (Defoe) to great literature (the George Eliot of F. R. Leavis' "The Great Tradition"). Instead, through her frame narrative of the reader scanning her shelves to find the next book to read, she evokes the active and desiring reader who reads, not to follow historical literary development in a strictly linear fashion, but to satisfy the cravings created by previous reading. The desire for prose and the desire for more poetic writing alternate as one reads. Rather than emphasize a strictly chronological hierarchy of literary development then, "Phases of Fiction" emphasizes context and readerly desire. "Phases of Fiction" traces the longing which the lack in each book or type of writing creates, from the realists or "truth tellers" (Defoe, de Maupassant, Trollope), to the "Romantics" who fulfill a desire for music and distance (Scott, Stevenson, Radcliffe), to "Character-mongers and comedians" (Dickens, Austen, Eliot), to the true "Psychologists" (James, Proust, Dostoevsky), to the "Satirists and

---

writes, "the significance of literature for feminism . . . gives a particular place to those writers whose work spans both feminist polemic and fiction or poetry, including Mary Wollstonecraft, Simone de Beauvoir, Adrienne Rich, and, preeminently, Virginia Woolf" (209).

[14]Originally intended as a book for Hogarth Press Lectures on Literature, the "book never appeared in the series..., but was eventually published as three articles under the title 'Phases of Fiction' in the New York *Bookman* 1929" (Anne Olivier Bell, *D3* 50 n6). The essay-version was later reprinted in *Granite and Rainbow* in 1958.

Fantastics" (Peacock, Sterne), to the "Poets" (Sterne, E. Brontë, Meredith, Hardy). The essay ends with an invocation of prose's relative infancy and the reader's endless desire to read more and different writing ("Phases of Fiction" 97). Sterne, uniquely among the writers considered in this long essay, crosses over two subdivisions, ending the section on "Satirists and Fantasists" and beginning that on "Poets." Once again, Sterne is her model of successful formal inclusiveness.

Woolf's emphasis on the reader's desire as a structure for a theory about literature's history and development echoes eighteenth-century debates about the importance and dangers of reading. Reading according to desire, especially for eighteenth-century women readers, was particularly hotly debated. Eighteenth-century novels are rife with fathers choosing appropriate reading material for their children (particularly daughters), and with admonitions and examples of the dangers of allowing young people or servants to read according only to their own desires.[15] *Tristram* exemplifies the difficulties and dangers of reading according to personal taste most overtly in Walter Shandy's ludicrous plan to educate his son according to his own eccentric reading. On the other hand, Sterne's *Tristram Shandy* particularly castigates passive reading practices, what Tristram terms "a vicious taste . . . of reading forwards, more in quest of the adventures than of the deep erudition and knowledge which a book of this cast . . . would infallibly impart to [the readers]" (Sterne 43). Thus, *Tristram* is an important site for Woolf's efforts to recast literary history as reading practice; Woolf's reading notes return obsessively to *Tristram Shandy*'s emphasis on the reader's part in making the text work, a kind of reader-response *avant la lettre*. Woolf's notes cite *Tristram Shandy*: "and that all good people, both male and female, from example, may be taught to think as well as read!" (Holograph Reading Notes). The added exclamation point stands as Woolf's comment on and agreement with Sterne's point so precisely quoted. Sterne's actual words vary slightly: "and that all good people, both male and female, from *her* example, may be taught to think as well as read" (Sterne 44, emphasis added). Here Tristram explains why he has sent "Madam," the woman-reader, back to reread an entire chapter, and tells his

---

[15]Some examples of eighteenth-century novels which contain warnings about reading novels and romances include Charlotte Lennox's *The Female Quixote*, Jane Austen's *Northanger Abbey*, Henry Fielding's *Shamela*, Elizabeth Inchbald's *A Simple Story*, Mary Hays's *Memoirs of Emma Courtney*, and Mary Wollstonecraft's *The Wrongs of Woman*. One could even make a case for Mary Godwin Shelley's *Frankenstein, or the New Prometheus* as centering on the dangers and pleasures of reading unguidedly or well in the different reading matter of Frankenstein and the monster.

readers, both male and female, that they are guilty of similar faults. Woolf's revision of Sterne highlights the connection between reading and thinking for both genders. Moreover, in her rewording, deleting "her" from the text's "from example" de-emphasizes Tristram's scapegoating of "Madam," the inadequate reader, in order to stress the creation of a positive example, a "common reader" who is also an engaged and "writerly" reader. Since Woolf's reading notes explicitly recognize Sterne's misogyny, this erasure is an active choice in her writing, not merely a glossing of Sterne's foibles. This is an example of Woolf's critical writing as active re-reading. Writing on Sterne, Woolf teaches the reader how to read *Tristram*, marking reading practice as itself politically and aesthetically inflected.

Woolf frequently cites Sterne's novel directly and without comment in her reading notes for the essay on Sterne: "'I wd go 50 miles on foot . . . to kiss the hand of that man whose generous heart will give up the reins of his imagination into his author's hand—be pleased he knows not why, and cares not wherefore'" (Holograph Reading Notes, ellipses in original). Most writers would, I imagine, be in sympathy with this description of the ideal reader, engaged, yet willing to grant temporary authority to the author. Given Woolf's constant immersion in critical discourse as both producer and recipient, and the regular round of criticism to which her books were subjected, this fantasy of readerly complicity may well have seemed particularly appealing. *Tristram Shandy*'s continued voicing of writerly anxiety and struggle with critical readerships resonated powerfully for Woolf. But, even more importantly, reading Sterne as a figure for the writer who demands a reflecting reader and who trains the reader to read critically was important to Woolf's own careful use of intertextual references and formal structure. Reiterating elements and images from book to book, interpolating verses and references to other literary texts, Woolf's own novels demand a reader who reads alertly and with an eye to repetition and the contexts of the repetition.

Art and Social Context

Silver has argued that Woolf's work shows an increasing interest in and awareness of the pressure which social history exerts upon artistic creation: "At the end of her life, when she began to write her own history of English literature, she repeatedly emphasized the need to write as well the history of the society that produced and responded to the art" (*Reading Notebooks* 7-8). This squares well with Woolf's repeated attempts to combine a political-social vision with a sense of art as developing and changing through history. One thinks of the woman writer in *A Room of One's Own* who is buried at the crossroads in Elizabethan England, confined in the Victorian household, writes "Chloe liked Olivia" in the early twentieth century, and is on her way to being a great poet in the literary future. While *Three Guineas* and *Between the Acts* are Woolf's most profound meditations on the connection between social history and literary art, most of Woolf's literary essays reveal this driving concern to combine social history, psychology, and artistic creation. Practicing what she preaches, Woolf's essays frequently use narrative form, telling stories rather than merely arguing logical points. Her essays use narrative tropes including metaphor ("the narrow bridge of art") and metonymy ("words flick their tails" like birds in "Words Fail Me"). This represents a different strategy of argument through narrative tale, an argumentative strategy more accessible to the "common reader." Rather than operating through logical persuasion and formal argument, this essay form works through sympathy, forging emotional and imagistic connections between the essayist's point of view and the reader's imagination.

Called the "Age of Sensibility" by some critics, the later eighteenth-century emphasized "sensibility" as both the locus of human social connection and as the road to developing right reason. The belief that emotional feelings could lead individuals to right reason through an instinctive swelling of sympathy with others undergirds many eighteenth-century novels' use of narrative to make moral arguments. The philosophical tale, the fable, and the interpolated personal narrative are common forms of didactic narrative eighteenth-century literature, and all make their appearance in *Tristram Shandy*. Each of these genres depends upon imaginative sympathy between audience and object, between observer or reader and suffering subject for its didactic power. Moreover, *Tristram Shandy* reveals that the bonds of sympathy (between men) are stronger than the persuasive power of formal rhetoric and logic. For example, although Walter's philosophical arguments never reach his brother Toby's understanding, the interpolated stories of Le Fever and Yorick are more effective in drawing connections between individuals, evidenced by the tears which their audience sheds and in which the reader is expected to share.

Woolf's critical writing which emphasizes the connection between social history and literary art borrows from the affective power of story-telling to make a politically inflected point tied to an aesthetic argument. "Sterne's Ghost" is a fine example of the essay as short story. In this essay, Woolf tells the story of Eliza Mathews's love match, and her efforts to surprise her husband by earning money for him from her writing. Living in rooms which the landlady assures them housed Laurence Sterne himself while writing *Tristram Shandy*, Eliza believes genius will visit her. She takes a mysterious midnightly knocking on the wall as Sterne's ghostly return, urging her on. Eliza becomes ill from overwork and nervousness, and dies. Years later her husband and his new wife discover that the knocks on the wall were in fact made by a neighbor who feared thieves and developed this ritual to frighten them away. In telling the story of Eliza Mathews's writing, illness and death, Woolf tells us much about the costs of women's exclusion from profitable labor, and makes an oblique comment upon Sterne's legacy of sentimentality. What is pleasurable sensibility for Sterne in the 1760s, returning in the 1800s as a ghost to "dip its handkerchief once more in the tears of lovers" becomes more insidious and even fatal for women in the nineteenth century (Woolf, "Sterne's Ghost" 98). Eliza Mathews's desire to rescue her husband without his knowledge leads her to work herself literally (and literarily) to death. The cost of unreflective sensibility for those already disempowered may be very high. This essay, then, is partially a tribute to the continuing importance of Sterne as an imaginative source for artistic inspiration. However, the essay also marks the restrictions of the woman writer in the nineteenth century, and the danger of seeing eighteenth-century male forefathers as directly imitable. One must also live in one's own time to survive as an artist, a fact of which Woolf's writing is very much cognizant. Hence, literary form and artistic style may be borrowed, but the material conditions of historical location limit and shape artistic production.

Representing Subjectivity

Woolf's project of representing "reality," "life," or "the soul" is in fact, a mode of representing subjectivity; both an inner sense of self and the outer material and social pressures which constrain and construct that self. Woolf's concern with the material as it is experienced through the psychological is not only very much in tune with Sterne's project in *Tristram Shandy*, but is a significantly feminist variation. In Sterne, the materiality and experience of the male body as permeable subvert the emerging modern conception of the masculine-sexed body as an opposite species to feminine-sexed bodies.[16] For Sterne, the male body's vulnerability and corporeality opens a space for imagining alternate masculinities. However, for Woolf, the body itself is a problematic site of gendered and sexed containment, particularly for women. The metavoices of *The Waves* generally resist the body's call to immanence and materiality through an emphasis on voice and relational definition rather than fixed corporeality. Flight into the psychic allows Woolf to achieve fluid representations of subjectivity in much of her novelistic writing, from *Jacob's Room* through *Between the Acts*. The indirection of Woolf's style in her essays, then, is more than coy femininity or solely a strategy for voicing feminist claims within an oppressive cultural regime. That indirection allows her writerly persona to evade specific gendered and sexed

---

[16] See Wallace, "Gender Bending" 188-91, and Thomas Laqueur, *Making Sex*.

locations, and so a novel like *The Waves* can evade the bodily limitations which her more realist novels (such as *The Years*) detail. The problem of women's reduction to their bodily capacity for reproduction and their association with physicality has plagued feminists at least since Mary Wollstonecraft recognized it in *A Vindication of the Rights of Woman* in 1792. For such divergent writers as Wollstonecraft, Simone de Beauvoir, and Woolf, women's bodily capacity for pregnancy has seemed to risk limiting them to the role of supporting art, rather than creating it. A move to a style of writing which seems to move beyond bodily specificity, one located in a kind of internal psychological flux must have felt liberating to an artist who both recognized and resisted the material limitations of her gendered corporeality.

Woolf's hyper-conscious awareness of the historical and cultural constraints placed upon the artist is frequently marked in her journals:

> As for the soul: why did I say I would leave it out? I forget. And the truth is, one can't write directly about the soul. Looked at, it vanishes: but look at the ceiling, at Grizzle, at the cheaper beasts in the Zoo which are exposed to walkers in Regents Part, & the soul slips in. It slipped in this afternoon. I will write that I said, staring at the bison . . . (*D3* 62)

Woolf suggests that the way to capture what she calls "soul," the elusive sense of individual lived reality, is not to focus directly on it, but to focus on the sense of a moment in flux, on the objects around it. Hermione Lee identifies this strategy as something Woolf recommends in her essays to writers of fiction: "Her radicalising programme to undo what she saw as the heavy-weight materialism, the over-stuffing, the literal detail and the thick plotting of the English novel is embodied in her critical preference for indirection and suggestion" (*Essays* 102). This mode of representing psychic interiority by focusing on external events, actions, and objects, leads to novelistic practice, as in *The Waves*' metonymic narrative strategy. *The Waves* moves through repeated images, events, and metaphors which travel from one voice to another or from the interstices to the voices, as for example, the birds spearing snails which are echoed by Rhoda's experience of social intercourse. This representational strategy, moreover, is one Woolf noted in *Tristram Shandy*, citing Tristram's claim that his digressions are actually a more effective way of drawing his Uncle Toby's character. Woolf's Holograph Reading Notes cite *Tristram*'s argument in favor of digression nearly directly from the text:

digressions "are the sunshine, —— they are the life the soul of reading: all the dexterity is in the good working and management of them . . . whats (sic) more, I shall be kept a-going these forty years, if it pleases the Fountain of health——
. . . ['] That [illegible] seem to me true: that he wrote from hand to mouth.
    Notwithstanding all this . . . the drawing of my U. T's character went on all the time. [17]

Woolf borrows Sterne's digressive technique, not to argue for hobby horses or John Locke's association of ideas, but to invoke a specific feminist attention to the fragmentary nature of human experience and the knowledge embedded in daily experience. She notes in *A Room of One's Own* that, to write of women necessitates a sidelong glance rather than a direct one: "women . . . are suspicious of any interest . . . so terribly accustomed to concealment and suppression, that they are off at the flicker of an eye turned observingly in their direction." She advises the novelist Mary Carmichael to "talk of something else, looking steadily out of the window, and thus note ... in the shortest of shorthand, in words that are hardly syllabled yet, what happens when Olivia . . . feels the light fall on [her], and sees coming her way a piece of strange food—knowledge, adventure, art" (*AROO* 84-5). The kind of observation needed by the new novel writer which she imagines is not the long steady look, but the kind of digressive subtlety for which Sterne mockingly argues. Sterne's technique of metonymic characterization is one which Woolf borrows and adapts to fit her own purposes, for example in her "tunneling" stream-of-consciousness in *Mrs. Dalloway*, and in the way other characters' insights complete the reader's view of Neville, Bernard, Rhoda, and Susan in *The Waves*.

---

[17]The relevant passages from *Tristram* are from Chapter XXII, Vol. I:

> Digressions, incontestably, are the sunshine—they are the life, the soul of reading;—take them out of this book for instance,—you might as well take the book along with them;....
> All the dexterity is in the good cookery and management of them, so as to be not only for the advantage of the reader, but also of the author, whose distress, in this matter, is truly pitiable....
> —This is vile work.—For which reason, from the beginning of this, you see, I have constructed the main work and the adventitious parts of it with such intersections, and have so complicated and involved the digressive and progressive movements, one wheel within another, that the whole machine, in general, has been kept a-going;—and, what's more, it shall be kept a-going these forty years, if it pleases the fountain of health to bless me so long with life and good spirits. (Sterne 55)

Gender and Literary History

Woolf used both the history of literature and her own reading practices to shape a specific sense of history as non-developmental in counter-distinction to an Enlightenment masculinist narrative of historical progress. She treats reading as a kind of practical self-education which substitutes for the education she always believed she had been denied because of her sex. In addition, by focusing on her own readerly experience traced through the sequence of her reading, Woolf highlights and exemplifies the special perspective which she believed gendered exclusion brought. This ambivalent sense of both a cost and a gain marks the double-bind of the woman-reader and the woman-writer under an unacknowledged system of gendered difference.

Woolf's novels progressively struggle with the difficulty of reconciling personal with national history. A central site of resistance and anxiety in Woolf's writing is education.[18] The system of English education from which Sterne himself had benefited was still unavailable to women when Woolf was of an age to attend university. *Tristram Shandy* displays all the standard marks of the "educated" Englishman: schoolboy Latin jokes, a mocking reiteration of the Grand Tour, and jokes only accessible to those with the classical education of Oxbridge. It is clear that the "right reader" of Sterne's novel is the classically educated gentleman, the one to whom the jokes are directed. By contrast, while Woolf lamented her lack of the traditional English education her brothers received, and sought through reading the classics and studying Greek to rectify what she persistently referred to as a lack, Woolf also valued the "outsider's" perspective she felt her exclusion developed. In her record of a discussion with Lytton Strachey about her literary method, Woolf represents herself as both anxious to defer to his judgement, and at the same time reserving her outsider's "situated knowledge"[19] in the face of Strachey's valued judgement. She writes:

[18]One could certainly argue that it is Woolf's arguments for better and more equal education for women that align her with both earlier eighteenth-century feminist apologists such as Mary Wollstonecraft, and with more recent twentieth-century feminist insistence on the cultural construction of gender through education. Woolf's frustration with her own lack of classical education and her suspicion of the effects of that education echo ongoing feminist debates, and highlight a problem which has long haunted feminism: what kind of education ought women to receive and whose purposes does that education serve? It is worth remembering that Woolf turned down at least two honorary degrees in her lifetime.

[19]For an important discussion of the term "situated knowledges" see Donna Haraway's "Situated Knowledges: The Science Question in Feminism as a Site of Discourse on the Privilege of Partial Perspective."

> I think as a whole, the book [*Mrs. Dalloway*] does not ring solid; yet, he [Strachey] says, it is a whole; & he says sometimes the writing is of extreme beauty. What can one call it but genius? he said! Coming when, one never can tell. Fuller of genius, he said than anything I had done. Perhaps, he said, you have not yet mastered your method. You should take something wilder & more fantastic, a frame work that admits of anything, like Tristram Shandy. But then I should lose touch with emotions, I said. Yes, he agreed, there must be reality for you to start from. Heaven knows how you're to do it. But he thought me at the beginning, not at the end. (*D3* 32)

Lytton Strachey is portrayed here as a trusted critic. Woolf seems willing to consider foregrounding her own questions about her developing artistry through the form of *Tristram Shandy* as an exemplar of inclusion. That *Tristram* is judged a model of inclusion by Strachey, a classically educated Englishman, is not surprising; that Woolf should take the suggestion seriously enough to consider what might be lost in such an experiment seems surprising on the surface. However, if we locate *Tristram* as a site of a tension between gender-blind Enlightenment assumptions about historical and scientific progress and Rousseauian attention to the insights of sympathy, we can trace the complex ambivalence Woolf's writing displays toward literary heritage.

While ideas of sensibility and sympathy are central to arguments for attention to women's distinct experiences and specific knowledges, the Enlightenment conception of the humanist subject denies that specificity. Yet, it was Enlightenment emphasis on the individual's self-judgement which enabled the feminist critique in the first place and established the idea of the individual artist to which Woolf was at least partially committed. Woolf's problem as writer and critic is to write herself into literary history as an important and individual artist, yet to use the insights which come from belonging to the "outsiders." *Tristram*'s own balancing act between Augustan wit and mid-century sentimentality plays out a similar problem in literary form. Balancing wit and sentiment against each other, *Tristram Shandy* achieves both an ideal of connection through shared emotion and marks that connection as extra-linguistic—all through written language. Woolf's problem is how to use writing to explore those aspects of the human psyche which evade language in a fundamentally linguistic medium. Woolf's concern with keeping the insights of emotion (or psychology) central in her writing points through *To the Lighthouse* to Woolf's ultimate experiment with formal psychological inclusiveness, *The Waves*. Even in her most formally experimental works, Woolf is careful to trace the emotional costs of material consequences, in Rhoda's inability to become a poet, Susan's vulnerability to the imperial ideal of motherhood, Neville's fear of sharing his poem except privately with Bernard.

While I am arguing that Woolf's successful strategies of exploring psyche through literary form draw upon her eighteenth-century predecessor, it would seem more intuitively obvious to explore the literary experiments of contemporaneous modernist writers, as many critics have done.[20] For example, Woolf's anxiety that "emotion" not be lost also echoes her critique of *Ulysses*, where she argues that her contemporary, James Joyce, privileges form and method over human psychology. It is this concern with balancing artistic form and style with attention to psychology which both marks Woolf's work as Modernist, and reveals the difference gender makes in her writing. Woolf distinguishes her project from what she takes to be that of her famous contemporary. Her reading of the tension between formal style and psychological truth in *Tristram* partially enables her own project and undergirds her critique of what she views as Joyce's arid emphasis on form and style alone.

Ulysses and *Tristram Shandy*

If Woolf was able to use Sterne and the eighteenth century generally as inspirations despite their historically specific limitations, why was she not so prone to use the writers of her own time in this manner? The novel which has signally come to represent "modernism" to generations of critics and students, James Joyce's *Ulysses*, was not only available to Woolf; we have evidence that she read it both in early serial form in *The Little Review* in 1919 and in full novel form when it was published by Shakespeare and Company in 1922.[21] Woolf's essays, "Modern Fiction" and "The Narrow Bridge of Art," her diaries, and her reading notes for "Modern Fiction" offer some insight into how Joyce's work was situated for his contemporary.

Curiously, Sterne-critics who see connections between Sterne and the modernist project have long looked to James Joyce's *Ulysses* as the logical inheritor

---

[20]My goal in this essay is not to compare Woolf's work with Joyce's, although such comparisons are critical commonplaces. See for example Maria DiBattista's "Joyce, Woolf, and the Modern Mind," Teresa Fulker's "Virginia Woolf's Daily Drama of the Body," Harvena Richter's "The *Ulysses* Connection: Clarissa Dalloway's Bloomsday," Molly Hoff's "The Pseudo-Homeric World of Mrs. Dalloway," and Michael Tratner's *Modernism and Mass Politics: Joyce, Woolf, Eliot, Yeats.*

[21]Critics have tended to champion either Joyce or Woolf, as though modernism requires a primal allegiance. Molly Hoff traces critical responses to Woolf's work as somehow lesser than or plagiarism of Joyce's *Ulysses*, beginning with Wyndham Lewis's attack in 1934 and William Jenkins's "Virginia Woolf and the Belittling of *Ulysses*," through the either/or choices of Maria DiBattista's "Joyce, Woolf, and the Modern Mind" and Richard Pearce's "Who Comes First, Joyce or Woolf," and ending with Kelly Anspaugh's "Blasting the Bombardier: Another Look at Lewis, Joyce, and Woolf" in 1994 (203 n1).

of Sterne's innovations; indeed, Woolf herself invokes *Tristram Shandy* in her own evaluations of *Ulysses* (Holograph Reading Notes, "Modern Novels [Joyce],"[22] "Modern Fiction," and *D*3). Woolf's continuing critique of *Ulysses* then becomes doubly interesting. As a self-professed "modern/Georgian" writer, Woolf's assessment of what has become the cult-text of high modernism bears particular weight and freights the assessment of her own contribution, particularly *The Waves*, which some critics invoke as her most modernist experiment in fiction. In her reading notebook for "Modern Novels," Woolf's notes on *Ulysses* refer to *Tristram Shandy*:

> Always to keep moving our only chance.
> Tristram Shandy.
> Novels in Letters.
> the desire to be more psychological——get more things into fiction.
> Everything can go in.
> Gertrude Stein.
> (Holograph Reading Notes, "Modern Novels
> [Joyce]")

The tenor of Woolf's notes suggest that she saw *Ulysses* as an experimental work, in line with the kind of rupture *Tristram Shandy* had attempted in the eighteenth century. In her notes, Woolf importantly links Sterne's work with a move towards psychological representation. Her most telling criticism of *Ulysses* is that the psychology seems driven by the desire to experiment and shock, rather than the experimentation being driven by the effort to better represent psychology: "Here we come to Joyce. And here we must make our position clear as bewildered, befogged. We don't pretend to say what he's trying to do. We know so little about the people" (Holograph Reading Notes, "Modern Novels [Joyce]"). Woolf's notes here express a concern that Joyce's work experiments with form merely for the sake of formal experiment, and that this results in a loss of deeper or truer representation of human consciousness. Whether or not one agrees with this assessment of *Ulysses*, it is certainly a viable critique of much of what we now identify as "Modernism."[23]

---

[22]See also Suzette Henke for a transcription of this notebook.

[23]Woolf's diary shows that she had read episodes of *Ulysses* as they were published in *The Little Review* (1919), but her reading notes for 'Modern Fiction" are notes for the whole novel and her essay is based upon the novel as a whole (1922). For the most part, her assessment of the chapters which had come out in *The Little Review* appear to have been wholly positive, while her assessment of the novel after the trip to the cemetery is quite critical.

The essay "Modern Fiction" itself is more positive about Joyce's novel as a marker of the kind of fiction which the modern age should be writing. Comparing Joyce to the "materialists," H. G. Wells, Arnold Bennett, and John Galsworthy, Woolf calls Joyce "spiritual" and "concerned at all costs to reveal the flickerings of that innermost flame which flashes its messages through the brain" ("Modern Fiction" 107).[24] She goes on to say that he "disregards with complete courage whatever seems to him adventitious, whether it be probability, or coherence, or any other of these signposts which for generations have served to support the imagination of a reader when called upon to imagine what he can neither touch nor see" ("Modern Fiction" 107). In particular, she admires the last scene published in the *Little Review*, the cemetery scene with "its sudden lightning flashes of significance, [which] does undoubtedly come so close to the quick of the mind that, on a first reading at any rate, it is difficult not to acclaim a masterpiece. If we want life itself, here surely we have it" ("Modern Fiction" 107). Here Woolf admires in particular the way in which Joyce's formal fracturing of narrative enables a new representation of internal psychic experience. She places Joyce interestingly in the company of Sterne and Thackeray in terms of the effect which his new "method" produces, arguing that:

> [a]ny method is right ... that expresses what we wish to express, if we are writers; that brings us closer to the novelist's intention if we are readers. This method has the merit of bringing us closer to what we were prepared to call life itself; did not the reading of *Ulysses* suggest how much of life is excluded or ignored, and did it not come with a shock to open *Tristram Shandy* or even *Pendennis* and be by them convinced that there are not only other aspects of life, but more important ones into the bargain." ("Modern Fiction" 108)

Again, *Tristram* is used as a model of literary method which is attentive to the reader's effort to uncover textual truth. If Woolf finds *Ulysses* remarkable, it is because of its shared interest with *Tristram* in using formal method to reveal psychological depth.

Woolf's objections to *Ulysses* in her diary entries and notes also rested upon her dissatisfaction with its explicit attention to bodily functions, what she termed "indecency." This is more than merely an example of lingering Victorianism. While Woolf notes "indecency frequent" in her reading notes on *Tristram*

---

[24]This essay was published in 1919 while *Ulysses* was first appearing in *The Little Review*. *The Little Review* only published *Ulysses* up through the early chapters. *The Egoist* also attempted publications, but only got as far as the "Wandering Rocks" section. Seizure and attacks for obscenity kept the novel from full publication until Shakespeare and Company's first edition in 1922, which was smuggled into both England and the USA. See Sylvia Beach, *Shakespeare and Company*.

Shandy, she does not dwell on this aspect as critically as she does with Joyce. Her concern with Joyce is that "whole question of indecency." Sketching her article, she wrote, "Must get out of the way of thinking that indecency is more real than anything else—a dodge now because of the veil of reticence, but a cheap one" (Holograph Reading Notes, "Modern Novels [Joyce]"). In her notes, she asks "Would my objection apply to T. S? Don Juan. I believe Johnson was outraged by TS T. S. has a warmer temperature than Ulysses" (Holograph Reading Notes, "Modern Novels [Joyce]"). It is not merely the "indecency" which gave her pause, but attention to bodily functions in an attempt to shock the reader rather than as an attempt to connect the reader more intimately to the imaginative world, or with a sort of sympathy and sensibility to which she clings. Woolf apparently found *Ulysses* too calculating in its efforts to shock the reader and too uninterested in readerly engagement to serve as a model for her own project as a writer.[25]

Written after the essay "Modern Fiction" (1919), Woolf's diary entries in 1922 mark her struggle as a critical reader to give *Ulysses* its due and yet to hold to her own judgements about the novel's successes and failures:

> I should be reading Ulysses, & fabricating my case for & against. I have read 200 pages so far—not a third; & have been amused, stimulated, charmed, interested, by the first 2 or 3 chapters—to the end of the Cemetery scene; & then puzzled, bored, irritated & disillusioned by a queasy undergraduate scratching his pimples. And Tom [T. S. Eliot], great Tom, thinks this on a par with War and Peace!... I may revise this later. I do not compromise my critical sagacity. I plant a stick in the ground to mark page 200. (*D2* 188-89)

She takes her final critical stand on Wednesday, September 6, saying:

> I finished Ulysses, & think it a mis-fire. Genius it has, I think; but of the inferior water. The book is diffuse. It is brackish. It is pretentious. It is underbred, not only in the obvious sense, but in the literary sense. A first rate writer, I mean, respects writing too much to be tricky; startling; doing stunts. I'm reminded all the time of some callow board school boy, . . . full of wits & powers, but so self-conscious & egotistical that he loses his head, becomes extravagant, mannered, uproarious, ill at ease, makes kindly people feel sorry for him, & stern ones merely annoyed; & one hopes he'll grow out of it; but as Joyce is 40 this scarcely seems likely. (*D2* 199-200)

---

[25]Woolf's diaries bear witness to her concern with reaching a broad readership and suggest greater sensitivity on her part to accusations of obscurity and elitism than Joyce's work would suggest of him. Joyce initially thought a first edition run of a thousand copies would be far too large to sell: in other words, he did not intend or expect the book to reach a broad readership (Beach 96).

Even here she defensively notes that she has only read it once, and not carefully, and "it is very obscure; so no doubt I have scamped the virtue of it more than is fair" (*D2* 199-200). She then records both self-questioning and determination to hold to her stand: "Having written this, L. put into my hands a very intelligent review of Ulysses, in the American Nation; which for the first time, analyses the meaning; & certainly makes it very much more impressive than I judged. Still I think there is virtue & some lasting truth in first impressions; so I don't cancell [sic] mine" (*D2* 200).

Woolf's judgement of *Ulysses* is revealing, not only of her own residual class and national prejudices, but more interestingly of her anxiety concerning her own merit as a writer. She makes a strong and coherent critique of Joyce's novel, and then retreats by saying that she's only read it once, and quickly at that. The influence of critical discourse is evident in Woolf's alternating stances, both admitting that she may have judged it too harshly too quickly and claiming that her own first impressions still retain validity. Both T. S. Eliot's judgement and the *Nation*'s give her pause and lead her to soften her stand, but she nevertheless holds her place. It seems that Woolf's recorded reactions to *Ulysses* are quite overtly related to gender as well as to class; Woolf's judgement conflates her own class privilege with her sense of disenfranchisement as a woman denied a formal education, calling the book both "underbred" and the work of a "queasy undergraduate scratching his pimples." Woolf's reaction, both defensive and just, classist and feminist, marks the complex relation of a writer to the literature of her own time. Woolf's own tenuous positioning as writer and critical authority is revealed more clearly in her confrontation with this contemporary artist than in her judgements on the "classics."[26]

Part of the emotional disconnect Woolf as a reader felt with *Ulysses*, then, is a gendered response. While *Tristram Shandy* is arguably misogynistic and leaves little space for the consciously female reader (a fact which Woolf notes in her reading notebook), it is also distanced by time and style. Reading across historical periods creates a kind of distance and containment. Contemporary misogyny is more immediate and more painful to negotiate; it is a direct attack. Woolf's

---

[26]From the late twentieth century vantage of post-colonial critique, it is possible to read *Ulysses* as a formal experiment to explore the alienation and complexities of Irish post-colonial subjectivity. This is also a way of making sense of the layering of Irishness, Jewishness and femininity in the novel. However, this perspective would have been a difficult one for Woolf to have espoused in the 1920s and 30s, despite her feminist consciousness and her socialist allegiances. See for examples of current readings of Joyce as problematically postcolonial: Vincent Cheng, *Joyce, Race, and Empire* and "Of Canons, Colonies, and Critics: The Ethics and Politics of Postcolonial Joyce Studies," and David Attridge and Marjorie Howes, *Semicolonial Joyce.*

lenience towards *Tristram Shandy* (which frequently performs similar moves; as Woolf's reading notes point out, "Mrs. S. never speaks,") and her criticism of *Ulysses* mark the different ideological stakes across time. That is, the ideological work of *Ulysses* is more overtly dangerous and threatening to a modern British middle-class woman writer than the ideological work of *Tristram Shandy* as it reaches across a historical distance.

Conclusion

The historical distance Woolf drew upon in her criticism and analysis of older literature aided the kind of engaged and attentive reading she promoted through her critical essays. Joyce, as a contemporary and potential rival, was more difficult to negotiate than Sterne. The gender privilege Joyce enjoyed as a writer was combated by Woolf with her own class and ethnic privilege. A similar dynamic surfaces in her comments on T. S. Eliot as a "shopkeeper's son." That Woolf-the-writer felt embattled as well as challenged by the male Oxbridge writers is clear in her writings and amply documented.[27] I suggest that this dynamic was productive as well as debilitating, and that part of Woolf's strategy as a writer for negotiating the competition she felt involved her turn to literary history both for models and material in her efforts to construct "Virginia Woolf, the great artist."

Finally, then, Woolf's work must be read not only in the context of her feminism, her contemporaries, her artistic connections, but also in the context of the literary and cultural history which she both inherited and constructed. Woolf marks out active reading practices and writing literary history as important in constructing an alternative feminist subject position for women. To neglect the imaginative space of eighteenth-century literary ancestors is to neglect an important cultural heritage which was often productive for Woolf as a writer. Western feminism and feminist literary production have long roots, and those roots are neither exclusively modern, nor restricted to female-authored texts. In particular, *Tristram Shandy* holds a special place in Woolf criticism, as Sterne-the-writer and the historical figure did for Woolf-the-writer. This suggests that to dismiss Sterne's novel as misogynistic or to focus exclusively on the representation of women in that novel is to miss the possibilities and power of engaged feminist re-reading and critique. Woolf's artistic efforts to rework her own literary tradition and to write herself into literary history mark the complexity and high stakes of defining feminist critical reading and writing practices. Our job is not only to expand the content of the literary canon, but also to understand our own reading

---

[27]See for example, Jane Marcus, "Niece of a Nun," and "Liberty, Sorority, Misogyny."

and writing as actively shaping literary history and imaginative possibilities. Following Woolf's lead, we must enact our own readings as active interventions in literary history and the cultural construction of meaning.

Works Cited

Anspaugh, Kelly. "Blasting the Bombardier: Another Look at Lewis, Joyce, and Woolf." *Twentieth Century Literature* 40.3 (1994 Fall): 365-78.

Attridge, David, and Marjorie Howes, ed. *Semicolonial Joyce*. Cambridge: Cambridge UP, 2000.

Barker-Benfield, G. J. *The Culture of Sensibility: Sex and Society in Eighteenth-Century Britain*. Chicago: U of Chicago P, 1992.

Barrett, Michèle. Introduction. *Virginia Woolf: Women and Writing*. New York: Harcourt Brace Jovanovich, 1979. 1-35.

Battesin, Martin. "Sterne: The Poetics of Sensibility." *Laurence Sterne's* Tristram Shandy. Ed. Harold Bloom. New York: Chelsea House Publishers, 1987. 59-86.

Beach, Sylvia. *Shakespeare and Company*. New York: Harcourt Brace and World, 1959.

Booth, Alison. *Greatness Engendered: George Eliot and Virginia Woolf*. Ithaca: Cornell UP, 1992.

Brady, Frank. "*Tristram Shandy*: Sexuality, Morality, and Sensibility." *Approaches to Teaching Sterne's* Tristram Shandy. Ed. Melvyn New. New York: MLA, 1989. 77-93.

Caughie, Pamela. *Virginia Woolf and Postmodernism: Literature in Quest and Question of Itself*. Urbana: U of Illinois P, 1991.

Cheng, Vincent. *Joyce, Race, and Empire*. Cambridge: Cambridge UP, 1995.

———. "Of Canons, Colonies, and Critics: The Ethics and Politics of Postcolonial Joyce Studies." *Cultural Critique* 35 (1996-97 Winter): 81-104.

DiBattista, Maria. "Joyce, Woolf, and the Modern Mind." Ed. Patricia Clements and Isobel Grundy. *Virginia Woolf: New Critical Essays*. Totowa: Barnes and Noble, 1983. 96-114.

Dubino, Jeanne. "Rambling Through *A Room of One's Own* versus Marching Through I. A. Richards' *Practical Criticism*: On the Essay as an Anti-Institutional Form." *Virginia Woolf and the Arts: Selected Papers from the 6th Annual Conference on Virginia Woolf*. Ed. Diane Gillespie and Leslie Hankins. New York: Pace UP, 1997. 283-91.

———, and Beth Carole Rosenberg, ed. *Virginia Woolf and the Essay*. New York: St. Martin's Press, 1998.

Dusinberre, Juliet. *Virginia Woolf's Renaissance*. Iowa City: U of Iowa P, 1999.

Fernald, Anne E. "Pleasure and Belief in 'Phases of Fiction.'" *Virginia Woolf and the Essay*. Ed. Beth Carole Rosenberg and Jeanne Dubino. New York: St. Martin's Press, 1998. 193-211.

Fox, Alice. *Virginia Woolf and the Literature of the English Renaissance*. Oxford: Clarendon P, 1990.

Fulker, Teresa. "Virginia Woolf's Daily Drama of the Body." *Woolf Studies Annual* 1 (1995): 3-25.

Gualtieri, Elena. *Virginia Woolf's Essays: Sketching the Past.* New York: St. Martin's P, 2000.

Haraway, Donna. "Situated Knowledges: The Science Question in Feminism as a Site of Discourse on the Privilege of Partial Perspective." *Feminist Studies* 14.3 (1988): 575-99.

Hawkes, Ellen. "Woolf's 'Magical Garden of Women.'" *New Feminist Essays.* Ed. Jane Marcus. Lincoln: U of Nebraska P, 1981. 31-60.

Henke, Suzette. "Virginia Woolf (1882-1941), The Modern Tradition." [Transcription] "Modern Novels (Joyce)" In Bonnie Kime Scott, ed. : 642-45.

Hoff, Molly. "The Pseudo-Homeric World of Mrs. Dalloway." *Twentieth-Century Literature* 45.2 (Summer 1999): 186-209.

Jefferson, D. W. "Tristram Shandy and the Tradition of Learned Wit." *Approaches to Teaching Sterne's* Tristram Shandy. Ed. Melvyn New. New York: MLA, 1989. 17-35.

Jenkins, William D. "Virginia Woolf and the Belittling of *Ulysses.*" *James Joyce Quarterly* 25.4 (1988): 513-19.

Laqueur, Thomas. *Making Sex: Body and Gender from the Greeks to Freud.* Cambridge, MA: Harvard UP, 1990.

Lee, Hermione. "Virginia Woolf's Essays." *The Cambridge Companion to Virginia Woolf.* Ed. Sue Roe and Susan Sellers. Cambridge: Cambridge UP, 2000. 91-108.

——. *The Novels of Virginia Woolf.* New York: Holmes and Meier, 1977.

Marcus, Jane. *Virginia Woolf and the Languages of Patriarchy.* Bloomington: Indiana UP, 1987.

——, ed. *Virginia Woolf: A Feminist Slant.* Lincoln: U of Nebraska P, 1983.

——, ed. *New Feminist Essays on Virginia Woolf.* Lincoln: U of Nebraska P, 1981.

——. "Thinking Back Through Our Mothers." *New Feminist Essays.* Ed. Jane Marcus. Lincoln: U of Nebraska P, 1981: 1-30.

——. "The Niece of a Nun: Virginia Woolf, Caroline Stephen, and the Cloistered Imagination." *Virginia Woolf: A Feminist Slant.* Ed. Jane Marcus. Lincoln: U Nebraska P, 1983: 7-36.

——. "Liberty, Sorority, Misogyny." *The Representation of Women in Fiction.* Ed. Carolyn Heilbrun and Margaret Higgonet. Baltimore: Johns Hopkins UP, 1983: 60-97.

Marcus, Laura. "Woolf's Feminism and Feminism's Woolf." *The Cambridge Companion to Virginia Woolf.* Ed. Sue Roe and Susan Sellers. Cambridge: Cambridge UP, 2000. 209-244.

Meisel, Perry. *The Absent Father: Virginia Woolf and Walter Pater.* New Haven: Yale UP, 1980.

Moglen, Helene. *The Philosophical Irony of Laurence Sterne*. Gainesville: U of
   Florida P, 1975.
Moore, Madeline. *The Short Season Between Two Silences: The Mystical and the
   Political in the Novels of Virginia Woolf*. Boston: George Allen and Unwin,
   1984.
Mullan, John. *Sentiment and Sociability: The Language of Feeling in the
   Eighteenth Century*. Oxford: Clarendon P, 1988.
New, Melvyn, ed. *Approaches to Teaching Sterne's* Tristram Shandy. New York:
   Modern Language Association of America, 1989.
Pearce, Richard. "Who Comes First, Joyce or Woolf?" *Virginia Woolf: Themes
   and Variations*. Ed. Vara Neverow-Turk and Mark Hussey. New York: Pace
   UP, 1993. 57-67.
Rich, Adrienne. *On Lies, Secrets and Silence: Selected Prose 1966-78*. London:
   Virago, 1980.
Richter, Harvena. "The *Ulysses* Connection: Clarissa Dalloway's Bloomsday."
   Studies in the Novel 21.3 (Fall 1989): 305-19.
Rodgers, James. "Sensibility, Sympathy, Benevolence: Physiology and Moral
   Philosophy in *Tristram Shandy*." *Languages of Nature: Critical Essays on
   Science and Literature*. Ed. L. J. Jordanova. New Brunswick: Rutgers UP,
   1986. 117-158.
Rosenberg, Beth Carole. *Virginia Woolf and Samuel Johnson: Common Readers*.
   New York: St. Martin's Press, 1995.
———. "Virginia Woolf's Postmodern Literary History." *Modern Language Notes*
   115.5 (2000): 1112-1130.
Schlack, Beverly Ann. *Continuing Presences: Virginia Woolf's Use of Literary
   Allusion*. College Station: Pennsylvania State UP, 1995.
Schwartz, Beth C. "Thinking Back Through Our Mothers: Virginia Woolf Reads
   Shakespeare." *ELH* 58.1 (1991). 721-46.
Scott, Bonnie Kime, ed. *The Gender of Modernism: A Critical Anthology*.
   Bloomington: Indiana UP, 1990.
Showalter, Elaine. *A Literature of Their Own: British Women Novelists from
   Brontë to Lessing*. Princeton. Princeton UP, 1977.
Silver, Brenda. *Virginia Woolf's Reading Notebooks*. Princeton, NJ: Princeton
   University Press, 1983.
———. "Cultural Critique." *The Gender of Modernism: A Critical Anthology*. Ed.
   Bonnie Kime Scott. Bloomington: Indiana UP, 1990. 646-658.
Sterne, Laurence. *The Life and Opinions of Tristram Shandy, Gentleman*. (1760-
   1767). Riverside Edition. Ed. Ian Watt. Boston: Houghton Mifflin, 1965.
Todd, Janet. *Sensibility: An Introduction*. London: Methuen, 1986.
Tratner, Michael. *Modernism and Mass Politics: Joyce, Woolf, Eliot, Yeats*.
   Stanford: Stanford UP, 1995.
Wallace, Miriam L. "Gender Bending and Corporeal Limitations: The Modern
   Body in *Tristram Shandy*." *Studies in Eighteenth Century Culture* 26. Ed.
   Syndy M. Conger and Julie C. Hayes. Baltimore: Johns Hopkins UP, 1997.

189-207.

——. "Theorizing Relational Subjects: Metonymic Narrative in *The Waves*." *Narrative* 8.3 October (2000): 294-323.

Woolf, Virginia. "The Art of Fiction." *Collected Essays*. Vol. 2. New York: Harcourt, Brace, and World, 1967. 51-55.

——. *Collected Essays*. 4 Vols. New York: Harcourt Brace Jovanovich, 1967.

——. *The Diary of Virginia Woolf*. Ed. Anne Olivier Bell. Four vols. New York: Harcourt Brace and World, 1980.

——. "Eliza and Sterne." *Collected Essays*. Vol. 3. New York: Harcourt, Brace, and World, 1967. 100-104.

——. Holograph Reading Notes, on *Tristram Shandy*, unpublished MS, Reading Notebook 14. Berg Collection of the New York Public Library.

——. "Modern Novels (Joyce)." In Scott: 642-45.

——. "Modern Fiction." *Collected Essays*. Vol. 2. New York: Harcourt, Brace, and World, 1967. 103-110.

——. "The Narrow Bridge of Art." *Collected Essays*. Vol. 2. New York: Harcourt, Brace, and World, 1967. 218-229.

——. "Phases of Fiction". *Collected Essays*. Vol. 2. New York: Harcourt, Brace, and World, 1967. 56-102.

——. *A Room of One's Own*. New York: Harcourt Brace Jovanovich, 1957.

——. "The *Sentimental Journey*." *Collected Essays*. Vol. 1. New York: Harcourt, Brace, and World, 1967. 95-101.

——. "Sterne." *Collected Essays*. Vol. 3. New York: Harcourt, Brace, and World, 1967, 86-93.

——. "Sterne's Ghost." *Collected Essays*, Vol. 3. New York: Harcourt, Brace, and World, 1967. 94-99.

——. *The Waves*. Harvest/HBJ Edition. New York: Harcourt Brace Jovanovich, 1978.

Virgina Woolf's Holograph Reading Notebooks are cited with permission from the Berg Collection, The New York Public Library, Astor, Lenox and Tilden Foundation. I am grateful for permission to cite them and for access to these unique materials.

Feminist Elegy/Feminist Prophecy: *Lycidas, The Waves*, Kristeva, Cixous

> What woman hasn't flown/stolen? Who hasn't felt, dreamt, performed the gesture that jams sociality? Who hasn't crumbled, held up to ridicule, the bar of separation? Who hasn't inscribed with her body the differential, punctured the system of couples and opposition? Who, by some act of transgression, hasn't overthrown successiveness, connection, the wall of circumfusion?
> A feminine text cannot fail to be more than subversive. It is volcanic; as it is written it brings about an upheaval of the old property crust . . . in order to smash everything, to shatter the framework of institutions, to blow up the law, to break up the 'truth' with laughter.
> —Hélène Cixous, *"The Laugh of the Medusa"*

In an essay written in 1916, Woolf describes *Lycidas* as having a "complete finality" about it. It bears the capacity, she writes, for a reader's repeated return without diminishment of its appeal (*E2* 60). In a diary entry composed fourteen years later, Woolf writes that when William Butler Yeats asked her if there is any poem in the language that she could come back to unsated, she said yes, one poem: *Lycidas* (*D3* 330).

One of the great myths of contemporary literary criticism is that Woolf disliked Milton. But Woolf did not dislike Milton (or not wholly) and she certainly did not dislike what he wrote. She admired his genius for language; she revered his lifelong pursuit of English liberty; *Areopagitica*'s argument for freedom of speech underlies *Three Guineas*; and Woolf describes *Comus* and *Lycidas* as among her three or four favorite poems in the language. But Woolf did dislike Milton's Christian patriarchalism. Woolf's ambivalence toward Milton; her double, Blake-like response of at once idolizing and wishing to correct, is apparent in *The Waves*, an experimental novel which this essay sees as a revision of *Lycidas*. If Woolf loved *Lycidas* as elegy and—as I shall argue here-as feminist elegy, she was troubled by its Christian patriarchalism and its apparent masculine homosociality. This essay discusses *The Waves* as both a tribute to and correction of *Lycidas*. It uses Woolf's autobiographical "A Sketch of the Past" and Kristeva's ideas of the semiotic to help explain the intensity of Woolf's attraction to *Lycidas*. It also uses Cixous's ideas of the laughter of the Medusa and the flight of women writers through the house of the past to suggest some of the ways in which Woolf deconstructs the Christian metaphysics and homosocial exclusivity of *Lycidas*.

I Theory

For Kristeva, who predicts the end of the "reign of metaphysicals," a new woman's writing has emerged in the past one hundred years. This new woman's writing has a different notion of time, and is connected to the pre-Oedipal, pre-symbolic semiotic world of the maternal.   "Essentially interested in the specificity of female psychology and its symbolic realizations," the new woman's writing seeks in new and experimental, subversive and revolutionary language, "the fluid and infinitesimal significations of the [woman's] relationship with the nature of [her] own body [and], that of the child, another woman, or a man." For Kristeva, the "new woman" writer is engaged in a *recherche de la mère perdu*, an "active research . . . always dissident . . . to break the code, to shatter language," to find "a specific discourse closer to the body and emotions, to the unnameable repressed by the social contract" (36-37, 42-43).

The recovering of *la mère perdu* through the shattering of patriarchal language aptly describes Woolf's lifelong effort as a writer.   For Makiko Minow-Pinkney, Woolf's work enacts an always feminist "subversion of the formal principles"; the very "definitions of narrative" that constitute and maintain the "patriarchal social order."   Fluid and unstable, Woolf's not-always-easily identifiable, always shifting subject undermines "the authoritarian rigidity of the male ego," even as it remembers a world "beneath consciousness: deep, sunk, savage, primitive" (x, 193, 195). Gillian Beer describes Woolf's project in *The Waves* similarly. In *The Waves*, Beer writes, Woolf rejects the linear Aristotelian plot and exploits in its stead the pre-Oedipal, pre-syntactical logic of the female. *The Waves* uses "women's time" as its organizing principle, evoking cycle and recurrence in a menstrual relation to time and the tides. "In her fascination for the sea," Woolf seeks not only "a recovery of the mother," Beer writes, but "a way out of sexual difference itself"; not only a "continuity with lost origins" but an "acceptance of oblivion" (135, 170).   It is this, I would argue--the acceptance of oblivion in *The Waves*--that permits Woolf finally to fly outside the psycho-symbolics of western Christian patriarchy. Instead of a fantasy of transcendence, Woolf offers death as a return to the mother, and, exactly as Kristeva predicts someone will, Woolf reopens the question of religion from a woman's point of view.

II Recovering the Mother

No critic has yet commented substantially on the relationship between Milton's *Lycidas* and Woolf's *The Waves*, but even brief investigation demonstrates similarities: both "poems" are elegies lamenting the untimely death of a loved one. Both make a hero of the Cambridge scholar they lament. Both are set in Cornwall, overlooking the Irish Sea. Both are written in dauntingly abstract language, off-putting to the common reader. Both are autobiographical elegies, investigating the problem of death. Both have been described as incantatory and soothing, and yet—apparently contradictorily—as cool and impersonal. For both, water imagery dominates. Indeed, in both *Lycidas* and *The Waves*, water is used as a baseline against which horror and consolation are played out. These correspondences might be thought accidental, but they are not. Rather in *The Waves*, Woolf rewrites *Lycidas* in a feminist key.

Though recent criticism on Woolf has justly emphasized Woolf's wish to "think back through her mothers," it would be a mistake to conclude—as Ellen Hawkes does—that writing produced by men was unimportant to Woolf.[1] Of *Lycidas*, Milton's great pastoral elegy, Woolf was more than fond.[2] In "Hours in a Library" (*E2* 60), Woolf describes *Lycidas* as having a sense of inevitability about it. The poem summons "all our faculties to the task of reading" and "as in the great moments of our own experience" some "consecration descends" upon us from its hands "which we return to life, feeling it more keenly and understanding it more deeply than before."

Woolf's fascination with *Lycidas* comes in part, I would argue, from the effectiveness of its evocation of the mother. This project—evoking the mother—is central to all of Woolf's work. Jane Marcus has remarked that all Woolf's works are elegies. More precisely, one could argue that all Woolf's works are elegies *for the lost mother*. This mother may be conceived in literal or symbol-

---

[1]See Hawkes, Marcus ("Thinking Back"), Hanley, Silver, and Fox for discussions of this intimidation. While Hawkes may oversimplify when she refers to Woolf's "caustic dismissal of masculine influence on women writers" (31), I, by no means, wish to underestimate Woolf's troubled relationship to the male tradition. Hanley tells us that by the time she had come to write *Three Guineas*, Woolf had begun "to regard educated men as dangerous to herself, her sex, and the human race" (48), and Marcus reminds us that Woolf was from the beginning so afraid to "trespass" on male territory that she feared as punishment "'instant dismemberment by wild horses'" ("Thinking Back" 1). Alice Fox describes "the torments she experienced for usurping her father's prerogatives" (31), and tells us that Woolf's "sense of inadequacy owing to her lack of a formal education" was sometimes overwhelming, so much so that "often when she tried to read a book she gave up because she felt that as a woman she had no rights" (2). In particular, we should bear in mind, Woolf felt the Elizabethan period, the great golden age of English literature, to be a "male preserve" (26).

[2]In this, Woolf repeats the sentiments of other literary women who, troubled by *Paradise Lost*'s Eve, are nevertheless drawn to Milton's shorter poems: *Comus*, *Lycidas*, and *L'Allegro* and *Il Penseroso*. See Cafarelli.

ic terms. Woolf's own mother, Julia Stephen, died when Woolf was thirteen, and Woolf never fully recovered from the loss. Further, Kristeva has theorized that "woman" in general is absent from history, for the woman/mother is the "unnameable repressed" of patriarchal language (43).

In "A Sketch of the Past," Woolf writes that her first memory is of sitting in her mother's lap (the vision of red and purple flowers tells us how closely Woolf's face is pressed to her mother's chest, a perspective that evokes infant dependency). Woolf's placement of the mother first in her "portrait of the artist as a young woman" signals her displacement of the paternal in favor of the mother-child relation. If for Lacan "consciousness, the ego and identity are all premised on the intervention of the symbolic in the mother-child relation" (Lechte 130), in "A Sketch" (as quite obviously in *The Waves* and *To the Lighthouse*), Woolf insists instead on an uninterrupted connection between the mother and child (a connection epitomized by the image of James in Mrs. Ramsay's lap throughout section one of *To the Lighthouse*). Later in the "A Sketch," Woolf describes the lost Julia Stephen more mythically still as a cathedral in which her mind sat for all of its life.

Significantly for our understanding of *The Waves* (and for my study of the relation between *The Waves* and *Lycidas*) Woolf's memory of her mother (which is her very first memory) is immediately connected to her memory of water (her second memory). "Perhaps we were going to St Ives," Woolf writes; "perhaps we were coming back to London" (*MOB* 64). With the idea of St. Ives—that town in Cornwall on the western edge of England that faces the Irish Sea (that place, incidentally, off the shore of which Lycidas drowned)—Woolf is led to the second, more comprehensive memory, also of water. "For if life has a base that it stands upon," she writes,

> if it is a bowl that one fills and fills and fills—then my bowl without a doubt stands upon this memory. It is of lying half asleep, half awake, in bed in the nursery at St Ives. It is of hearing *the waves* breaking, one, two, one, two, and sending a splash of water over the beach; and then breaking, one, two, one, two, behind the yellow blind. It is of hearing the blind drawing its little acorn across the floor as the wind blew the blind out. It is of lying and hearing this splash and seeing this light, and feeling, it is almost impossible that I should be here; of feeling the purest ecstasy I can conceive (*MOB* 64).

In the convergence of the two memories—of the mother and of the waves (Woolf writes later that the two memories are indeed indistinguishable)—the mother is at once distinct (Julia Stephen) and reformulated in larger terms, as a part of the waves. The mother merges with water—the waves, the sea—and both merge with the ocean of possible forms out of which, according to Darwin, we were born. In Kristevan terms, the connection between the mother and water suggests the *chora*, the embryo-like "receptacle" which is itself " . . . connotative of the mother's body" (Lechte 128). Perhaps because we are comprised mainly of water; perhaps because, as Darwin suggests, we come from the sea; perhaps because, within the individual life, we come from the amniotic watery sea-sac and breathe, in the womb, like fish, mother and water are indistinguishable.

Kristeva describes the *chora* as pre-linguistic; it is a "nonexpressive totality formed by the drives and their stases in a motility that is as full of movement as it is regulated" (128). As such, the *chora* is a kind of amniotic sea sac or miniature ocean which moves with, but ultimately contains, the child. The *chora* is like the waves which provide the dominant pattern of cycle and return in *The Waves*. Woolf's first and happiest memories—of her mother and the waves— evoke the *chora* which is prior to linguistic consciousness, the Lacanian symbolic. In the solution and dissolution of waves that is the *materia materna* of the nine interludes that organize the novel; in the crashing of the progeny-delivering waves on the shore (Beer 170),[3] Woolf recovers the mother, in part by replicating the birth process itself, the moment of individuation and ideation. She imagines the washing of the not-fully-formed human body up against the pelvic rock, and the pushing of the self into the world through the hole at the scene of deaths and entrances. More mythically and scientifically, in the rhythmic rise and fall of the waves, Woolf reopens the question of theology from a woman's point of view, for the waves are the source and as such, they embody Woolf's material/maternal theology of human formulation and return. If for the Christian patriarch the world is a fallen place from which the spirit must escape to its true home, for Woolf, the self is not only embodied in, but finds its home, in the *materia materna* of mother/nature. We are not destined for heaven. Rather—and not entirely tragically—we are destined by biological birth fact to die; to sink, like Lycidas's head, barely formed, in time not formed at all, beneath the fluid oblivion of the oblivious and obliterating, but always materializing waves.

For Woolf—and I think this explains the pleasure she takes in the poem— this feminist ideology of the *materia materna* is anticipated in *Lycidas*, Milton's oceanic elegy about the early death by drowning of a beloved friend and fellow poet. Like *The Waves*, *Lycidas* is woven through with wave imagery. Indeed, is there any other poem in the English language—with the possible exception of

---

[3]Beer writes (170) that "in an early version of *The Waves* [Woolf] wrote of the waves as "sinking and falling, many mothers, and again, many mothers, and behind them, many more, endlessly sinking and falling."

Woolf's novel/poem *The Waves*—so water laden? Waves recur cyclically from one end of *Lycidas* to the other, rocking the poem like a boat or a cradle. The dead Lycidas floats on the "wat'ry bier" (12); Milton composes for the dead Lycidas, a "melodious tear"(14); Orpheus's "gory visage" (62) floats down the river to the Lesbian shore; the Swift Hebrus (63) and the Rivers Cam (103) and Alpheus (132) join the Fountain Arethuse (85) to wash through the poem; Lycidas's body sinks in the "remorseless deep" (50); the "shores and sounding [Irish] seas" (154) wash Lycidas's bones "far away . . . under the whelming tide" (155, 157) where he visits "the bottom of the monstrous world" (158). Even in heaven, Lycidas washes his "oozy locks" (175) saved at last by "the dear might of him that walk'd *the waves*" (173; italics mine). The "melodious tear" (14) remembered at poem's end in the wiping of the tears forever from Lycidas's eyes (181), is Milton's metonymical description for poetry itself and for *Lycidas* in particular.

Lycidas is an elegy for a loved one drowned in the Irish Sea. It is situated, like *The Waves*, off the coast of Cornwall, at the foggy intersection of land, sea, and sky, the seemingly preternatural site of deaths and entrances. It is a meditation on the mysterious fact of death—one that tries to come to terms with the grief that attends death, obsessively and painfully addressing the question of what to do in such a world. It is saturated in the water imagery of the maternal (whether of tears or the sea). It uses the fluid mechanics of the waves as its thematic center, its protection against death and resolution to despair.   Given these conditions, it is unsurprising that *Lycidas* was Woolf's favorite poem, the one poem to which she could return, in a curiously maternally associated word, "unsated" ("and then," she writes of her conversation with Yeats, "discussing what poems we could come back to unsated, I said Lycidas" [*D3* 330]).   In its imagery of waves and in the regular pulse that its waves promise of the return of the mother, Woolf found in *Lycidas* not only consolation, but the fluid mechanics for a feminist poetic.

Both *Lycidas* and *The Waves* have been described as elegies of enormous emotional power.   Shumaker writes, for example, that praise for *Lycidas* is "couched often in language so high-pitched that it absorbs easily adjectives like 'exquisite,' 'thrilling,' 'tremendous,' and 'supreme'" (129). Similarly, Marilyn Zucker describes *The Waves* as "incantatory" (106) and Carol Ascher describes *The Waves* as "that rhythmic ode to the ocean" in which a "rolling succession of soliloquies reproduces the ceaseless roll of waves."   For Ascher, *The Waves* is "about the imagination itself," not only "as flight" and "reach for order," but "as relief from pain" (51, 54).

At the same time, and seemingly paradoxically, both works are described as so abstract and impersonal as to be almost indecipherable. James Holly Hanford writes, for example, that "It is doubtful whether anyone, approaching *Lycidas* for the first time, fails to experience a feeling of strangeness" (Hanford 31) and Wayne Shumaker writes similarly that "more insistently, perhaps, than any other poem in English, *Lycidas* raises the purely aesthetic problem of how the emotions may be stirred by lines which at first are much less than perspicuous to the intellect" (129). David Daiches describes *The Waves* in similar terms as "a curiously artificial piece of work" whose technical difficulty makes it, "at once the subtlest and the most rigid, the most eloquent and the least communicative of Virginia Woolf's novels" (105, 111).

One explanation for the paradox of indecipherability that is nonetheless comforting (and it has surfaced from critics on both sides) is this: in *Lycidas* and *The Waves* Milton and Woolf discover a strategy to describe "the essence of [affective] consciousness itself" (Briggs 111). John Briggs likens the "wavelike movement of consciousness" that Woolf replicates in *The Waves* to a "musical theme" that recurs throughout a larger piece of music (110, 113). Critics have referred to a similar affect in *Lycidas*. Wayne Shumaker describes the "affective connotations of words, phrases, and images" which blend in *Lycidas* into formal strands like "musical themes" to create "a total emotional harmony both massive enough and piercing enough to be overpowering" (129).

Authorial impersonality—connected for Kristeva to the semiotic—may also contribute to the paradoxical affect—of linguistic difficulty, but of emotional satiation/satisfaction—of *Lycidas* and *The Waves*. One of the staples in *Lycidas* criticism is the question of its anonymity. In "*Lycidas*: A Poem Finally Anonymous," Stanley Fish argues that while we are reminded throughout *Lycidas* of Milton's "fierce egoism," in the end the poet transcends himself, denying "the privilege of the speaking subject, of the unitary and separate consciousness" in favor of anonymity (340, 339). In Kristevan terms, the denial of the privileged speaking subject marks an affiliation to the semiotic. If "the subject's entry into the symbolic" is "signalled . . . by the mastery of language" (Lechte 132) and the "capacity to posit difference" [the mastery of the pronouns I and you], it is precisely the inability (or refusal) to master the difference between "I" and "you" that marks Milton's poem, for in *Lycidas*, as Fish points out, the subject shifts inexplicably at the end from the first person "I" of the body of the poem, to the second person "you" of Apollo's intervention, to the third person "he" of the coda.

A similar condition of anonymity, of the refusal of division between subject and object, is characteristic not only of Woolf's *The Waves* (perhaps best characterized by six liquefied protagonists who blend into one another and back again, unsuppressed by bodily form or psychic distance) but of Woolf's attitude toward art and poetry in general. If to Woolf Milton was the consummate *poet* (in some senses, greater even—at least as a poet—than Shakespeare[4]), the peculiarity of Milton's greatness, for Woolf, comes from the impersonality of his style.[5] In *The Waves*, Woolf also strives for impersonality. She wants to represent not her life but "the life of anybody" (DeSalvo 179). "This shall be childhood," she writes, "but it must not be *my* childhood" (*D3* 236). The narrator "should have no name," Woolf writes, "I dont want a Lavinia or a Penelope: I want 'She'" (*D3* 229-30). Such namelessness permits at once a dissolution of self and a form of transcendence connotative of maternal deity. In the first holograph draft, Woolf describes her narrator as "the seer . . . the force that arranges . . . the thing in which all this exists" (Marcus, *Art* 200). This seer—whether the woman with the lamp that brings light from the bottom of the sea or the Woman of Elvedon—is the organizing principle of the novel, the living, thinking, writing being around whom the fluctuating novel-poem flows like a sea.

Both poems speak from the remembered language of the maternal repressed. According to Kristeva, the semiotic is constituted more by drives, sounds, and impulses, than linearity and coherence. While the symbolic relies on linear "syntax, grammar, meaning, and logic," the ungrammatical, imagery-dense pre-Oedipal semiotic represents "heterogeneous rupture . . . a challenge to, if not the transgression of, the existing historical form of the symbolic" (Lechte 139). Poetic language "wipes out" the symbolic, "attack[ing] denotation and meaning" (135). In poetry this rupture is enacted phonetically, for primitive sounds—sounds heard by the fetus in the body of the mother—have the power to enlist,

---

[4]Of *Paradise Lost* Woolf writes, "But how smooth, strong & elaborate it all is! What poetry! I can conceive that even Shakespeare after this would seem a little troubled, personal, hot & imperfect. I can conceive that this is the essence, of which almost all other poetry is the dilution" (*D1* 193).

[5]In the well-known diary entry of September 10, 1918, Woolf comments on "the sublime aloofness & impersonality of the emotions" in *Paradise Lost* (1:192), and in a letter to Lytton Strachey she writes, "I have read the whole of Milton, without throwing any light upon my own Soul" (*L2* 282). Woolf at times interprets this "impersonality" in negative terms: "Don't you think it very queer though" she writes in the letter to Strachey, "that [Milton] entirely neglects the human heart?" At the same time, for Woolf, "impersonality" is the most significant characteristic of great poetry. In *A Room of One's Own*, for example, Woolf wonders why women have written novels but not yet poetry, indicating that poetry was the "original impulse" (*AROO* 71) and should be the direction in which women move, and in "Women and Fiction," similarly, she chastises women writers for being too personal, for writing too close to the bone of the self, and therefore, for not yet writing *poetry*. As the female artist matures she will become less autobiographical, Woolf writes for "the greater impersonality of women's lives will encourage the poetic spirit . . ." and women will begin to look "to the wider questions which the poet tries to solve . . ." (*GR* 83).

within the symbolic, associations from the primordial.   Semiotic devices—
rhythm, repetition, and metonymy—express the "pre-Oedipal drive activity that
underlies the symbolic order," for the "acquisition of language involves a period
in which drive activity dominates the production of sounds."   Thus [for exam-
ple], for Kristeva, the "m" of mama is evocative of sucking, while the "p" of papa
is exploratory, anal (143).

   Lycidas and *The Waves* both articulate this phonetic primordiality.   James
McGavran argues that William Wordsworth precedes Woolf in connecting a
shoreline with childhood and birth.   But in this Milton anticipates Woolf and
Wordsworth both.   *Lycidas* not only depicts, but auralizes the shoreline of birth
and death.   In a system of masculine end rhymes which exploit the terrifying but
also comfortingly incantatory repetition of waves, *Lycidas*'s imagery enacts
Kristeva's condition of primordiality and pulverization of language.   One obvious example is the eerie "or" sound which provides an underlying musical
phrase.   The poem's frequent repetition of "Shore," "door," "floor," "no more,"
and "yet once more" in midst of the visual description of the misty/mystifying
juncture of earth, sea, and sky, presents the sea as a "door" and as the terrifying-
comforting, alien-familiar maternal body.   This "door" is the mediating zone in
which, in a few terrifying moments, the living Edward King drowns.   The word
"floor," similarly, suggests both the sea's bottom where the bones of Edward
King are tossed with supreme and disturbing indifference and the sea's surface
from which King rises in his redemption.

   Woolf creates similar effects in *The Waves*.   The nine interludes in which the
waves predominate, assuming form before breaking on the shore, replicate the
rhythms of birth and death.   The waves stampede and trample, they break and
toss, they lap at the drowned ship at the bottom of the sea.   Rhoda imagines herself drowning at the close of the novel's odd-numbered episodes 1, 3, 5, 7 (and
by extension in Bernard's soliloquy in 9).   If in *Lycidas* water is used as a kind
of musical theme, a bass note of dread and solace throughout, and if the manner
of Lycidas's death—by drowning in the Irish Sea—is never fully suppressed, but
is always, terrifyingly, within reach of the reader's consciousness (Shumaker
134-35), so also Woolf uses sound and rhythm to replicate the sea, the memory
of mother, and the foreshadowing of death, and so to play a similarly frighten-
ing-comforting role in *The Waves*.   If, on the one hand, the waves sing a lullaby,
promising renewal with their cycle of rising and falling and rising again, and if
in this sense they are likened to the rhythmic motility of the fetus in the body of
the mother (Schwartz 106), on the other hand, the waves are an unsympathetic
force, carrying within them an indifference and anonymous violence that can
only be terrifying.

In both works, the water that symbolizes/represents the remembered maternal *chora* is appealed to phonetically on a primordial level to suggest both that with which we automatically identify and that of which we are unspeakably afraid. Our genesis is in the mother's womb, a watery base in which we float, both alive and not alive, before birth. We evolved from the sea, but once born, we drown in the waves. Both enacting and deferring the pain of death associated with the waves, both works use rhythms, sounds, and images characteristic of the semiotic to evoke the sea, and to disturb, calm, and then disturb again, feelings of fear and pleasure associated with the mother.

III Flying Through the House of the Past

Woolf's identification with *Lycidas* is more thorough perhaps than with any other poem in the language. It is the one poem she can return to *unsated*. As we have seen, this identification occurs psychoanalytically on the level of a shared access to the semiotic. At the same time, that identification with *Lycidas* is interfered with, for in *Lycidas* the soothing/terrifying voice of the mother is ultimately overthrown by the law of the father. Cixous writes that as a child she identified with freedom fighters Hercules and Ulysses. It was only later that she realized that to them she was not a comrade, but a mere woman (572). So also on some level, *Lycidas* is the admired but ultimately woman-excluding poem Woolf must revise. It is that beloved maternal, but also disturbingly masculine polemic against which Woolf must construct her own elegy/prophesy for women. If *The Waves* pays tribute to and extends the "fluid mechanics" of *Lycidas*, it also breaks its woman-excluding patriarchal laws and smashes its Christian untruths. Not only in *A Room of One's Own*, but in *The Waves*, Woolf's mission is to break the language vessel that holds the father's law intact.

In "A Poem Nearly Anonymous," John Crowe Ransom argues that the pastoral elegiac tradition is "extremely masculine" (70). In addition to demonstrating manly restraint in the face of death, pastoral elegies construct a woman-excluding buddy-buddy system that depicts one male poet aggrandizing another. In *Lycidas* Milton idealizes his dead classmate, Edward King, even as he hopes that "some [future] Muse," presumably male, will turn to bid his grave a similar "fair peace" (19, 22). Pastoral elegy provides the archetypal genre for authorizing the homosocial bonding, performed over the body of woman, theorized by Eve Kosofsky Sedgwick.

Pastoral elegies are sophisticated productions. To write, even to read, the form one needs to be highly literate, part of an educated elite. As Woolf demonstrates when she imagines herself blocked from the library door in *A Room of One's Own*, such literacy is—and is meant to be—literally impossible for women to achieve, for the patriarchy constitutes itself precisely by the exclusion of

women, and in some senses, most fundamentally, by the refusal of their education.   The writer of elegies is a male, because only males have access to the
education needed for the elite form.   Similarly, the reader to whom elegies are
directed is also male.   The subject of elegy, the disposed-of, is woman.   Woolf's
insight into this exclusion, her peek behind the male door which her father's
long-ago violation of the Law of the Father allowed (for the virgin Woolf could
roam *his* library unattended), reveals to her, and by extension to the female reader to whom she directs her oratorical-poem, the further revelation that the
conventions themselves of pastoral elegy are misogynistic.

If an elegy in general is a "formal and sustained poem of lament for the death
of a particular person," the most prestigious of elegies, the *pastoral* elegy, depicts
a male poet-shepherd mourning the loss of a fellow male poet-shepherd through
the use of elaborate and *gendered* conventions. These gendered conventions
include an invocation to the *female* muses; a depiction of a grieving but *feminized*
nature; an accusation against the *female* nymphs for failing to protect the loved
one; a procession of *masculine* mourners; a casting of *feminine* flowers on the
loved one's grave; and, in Christian elegies, a closing consolation asserting both
heavenly redemption and eternal fame for the lost poet.[6] Taken together these
conventions contrast a female and killing, but ultimately impotent nature against
a masculine poet and his savingly potent, also masculine, heaven-residing God.
In effect, having been excluded historically and materially, women are further
excluded by the all-male linguistic in-crowd whose most priestly inner sanctum
is the pastoral elegy.

In *A Room of One's Own*, Woolf rewrites elegy by burying *Lycidas* (the
poem she is prevented from seeing in the first few paragraphs of that polemic)
under a restored community of female writers, for a Kristeva-like *recherche de
la mère perdu*, the uncovering of a Lost Atlantis of female writers is the priority
of *A Room*. Rejected at the library door, refused entrance to the male canon epitomized in *Lycidas*, Woolf replaces *Lycidas* with a *female* and feminist elegy. In
A Room, Woolf mourns not a male, but a female tradition, a lost Atlantis that, dug
up, could mark the beginning of a centuries-long archaeological project.
Forgotten but foundational women writers in England include, for Woolf, the
Duchess of Newcastle, Dorothy Osborne, Aphra Behn, Eliza Carter, Fanny
Burney, Jane Austen, and George Eliot (among others). "Rearranging the furniture" of pastoral elegy, Woolf describes a host of women writers as forerunners
to one another, even as she asks each to throw tribute-bearing flowers upon one
another's graves:

[6]To my knowledge, the gendered character of pastoral elegiac conventions has not
yet been demonstrated. My list follows but genders Abrams's basic list of pastoral conventions.

> Without those forerunners [Newcastle, Carter, Behn, and so forth] Jane Austen and the Brontes and George Eliot could no more have written than Shakespeare could have written without Marlowe, or Marlowe without Chaucer, or Chaucer without those forgotten poets who paved the way . . . For masterpieces are not single and solitary births; they are the outcome of many years of thinking in common, of thinking by the body of the people, so that the experience of the mass is behind the single voice. Jane Austen should have laid a wreath upon the grave of Fanny Burney, and George Eliot done homage to the robust shade of Eliza Carter . . . All women together ought to let flowers fall upon the tomb of Aphra Behn. (*AROO* 70-71)

As in *Lycidas* Milton lays a wreath on King's urn, and hopes, in time to come, for yet another latter-day poet to lay a wreathe on his, so here Woolf imagines women writers as a procession of mourners celebrating their forerunners. As the whole function of pastoral elegy is to prevent the isolation and demise of individual masculine poets by placing them within the protection of a larger and immortalizing institution, so Woolf, in *A Room of One's Own*, refuses to isolate "single" and "solitary" women writers, but creates instead an ongoing community among them in which "the experience of the mass is behind the single voice."[7]

IV Peeking in on Masculine Homosociality

In *The Waves* (1931), Woolf's first major work to follow *A Room of One's Own* (1929), Woolf further tears down the false laws and horrid "truths" of the patriarchy. There is much in *The Waves* that simply establishes it as a successor to *Lycidas*. Woolf reproduces, for example, Milton's three-part structure of childhood, loss, and recovery; she uses nature (particularly the sun and the waves) as a backdrop against which the individual life is given apocalyptic scope; she offers, in her six protagonists, a procession of pastoral mourners, and in her portrait of Percival and the British educational, military, and imperialistic systems, she practices political invective, exemplifying her distaste for corruption. She employs the impersonality of an all-but anonymous narrator whose removal from the scene of grief imitates nature's indifference; and most importantly, she echoes and so pays tribute to *Lycidas* by way of "the waves," which, as in *Lycidas*, are presented as both terrifying and comforting. Still, Woolf establishes many of these motifs only to criticize the masculine values they express.

---

[7]In a similar vein, Ransom (78) writes that *Lycidas* is "the climax of a tradition, and is better than the work of any earlier artist in the series."

Of the masculine values that dominate *Lycidas*, Woolf deconstructs the two most damaging in *The Waves*: the homosocial bonding that underwrites the pastoral elegiac idiom (in effect, the Law of the Father itself) and the Christian metaphysics which offer philosophical grounding for such homosociality.

Woolf's challenge to the homosocial bonding of the pastoral elegiac idiom—not only to the collusion of poets and poetry with sexism, but to the very inscription of sexism within the poetic domain—occurs throughout the novel, but most obviously in her satiric portrayal of Cambridge culture, and, at its center, the friendship between Neville and Bernard.

Through their shared interest in poetry, the elitely educated, upper class Neville and Bernard bond with and hope to immortalize one another. But such bonding and attempted self-immortalization is constructed over the body of woman. The third episode of *The Waves* finds Bernard reading Gray's pastoral "Elegy in a Country Churchyard." The poem inspires Bernard, and in Neville's company, Bernard begins to feel "among the most gifted of men." "I am filled," he says, "with the delight of youth, with potency, with the sense of what is to come" (*TW* 233). After this, he says that he *owes* "these Latin words" to Neville. Neville responds immediately to such poetic warmth, saying to Bernard, in what forms a dramatic climax, "give me your poems. . . let us go back together, over the bridge, under the elm trees, to my room" (*TW* 234). In the Cambridge dorm, Bernard and Neville, closeted with one another, shut out the women, "these distracting voices . . . these pert shop-girls . . . these shuffling, heavy-laden old women . . . Jinny . . . Susan . . . [and] Rhoda" (*TW* 234). There, the voice and smell of women—all women, young and sexual ("these pert shop-girls"), old and no longer sexual ("these shuffling, heavy-laden old women"), and even one's friends (Jinny, Susan, and Rhoda) can be excluded. In fact, amid the beautiful architecture of Cambridge, Neville can not bear the thought of women, who fill him with contempt: "When there are buildings like these . . . I cannot endure that there should be shop-girls. Their titter, their gossip, offends me; breaks into my stillness, and nudges me, in moments of purest exultation, to remember our degradation" (*TW* 234). Women—associated with nature and the body and excluded from the immortalizing function of poetry—degrade Neville, for, ultimately, they represent the maternal body that reminds Neville of his own, necessarily denied death. Bernard also associates women with death. In episode four, Bernard notices the common shop-girls who "ignoring their doom, look in at the shop-windows." Meanwhile Bernard believes the Christian metaphysical delusion that his life will be "mysteriously prolonged" for he will "cast a fling of seed wider, beyond this generation, this doom-encircled population" (*TW* 254).

Away from the shop-girls and laden old women, Neville and Bernard become "masters of tranquility and order" as well as "inheritors of proud tradition" (*TW* 234). "If I think of you in twenty years' time," Neville "says" to Bernard, in a direct allusion to the conventions of pastoral elegy, "when we are both famous . . . I shall weep for you if you are dead" (*TW* 235). Remembering Catullus, whom he "adore[s]" (*TW* 235), Neville says it would be "a glorious life, to addict oneself to [such] perfection" (*TW* 235)—a perfection wholly outside and above the imperfect, mute mortality of silent (and silenced) women. Thinking again of that perfection, and longing to join the parade of immortals of which pastoral elegists Bion, Moschus, Theocritus, Virgil, Spenser, and Milton are already a part, Neville asks Bernard, "Am I a poet?" (*TW* 236).   But Neville's poetry, conventionally elitist, and, in some ways, far from the *materia materna* of *Lycidas* itself, condemns the "vulgarity" (*TW* 236) of shop-girls. Tossing his poem at Bernard, Neville says, "Take it . . . the thing I aim at: shop-girls, women, the pretence, the vulgarity of life . . . catch it—my poem" (*TW* 236).

Bernard responds ecstatically to Neville's gift, and behind the curtain where Woolf is peeping, we hear her laughing: "He has left me his poem," Bernard exalts, and then, on a surge of emotion not found elsewhere in the novel, he cries: "O friendship, I too will press flowers between the pages of Shakespeare's sonnets! O friendship, how piercing are your darts—there, there, again there. He looked at me, turning to face me; he gave me his poem" (*TW* 236). Moments later, in imagery that suggests the underlying narcissism that characterizes, for Woolf, the masculine pastoral elegiac tradition, Bernard says, "Like a long wave, like a roll of heavy waters, he went over me, his devastating presence—dragging me open, laying bare the pebbles on the shore of my soul" (*TW* 236).

Because he is cut off from fellowship with his more elite peers, Bernard and Neville, Woolf is sympathetic to the lower-class Louis.   Nevertheless, like Neville and Bernard, Louis uses poetry to elevate himself narcissistically and snobbishly, at others' expense. Louis is the greatest poet among them, for as Bernard tells us, "When Louis is alone he sees with astonishing intensity, and will write some words that may outlast us all" (*TW* 267). Louis is most closely associated with Rhoda (for as poets and lovers, Louis and Rhoda meet secretly and repeatedly to meditate a *Lycidas*-like pastoral urn), but Louis is nonetheless a snob.   Unable to attend Cambridge (for his father was merely a banker in Brisbane); relegated to the quotidian, vulgar business world to which he does not psychically belong, Louis is alienated from all people who do not rise to the heights of poetic grandeur. He cries out in *Lycidas*-echoing language, "Bring us back to the fold, we who pass so disjectedly" (*TW* 240), and looking from a restaurant window upon the passers-by on the street, above all of whom he feels superior, again he cries, "Poetry. You, all of you, ignore it. What the dead poet said, you have forgotten." But "I, the companion of Plato, of Virgil," shall not forget (*TW* 240).

From all this poeticizing women are excluded. Susan is condemned to a life of maternity, of natural beauty only, of which she early grows weary, and Jinny is doomed to an attachment to tinsel and string, the vanities of a rapidly turning-to-dust beauty. Between them, Susan and Jinny signify the bodily mortality to which women are condemned, and within which women have traditionally been identified by men.[8] Most pointedly, the psychologically and linguistically violated Rhoda (described repeatedly in direct allusion to *Lycidas* as Arethuse, "the [raped] nymph of the fountain always wet"), who might have been a great poet, who is in every way described as a poet—related to Shelley, to Keats, and to Milton—suffers a death that goes almost entirely unnoticed. In fact, it is only in Bernard's final soliloquy, when he describes Rhoda as flying through the sky with neck outstretched (*TW* 371), that we learn of her suicide and even then we do not discover the means. Did she hang herself? Did she leap from a tall building? Did she drown in the waves? Rhoda is the abandoned intellectual, Woolf's sinister substitute, a poet manqué whose career is cut short by the mere fact of her femaleness. In Rhoda's unsolemnized death—opposed directly to the noisy fanfare of Percival's much (and publicly?) mourned death—Woolf attacks the male-dominated social institutions which exclude her. Rhoda "reminds us," Ruddick writes, "in her experiences, images, fears and gifts of Woolf herself" (209). Through Rhoda's suicide, Woolf demonstrates that however much she loved, admired, and even adored Percival/Thoby, she also resented the masculine privileges he enjoyed and comfortably assumed: a Cambridge education, literate peers, privilege, prominence, and above all, the right to be taken seriously that Milton and his dead friend, Edward King, also enjoyed.

V A New Religion

In some ways, Woolf's principal objective in *The Waves* is to unravel the Christian metaphysics that are supremely represented in *Lycidas*. Both poems are haunted, even horrified by death. *Lycidas* records the mind-numbing shock ("For *Lycidas* is dead, dead ere his prime" [8]) of hearing of Lycidas's death by emphasizing the ear, the organ to which the revelation is delivered: "As killing as the Canker to the Rose," Milton laments, "Such, *Lycidas*, thy loss to Shepherd's *ear*" (45, 49; emphasis on "ear" mine). He pictures over and over the manner of Lycidas's death. He thinks, for example, of Lycidas's "gory visage" as if it were Orpheus's beheaded mask sent downstream amidst a "hideous roar" by the female Bacchantes (62, 61); he sees the "remorseless deep" closing over the head of his beloved Lycidas (50); and he imagines Lycidas's dead body

[8]In *The Singing of the Real World* (8, 9) Mark Hussey writes that Jinny "relates to others solely through her body" and that "Susan lives her body almost as completely embodied as Jinny."

hurled "under the whelming tide" to the bottom of the sea, that "monstrous world" where eye-to-eye Lycidas meets the monsters of the deep (157, 158). To emphasize the terror and randomness of death, Milton alludes to the blind female fury Atropos who "slits" the poet's "thin-spun life" with her "abhorr'd shears" (75-76) just when the poet, after years of preparation, hopes to blaze out into sudden fame.

The Waves is similarly haunted by news and imagery of death. Denied a view of the dead body, Bernard is nevertheless tormented by imagined sightings of the dead Percival. His friend lies perhaps "pale and bandaged in some room" (*TW* 281). Bernard further fantasizes "the hospital; the long room with black men pulling ropes . . ." (*TW* 282-83). In his final soliloquy Bernard says: "What torments one is the horrible activity of the mind's eye—how he fell, how he looked, where they carried him" (*TW* 360). Again, it is not only images of the dead body, but terror at the randomness of death that haunt Bernard. In one of the more obvious allusions to *Lycidas* in *The Waves*, Bernard calls to mind Atropos' "ab'horred sheers" (*Lycidas* 75), when he sits in his final soliloquy to have his hair cut by the barber:

> The hairdresser began to move his scissors to and fro. I felt myself powerless
> to stop the oscillations of the cold steel. So we are cut and laid in swathes, I said;
> so we lie side by side on the damp meadows, withered branches and flowerings.
> (*TW* 371)

A few pages earlier, Bernard prepares for the allusion to the Miltonic Atropos when he wonders why there should be "universal determination to go on living, when really . . . any slate may fly from a roof, any car may swerve, for there is neither rhyme nor reason when a drunk man staggers about with a club in his hand" (*TW* 361).

Both poems register the strange, mystifying psychological disturbance of death, but for Woolf death is inevitable and final, an oblivion to be accepted. Bernard says, for example, "I scoff . . . [at] eternal life" (*TW* 372). For Milton, on the other hand, death—equivalent to relegating the human body-mind to the maternal natural world only—is what the celibate, studious, elite poet must escape. *Lycidas* holds nature responsible for mortalizing what otherwise would be the poet's immortal soul. In the wake of this accusation, the gynocidal poet leaves woman behind; indeed, builds his Noah's Ark from her remains, and turns, for self-rescue, to the masculine paternal otherworldly force of the Christian God, a vertical, hurry-climb-up-this-ladder elevation found at the still point of a no longer revolving world.

In an outpouring of grief ("But O the heavy change, now thou art gone, /Now thou art gone, and never must return!" [37-38]), Milton laments the maternal, earth-world change which has resulted in King's death. In a classic instance of pathetic "ph"allacy, Milton depicts the female-identified woods and caves as able to sympathize with but not to convert Lycidas's fate. Not only the female nymphs and Calliope are blamed for neglecting Lycidas, but the female Bacchantes are charged with *causing* his death. "Where were ye Nymphs," Milton questions, "when the remorseless deep / Clos'd o'er the head of your lov'd *Lycidas*?"; but "what could that have done?"

> What could the Muse herself that *Orpheus* bore,
> The Muse herself, for her enchanting son
> Whom Universal nature did lament,
> When by the rout that made the hideous roar,
> His gory visage down the stream was sent,
> Down the swift *Hebrus* to the *Lesbian* shore? (50-51; 57-63)

First as neglectful, then as helpless, and finally as destructive, the feminine is implicated in this passage in her paradoxical incarnations as madonna and as whore, for neither the Nymphs (who should have been watching and guarding the waters to prevent King's death), nor Calliope herself (who, impotently female, could do nothing to save her poet son Orpheus from death), nor the female Bacchantes (who savagely murdered Orpheus in their jealous frenzy) either did or could or wished to prevent King's death. Only the removed, potent, rational, Christian God can save man from the dreaded cycle of birth and death which female nature otherwise forces man to occupy. So Apollo reassures the frightened Milton that even in death a poet's fame will be "no plant that grows on mortal soil," but will "live[ ] and spread[ ] aloft" before the "pure eyes / And perfect witness of all-judging *Jove*" (78, 81-82).

With the intervention of Apollo's reassuringly masculine voice the lamenting Milton is brought up short, reminded of the transcendent God, and in the poem's final transformation, King is declared not dead—not confined to this mortal world of the doomed body (the rigged human ship built in the eclipse of flesh and bone)—but, rather, "through the dear might of him [Christ] that walk'd *the waves*" (italics mine 173), miraculously resurrected in a fantasy of transcendence, otherness, difference from woman:

> Weep no more, woeful Shepherds weep no more,
> For *Lycidas* your sorrow is not dead,
> Sunk though he be beneath the wat'ry floor
> So sinks the day-star in the Ocean bed,
> And yet anon repairs his drooping head,
> And tricks his beams, and with new-spangled Ore,
> Flames in the forehead of the morning sky. (165-172)

As the male sun sinks in the ocean bed but miraculously rises on the following day to flame in the "forehead of the morning sky,"[9] and as *the* son, Christ, walks on water, demonstrating his superiority to the merely natural waves, so Lycidas—a member of the masculine brotherhood of poet-shepherds—shall be lifted from the destructive but ultimately impotent maternal waves not only to be celebrated, but to be immortalized aloft before the all-judging eyes of Jove/God.

In *The Waves*, Woolf refutes such masculine pipe dreams. Instead, Woolf laughs at the Masculine Word—whether expressed in the male fantasy of authoritarian, patriarchal Christian theology or in the self-delusions of pastoral elegy—and accepts in its stead loss, mortality, and the female body with which they are associated. Where for Milton death is that maternal which must be overcome by way of the masculine Word, for Woolf, death is the (if anything masculine) nemesis against which one must hurl oneself bravely, for nothing lasts and we enjoy, at best, "momentary alleviation[s]" (*TW* 335). It is in this context that we should see Bernard finally cast aside his writer's notebook, and in this context that we should hear him say, mockingly, that it is only as "children" that "we tell each other stories . . . make up these ridiculous, flamboyant, beautiful phrases" (*TW* 341). It is in this context, finally, that we should hear Bernard—who, after Percival's death, solaces himself with words—reject, finally, the "false surmise" (*Lycidas* 153) of the masculine symbolic "immortalized" in pastoral elegy: "Let us commit any blasphemy," he says, "rather than exude this lily-sweet glue; and cover him with phrases" (*TW* 360). In the end for Bernard, words console but only temporarily, for there is no promise of resurrection, no father god, and no certainty on earth or heaven. If Blake finalized the transmission of the idea of God and the devil from the skies to the human mind, Woolf finalizes, annihilates the fantasy of the transcendent ego, the thetic self, constructed for Woolf in the myths and self-flatteries of symbolic language. If once Neville threw a poem at his head, allowing Bernard to feel "a sudden conviction of immortality," now that, too, "has gone" (*TW* 334).

Both *Lycidas* and *The Waves* are elegies, meditations meant to exorcise the early, unexpected death of a person of symbolic and emotional importance to their respective authors,[10] and both, as elegies, are sublimely effective, especially in the use of an experimental language—expressed most sensitively through choric water imagery—to recreate and then sublimate the fear of death. If the

---

[9]"Forehead" implies the masculine machinery of the brain, both the poet's soon-to-be immortalized brain and the brain of God, superior to the body of mother nature.

[10]As Ruddick tells us (190), Woolf was devastated by the unexpected death, at twenty-six, of her brother Thoby whom she nursed in his illness. "He became for her the prototype of a beautiful, privileged young male whose character can never be assessed."

sub-dominant voice of *Lycidas* yearns for the repressed maternal, its dominant voice is vertical, Christian, and supremely patriarchal. *The Waves* detaches itself from *Lycidas'* fantasies of domination, positioning itself instead along the horizontal, secular, and matriarchal line of the all seeing, earth-present Woman of Elvedon and the woman with the lamp of hours and days, rising from the bottom of the sea. If, for Milton, we are born of the inferior woman but saved at last by a nature-transcending and soul-redeeming father-God, for Woolf such transcendence is neither possible nor desired.[11] Articulating "the vision of an omnipercipient, androgynous, but recognizably female narrator" (Marcus, *Art* 20), Woolf describes not Jove, but the all-powerful woman beneath the sea as the *female* deity who raises the lamp that raises the sun, even as—in praise of female creativity—the waves sweep forward to deposit their children on the shore. If the whole of *Lycidas* leans toward redemption, the male-centered apocalyptic conclusion to this female-centered life, *The Waves* flows otherwise—from childhood—that series of moments in which, close to our maternal/material beginnings, we discover that we are and shall be nothing and all.

As Ruddick, among others, suggests, Woolf loved her father, but hated his tyrannies (195). I argue here that she felt similarly toward Milton, her literary father. She loved that aspect of his poetry that articulated struggle, that uncovered and passionately married the *materna materia* buried beneath patriarchal civilization; but insofar as his poetry's dominant voice insists on the woman-depriving masculine, "Defac't, deflow'r'd, and now to Death devote" (*PL* 9:901), Milton becomes for Woolf a nodal point of rage and a source of laughter. In *The Waves*, though without the iconoclastic fury of a Cromwell, Woolf tears through *Lycidas*, turning that great poem's furniture upside-down, smashing its laws, breaking its untruths with laughter. In the pastoral politics, religious ideologies, and aesthetics of *Lycidas*, as Woolf saw it, Milton's dominant voice not only excluded women, but transformed them into bogeys who steal from men the immortality they would otherwise enjoy. In *The Waves*, Woolf restores woman, but only partially at men's expense. While the failed poet Bernard can find no lullaby suitable to sing Percival "to [his] rest" (*TW* 345), the generous, lamb-like Rhoda throws withered violets on Percival's sea-grave. Through Rhoda especially—whose hungry face looks up throughout *The Waves* but is not fed—the embittered, satiric, triumphant, *mild* Woolf smears female blood on what she hopes is the hearse of the Cambridge pastoral tradition of male poetic self-immortalization.

---

[11]Woolf claims transcendence for Bernard according to Mark Hussey (*Singing* 94), but this is hardly the case. Rather, Bernard has a self-deluding moment of perceived transcendence in episode nine, an illusion almost immediately smashed.

Works Cited

Abrams, M. H. *A Glossary of Literary Terms*. New York: Holt, Rinehart and Winston, 1971.

Ascher, Carol. "Reading to Write: The Waves as Muse." *Virginia Woolf Miscellanies:Proceedings of the First Annual Conference on Virginia Woolf*. Eds. Mark Hussey and Vara Neverow-Turk. New York: Pace UP, 1992. 47-56.

Beer, Gillian. *Arguing with the Past: Essays in Narrative from Woolf to Sidney*. London: Routledge, 1989.

Briggs, John. "Nuance, Metaphor and the Rhythm of the Mood Waves in Virginia Woolf." *Virginia Woolf Miscellanies: Proceedings of the First Annual Conference on Virginia Woolf*. Eds. Mark Hussey and Vara Neverow-Turk. New York: Pace UP, 1992. 107-18.

Cafarelli, Annette Wheeler. "How Theories of Romanticism Exclude Women." *Milton,The Metaphysicals and Romanticism*. Eds. Lisa Low and Anthony John Harding. Cambridge: Cambridge UP, 1994. 84-113.

Cixous, Hélène. "Sorties: Out and Out: Attacks/Ways Out/Forays." *Contemporary Critical Theory*. Ed. Dan Latimer. San Diego: Harcourt Brace, 1989. 558-78.

Daiches, David. *Virginia Woolf*. Norfolk, Ct: New Directions, 1963.

DeSalvo, Louise. *The Impact of Childhood Sexual Abuse on Her Life and Work*. New York: Ballantine, 1989.

Fish, Stanley. "Lycidas: A Poem Finally Anonymous." *Milton's* Lycidas*: The Tradition And the Poem*. Ed. C. A. Patrides. Columbia: U of Missouri P, 1983. 319-40.

Fox, Alice. *Virginia Woolf and the Literature of the English Renaissance*. Oxford: Clarendon, 1990.

Goldman, Jane. "'Purple Buttons on Her Bodice': Feminist History and Iconography in *The Waves*." *Woolf Studies Annual* 2 (1996): 3-25.

Hanford, James Holly. "The Pastoral Elegy and Milton's Lycidas." *Milton's* Lycidas*: The Tradition and the Poem*. Ed. C. A. Patrides. Columbia: U of Missouri P, 1983. 31-59.

Hanley, Lynne. *Writing War: Fiction, Gender, and Memory*. Amherst: U of Massachusetts P, 1991.

Hawkes, Ellen. "Woolf's 'Magical Garden of Women.'" *New Feminist Essays on Virginia Woolf*. Ed. Jane Marcus. Lincoln: U of Nebraska P, 1981. 31-60.

Hussey, Mark. *The Singing of the Real World*. Columbus: Ohio UP, 1986.

Katz, Tamar. "Modernism, Subjectivity, and Narrative Form: Abstraction in *The Waves*."*Narrative* 3 (1995): 232-51.

Kristeva, Julia. "Women's Time." *Feminist Theory: A Critique of Ideology.* Eds. Nannerl O. Keohane et al. Chicago: U of Chicago P, 1982. 31-53.

Irigaray, Luce. *This Sex Which is Not One.* Trans. Catherine Porter. Ithaca: Cornell UP, 1985.

Lechte, John. *Julia Kristeva.* London: Routledge, 1990.

Marcus, Jane. *Art and Anger: Reading Like a Woman.* Columbus: Ohio UP, 1988.

——, ed. *New Feminist Essays on Virginia Woolf.* Lincoln: U of Nebraska P, 1981.

——. "Thinking Back Through Our Mothers." *New Feminist Essays on Virginia Woolf.* Ed. Jane Marcus. Lincoln: U of Nebraska P, 1981. 1-30.

McGavran, James Holt. "'Alone Seeking the Visible World': the Wordsworths, Virginia Woolf, and *The Waves.*" *Modern Language Quarterly* 42 (1981): 265-91.

Milton, John. *Complete Poems and Major Prose.* Ed. Merritt Y. Hughes. Indianapolis: Odyssey P, 1953.

Minow-Pinkney, Makiko. *Virginia Woolf and the Problem of the Subject.* New Brunswick: Rutgers UP, 1987.

Paccaud-Huguet, Josiane. "The Crowded Dance of Words: Language and Jouissance in *The Waves.*" *Q/W/E/R/T/Y: Arts, Litteratures, Civilisations du Monde Anglophone* 5 (1995): 337-40.

Ransom, John Crowe. "A Poem Nearly Anonymous." *Milton's* Lycidas: *The Tradition and the Poem.* Ed. C. A. Patrides. Columbia: U of Missouri P, 1983. 68-85.

Roe, Sue. "The Mind in Visual Form: Sketching *The Waves.*" *Q/W/E/R/T/Y: Arts, Litteratures & Civilisations du Monde Anglophone* 5 (1995): 227-40.

Ruddick, Sarah. "Private Brother, Public World." *New Feminist Essays on Virginia Woolf.* Ed. Jane Marcus. Lincoln: U of Nebraska P, 1981. 185-215.

Schwartz, Beth. "'A Rope to Throw the Reader': The Reading of Rhythm in Virginia Woolf." *Virginia Woolf Miscellanies; Proceedings of the First Annual Conference on Virginia Woolf.* Eds. Mark Hussey and Vara Neverow-Turk. New York: Pace UP, 1992. 105-07.

Sedgwick, Eve Kosofsky. *Between Men: English Literature and Male Homosocial Desire.* New York: Columbia UP, 1985.

Shumaker, Wayne. "Flowerets and Sounding Seas: A Study in the Affective Structure of *Lycidas.*" *Milton's* Lycidas: *The Tradition and the Poem.* Ed. C. A. Patrides. Columbia: U of Missouri P, 1983. 129-39.

Silver, Brenda. "The Authority of Anger: *Three Guineas* as Case Study." *Signs: A Journal of Women in Culture and Society* 16 (1991): 340-70.

Vandivere, Julie. "Waves and Fragments: Linguistic Construction as Subject

Formation in Virginia Woolf." *Twentieth Century Literature*. 42 (1996): 221-33.

Woolf, Virginia. *The Diary of Virginia Woolf. Volume One 1915-1919*. Ed. Anne Olivier Bell. San Diego: Harcourt Brace, 1977.

——. *The Diary of Virginia Woolf. Volume Three 1925-1930*. Ed. Anne Olivier Bell. New York: Harcourt Brace, 1980.

——. *The Essays of Virginia Woolf. Volume Two 1912-1918*. Ed. Andrew McNeillie. San Diego; Harcourt Brace, 1987.

——. *Granite and Rainbow*. New York: Harcourt Brace, 1958.

——. *Jacob's Room and The Waves*. New York: Harcourt Brace, 1959.

——. *The Letters of Virginia Woolf. Volume Two 1912-1922*. Eds. Nigel Nicolson and Joanne Trautmann. New York: Harcourt Brace, 1976.

——. *Moments of Being*. San Diego: Harcourt Brace, 1985.

——. *A Room of One's Own*. New York: Harcourt Brace, 1929.

——. *A Writer's Diary*. Ed. Leonard Woolf. New York: Harcourt Brace, 1954.

Zucker, Marilyn. "'A Rope to Throw the Reader': The Reading of Rhythm in Virginia Woolf." *Virginia Woolf Miscellanies; Proceedings of the First Annual Conference on Virginia Woolf*. Eds. Mark Hussey and Vara Neverow-Turk. New York: Pace UP, 1992. 105-07.

Guide to Library Special Collections

This guide updates the information in volume 8.

Name of Collection: The Beinecke Rare Book and Manuscript Library

Contact: Vincent Giroud, Curator of Modern Books and Manuscripts
Patricia Willis, Curator of American Literature

Address: Yale University Library
P.O. Box 208240
New Haven, CT 06520-8240

Hours: Mon.-Fri. 8:30AM-5PM

Access Requirements: Register at the circulation desk on each visit.

Holdings Relevant To Woolf: General Collection includes autograph manuscript of "Notes on Oliver Goldsmith." Comments on Edward Gibbon, William Beckford Collection. Letters from Virginia Woolf in the Bryher Papers, the Louise Morgan and Otto Theis Papers, and the Rebecca West Papers. Related material: 41 letters from Vita Sackville-West to Violet Trefusis; files relating to Robert Manson Myers's *From Beowulf to Virginia Woolf* in the Edmond Pauker Papers.

Yale Collection of American Literature includes typewritten manuscripts of "The Art of Walter Sickert," "Augustine Birrell," "Aurora Leigh," "How Should One Read a Book?" "Letter to a Young Poet," "The Novels of Turgenev," "Street Haunting." Dial/Scofield Thayer Papers: manuscripts of "The Lives of the Obscure," "Miss Ormerod," and "Mrs. Dalloway in Bond Street." Letters from Virginia Woolf in the William Rose Benet Papers, the Benet Family Correspondence, the Henry Seidel Canby Papers, the Seward Collins Papers, the Dial/Scofield Thayer Papers, and the *Yale Review* archive. Material relating to translations of Woolf in the Thornton Wilder papers. Related material: Clive Bell, "Virginia Woolf" (Dial/Scofield Thayer Papers); 43 letters from Leonard Woolf to Helen McAfee (*Yale Review*); 11 letters from Leonard Woolf to Gertrude Stein.

Name of Collection: The Henry W. and Albert A. Berg Collection of English and American Literature

Contact: Isaac Gewirtz, Curator

Address: New York Public Library, Room 320
Fifth Avenue & 42nd Street
New York, NY 10018

Telephone: 212-930-0802
Fax: 212-930-0079
E-mail: igewirtz@nypl.org

Hours: Tues./Wed. 11AM -5:45PM
Thurs.-Sat. 10AM-5:45PM
Closed Sun., Mon. and legal holidays

Access Requirements: Apply for card of admission at Office of Special Collections, Room 316. Traceable identification required. Undergraduates working on honors theses need letter from faculty advisor.

Restrictions: Virginia Woolf's MSS are now made available on microfilm. N.B. *All the Berg's Woolf MSS are on microfilm published by Research Publications and available at many research libraries.*

Holdings Relevant
To Woolf: Manuscripts of *Between the Acts, Flush, Jacob's Room, Mrs. Dalloway* (notes and fragments), *Night and Day, To the Lighthouse, The Voyage Out, The Waves, The Years*; 12 notebooks of articles, essays, fiction and reviews, 1924-1940; 36 volumes of diaries; 26 volumes of reading notes; correspon-

dence with Vanessa Bell, Ethel Smyth, Vita Sackville-West and others. Su Hua Ling Chen's Bloomsbury correspondence.

Name of Collection: The British Library Manuscript Collections

Contact: Manuscripts Enquiries

Address: 96 Euston Road
London NW1 2DB
England

Telephone: 0207-412-7513
Fax: 0207-412-7745
E-mail: mss@bl.uk

Hours: Present Hours: Mon 10:00-5:00PM
Tue-Sat: 9:30-5:00PM

Access Requirements: British Library Reader Pass (signed I.D. required and usually proof of post-graduate academic status, or other demonstrable need to use the collections— see www.bl.uk). In addition, access to most literary autograph material only available with letter of recommendation.

Restrictions: Paper Copies, Microfilms, and Photography of selected items available upon receipt of written authorization for photo duplication from the copyright holder.

Holdings Relevant
To Woolf: Diaries 1930-1931 (microfilm); Mrs. Dalloway and other writings (1923-1925) three volumes; letter from Leonard Woolf to H. G. Wells (1941); two letters from Virginia Woolf and three letters from Leonard Woolf to John Lehmann (1941); letter written on behalf of Leonard Woolf to S. S. Koteliansky (1946); notebook in Italian kept by Virginia Woolf;

notebook of Virginia Stephen (1906-1909); A sketch of the past revised ts (1940); letters from Virginia Woolf in the correspondence files of Lytton and James Strachey; letter from Virginia Woolf to Mildred Massingberd; letter from Virginia Woolf to Harriet Shaw Weaver (1918); letters from Virginia Woolf to S. S. Koteliansky (1923-27); letter from Virginia Woolf to Frances Cornford (1929); letter from Virginia Woolf to Ernest Rhys (1930); correspondence of Virginia Woolf in the Society of Authors archive (1934-37); letter and postcard from Virginia Woolf to Bernard Shaw (1940); three letters (suicide notes) from Virginia Woolf (1941); two letters from Virginia Woolf and three from Leonard Woolf to John Lehmann (1941).

Collection of RPs ("reserved photo copies"–copies of manuscrips exported, some subject to restrictions).

Recent Acquisitions:	"Hyde Park Gate News" 1891-92, 1895 (add. MSS 70725, 70726). Letters of Virginia and Leonard Woolf to Lady Aberconway, 1927-1941. Letter from Virginia Woolf to Frances Cornford.
Name of Collection:	Harry Ransom Humanities Research Center
Contact:	Research Librarian
Address:	The University of Texas at Austin P.O. Box 7219 Austin, TX 78713-7219
Telephone:	512-471-9119
Fax:	512-471-2899
E-mail:	reference@hrc.utexas.edu
URL:	www.hrc.utexas.edu/fa/woolf.virginia.html
Hours:	Mon.-Fri. 9AM-5PM Sat. 9AM-NOON

Closed holidays; intersession Saturdays; one week each in late May and late August.

Access Requirements: Completed manuscript reader's application; current photo identification.

Restrictions: Photocopies of selected items available upon receipt of written authorization for photoduplication from the copyright holder.

Holdings Relevant To Woolf: The manuscript collection includes the typed manuscript with autograph revisions of *Kew Gardens,* and the typed manuscript and autograph revisions of "Thoughts on Peace in an Air Raid." The Center holds 571 of Woolf's letters, including correspondence to Elizabeth Bowen, Lady Ottoline Morrell, Mary Hutchinson, William Plomer, Hugh Walpole and others. Further mss. relating to Virginia Woolf include letters to her from T. S. Eliot and reviews of her work. A substantial collection of the first British and American editions of Woolf's published works, as well as 130 volumes from Leonard and Virginia Woolf's library and a collection of books published by the Hogarth Press, is also housed. An art collection holds a landscape painting of Virginia's garden and a series of Cockney cartoons in a sketch book, signed "V.W." The center also has extensive holdings of materials related to Leonard Woolf, Ottoline Morrell, Mary Hutchinson, Lytton Strachey, Dora Carrington, E. M. Forster, Clive Bell, Roger Fry, Vanessa Bell, Bertrand Russell, Elizabeth Bowen, William Plomer, Stephen Spender and Hugh Walpole.

Name of Collection: King's College Archive Centre

Contact: Rosalind Moad, Archivist

Address: King's College
Cambridge CB2 1ST

Telephone: 01223-331444
Fax: 01223-331891
E-mail: archivist@kings.cam.ac.uk

Hours: Mon.-Fri. 9:30AM-12:30PM and 1:30PM-5:15PM. *Closed during public holidays and the College's annual periods of closure.*

Access Requirements: Proof of ID, letter of introduction, appointment in advance.

Holdings Relevant To Woolf: Woolf MSS and letters: Minute book, written up by Clive Bell, of the meetings of a play-reading society, with cast lists and comments on performances by CB. Dec. 1907-Jan. 1909, Oct. 1914-Feb. 1915. Players included variously Clive & Vanessa Bell, Roger & Margery Fry, Duncan Grant, Walter Lamb, Molly MacCarthy, Adrian & Virginia Stephen, Saxon Sydney-Turner. *Freshwater, A Comedy*–photocopy of editorial typescript prepared from the MSS at Sussex University and Monk's House; photcopy of covering letter from the publisher to "Robert Silvers," 1.29.1976. Papers relating to the Virginia Woolf Centenary Conference held at Fitzwilliam College, Cambridge, 9.20-22.1982. TS with corrections of "Nurse Lugton's Curtain." Typed transcript of R. Fry's memoir of his schooldays. Correspondence with Clive Bell, Julian Bell, Vanessa Bell, Richard Braithwaite, Rupert Brooke, Mrs. Brooke, Katharine Cox, Julian Fry, Roger Fry, John Davy Hayward, J. M. Keynes, Lydia Keynes, Rosamond Lehmann, Charles Mauron, Raymond Mortimer, G.

H. W. Rylands, J. T. Sheppard, W. J. H. Sprott, Thoby Stephen, Madge Vaughan. Woolf-related archival collections held: Charleston Papers; Rupert Brooke Papers; E. M. Forster Papers; Roger Fry Papers; J. M. Keynes Papers; J. T. Sheppard Papers; W. J. H. Sprott Papers. Various works of art by Vanessa Bell, Duncan Grant, and Roger Fry, held in various locations around King's College. Access via Domus Bursar's secretary.

Recent Acquisitions: Roger Fry Papers: sketchbooks, 1880s-1920s. The papers of George Humphrey Wolferstan ('Dadie') Rylands (1902-99).

Name of Collection: The Lilly Library

Contact: Breon Mitchell, Director
Saundra Taylor, Curator of Manuscripts

Address: The Lilly Library, Indiana University
1200 East Seventh Street
Bloomington, IN 47405-5500

Telephone: 812-855-3143
Fax: 812-855-3143
E-mail: liblilly@indiana.edu, mitchell@indiana.edu
taylors@indiana.edu

Hours: M-F 9-6; Sat. 9-1; Closed Sundays and Major Holidays

Access Requirements: Valid photo-identification; brief registration procedure.

Restrictions: Closed stacks; material use confined to reading room; wheelchair accessible reading room and exhibitions (but no wheelchair-accessible restroom)

Holdings Relevant to
Woolf: Corrected page proofs for the British edition of *Mrs Dalloway*; letters to Woolf from Desmond and Mary

(Molly) MacCarthy; 77 letters (published in *Letters*) from Woolf to correspondents including Donald Clifford Brace, Robert Gathorne-Hardy, Barbara (Strachey) Halpern, Richard Arthur Warren Hughes, Desmond MacCarthy and Molly MacCarthy; "Preliminary Scheme for the formation of a Partnership between Mr Leonard Sidney Woolf and Mr John Lehmann to take over The Hogarth Press" (includes contract signed by Lehmann, LW, and VW, and receipt for Lehmann's payment to VW to purchase VW's share in the Hogarth Press); photographs of VW, LW, Lytton Strachey, Strachey family, Roger Fry, and Vanessa Bell (Hannah Whitall Smith mss.); (Richard) Kennedy mss. (four hand-colored lithographs of VW: artist's proofs for RK's portfolio, VIRGINIA WOOLF: "AS I KNEW HER"; Sackville-West, V. mss. (10,529 items: includes the correspondence of Vita Sackville-West, and Harold Nicolson); MacCarthy mss. (ca. 10,000 items: papers of Desmond and Molly MacCarthy); correspondence between LW and Mary Gaither regarding publication of *A Checklist of the Hogarth Press* (1976, repr. 1986); Todd Avery, *Close and Affectionate Friends: Desmond and Molly MacCarthy and the Bloomsbury Group* (The Lilly Library / Indiana University Libraries, 1999).

Name of Collection: Archives and Manuscripts, University of Maryland, College Park, Libraries

Contact: Beth Alvarez, Curator of Literary Manuscripts

Address: University of Maryland Libraries
College Park, MD 20742

Telephone: 310-405-9298
E-mail: ra60@umail.umd.edu
Hours: Mon.-Fri. 10AM-5PM, Sat. Noon-5PM.

Access Requirements: Photo ID.

Holdings Relevant to Woolf:	Papers of Hope Mirrlees contain five autograph letters and postcards (1919-28) from Virginia Woolf to Mirrlees. Also in the collection are 113 letters from T. S. Eliot to Mirrlees, and three letters from Lady Ottoline Morrell to Mirrlees.
Name of Collection:	Monks House Papers/Leonard Woolf Papers/Charleston Papers/Nicolson Papers
Contact:	Dorothy Sheridan, Head of Special Collections
Address:	University of Sussex Library Brighton Sussex BN1 9QL England
Telephone:	01273-678157
Fax:	01273-678441
E-mail:	Library.Specialcoll@sussex.ac.uk
Hours:	By appointment
Access Requirements:	Letter, to be received *before* visiting. Photocopying strictly controlled.
Holdings Relevant to Woolf:	The University of Sussex holds two large archives relating to Leonard and Virginia Woolf: The Monks House Papers, primarily correspondence and MSS of Virginia Woolf, including the three scrapbooks relating to *Three Guineas*; and The Leonard Woolf Papers, primarily correspondence and other papers of Leonard Woolf. (Monks House Papers are available on microfilm in many research libraries.) The Charleston Papers consist in the main of letters written to or by Clive and Vanessa Bell and Duncan Grant which had accumulated in their home; the library houses Quentin Bell's photocopied set. Also included are c. 900 letters from Maria Jackson to Julia and Leslie Stephen (Charleston Papers Ad. 1); letters from Roger Fry, Maynard Keynes, Lytton

Stachey, Virginia Woolf, Vita Sackville-West, E. M. Forster, T. S. Eliot, Frances Partridge and others. The Nicolson Papers complement these three Sussex archives relating to the Bloomsbury Group, and consist of Nigel Nicolson's correspondence relating to his editorial work as principal editor of the six-volume *Letters of Virginia Woolf*, published between 1975 and 1980.

The Bell Papers. A. O. Bell's correspondence relating to her editorial work on Virginia Woolf's Diaries. A parallel collection to Nicolson Papers.

Collection level descriptions may be accessed at www.archiveshub.ac.uk

Name of Collection: Archives & Manuscripts

Contact: Michael Bott, Keeper of Archives & Manuscripts

Address: The University of Reading, The Library,
Whiteknights
P.O. Box 223
Reading RG6 6AE
England

Telephone: 0118-931-8776
Fax: 0118-931-6636
E-mail: g.m.c.bott@reading.ac.uk

Access Requirements: Appointment needed to consult material. Permission required to consult or copy material in the Hogarth Press and Chatto & Windus collections from Random House, 20 Vauxhall Bridge Road, London SW1V 2SA, UK.

Holdings Relevant to
Woolf: Hogarth Press (MS2750): editorial and production correspondence relating to publications of the Press including Woolf's own titles. Production ledgers 1920s-1950s. Correspondence between Leonard Woolf and Stanley Unwin about progress with his collected edition of the works of Freud.

Chatto & Windus (MS2444): small number of letters 1915-25; 1929-31.

George Bell & Sons (MS1640): 5 letters from Leonard Woolf 1930-66.

Routledge (MS1489): Reader's report by Leonard Woolf on George Padmore's "Britannia rules the blacks" (1935); "How Britain rules Africa."

Megroz (MS1979/68): 2 letters from LW, 1926.

Allen & Unwin (MS3282): Correspondence with LW 1923-24; 1939-40; 1943; 1946; 1950-51, including letters concerning a reprint of *Empire and Commerce in Africa*, and concerning ill-founded rumors about the Hogarth press.

Name of Collection: Frances Hooper Collection of Virginia Woolf Books and Manuscripts/Elizabeth Power Richardson Bloomsbury Iconography Collection.

Contact: Karen V. Kukil, Associate Curator of Rare Books

Address: Mortimer Rare Book Room
William Allan Neilson Library
Smith College
Northampton, MA 01063

Telephone: 413-585-2906
Fax: 413-585-4486
E-mail: kkukil@smith.edu

Hours: Mon.-Fri. 9AM-5PM

Access Requirements: Appointment to be made with the Curator.

**Holdings Relevant
to Woolf:**   The Hooper Collection emphasizes Woolf as an essayist but also includes many Hogarth Press first editions, limited editions of Woolf's works, and translations. The collection includes page proofs of *Orlando*, *To the Lighthouse*, and *The Common*

Reader, corrected by Woolf for the first American editions, a proof copy of *The Waves* that Woolf inscribed to Hugh Walpole, and the proof copies of *The Years* and of *Flush*. The Collection also has one of the deluxe editions of *Orlando* that was printed on green paper. Other items include twenty-two pages of reading notes from 1926, three pages of notes on D. H. Lawrence's *Sons and Lovers*, thirty-three pages of notes for *Roger Fry*, a six-page ms. "As to criticism," a five-page ms. of "The Searchlight," and a fourteen-page ms. of "The Patron and The Crocus." The Hooper Collection also owns 140 letters between Woolf and Lytton Strachey as well as other correspondence, including a 13 February [1921] letter to Katherine Mansfield and ten letters to Mela and Robert Spira.

The Richardson Collection is a working collection of books and materials used by Richardson in preparing her *Bloomsbury Iconography*. It includes Leslie Stephen's photograph album, ninety-eight original exhibition catalogs dating back to 1929, clippings and photcopies of such items as reviews of early Woolf works, and Bloomsbury material from British *Vogue* of the 1920s. The Collection also has three preliminary pencil drawings by Vanessa Bell for *Flush*.

The Mortimer Rare Book Room also owns Woolf's 1916 Italian ms. notebook and her corrected type-scripts of "Reviewing" and "The Searchlight." In addition, there is a 1923 photograph of Woolf at Garsington. Original cover designs for Hogarth Press publications include *The Common Reader*, *On Being Ill*, and *Duncan Grant*. The Mortimer Rare Book Room also has a Sylvia Plath Collection that includes eight of Woolf's books from Plath's library, several of which are underlined and annotated, as well as Plath's notes from her undergraduate

English 211 class at Smith (1951-2) in which she studied *To the Lighthouse*.

Name of Collection: Woolf/Hogarth Press/Bloomsbury

Contact: Robert C. Brandeis

Address: Victoria University Library
71 Queens Park Crescent E.
Toronto M5S 1K7
Ontario
Canada

Hours: Mon.-Fri. 9AM-5PM
URL: http://library.vicu.utoronto.ca/special/bloomsbury.htm

Access Requirements: Prior notification; identification.

Restrictions: Limited photocopying.

Holdings Relevant to Woolf: This collection, the most comprehensive of its kind in Canada, contains all the work of Virginia and Leonard Woolf in various editions, issues, variants and translations; all the books hand printed by Leonard and Virginia Woolf at the Hogarth Press, including many variant issues and bindings, association copies and page proofs; a nearly comprehensive collection of Hogarth Press machine printed books to 1946 (the year Leonard Woolf and the Press joined Chatto & Windus) including presentation copies, signed limited editions, page proofs, variants as well as substantial amounts of ephemera. The collection is also very strong in Bloomsbury art, especially the decorative arts, and contains important examples of Omega Workshops publications and exhibition catalogues. Vanessa Bell correspondence/MSS; Leonard Woolf correspondence; Ritchie family materials and correspondence re: Anne Thackeray Ritchie/Stephen family. Vanessa

Bell dustwrapper designs for Woolf novels; Quentin Bell correspondence; S. P. Rosenbaum mss. 97 additional items: Ephemera Collection. Bronze bust of Lytton Strachey by Stephen Tomlin (1901-37). A companion piece to Tomlin's bronze of Virginia Woolf already in the collection. More than 100 additional items including translations of Virginia Woolf's work.

Recent Acquisitions: More than 150 additional items including Hogarth Press variant bindings and proof copies; translations of Virginia Woolf and Leonard Woolf; ephemera; including Hogarth Press: Complete Catalogue of Publications to 1939 with annotations by Leonard Woolf; materials relating to Bloomsbury Art and Artists including the catalogue of the second post impressionist exhibition, 1912, and catalogues relating to Vanessa Bell and Duncan Grant exhibitions.

Name of Collection: Library of Leonard and Virginia Woolf (Washington S U)

Contact: Laila Miletic-Vejzovic, Head Manuscripts, Archives and Special Collections

Address: Washington State University Libraries Pullman, WA 99164-5610

URL: www.wsulibs.wsu.edu/holland/masc/masc.htm

Hours: Mon.-Fri. 8:30AM-5PM

Access Requirements: Letter stating nature of research preferred; student or other identification.

Restrictions: Materials must be used in the MASC area under supervision. Photocopying or photographing is permitted only when it will not harm the materials and is permitted by copyright.

Holdings Relevant to Woolf: WSU has the Woolfs' basic working library including many works which belonged to Virginia's father, Sir Leslie Stephen, and other family members. Over 800 titles came from their Sussex home, Monks House, including some works bought at auction soon after Leonard Woolf died in 1969. Later additions include: 1,875 titles from his house in Victoria Square, London; 400 titles from his nephew Cecil Woolf; and over 60 titles from Quentin and Anne Olivier Bell. WSU has been actively collecting: all works in all editions by Virginia; all titles by Leonard; works published by the Woolfs at the Hogarth Press through 1946; books by their friends and associates, especcially those by Bloomsbury authors and about Bloomsbury artists; relevant correspondence and original works of art. Original artwork by Vanessa Bell; scattered letters by Vanessa Bell, E. M. Forster, Roger Fry, Leslie Stephen, Lytton Strachey, and Leonard Woolf. Original artwork by Richard Kennedy for illustrations in his book *A Boy at the Hogarth Press*; scattered letters by Roger Fry, Leslie Stephen, Ethel Smyth, and Leonard Woolf. Virginia Woolf's initialed copy of *Cornishiana*; Leonard Woolf's annotated copy of *An Anatomy of Poetry* by A. William-Ellis; Leslie Stephen's copy of *Lapsus Calami and Other Verses*, inscribed by James Kenneth Stephen. Several letters from Virginia Woolf, including two written in 1939 to Ronald Heffer, and a letter to Edward McKnight Kauffer. New in the Hogarth Press Collection are a copy of E. M. Forster's *Anonymity, an Enquiry*, bound in cream paper boards, and what Woolmer calls the third label state of Forster's *The Story of the Siren*.

Name of Collection: Yale Center for British Art

Contact: Elisabeth Fairman, Associate Curator forRare Books

Address: 1080 Chapel Street
P.O. Box 208280
New Haven, CT 06520-8280

E-mail: elisabeth.fairman@yale.edu

Hours: Tues.-Fri. 10AM-4:30PM

Access Requirements: Permission needed in order to reproduce.

Holdings Relevant to
Woolf: Rare Books Department: 94 letters from Vanessa Bell
and Duncan Grant to Sir Kenneth Clark. Prints &
Drawings Department: 2 designs by Vanessa Bell and
2 studies by Duncan Grant. Paintings Department: 1
painting by Vanessa Bell, 2 by Duncan Grant (including a portrait of Vanessa Bell).

Reviews

Sex Drives: Fantasies of Fascism in Literary Modernism
Laura Frost (Ithaca and London: Cornell University Press, 2002)

For anyone wondering why television is about to bring us a glut of movies and documentaries about Hitler—a CBS miniseries, "Young Hitler," covering the years 18 to 34; a BBC drama on Hitler as a struggling painter in Vienna; an independent feature film focusing on the relationship between a Jewish art dealer and the mass murderer[1]—then Laura Frost's interesting new book, *Sex Drives: Fantasies of Fascism in Literary Modernism*, is an excellent place to begin. While many will simply protest that any sympathetic portrayal of Hitler is anathema, Frost's analysis helps us to understand why those who oppose the proliferation of Hitler projects are likely to tune in to their local Hitler movie-of-the-week. *Sex Drives* provides us with the tools to read this schizophrenic cultural obsession—part repudiation, part fascination—with the world's most famous fascist; her book, moreover, implicitly explains not only why TV executives are eager to play the Nazi card today, but why Hitler himself is still a hot and sexy commodity, almost sixty years after his death. Frost's central question—What does it mean when an author simultaneously eroticizes fascism and repudiates it politically?—provides us with one window into the current Hitler conundrum, demonstrating the extent to which our collective psyche is arguably fraught with contradictory and transgressive impulses that often eroticize the very behaviors and prohibitions that we consciously revile. Although Frost is careful to distinguish between actual fascist violence and fantasies of erotic sadomasochism, her focus is not with historical fascism per se but with the myriad ways in which (primarily male) writers have been repeatedly seduced by the lure of "nonfascist eroticized fascism" (5).

Frost's intriguing premise is that current representations of "sexualized fascism" (3) were not conceived or developed by television executives or design studio talking heads, but rather, that they have their roots in an artistic form not ordinarily associated with contemporary popular culture: literary modernism. *Sex Drives* traces the literary genealogy of eroticized images of fascism and explores why brutal European dictatorships became so widely associated with

---

[1]See Maureen Dowd's editorial, "Swastikas for Sweeps" (*The New York Times* Op-Ed, July 17, 2002): A 23.

eroticism and sexual deviance in the early to mid-twentieth century. Invariably, when the book utilizes "fascism" it means to signal "Nazism" (8). What's compelling about Frost's analysis is her focus on a large number of writers—D. H. Lawrence, Georges Bataille, Hans Bellmer, the pseudonymous "Vercors," Jean Genet, Marguerite Duras, and Sylvia Plath—who do not subscribe to fascist ideology but nevertheless produce sexualized representations of fascism in their work. Frost argues that these authors adopt many of the same strategies as the so-called fascist modernists (e.g. Ezra Pound, Wyndham Lewis, F. T. Marinetti), but they do so alongside a rejection of fascist politics. This is not a book that constructs an overarching chronological continuum or a single narrative focus; rather, it usefully looks at a number of historical moments—Britain and France during World War I and the interwar period; France during the Occupation and immediately after Liberation; the United States ten and forty years after WWI—in order to show how "differences in the proximity to fascism . . . culminate in different way of imagining fascism in fiction" (7).

Frost's central questions: Where do images of eroticized fascism come from? Why is fascism privileged as a particularly sexual ideology? prompt her to unearth a wide range of fascinating historical materials (such as children's books, political cartoons, fairytales, visual propaganda) which contrast the "perverse authoritarian libido" (17) of Germans during World War I with the "normative democratic libido" (17) of the anti-fascists. She draws, for example, upon Wilhelm Reich's descriptions of fascist psychology in his 1933 *Mass Psychological Structure of Fascism* as a way of interpreting the sadomasochistic fantasies in Genet's novel, *Funeral Rights* (1949), in which Nazis are represented as fetishized objects of desire. While Frost utilizes psychoanalytic concepts such as intersubjectivity freely, she claims that her primary methodology in *Sex Drives* is explicitly not psychoanalytic because "psychoanalytic discourse itself participates in the eroticization of fascism and hence is part of the phenomenon rather than an explanatory tool" (6). That may indeed be true, but her book nonetheless focuses on the often unconscious libidinal dynamics that are shared by the disparate group of authors she foregrounds: "prohibition, fetishism, and sadomasochism" (12).

At the same time, the book carefully historicizes its engagement with fascist politics, demonstrating how the early twentieth-century perception of Germany as a "violently atavistic nation" (16) is linked to anti-German propaganda such as William S. Sadler's study, *Long Heads and Round Heads: or What's the Matter with Germany* (1918), a phrenological comparison of Neanderthal and Cro-Magnon heads with those of Germany's military leaders during World War I. Frost shows how Sadler's influential argument, that Germany during World War I was in effect a "nation of rapists and sadomasochists" (20) which threatened a feminized Britain and France, is taken up and revised by writers such as Leonard Woolf during the interwar period. Frost convincingly argues in chapter one that Woolf's political treatise, *Quack, Quack!* (1935), borrows from Sadler's format in *Long Heads and Round Heads*, which juxtaposes photographs of authoritarian German leaders with images of "primitive" people. In *Quack, Quack!*, Woolf places photographs of Hitler and Mussolini alongside effigies of the Hawaiian war-god Kukailimoku (23) in order to highlight the savagery and monstrousness of fascism. Frost demonstrates how such primitivist allegations are echoed by D. H. Lawrence, who similarly concurs that "authoritarianism enacts an atavistic return to a premodern and nondemocratic state" (43). But in contrast to Leonard Woolf, who relishes rationality as the basis of civilization, Lawrence both condemns authoritarianism and opportunistically recuperates it as the phallic source of an erotically liberatory politics. Frost effectively illustrates how Lawrence manipulates the same metaphors of regression and atavism show-cased in Sadler's propagandistic *Long Heads and Round Heads*, but instead of fearing this regression, Lawrence celebrates it and suggests that a manly primal libido has the potential to reinvigorate modern life. As in other chapters, Frost is interested here in unpacking the discursive structures of propaganda in fictions that do not appear to be primarily fascist in order to interrogate "those regulative democratic, liberal politics that . . . construct a sexually deviant fascism in rela-tion to a sexually normative, idealized politics" (125).

Frost's larger objective, stated broadly, is to recuperate fascism from its long association with deviant sexuality and perversity, a move which is admirable for its attempt to widen our narrow perceptions of desire, but that unfortunately necessitates both the marginalization of female modernists in general and the excoriation of twentieth-century feminism in particular. (Of her six chapters, one is devoted to postmodern women writers, with Virginia Woolf being the only female modernist of note.) Within this equation, Woolf plays an inevitably salient role as the paradigmatic uptight female modernist who, unlike her more sexual-ly adventurous male peers, "limits her purview of fascism and patriarchy to dynamics in which women have no sexual identification with or libidinal desire for the patriarch/dictator" (130). Frost recounts the moment in *Three Guineas* when Woolf describes the dictator in the flesh—"His body, which is braced in an unnatural position, is tightly cased in a uniform...His hand is upon a sword"[2]— and argues that the language here suggests Woolf's "libidinal identifications . . . [with] the displayed fascist body . . . as simultaneously oppressive and poten-tially erotic" (129). This point is of course debatable, but what Frost wants to foreground is Woolf's alleged "blind spot" (131), that is, her problematic evasion

[2]Virginia Woolf, *Three Guineas*, (New York: Harcourt Brace, 1938), 142.

of women's erotic craving for submission or domination. Within Frost's framework, women writers (such as Duras and Plath) who repudiate the kind of bifurcation of male aggression and female submission that Woolf delineates in *Three Guineas* are the most politically progressive. Hence, Sylvia Plath's 1962 poem "Daddy," which similarly links fascist and patriarchal oppression but then "infuses both terms of the analogy with sadomasochistic erotics" (141), is upheld by Frost as a positive model of what happens when women no longer disavow their libidinal impulses—what they lose in ideological purity, she suggests, they gain in analytic complexity. The problem with Frost's analysis is not her claim that "a woman who is 'sexually awakened' may still harbor fantasies of submission and domination with a distinctly authoritarian character" (150), but rather, that female sexual liberation repeatedly and relentlessly hinges upon (as in the case of Plath) the expression of "sadistic and masochistic impulses" (147) that function as "the substance of eroticized fantasy, [and are] linked to fascism" (149).

My irritation is both with Frost's reductive and dismissive stance toward well-known early twentieth-century women writers, such as Woolf, and lesser known writers such as Katherine Burdekin (the author of *Swastika Night* [1937]), and her tendency to treat the majority of feminist theorists since Simone de Beauvoir as avatars of a contemporary sexual purity movement. How much more nuanced and complicated Frost's analysis could have been, from a feminist perspective, if she had considered, for example, the bisexual English modernist Mary Butts, whose xenophobia, virulent anti-Semitism, and racism enable us to read her as a proto-fascist—even though she vehemently rejected the macho ethos of militarism and technology. It is perhaps unfair to reproach an author for what she hasn't written, but certainly the materials that Frost does examine could have benefited from greater attention to Woolf's observation that women modernists' fiction will exhibit "infinite differences in selection, method and style,[3] the better to compare male and female fantasies and approaches. Thus one wonders, for example, how Frost's interpretation of Hans Bellmer's surreal, eroticized serial photographs of quasi-pornographic jointed dolls would have shifted had she read them alongside Jean Rhys's own preoccupation with dolls and female automatons in *Good Morning Midnight*. There, within the context of the novel's larger preoccupation with the links between fascism and sexual violence against women, a drunken Sasha Jensen hallucinates a grotesque, futurist image of female artifice in the form of an enormous, mechanized female body with emphatically feminized prosthetic limbs that sprout mascara-caked eyes. If, as Frost contends, female modernism is invariably aligned with social regulation

[3]Virginia Woolf, "Women Novelists," *Women and Writing*, ed. Michèle Barrett, (New York: Harcourt Brace, 1979), 71.

and the effacement of desire, then how are we to read Rhys's own masochistic image of feminine narcissism here?

Frost claims that "representations of fascism are not limited to a particular gender or sexual orientation but are rather part of [an author's] larger response to [his or her own] culture's strategic constructions of fascism" (141), yet, in *Sex Drives*, it is primarily male authors who display an interest (whether hetero- or homosexual) in eroticized fascism. Frost expresses a suspicion of ideologies of sexual normativity, but oddly does not speculate on the meaning of lesbian sexuality within fascism even when her material invites the analysis. For example, when she reads Hans Bellmer's provocative photograph of two intertwined semi-naked female bodies, "La croix gamahuchée" (1946), in which one woman's fingers are inserted into the vagina of the other (77), Frost persuasively argues that the composition of Bellmer's contorted image invokes an erotically charged swastika, yet she never addresses the lesbian content of this Nazi iconography. Elsewhere, in her brief reading of *Mrs. Dalloway*, Frost discusses Miss Kilman's fantasy of "subduing" Clarissa and "bring[ing] her to her knees,"[4] but she never addresses the homoerotic subtext of this libidinally charged moment. What's strange about Frost's book is that it seeks to free sexual "abnormality" and topple sexual hierarchies, while simultaneously establishing its own rigid orthodoxy of transgressive liberation. This is a book that puts the dissenting reader (and critic) into the uncomfortable position of not being able to critique Frost's premise unambivalently because the implicit implication is: you are a repressed, retrograde, prurient feminist who is aligned with liberalism and democracy (categories which Frost excoriates). *Sex Drives* self-consciously positions itself against political correctness but nonetheless ends up reproducing the same kinds of strict parameters that it purports to reject. Despite these reservations, however, I am still grateful to Frost for successfully demonstrating how fictions of eroticized fascism cannot adequately be explained as a generalized expression of sexual dominance, and for showing how such fictions are part of an antifascist culture which "persistently sexualizes fascism" (6).

—Jane Garrity, *University of Colorado, Boulder*

.

[4]Virginia Woolf, *Mrs. Dalloway* (New York: Harcourt Brace, 1981), 125.

The Artist as Outsider in the Novels of Toni Morrison and Virginia Woolf
Lisa Williams
(Westport: Greenwood P, 2000) 194 pp

Having taken a seminar focusing on the works of Toni Morrison and Virginia Woolf several years ago, I approached Lisa Williams's *The Artist as Outsider* eagerly. I was quite anxious for the opportunity to continue my studies of Morrison and Woolf outside of a classroom environment. I was also hopeful that I would discover a rereading of the texts that shed new insights on the similarities in the works of these two literary giants. The *Artist as Outsider* delivered on both counts.

In her carefully crafted intertextual analysis, Williams argues that both Morrison and Woolf "create narrative structures that emphasize the severe obstacles the female artist must encounter and overcome in order to create" (1). Williams engages with a wide range of contemporary critics on race, gender, and culture; and she presents a provocative study of the connections between the literary and cultural aesthetics of Morrison and Woolf. Focusing on Woolf's *The Voyage Out*, *Mrs. Dalloway*, and *To the Lighthouse* and on Morrison's *The Bluest Eye*, *Sula*, and *Beloved*, Williams argues that Woolf and Morrison offer important insights into the effect abuse and domination have on black and white female artists. Throughout an analysis informed by the critical essays of Woolf and Morrison, Williams illustrates how in their fiction both writers "strive to give form to the muted and silenced voices that have been left out of history" (7).

In her Introduction, Williams describes her book as a comparative women's studies project and explains how she will examine the similarities that connect these women despite differences of race, class, history, and nation . Williams acknowledges that while Virginia Woolf was clearly writing to express the female perspective she was "for the most part, blind to issues of race"(1). Thus Williams turns to critical work on race, including the work of Morrison, to call attention to the ambiguities in Woolf's writing about race, class, and sexuality. Conversely, Toni Morrison's intention "was to create a distinctly black aesthetic that would capture the experiences of black women who had been left out of literature" (1). Since Morrison writes her novels for an audience similar to the people who populate her fiction, she resists the state of double-consciousness. Instead, her novels bear witness to the experience of the African-American com-

munity in general and the African-American woman in particular. The most striking similarity, then, between the two writers is their shared   attention to the
female artist. Williams contends that the artist figures that Woolf and Morrison
create struggle to "subvert the larger racist and sexist structures of hierarchy and
domination" (2). In their novels, both writers depict their characters' tragic loss
of and exclusion from language; at the same time, they both strive to create language that will effectively challenge the discourse of dominance.

In Part I, Williams pairs Woolf's *The Voyage Out* with Morrison's *The Bluest
Eye,* and through the characterizations of Rachel Vinrace and Pecola Breedlove
examines how each author's first novel conveys the story of female initiation into
patriarchy and the ideology of racism. Williams shows how the issue of race
plays a pivotal role in the lives of the female artists in both novels. She argues,
for instance, that Rachel and Pecola fail as artists and fall victims to madness
because they are both trapped in what Morrison identifies in her essay "Home"
as a "racist home." In the case of Pecola, a poor black girl, the actual home is a
site "where the very hatred of her blackness is dominant" (25). On the other
hand, Williams characterizes Rachel's "racist home" as her status as a "homeless
traveler, [who] is blind to the inequities of race" (25). Williams explains that the
young Pecola remains in a racist home because she "longs to be white; Rachel
remains because she can never disassociate herself from the privileges of white
femininity despite her wish to establish an independent, artistic identity" (25).
Eventually both Pecola and Rachel are silenced, Pecola through madness and
Rachel through madness and death. Neither is able to give voice to her artistic
inclination because both "from their very different subject positions define themselves through the insidious gaze of whiteness" (25).

Throughout her discussion of *The Voyage Out*, Williams uses Morrison's
Playing in the Dark to analyze how Woolf racializes the plot of her first novel.
Building on the work of other critics, she shows how Woolf indicts British colonialism in the private home as well as the public Empire. By situating her
heroine's coming-of-age story outside the boundaries of England, Woolf reveals
how easily the ideology of imperialism and patriarchy expand through geo-
graphic as well as psychic space. In the first part of the novel, Rachel recognizes
her status as the sexual prey of such male characters as Richard Dalloway. She
succumbs to the marriage proposal of Terence rather than act upon her attraction
to Helen. But, as Williams notes, when shortly after her engagement Rachel
turns her gaze upon the women in the South American village, she becomes initiated into the reality of white upper-middle class English marriage and the
troubling prospect of her own entrapment. Although Rachel participates in the
objectification of these women, by observing them she recognizes how she, too,
is sexually colonized. Throughout her discussion Williams details how Woolf

wavers between racist attitudes and racial insights. As Williams contends, "These contradictions inherent in the text reflect the cultural biases that Woolf, as a citizen of England living in an historical time of colonialism, had internalized" (48).

Morrison's *The Bluest Eye* directly depicts how racist invisibility and incestuous rape lead to Pecola's demise. Williams is especially skillful at showing the parallel ways in which both writers use lyrical language to break the silences that surround their characters' retreats into madness. But whereas Woolf's novel ends with the death of Rachel, Morrison presents Pecola's story through the narrative of Claudia, the young girl who rejects the racist aesthetics of the white world. As Williams concludes, with Pecola's madness Morrison represents the fragmentation of broken silence. Through Claudia's storytelling, she provides a "shape that can transform loss into language" (73).

In Part II, Williams pairs *Mrs. Dalloway* and *Sula*, an especially interesting juxtaposition in light of the fact, which Williams notes, that Morrison wrote a chapter of her MA thesis on alienation in *Mrs. Dalloway*. Williams attends to Woolf and Morrison's reconfiguration of self-identity within a narrative structure that "examines the conditions necessary for the creation of art"(77). She traces the suggestive connections between the two veterans of World War I, Septimus and Shadrack, and the light they shed on the female characters. She also addresses the parallel sexual tensions between Clarissa and Sally and between Sula and Nel. Both of these works insist, Williams argues, that the female artist find sources of creativity outside the confines of marriage and home. She highlights the vehicle for this exploration as the party in *Mrs. Dalloway* and the carnivalesque in *Sula*. In *Mrs. Dalloway*, Woolf uses Clarissa's party as a narrative structure within which to suggest the chaos of war and the plot of female development. For Williams, the party symbolizes Clarissa's desire "to reclaim the static language" of patriarchy. Party giving, then, is the affirmation of life and an opposition to war. At the same time, Williams calls our attention to the limitations of such parties. After all, Clarissa's party fails both to escape the privileges and oppressions of upper-class British life, and to recapture the lesbian eroticism of Bourton. Although Woolf explores issues of voice and voicelessness, silence and speech, her heroine remains entrapped in her conventional world.

Sula Peace challenges all conventions in a novel that, as Williams describes it, "emphasizes the importance of female friendship rather than the primacy of heterosexual relationships" (102). As Woolf pairs Clarissa with Septimus, Morrison pairs Sula with Shadrack, another damaged veteran. Whereas Woolf uses the party as a narrative frame, according to Williams, Morrison creates a Bakhtinian carnivalesque that questions the community's reactions to the unconventionality of Shadrack and Sula. Nel's conventionality, then, parallels Clarissa's; with Sula's death Morrison "shows how difficult rebellion is against entrenched structures that uphold domination" (121). While provocative, Williams's arguments in this part are by no means flawless. For instance, she contends (and I would strongly disagree) that "the friendship between Sula and Nel does not have the homoeroticism that exists between Clarissa and Sally" (98). In fact, Nel's repressed lesbian desire much like Clarissa's leads her to reject not only Sula but also the essential aspect of herself.

In Part III, Williams compares *To the Lighthouse* and *Beloved*. Whereas she acknowledges the dramatic differences between Mrs. Ramsay and Sethe who represent the opposing positions of Madonna and whore, Williams focuses on the relationship between the mother/daughter bond and artistic identity that runs through both novels. Recognizing that both narratives are elegies, Williams also draws our attention to the significance Woolf and Morrison place on memory as an act of healing. As Williams puts it, both writers "employ narrative strategies that disrupt linear notions of time and space as the dead arise from the past to find their rightful place in the present moment"(129).

Following the lead of the critics who precede her, Williams shows how through Mrs. Ramsay Woolf represents the destructive self-abnegation at the core of Victorian motherhood that Woolf's narrative must destroy. At the same time, Mrs. Ramsay is the inspiration of Lily's art and the subject of her memory. Through remembering and re-envisioning Mrs. Ramsay in her art, Lily replicates Woolf's own narrative and "captures the still silence of death that defies linear notions of past, present, or future" (148). Whereas Lily remembers Mrs. Ramsay and momentarily recreates her ghostly presence, Sethe unwillingly re-members Beloved, bringing her into her present day life. This painful process entails recalling the tragic suffering of slavery and bringing the fragments of her dead daughter to life, a necessary passage for Sethe.

In this final part of the *The Artist as Outsider*, I found Williams's project to be most promising. Whereas other critics have shown that *To the Lighthouse* is Woolf's attempt to "dismantle the Victorian ideal of womanhood," Williams's work analyzes how "Mrs. Ramsay is an artist figure with no art form other than the lovely dinner party her cook prepares" (135). Her argument that *Beloved* describes how the institution of slavery leads to the destruction not only of a people but also of language, culture, and identity has profound implications. Yet her discussion of how memory functions to heal the wounds and enhance the artistic process begs for further analysis. Both Woolf and Morrison create a language of rememory, to use Sethe's phrase, that empowers their female artists/outsiders to re-envision their worlds. Examining how these brilliant narratives accomplish this remembering would have enriched this thoughtful discussion.

Yet this is a flaw of omission. At the same time, Williams's arguments are thoughtful and engaging, buttressed by generous citations of letters, essays, and diary entries of Woolf and excerpts from essays and interviews with Toni Morrison. Those readers who long, as I do, for thoughtful readings of the text will not be disappointed by Williams. I found *The Artist as Outsider in the Novels of Toni Morrison and Virginia Woolf* to be a well researched, wonderful book that provides scholars and general readers with interesting ways to view how the works of these two great artists intersect.

—Jennifer D. King, *Mills College*

The Resurrection of Mary Magdalene: Legends,
Apocrypha, and the Christian Testament.
Jane Schaberg (New York and London: Continuum, 2002). 379 pp.

Jane Schaberg uses Virginia Woolf as her imagined mentor in this book on
the Biblical, Gnostic, apocryphal, and legendary Mary Magdalene. Schaberg's
Woolf is a feminist, a socialist, and a pacifist. This Woolf makes her primary
appearance in Chapter One, "Virginia Woolf and Mary Magdalene: Thinking
Back through the Magdalene," where Schaberg explains her role in the book.
Thereafter Woolf pops up in the epigraph to every chapter, and also periodically
in the text, where she makes brief comments that are sometimes very apposite
and sometimes less so. For example, Schaberg backs up her claim that Jewish
women's probable participation in Galilean village assemblies around the time of
Christ made them not insiders but outsiders, by quoting Woolf's remarks on tres-
passing (264).

In chapter one, Schaberg says that Woolf plays for her a role something like
the role played for other biblical scholars by thinkers like Heidegger, Marx,
Freud, Foucault, Lacan, Derrida, and others (21). Using Woolf in this way is an
interesting experiment—one wonders why Schaberg chooses her over the many
feminist theorists who have drawn from her and others to develop organized systems of thought, more comparable to those developed by the thinkers named
above. Woolf functions in the book less to provide a theoretical framework and
more as a sort of socialist feminist pacifist alter ego for Schaberg, who views herself as a brave outsider in the academy, partly because of her political views and
partly because she teaches at an underprivileged university—she tells us she has
tried and failed to get better jobs, and is now "standing again at Golgotha in
Detroit" (15).

From the second chapter to the seventh and final one, the book, as its title
indicates, focuses on Mary Magdalene. It proceeds from visits to Mary's now-
neglected village, Migdal, to a consideration of the medieval legends about her
(as, among other things, prostitute and ascetic) to Gnostic texts such as the
Gospel of Philip and the Gospel of Mary, some of which construct her as a specially beloved disciple (from which perhaps arise modern reconstructions of her
as Jesus' lover), and others of which show her as a leader opposed by Peter.
Schaberg privileges the Gnostic and apocryphal texts over the canonical Biblical

ones, reading the latter through the former, on the principle that the "canon is ... to be treated with tremendous suspicion" (203). She concludes by suggesting that the accounts of the risen Jesus' first appearance to Mary Magdalene, especially in the Gospel of John, may be part of an earlier tradition in which Mary, not John, was the Beloved Disciple, and in which Jesus appointed Mary (not Peter) his successor, much as Elijah did Elisha.

In mainstream Christian traditions encountered by lay people in church, the Gospel accounts of Jesus' appearance to Mary Magdalene and the accounts of her and other women discovering his empty tomb are seen as together exemplifying the miracle of resurrection. In a familiar Christian paradox, emptiness signifies not lack but fulfillment and triumph. A parallel Catholic tradition celebrates Jesus' post-resurrection to Mary, his mother—a moment often represented by European artists, although not recorded in the Bible.

Schaberg tells us that male Biblical scholars and the communities around them, influenced by sexist biases, have decided that the appearances and the empty tomb are two separate lines of tradition, and that "The appearances are associated with males and the empty tomb with females" (221). Schaberg therefore undertakes to uncover these biases and reinscribe the tradition of Jesus' first appearance to Mary. This undertaking may be puzzling to most lay readers of the Bible, to whom these particular male scholarly biases have not percolated down, and for whom Mary Magdalene's importance, both as discoverer of the empty tomb and as recipient of Jesus' post-resurrection appearance, has not been erased. For example, a large number of European paintings of the *Noli Me Tangere* moment testify to the fact that the Magdalene is associated not just with the empty tomb but also with Jesus' appearance. Schaberg, however, finds not only the scholarly tradition but also "the whole Magdalene tradition" oppressive (352) and sexist, and therefore attempts to destabilize dominant scholarly readings and suggest new lines of research.

As one of a series of introductory disclaimers, Schaberg warns against the risks inherent in recreating female figures from the past in one's own image: "Feminism's desire for a committed feminist and deeply political Woolf corresponds to its desire (or the desire of some feminists) for a feminist Mary Magdalene . . ." (36). This is a rare moment in the book when Schaberg implicitly acknowledges the existence of a range of feminisms and feminists, not all of whom might agree with her interpretations. Had I first encountered Woolf not through her own writings but in Schaberg's "committed feminist and deeply political" incarnation, I might have found her lacking in subtlety and sophistication, and therefore not sought out her writings.

Schaberg's representation of Woolf prepared me to be wary of her representation of other commentators, from the biblical to the contemporary. For example, the Gospel of Luke, which has long been thought of as "the women's gospel," and which I and many others teach in women's studies classes as an empowering text, is repeatedly and without qualification characterized as misogynist (100), and as depicting "women as subordinate, passive, and silent" (265). It might seem odd to accuse Luke of exercising "editorial techniques in his Gospel" that have the effect "of silencing women," (79) when his is the only Gospel that not only details the annunciation to Mary the mother of Jesus, and also the only Gospel that records the sole text in the New Testament the authorship of which is ascribed to a woman—Mary's song that came to be called the *Magnificat*. Much of later Mariology is based on Luke's account. One reason Schaberg does not see these and other elements in Luke's Gospel as empowering for women is that she sees Mary Magdalene as representing "resistance to gender subordination," and Mary mother of Jesus as representing gender subordination (127) in the tradition.

These clear-cut positions are not at all surprising, and have the predictable result of celebrating one female figure and combating some stereotypes about her (Magdalene) only to buy into stereotypes of others (Mary mother of Jesus, and Mary, sister of Martha). More troubling than this predictable outcome is Schaberg's assumption that she understands various ancient authors' intentions. For instance, she assumes that she correctly understands Luke's intentions to have been misogynist and that feminist readings of Luke that differ from her reading are therefore more subversive than exegetical. Citing primarily her own essay on Luke to dismiss his Gospel as misogynist, she notes that Hornsby's feminist reading of Luke is at odds with her own, but frames that note with these comments: "I think it is Luke's intent that she [the woman who anointed Jesus' feet, whom he does not name as the Magdalene but who later came to be identified with her] be seen as such [a prostitute—which Luke nowhere says that she is, though many readers have interpreted her as one] ... My suggestion is that... this attempt to degrade can be turned around into an opportunity for solidarity" (74-75 n40). But what if one does not read Luke's representation as an attempt to degrade? Is it possible to decide what Luke's intentions were? More importantly, do we need to speculate about his intentions?

One does not need to be a deconstructionist to wonder whether determining an author's intentions is a useful exercise. As St. Augustine points out in a remarkable passage in his *Confessions*, we can never recover the author's intentions nor do we need to do so, and to debate these intentions is futile. Shifting the focus from authorial intention to reader reception, Augustine argues that if we see meanings in the text that the author did not intend, so much the better—a creative author would be happy to have readers discover such meanings in the text. Using an image dear to Woolf, he figures the text as a fountain from which different drinkers derive similar and yet different types of sustenance.

Reception studies are often fascinating because of the range of responses to major texts and figures that they uncover. The impulse to categorize can, however, reduce and tame that fascination. Schaberg briefly sums up a range of responses to the Magdalene from the twelfth to the fifteenth centuries and places them in two categories—as a penitent and a contemplative, she was a model for all, and as an apostle and preacher, she was an exception to the rule that women were not to preach. Schaberg then remarks, "What can we say that is not utterly obvious about the sexual politics of these two medieval versions of her legend?" (97). She sees the focus on contemplation rather than on action as arising from a taming impulse, both in the case of Mary Magdalene and in that of Mary of Bethany (Martha's sister, who neglected housework to sit at Jesus' feet and listen to him).

This reading entirely misses the point that from at least Plato and Aristotle to at least the Renaissance, the life of contemplation was seen as an indisputably higher human life than the life of action. The Marys who were seen as choosing contemplation over action thus functioned not as models for domesticity (Martha was the model for domesticity) but as models for women who aspired to choose the life of the mind and the spirit over an endless round of childbearing and domestic drudgery. Schaberg dismisses the argument that this choice had liberatory potential for women by citing one essay that combats the argument, but she cites none of the studies that support it: "the power to tame her [Mary Magdalene] comes most strongly from the story [of Mary of Bethany] ... which many have thought of as promoting the liberation of women, but which Elizabeth Schüssler Fiorenza has shown promotes with dangerous subtlety the patriarchal separation and restriction of women" (96).

The book begins and concludes with Schaberg envisioning a new "Magdalene Christianity" or religion of Outsiders. By her account, this religion appears to be a type of socialist feminism rooted in Judaeo-Christian-Islamic traditions, and therefore is a religion already very much in existence. Transposing Woolf's famous anti-nationalist statement, "As a woman I have no country. As a woman I want no country," Schaberg argues that Woolf can teach us to say, "As a woman I have no religion. I am not Jew or Christian or Muslim or pagan—or— As a woman I am Jew, and Christian, and Muslim and pagan—" (40). This reformulation, it seems to me, echoes not so much Woolf as Mahatma Gandhi, a Hindu and therefore a "pagan" by this classification, who famously said, "I am a Hindu, a Muslim, a Christian, a Sikh and a Jew." Perhaps someone will soon write a book on Gandhi and Woolf, envisioning a Woolfian Hinduism.

—Ruth Vanita, *University of Montana*

> *Ethics and Aesthetics in European Modernist Literature:*
> *From the Sublime to the Uncanny*
> David Ellison (Cambridge: Cambridge UP, 2001) 290pp.
> *Literary Impressionism and Modernist Aesthetics*
> Jesse Matz (Cambridge: Cambridge UP) 278pp.

David Ellison's *Ethics and Aesthetics in European Modernist Literature: From the Sublime to the Uncanny* and Jesse Matz's *Literary Impressionism and Modernist Aesthetics* are two texts that extend the field of inquiry into the dynamics of modernism, albeit in diverse ways. That is, Modernism is understood by Ellison to be an ethical aesthetic practice whereas Matz argues for the political aesthetic of Modernism.

As one would expect in texts on Modernism, there is in each of these books a chapter on Virginia Woolf and Woolf scholars may be tempted to dip into the contents of these chapters as they could stand alone. The traditional philosophical journey from Kant via Kierkegaard to Freud taken by Ellison some may feel is unnecessarily lengthy and the painstaking intensity of Matz's theoretical progression (read slow) a little tedious. Yet despite these anticipated initial quibbles, a perusal of the entire works of each is rewarding in terms of the theoretical complexities not only of Modernism per se but also of Woolf's particular ethical and political contribution.

Ellison's book investigates the historical origins and textual practice of European literary Modernism. While stressing that the literary analysis in the latter part of the text is the most important, he commences with Kant, Kierkegaard and Freud. These philosophical chapters are well explained and will be accessible to those with even the smallest amount of philosophical knowledge. He argues, unlike Kant and Kierkegaard who saw the ethical as separate from the aesthetic, that the sublime and the uncanny are hybrid notions formed by the interplay of the aesthetic and ethical. It is this interplay that is the textual space in Modernist literature as uncanniness, *Das Unheimliche*, which is "both feared and desired, at times censored and prohibited from exerting its power but at other times allowed to function freely, dangerously, diabolically" (ix-x). His reading of Kant tends to merge the three critiques, as Deleuze read them together as a "condition of possibility" (4); the third critique can be read as an intermediary link, in that reflective judgement is the mediating link between understanding and reason (5). He proposes that the sublime and the beautiful are not simply a binary opposition; they are different but similar in that they "both tend toward the ethical" (13). For Kant the aesthetic is precarious and fragile, forever risking losing its territory for the sake of the ethical.

Kierkegaard also worked with the interplay of the aesthetic and the ethical, albeit with the difference that the religious is present. Ellison is interested in the second volume of *Either/Or* where Kierkegaard insists that "it is possible to conceive of an ethically grounded poetic life" (26). The text could, perhaps, work quite well without the inclusion of Kierkegaard as, near to his introduction on Freud, Ellison argues that "the uncanny is the sublime of our age—foreign and familiar" (53), which seems to suggest a plausible, more simplistic, connection between Kant and Freud.

For Ellison it is the Modernist novel that engages with the uncanny, *Das Unheimliche*, and enables the ethical. In the close analytical readings of Proust and Kafka, Conrad, Gide, and Woolf, he aims to locate the narrative traits of uncanniness. In Proust, Ellison recognizes a Jakobson (aphasic) type of the crossing of "metaphoric and metonymic" poles as that which deems uncanniness. Kafka's work is analyzed in terms of his use of certain key words that reveals an "openness within the act of writing itself" (146). The aesthetic brilliance of both Conrad and Gide "envelops an ethical labyrinth" (159) engaging with the large issues of responsibility and freedom, experience and understanding. These texts pose the fundamental question of immoralism in ways such as the inhuman appears as unframeable (166).

With regard to Woolf, while Ellison's focus is on the ethical, he makes some interesting comment on Woolf's fluid style of writing that could, also, be pertinent to further research on the politics of stream of consciousness. He sees the fluidity of Woolf's writing as related to an inner rhythm that enabled her to be released, willingly, into contact with an inner darkness. He argues that the tenuously fine line between autobiography and the writing of *To the Lighthouse* is significant. By examining certain points in a diary entry of 23 February 1926 where Woolf declares, ecstatically, her experience of writing *To the Lighthouse* ("I live entirely in it"), he claims it is the very thinness of this boundary that accounts for the emotion, that is, the uncanny sensation experienced by Woolf as she vacillates between aesthetic achievement and feelings of "darkness and death" (187). The very success of Mrs. Ramsay then, according to Ellison, is an experiential and existential fall into the uncanny. It is in making the dead come to life that the reader enters the "domain of the un-homelike, the alive-but-also-dead region of the uncanny" (189). We slip from the sublime into the uncanny. This uncanniness is ethical, for Ellison, because he believes that Mrs. Ramsay operates as harmony. She throws "an aesthetic veil over an ethical situation" at the expense of revealing the truth, that is, of her physical and emotional poverty (196). Woolf scholars will, of course, be reminded of the green shawl. However, the extensive space given to close analysis of "The Fisherman and his Wife" in this chapter is less interesting.

While Ellison's work is philosophically and stylistically dry in tone there are some amusing vignettes that lighten the theoretical load. For instance, he accuses Freud of "fiction envy"! He posits that Freud envied fiction writers their freedom: a reader of fiction engages in a "willing suspension of disbelief" (57) as does the teller of tales fall into the uncanny, *Das Unheimliche*; they fall into literariness. This explains why the uncanny is "diabolical," as it is a destabilizing threat to social norms and values, the ethical. Further amusing stylistic touches that break the dryness are worthy of mention. Whenever Ellison argues against a theorist, such as Freud, or Carolyn Heilbrun, to name a couple, he tends to commence his sentence with: "With apologies to ...." It somehow gives the impression of the polite (oh! so well known) formal 'academic' bow of the head—a pause—before he continues. At least this is my impression. However, my playful use of the term 'impression' is not to belittle the topic of Matz's text.

Jesse Matz's *Literary Impressionism and Modernist Aesthetics* is, as the title suggests, an exemplification of literary Impressionism. He argues that literary Impressionism is inherently different from pictorial Impressionism because it is associated with sociocultural life.

Matz's definition of the literary impression is extensive and spans many pages and, as does Ellison, he works from a traditional base by referring initially to Aristotle, Hume and Locke. His work is similar to Ellison in terms of Woolf and the politics of stream of consciousness. Unlike the pictorial, according to Matz, the literary impression has "no location, but conveys perception and understanding from one point to the next, like a miraculous analogy among distinct perceptual moments. It is neither sensation nor idea ... connects the mind to the body ... [as] timeless concept ... not concrete ...but spiritual" (7). He observes, via an analysis of prominent figures such as Proust, Pater and Woolf that Modernist writers very often turn to women and lower classes to politicize their aesthetic. For instance, Proust writes of his servant and servant's bedroom in a manner to express something that is free of external imperfection, that is, the non-pictorial.

He believes Pater to be a key figure in literary Impressionism for the way he is able to express homosexual desire through the impression, whereby capacities for judgement become incomplete. He describes it as "discovering self-alienation, and trying to correct the problem through engagement with another kind of person" (55).

An explanation of this concept becomes clearer, perhaps, in terms of Woolf's depiction of Mrs Brown. Matz argues that Woolf's non-pictorial Impressionism is to do with both class and gender politics and that Mrs Brown became the archetype of many later characters. In such context, he cites for instance, the charwoman, Sally Seton, Jinny and even Mrs. Ramsay so that the political aesthetic thereon is forever a result of deconstructing Mrs. Brown.

Matz defines Woolf's feminism as "standpoint" feminism in that, he argues, this type of feminist stance opposes perceptual divisions. However, this position could, perhaps, be substituted by any theory of representation that aims to replace subject for object in literary writing practice. His point is that social fallacies (such as inequalities between class, gender, sexuality) enforced by social divisions are then discredited. He notes that when

> Woolf discovers this isomorphism of social and perceptual division she can move beyond her merely negative interest in free play. Free play becomes important not simply because of its open indecision, but because it presents perception with a wholly different object (184).

In other words, he claims that with the free play of impressions there is always uncertainty. With regard to the political, he questions whether Woolf, as a self-designated snob, invokes Mrs. Brown as materiality "to draw matter into her art without leaving her high ground" (177). Yet later, such comment is modified in that, he says, Woolf perhaps implemented the indeterminacy of the impression for the sake of her preference for indeterminacy of class. The play of ambiguity seems to be an integral part of his project and indeed text. It is also related to his understanding of Woolf's desire to produce "life itself," while refusing "a philosophy" of writing in favor of "myriad impressions." He insists that no philosophy can define her writing but rather, merely locating it in what appear to be negative terms as "vague theory"(176). Terms such as "vague" and "indeterminate" become valorized to evoke the very "elected inconsistency" of perception, that is, the indeterminacy of literary Impressionism, or "myriad impressions" in Woolf's fiction.

As far as Woolf's feminist politics are concerned, he argues that by giving the impression of a female body as in Mrs. Brown there is marked a turning point in producing "life itself." This is extended further in *Jacob's Room* when it is the other way around. She gives the lower class woman in the railway car the job of investigating impressions of him.

Matz considers analogies between arts to be suspect and this may be considered a little antagonistic by some readers, considering the research already undertaken on this topic: There is, for instance the renowned work of both Jane Goldman and Diane F. Gillespie. The separation of literary and pictorial

Impressionisms is extended to a historical separation between Woolf and her sister Vanessa Bell (as in the sisterly connection in Diane F. Gillespie *The Sisters' Arts*). It is denied yet appears surreptitiously, so as to make the disconnection incomplete/indeterminate. That is, the sub-heading of one chapter and the title of another chapter is "The Sister Arts." The ambiguity is reinforced in that while the connection is being denied it is simultaneously acknowledged.

It seems that, despite certain anticipated reservations on the part of Woolf scholars, both Ellison and Matz make some worthy contribution to the ethics and politics of literary Modernism. In terms of Woolf scholarship the contribution is more specific in that both authors participate in further understanding of stream of consciousness writing as ethical and political, respectively. While this may, or may not be, the contemplative delight of "myriad impressions" it is certainly not "art for art's sake."

—Carolyn Abbs, *Murdoch University, Western Australia*

Literary Modernism and Musical Aesthetics: Pater, Pound, Joyce, and Stein
Brad Bucknell
(Cambridge: Cambridge UP, 2001) xii + 288 pp.

Brad Bucknell's *Literary Modernism and Musical Aesthetics*, as its title promises, examines modernist literature's relationship to music and, more particularly, to ideas of music and musical value. Focusing on a select group of writers for whom music carried particular weight, and whose work, he claims, illustrates the range of modernist approaches to music, Bucknell reveals music's crucial involvement in literary modernism's struggles to define as well as justify its experimental projects and epistemological questions. Chapters on Pater, Pound, Joyce, and Stein, explore the authors' theoretical ideas about music's significance, their various methods of incorporating musical styles, motifs, structures, and references in their literary work, and, in the case of Stein and Pound, their actual bringing together of music and words in the form of opera. Hesitant to impose any homogenizing thesis of continuity on their diverse perspectives, Bucknell nonetheless convincingly demonstrates the ways in which music becomes associated in each case with what he considers a defining tension of modernism: "the tension between interiority and artistic form." Music, for these writers, still carries its nineteenth-century promise to fuse subject and object, inside and outside, in a total and direct presentation of interiority, while it also raises doubts about the possibility of such a fusion for music or literature. Either by betraying its own conventionality—the possibility that it only creates that which it seems to express—or by remaining an ideal that language can never fully grasp, music ultimately reinforces rather than allays the "anxiety" of modernist formal experimentation.

Though the first of his authors is Pater, whom he sees as pivotal in relating music to the "scene of modernist difficulty of style and form," Bucknell sets the scene with Mallarmé's rejection of Wagner's notion of the *Gessamkunstwerke*. Where Wagner's project asserts the possibility of total expressivity in a fusion of language, gesture and music, Mallarmé conceives of music as artifice, an untranslatable surface that preserves the "mystery" of depth. His musical poetics rescues language from its doomed efforts to represent nature by turning back toward the surfaces of language itself. Rather than conceiving music as a source or model for literary expressiveness, "'true' music is already the 'written word'" (25) for Mallarmé, after whom, Bucknell claims, "writers can no longer view music as the trope of a secure inwardness" (36). In thus situating Mallarmé, rather than Wagner, at the beginning of modernism's engagement with music, Bucknell significantly revises a critical approach that has tended to see only the influence of the expressivist notion of music. (He cites as an example Alex Aronson—consistently misspelled as Aaronson—whose important *Music and the Novel: A Study in Twentieth-Century Fiction* is the only other monograph on music and literary modernism.)

But in restricting his own focus to the scene of "stylistic and formal difficulty" exemplified by Pound, Joyce, and Stein, Bucknell perhaps underplays the larger implications of his important revision. The tension he traces between belief in music's transcendent potential and awareness of music's implicatedness in the "problem of representation" can also be seen to inform, for example, the sometimes anxious relationship of African American modernists (Langston Hughes and James Weldon Johnson, for example) with "black music," imagined as both an expressive source and a cultural discourse. While Bucknell cannot be faulted for his narrower focus, his emphasis on modernist "difficulty" as the site of music-literary relations threatens to shut down some potentially illuminating extensions of his argument.

Pater's oft-cited pronouncement that all art "aspires to the condition of music" would seem to place him securely in the "expressivist" camp, but Bucknell reveals a much more complicated, and paradoxical, idea of music pervading *The Renaissance*, and linking Pater to modernism. While the "condition" to which all art "aspires" is, for Pater, a kind of removal from time that follows music's apparent fusion of "matter" and "form," he nonetheless recognizes that music exists and is experienced *in* time, by an historically conditioned listening subject. "Aspiring to the condition of music for the one beholding the work of art is not to conquer time," Bucknell writes, "but to refigure its loss, its surety, and its ephemerality" (49). Pater's music, then, is a "condition" of fullness and transcendence that dissipates in the moment of its perception, and, as such, "offers us yet another image of modernity's supplementary condition" (50).

The idea of supplementarity looms large in Bucknell's discussion of Pound, who most resembles Pater in his commitment to the idea of musical transcendence. At 70 pages, Bucknell's chapter on Pound offers a thorough exposition on the centrality of music (typically overshadowed by critical attention to visuality) to Pound's thinking, poetics, and experience (he was a reviewer, a concert organizer, and a composer as well as an aesthetician). After reviewing Pound's ideas about music expressed in the *Osiris* essays,"How to Read," and elsewhere, Bucknell turns to Pound's various attempts to turn theory into practice, from his opera, *Le Testament de François Villon* (of whose compositional methods Bucknell offers an illuminating analysis that may be lost on those who don't read music), to his incorporation of music and musical models in the *Cantos*. Pound conceives of music as "a kind of essential hierarchical structure, a truth beyond the merely material or materialistic," that promises to join consciousness with "the unthinking sentient or even insentient universe" (62). In this vein, he elaborates his notions of the "Great Bass" and "absolute rhythm" as the musical, and mystical, ground for his poetic practice. But lurking within such absolutist invocations of music as ground, Bucknell traces the problem of authority: who but the poet himself can authorize this ground, this essential structure? What if, indeed, the poet is only inventing this structure? And so, the poet-composer is left with the "process of a constant supplementarity that 'music,' in any of its various appearances, cannot stop, but of which it can only become a part" (120).

While Pound continues to strive for a musical poetics that will achieve a kind of "direct presentation," Joyce thoroughly ironizes expressivist ideas of music in his famously "musical" "Sirens" episode of *Ulysses*. The Joyce chapter was, for me, the most interesting in the book, as it illuminated Joyce's extreme sensitivity to the multi-layered presence of music in early 20th-century Dublin experience. Much of the existing criticism on the musicality of "Sirens" works to substantiate Joyce's own claims that he used the "fugue" or "fuga per canonem" as a model for his writing. In reviewing this literature, Bucknell points out the many problems inherent in any attempt to map musical onto narrative structure, particularly when it comes to identifying the "voices" of a fugue, which critics have seen in everything from the episode's characters, to the aural and rhythmic patterns in its language. Identifying the contradiction in Joyce's own statements about his method—"fugue" and "fuga per canonem" are not interchangeable—Bucknell suggests that, rather than the strict and rule-driven sixteenth-century "fuga per canonem," Joyce more likely was thinking of the nineteenth-century "fuga sciolta," whose compositional method combined "freedom and form." But rather than name the musical form that will unlock the episode's meaning, Bucknell stresses Joyce's more parodic approach to questions of musical meaning and music's relationship to language. The fugal qualities of "Sirens" ultimately underscore, for Bucknell, "the problem of finding complete meaning in sound," whether of language or music. While it pulls readers' attention away from the referentiality of language and toward its aural and rhythmic properties, this episode—like the singing voice that it references—insists that sounds and rhythms are inevitably heard, understood, and filtered through the conventions and circumstances of cultural context. Joyce thus refuses to invoke a musicality that transcends time and place, or that directly expresses "interiority," except as itself a clichéd—albeit powerful—form of listening.

Stein alone among Bucknell's modernists seems altogether uninterested in the "expressivist" idea of music, and least defined by the "tension between interiority and artistic form" that Bucknell sees as a driving force behind modernist formal experimentation. Instead, the illuminating tension driving modernist experimentation here lies in the encounter of her *Four Saints in Three Acts* with "history," first in the form of Virgil Thomson's music, and then in the historical scene and event of the opera's 1934 premiere with an all-black cast. Bucknell first demonstrates how the text reflects Stein's larger aim to produce writing that "creates its own time and space," and in particular to create by her writing a "continuous present" that opposes temporal conventions of causality, continuity and succession. Bucknell then approaches Thomson's very tonal score—which he deems "one of the most extensive responses to Stein's writing"—as the "perfect foil" for Stein's language. By giving the "tonal impression of causality," Thomson's music both "reveals and conceals" the grammatical and syntactical indeterminacy of Stein's language. (Bucknell offers a particularly compelling reading of Thomson's music as it plays with and against Stein's confusingly repetitive use of the word "fish" in the Prologue.) Bucknell provocatively suggests music and text trade places in this opera as Thomson's score takes the conventional place of language in its promise to anchor the opera's meanings in some kind of symbolic stability. But Stein's language refuses to be so anchored, as Thomson's music also performs its own Steinian breaks with predictability, suggesting a kind of "continuous present" by its constant gestures of restarting and redirecting the musical flow of the opera.

Bucknell brings his study beyond the examination of "ideas of music" in the final section of this chapter when he turns to the moment that Stein and Thomson's opera leaves the written page and becomes an event, relinquishing its meanings to those present at its 1934 premiere. Thomson insisted to Stein, who worried that the presence of "Negro bodies" would distract from her "theme," that his decision to use an all-black cast for the opera's first production had to do not with race, but with his sense of their "rhythm, their style and especially their diction" (qtd., 216). Bucknell suggests that, for reasons that have everything to do with race, the black cast served, in fact, along with Thomson's music, to make Stein's difficult text "socially acceptable," by visually marking the text's "otherness" for its white audience, and for the composer himself. More importantly for Bucknell, the all-black production enacts a certain "repressed element" of the music and words, namely the very historicity that Stein works to resist. In other words, this production, like any production, inevitably brings into play the "discourses and practices" of its particular time and place, in this case those surrounding the "vogue" of blackness in New York in the 1920s and 30s. Where music represented a horizon of meaning that words could only strive after in vain for Pound and Pater, here it occasions a "collision with the contemporary history of American culture itself," thus illuminating the silent presence of cultural narratives and meanings within Stein's writerly efforts to elide them.

Bucknell himself here finally collides with the concerns of cultural studies, and with the growing field of scholarly interest in music's cultural roles, effects and meanings. Indeed, several have written about the *Four Saints* premiere in terms of its participation in American racial ideology and in an American modernism more broadly conceived. Bucknell does not, however, engage with this work, or with the debates of "cultural studies," as he remains primarily concerned with how music, as idea or event, "tends to reinforce and amplify the anxiety of modernist formal experimentation" (224). But Bucknell's focused and highly nuanced project is, without question, an extremely important one—for both literary studies and cultural studies—as it not only establishes music's central and crucial place in literary modernism's conception of its own efforts and aims, but also gestures more generally toward its contradictory place in 20th-century experience.

—Cristina L. Ruotolo, *San Francisco State University*

Modernist Fiction, Cosmopolitanism and the Promise of Community
Jessica Berman (Cambridge, UK: Cambridge UP, 2001) x + 242 pp

In *Modernist Fiction, Cosmopolitanism and the Promise of Community*, Jessica Berman begins and ends by addressing the questions Raymond Williams poses in his late essay "When Was Modernism?" Commenting on the failures of a commercialized and institutionalized modernism, Williams considers the possibility of an alternative modernist tradition to be discovered in marginal works that might enable us to imagine community in the future. Disagreeing with Williams's insistence that such an alternative is nowhere to be found in high modernism, Berman argues that in the fiction of Henry James, Marcel Proust, Virginia Woolf, and Gertrude Stein community is re-imagined in response to historical and political transformations in the early twentieth century. She claims that although these four writers "develop radically different models for social organization, their narratives consistently place the notion of community at their core," returning repeatedly "to issues of commonality, shared voice, and exchange of experience, especially in relation to dominant discourses of gender and nationality" (3). These writers responded to the threat posed by various versions of totalitarian models of national community by constructing models of cosmopolitan communities. Berman's interdisciplinary project seeks to offer a theory of community that incorporates the narrative construction of community and that encourages a positive re-envisioning of the connotations of modernist fiction's "internationalism," arguing for modernism's political engagement in the issues of cosmopolitanism and community. She establishes a rich context for the works of Woolf, James, Proust, and Stein by juxtaposing them in telling (and often ironic) ways to other texts in the "discursive terrain."

Berman provides a helpful reading of current theories of cosmopolitanism and community. Although she agrees with Martha Nussbaum on the importance of literature in cultivating humanity and helping us to re-imagine relationships with others, she does not share Nussbaum's belief in the notion of a core self and a fixed identity. Berman's concept of community derives from the belief that subjectivity is incomplete, relational, and embedded in a social context. From this perspective, she interrogates the utopianism and universalizing tendencies of certain feminist theories of community. She also points to the inability of early and late forms of American pragmatism to conceive of community in any way except as national models of community. She finds that theorists of all stripes (including a host of Habermasians) avoid coming to terms with difference and fail to bring together the private and the public spheres. Berman, however, finds very useful Jean Luc Nancy's concept of community as "radically separate subjects in what he calls a process of 'compearance'" (14). She also builds productively on Homi Bhabha's concept of locations of culture, Arjun Appadurai's sense of situated community, and Bruce Robbins's contention that "actually existing cosmopolitanism is a reality of (re)attachment, multiple attachment, or attachment at a distance" (qtd. in Berman 16). Berman finds in Woolf, James, Proust, and Stein that community is always historically contingent, with their narratives conveying the process of "writing being-in-common and its limit" and of conceiving community "as both local and international, private and public at once" (20). Thus, she argues, in what is one of her central claims, that these modernists blur the supposed distinction between modern and postmodern culture. Through such narrative models that perform radically new forms of affiliation "we can begin to imagine community anew," which is the thesis—and the hope—of Berman's book.

Berman locates Henry James's texts in the changing attitude towards cosmopolitanism in the latter half of the nineteenth century, beginning with a compelling analysis of the magazine *Cosmopolitan* in its early years, the 1880s and 1890s. Her discussion is rife with the paradoxical complexity of James's texts. His pronounced nativism (with its close attention to regional differences and fear of miscegenation) is undercut and inflected by his use of an ideally feminized version of America that challenges the escalating imperialism and jingoism of the period. James uses the ideal feminine virtues of relationality and interdependence to undercut the aggressive individuality and insularity of America after the Spanish-American War as national expansion comes to trump cosmopolitan wanderlust. Believing that American males have become cultural barbarians involved only in commercial pursuits, James repeatedly claims that the cultivation of manners and the advancement of culture, what Berman calls "the pedagogical aspect of nation-building," has become the task of American women (57). James's woman-as-national-icon is a cosmopolitan patriot, who not only challenges the restrictions of the domestic sphere but also conveys in her person and her words the tension between a racially and socially striated America at the turn of the century and the perennial "narrative prescriptions of assimilative national identity" (71).

The chapter on Marcel Proust is fascinating in its provocative juxtaposing of Proust with the anarcho-Zionist, symbolist poet, and journalist Bernard Lazare—both of whom claimed to be the first Dreyfusard. Berman states, "[I]t is in the unlikely connection between [them], constituted within the embrace and re-figuration of pariahdom, and a Jewish pariahdom in particular, that the political implication of Proust's constructions of community become clear" (74). Hannah Arendt uses Lazare's argument for the political power of pariahdom to establish a dichotomy between the "conscious pariah" and the Jewish *parvenu*, who hastens the demise of his people (74). In the course of *A la recherche du temps perdu*, Proust interrogates this dichotomy between the *parvenu* and the pariah. In the end of the novel, when Marcel decides to live apart from those of his past in what becomes a reconnection, from a distance, with re-imagined others, Proust's text embraces the position of the contemplative pariah, while holding on to multiple, partial perspectives and imagining new forms of affiliation. Through his narrative model of a pariah, who is both eternally other and always connected to the world, "Proust rescues the social from the political ignominy to which Hannah Arendt consigns it. When she claims that the entrance of previously private concerns into the social realm, and the increasing predominance of the social over the political, are the downfall of modernity, Arendt neglects the possibility that new modes of affiliation might be born within that mix" (113).

The chapter "Steinian Topographies," which ranges across a number of texts from *The Making of Americans* to *Ida: A Novel*, begins with a discussion of the evolution of nineteenth-century geography into a human and cultural geography influenced by Darwinism at the beginning of the twentieth century. Berman claims that although her narratives have been read as "wandering" in the sexual sense, "Stein's writings also ask us to read these wanderings literally. . . . They inaugurate a complex series of connections between geography and identity, geography and nationality, and geography and nomadism that also ultimately raise the question of community and its relationship to cosmopolitanism" (158). Taking care not to equate Stein's "exile" with postcolonial migrancy, Berman points to the example of Stein's wandering narratives of a nomadic cosmopolitan community as a starting point for postmodern and postcolonial theories—another example of the blurring of the distinction between the modern and the postmodern. She also argues that Stein's attention to intersubjectivity in the ethical relationship implied in such texts as *Stanzas in Meditation* opposes a feminist ethics of intimacy to Emmanuel Levinas's ethics of radical alterity. Stein's texts offer us "an ethical model of social community" (186).

Engaging in a dialogue with such scholars as Melba Cuddy-Keane, Jane Marcus, and Gillian Beer, Berman reads Woolf's *Orlando* and *The Waves* in the context of Britain's political crises from 1929-1931. In these novels "we can see the way in which narrative action becomes praxis, the expansion of the subject substitutes for the consolidation of personal political power, and the construction of alternative models of community pushes a cosmopolitan ideal" (117). Woolf's feminist discourse radically reconstructs community on the model of a co-operative rather than a collective—a politics composed of diverse individuals working together. Berman sees Woolf as anticipating Nancy's idea of compearance, rejecting both the conception of affiliation as the free association of atomistic individuals or of the group as a homogeneous, monolithic whole (122). For Woolf, nationalism is always masculinist and patriarchal, which is why she came to prefer the micro-politics of the Co-operative Movement, especially the Women's Co-operative Guild (WCG), which refused to merge with the Labour Party. One of the most interesting aspects of Berman's chapter on Woolf is the discussion of the influence of the WCG on her writing. The WCG was structured as a federation of active, independent branches, rather than a federation. It is precisely this decentralization (as opposed to the more centralized structure of the Co-operative Movement) that enabled the WCG to be so radical and to focus on gender issues. And it was the Women's Guild that was the most vocal in supporting internationalism (127-28).

Berman makes a rather abrupt turn—after the fascinating discussion of the influence of the WCG on Woolf's political philosophy—to make the point that finally Woolf felt herself to be too distant from these working women. The kind of community envisioned in *Three Guineas, Orlando,* and *The Waves* is like the WCG in being a collective of independent affiliated subjects, yet it is a "being-with-others" that does not involve shared political agendas. Berman argues that in *Orlando*, Woolf "opens up a realm of liminal community," which indicates the failure of "conventional versions of history and national belonging to account for or to accommodate the shared experience" (136). Orlando's attraction to and distance from the gypsy women mirrors Woolf's own relationship to the women of the WCG. Neither Orlando nor Woolf is able to think back through a mother to a shared identity; rather, they must turn to an "imaginative presentation of the self" (138). Berman points out that *The Waves* starts from *Orlando*'s achievement as "internal fantasy" and extends beyond the self (139). Her analysis of *The Waves* persuasively argues that the novel "absolutely opposes most traditional models of family, proximity, and nation as well as the fascist call for the corporate self. Secondly, *The Waves* resists fascism by rejecting the idea of a charismatic leader in the form of the character Percival. And thirdly . . . by using gendered images of active natural power to contradict the ordered might of fascism" (141). The community of characters in *The Waves* is fragmented, in process, and never consolidates into a common being—much like Nancy's depiction of community. Berman claims that Woolf offers a model that makes cosmopolitanism possible and "is directly targeted at those in search of political answers to England's crisis" (149). In one of the delicious ironies of Berman's juxtaposing of incongruous perspectives, she reveals that in the premier issue of Oswald Mosley and Harold Nicolson's *Action* in 1931, Nicolson wrote a glowing review of *The Waves*, praising its "battering restlessness" and its "incessant renewals of shape and energy" (143).

There is much to admire in Jessica Berman's ambitious book, not the least of which is her construction of a rich interdisciplinary context in the chapters on the writers. These sections are so compelling that they could stand on their own. (In fact, one might argue—and this is a quibble—that there is occasionally a bit of a disjunction between context and texts, such as in the Stein chapter.) But what is most striking about this study is the way it brilliantly reflects in its structure the central theoretical concept of compearance—the being-in-common or affiliation of radically different writers all responding to the threat of a looming totalitarian nationalism. In *Modernist Fiction, Cosmopolitanism and the Politics of Community*, each writer is remade in this connection with the others.

—Molly Abel Travis, *Tulane University*

Material Modernism: The Politics of the Page.
George Bornstein (Cambridge: Cambridge UP, 2001) xii + 185 pp.

You flip open the book and the first thing you notice is the extraordinarily wide margins, over 15/8 inches. This space is attractive, it gives us visual pleasure, and it allows the text to breathe (the *Woolf Studies Annual* you are reading is not stingy; their 0.75 inches gives you space for your thumbs). This testifies at the outset to the importance the author places on the visual aspect of the page; we would expect no less from a scholar who has edited the excellent collection, *The Iconic Page in Manuscript, Print, and Digital Culture.* The margins invite us to make notes (carefully, in pencil—you're not going to scrawl in this text the way you would on a greasy photocopy); they become a place of dialogue, and this clearly is what Bornstein hopes to foster. The *mise en page* also shows that Cambridge University Press is a classy press, sparing no expense. Nor will you: the book is $55, what one commentator on Amazon.com called "forbiddingly priced."

The copyright page tells us the book is set in Monotype Baskerville. Baskerville, designed in England in the eighteenth century, is "the epitome of neoclassical rationalism" in type, more popular in France and America than in England where it was made. It has a rationalist—vertical—axis, rather than the humanist—oblique—axis of, say, Times New Roman. (What this means is if you look at an 'o' the thinnest parts of it will be off to the side, positioned at 11 o'clock and 5 o'clock, in Times New Roman, whereas in Baskerville the thinnest part of the stroke occurs at the top and bottom of the letter.) The typeface was admired by Ben Franklin, and it's partly because of him that it became more popular in the American colonies than it did in England. Typographer Robert Bringhurst argues that these "beautiful and calm" letters correspond to the federal style in American architecture. An appropriate typeface, then, for a book that is provocative, but calm and lucid in articulating those provocations.

But why then a British publisher? A publisher notorious for pricing its books out of the reach of the common reader, and even the common library? Much of Bornstein's early work was issued by the University of Chicago; more recently he has published with the University of Michigan, which has become the leading U. S. publisher of books related to print culture. Did he want the cultural cachet of CUP, even though he must have known the decision would have cost him readers? Or was he paid more? (Not likely, CUP is only generous with their margins.) And is it fair to ask these questions?

Well it is, because the book makes us address precisely these issues.

Bornstein opens with the engaging question, "If the Mona Lisa is in the Louvre, where is *King Lear*?" His point is that any literary work exists in many places at the same time, and thus "any particular version that we study . . . is always already a construction, one of many possible." Further, there may be multiple authorized versions of a text (a situation that faces any reader of Woolf). Older schools of bibliography were devoted to establishing one true text, but much recent editorial theory advocates a position that Emily Dickinson scholars describe as "choosing not choosing" (5)—which leads to the possibility that "the literary work might be said to exist not in any one version, but in all the versions put together" (6). This is turn leads to the importance of reading what Jerome McGann, D. F. McKenzie, and others have called the "bibliographic code": everything from cover design, ink, paper, page layout, spacing (i.e. the physical embodiment of a given text), to prefaces, notes, dedications, and the other texts of a periodical or book in which the work appears (i.e. related textual matter), to—moving now outside the book—publisher, print run, price, and audience. In short, anything that affects the reception and interpretation of the work. This "bibliographic code" is like Walter Benjamin's "aura," that which points to the work's presence in time and space. Bornstein argues that representations of a text beyond its first incarnation tend to isolate the text from its original time and place, making it an aesthetic rather than an historicized object, leading to a "withering of the aura" (7).

After laying out his principles, Bornstein moves quickly from theory to practice, offering us, as the title of his first chapter announces, an example of "How to read a page." He chooses four sonnets, one each by Keats, Emma Lazarus, W. B. Yeats, and Gwendolyn Brooks. He shows how the initial publication of Keats's "On looking into Chapman's Homer," in the left-leaning political and literary quarterly *The Examiner*, links the poem to Romantic revolutionary politics, an association lost when the poem is reproduced with footnotes in the *Norton Anthology*. More striking, Bornstein shows how Lazarus's sonnet "The New Colossus," with the famous lines "Give me your tired, your poor,/Your huddled masses yearning to breathe free," is first included, then excluded, from the *Norton* (where in any case it is misleadingly footnoted), and then gutted for the plaque in JFK airport in New York, with the line "The wretched refuse of your teeming shores" excised in the name of political correctness. Anyone who has ever railed against the *Norton* (is there anyone who has not?), or lamented the compromises any anthology must make, will find articulate and powerful arguments in Bornstein for how the footnotes and the page design substantially affect the literary meaning of the text.

Chapter two, "The once and future texts of modernist poetry," provides a useful overview of copyright, introduces the notion of a "contextual code" to deal with the arrangement of poems in collections, and discusses poems by Yeats, Ezra Pound, and Marianne Moore in various states, from their first editions to their digital reproductions. Again, his arguments have wider applications, for the principles apply to the once and future texts of all modernist works. What does it mean, for example, that the most-easily accessed text of *Jacob's Room* online has no space breaks in it? In return for machine searchability what are we losing? And what strange monsters are produced by the intersection of copyright restriction and easy electronic reproduction?

Chapters three and four focus on Yeats. Here Bornstein's remarks on the relation between the Cuala Press, with its hand-made paper and Caslon Old Face type ("At the material level of inscription, then, the book protests against those who fumble in a greasy till"), and the more commercial Macmillan publishers are fascinating in themselves, and also provide useful points of comparison with the Woolfs' Hogarth Press (61). The following chapter, "Pressing women: Marianne Moore and the networks of modernism," addresses the importance of women in producing modernist literature. Marianne Moore operated within, and beyond, a network created by such figures as Bryher, Harriet Shaw Weaver, Dora Marsden, Harriet Monroe, Margaret Anderson, Jane Heap, Nancy Cunard, and Virginia Woolf, and Bornstein operates from the assumption that, "The presses and magazines of these women carried distinctive bibliographic codes that marked the early incarnations of the works that they published" (83). He shows how Moore's poem "The Fish," which first appeared ten months after the end of the First World War in *The Egoist*, gradually loses its political valence and becomes, with its publication in the *Selected Poems*, edited by T. S. Eliot and published by Faber & Faber, "a highly wrought formal object."

Chapters six and seven, "Joyce and the colonial archive" and "Afro-Celtic connections," move in a new direction, taking up post-colonial issues in conjunction with questions of the material text. The first essay alone is worth the price of admission, for it's the first I've seen that not only explains how Gabler's synoptic edition of *Ulysses* works, but shows how we can work with it. Bornstein links postcolonial theory with genetic criticism to show how the text's construction of alterity, particularly of Black, Jewish, and Irish Nationalist identities, is itself constructed at a particular stage in the construction of the text, thus throwing into relief the linkages between these identities. The argument is interesting, but the procedure is fascinating for it provides an example of how we might use texts such as John Graham's edition of the two holograph drafts of *The Waves* in exploring questions of gender and identity, as well as other issues.

One of the chief delights of this book is that it is incisive and eminently lucid. It could have been much longer, but it reads as if it has been carefully honed. It is highly theoretical but the theory has been absorbed, so that if you have been following current debates in continental and Anglo-American editorial theory you will recognize Bornstein's negotiations with these debates, and if you haven't you will learn something but you will not feel excluded. It is an important work for any scholar of Modernism, and it also translates well to the classroom. I used "How to read a page" in my first-year literature class because it's a superb example of how to read a *book* as well as how to read a *text*; and I used the same essay in a graduate class as an introduction to print culture history. That said, it is disappointing that there is no bibliography, for the book is an excellent guide to the field, and it is surprising to see no mention of French theorists such as Pierre Bourdieu, Gerard Genette, and Louis Hay, particularly since, as one of the editors of *Contemporary German Editorial Theory,* Bornstein is clearly aware of continental editorial and book history theory.

Several of these essays have appeared elsewhere, but it is good to have them collected between hardcovers, even the expensive covers of CUP, and the newer material extends in useful ways the arguments of the earlier pieces. *Material Modernism* is a fine book; for either a personal collection or an institutional library, it's worth the money.

—Edward L. Bishop, *University of Alberta*

The Phantom Table: Woolf, Fry, Russell and the Epistemology of Modernism
Ann Banfield (Cambridge: Cambridge UP, 2000) xviii + 433 pp.

By 1975, when Ann Banfield taught the Woolf seminar at Berkeley in which her book has its origins, *Modern Fiction Studies* had devoted a special issue to Woolf (1972), Alice van Buren Kelley had published *The Novels of Virginia Woolf: Fact and Vision*, Nancy Bazin *Virginia Woolf and the Androgynous Vision*, and Carolyn Heilbrun *Toward a Recognition of Androgyny* (all in 1973); the two volumes of Quentin Bell's biography of Woolf were already being argued over by American feminist scholars, Harvena Richter's *Virginia Woolf: The Inward Voyage* had been available for five years, and Jane Novak's *The Razor Edge of Balance* was just published. In other words, that "critical celebration that has changed the perception of Woolf as a 'major author'" (Banfield x) was just gathering steam. Now, the international bibliography of Woolf studies is vast, probably exceeding any one person's ability to grasp it all. It is a body of work that according to Banfield "continues to ignore a central aspect of [Woolf's] work" (x).

The ignored aspect which this dense, learned book seeks to illuminate is Woolf's philosophical project, identified by Banfield as aligned quite precisely with the theory of knowledge expounded by Bertrand Russell. The first hundred pages of *The Phantom Table* painstakingly outline Russell's epistemology, with detours where necessary to discuss Moore, Wittgenstein, and the history of British philosophical thought with particular reference to Leslie Stephen. The early twentieth-century British articulation of the ancient debate between Realism and Idealism was an idiosyncratic one that Banfield argues is a "key to otherwise unexplained obsessions of the novels" (4). These "obsessions" with unperceived space, with the relations between subject and object, and with the ubiquitous kitchen table most famously referred to in *To the Lighthouse*, are linked also to Roger Fry's version of the history of art, in which Impressionism is the logical *telos* of representational painting and Post-Impressionism comes to wrestle with the new scientific worldview that dominated the early twentieth century.

Sandra M. Donaldson has explained how a "wide-ranging debate among the Victorians about logic and the significance of the syllogism" culminated in Russell and Alfred North Whitehead's three-volume *Principia Mathematica*, published 1910-13, "the new order of mathematicians officially displacing the old order of philosophers and seizing the imagination of a more complex society" (330-31). Donaldson succinctly notes that Woolf would likely have known "conventional notation and illustrations for the syllogism" (329), and Banfield, at much greater length, convincingly argues that Woolf's milieu would have immersed her in the debates about knowledge being conducted at Cambridge University where, of course, so many of her most intimate friends, acquaintances, and relatives had been educated and with which they were long associated. This theory of knowledge emerged during the first three decades of the twentieth century in the context of a nascent philosophy of science and of startling discoveries in physics that were also the context for Woolf's novels. Banfield places her own work as complement to Alex Zwerdling's *Virginia Woolf and the Real World*, and Elizabeth Abel's *Virginia Woolf and the Fictions of Psychoanalysis*, each concerned with specific milieux that fed Woolf's consciousness.

Bloomsbury's contribution to the philosophical and scientific context outlined by Banfield was the aesthetic sense and knowledge that Cambridge lacked; in this marriage, Fry, whose degree was in Natural Science and whose aesthetic, Banfield argues, is derived from analytic philosophy, acted as go-between. In contrast to received wisdom, Banfield identifies as Woolf's main philosophical interlocutor not Moore but Russell, a relationship most evident in *To the Lighthouse*'s reconciliation of Moore's common sense and Russell's scientific views in the kitchen table that Lily Briscoe thinks is an ordinary piece of furniture "and yet at the same time, It's a miracle, it's an ecstasy" (*TTL* 202). Banfield's Bloomsbury is one in which not the personal relations of Moore underpin its aesthetics but rather the impersonal science of Russell and the physicists. Her aim is to demonstrate "which philosophical system provides a convincing reading of Woolf's *oeuvre*" (46).

The book's detailed account of how the table has been the "paradigmatic object of knowledge in 'the history of English thought'" (66) provides a lens by which Banfield is able to focus her readings of a number of apparently disparate moments in Woolf's texts. Russell writes in *The Problems of Philosophy* (1912) that the discipline has treated a common object such as the table with

> the most complete liberty of conjecture. Leibniz tells us that it is a community of souls: Berkeley tells us that it is an idea in the mind of God; sober science, scarcely less wonderful, tells us it is a vast collection of electric charges in violent motion.
>
> Among these surprising possibilities, doubt suggests that perhaps there is no table at all. (Qtd. Banfield 43)

Furthermore, according to Banfield, "Cézanne through Fry made philosophy's and art's common object a kitchen table" (258). Fry's theory of Post-Impressionism gave an "eyeless dimension" to "the eye disburdened of thought" which Banfield argues entered Woolf's aesthetic by way of Fry's theory of Impressionism. In "A Sketch of the Past," she argues, the movement is recapitulated in Woolf's descriptions of her "shock-receiving capacity," mirroring the Impressionist's encounter with sense-data, and of the revelation of "pattern," recalling the post-impressionist's logical explanation of that data's underlying structure (Banfield 341). The table supporting the objects of a still life, then, or the table rendered "mystical" by the early-twentieth century physicists' descriptions of the subatomic realm is also that scrubbed and bare correlative for Mr. Ramsay's philosophy which his son Andrew provides for Lily's understanding in *To the Lighthouse*. With such a context established, Banfield is able to knit together numerous references to tables in Woolf's writings so that Woolf's concerns seem often to derive directly from Russell's.

Banfield's method, however, is troubling. Woolf's writing—letters, diary, short fiction, novels, book reviews, essays—all become a seamless "text" in her argument, as if the occasion of their writing, their time of composition, were irrelevant. For example, to illustrate her point that "Novel-writing becomes the imaginative construction and furnishing of private rooms" (112), Banfield quotes from *Jacob's Room*, *A Room of One's Own*, *To the Lighthouse*, "Reminiscences" (in *Moments of Being*), "Street Haunting," and "The Lady in the Looking-Glass: A Reflection" within a single paragraph as if any time Woolf uses the word "room" her intentions are the same. The method extends even to the stitching together of quotations from various sources into pastiche sentences of her own:

> "Spaces of complete immobility separated each of these movements" . . . "space-like intervals" and "time-like intervals" . . . dividing night from day as the horizon divides "the sea from the sky" . . . or miles divide both night from day and Cambridge from Turkey, where always "someone at this very moment, was seated in a minute speck of light somewhere to the east of her" . . . where "there are other centres of consciousness besides my own" (Banfield 113)

My ellipses hide, respectively, references to *Jacob's Room*, Russell's *The Analysis of Matter*, *The Waves*, *Night and Day*, and Leslie Stephen's "What is Materialism?" This blurring of distinctions among texts, authors, and genre is of a piece with Banfield's choice to refer to Woolf's essays only by their volume and page number in the out-of-print *Collected Essays*, without providing the essays' titles. Too often, suggestively joined quotations form a hybrid statement that is allowed to stand in place of argument: for example, the "flash of some terrible reality leaping" in *A Room of One's Own* is linked to the flash of the scimitar blade as which James imagines his father in *To the Lighthouse*, which is also somehow the "stroke" of the lighthouse beam. As Banfield herself remarks, "similarity of grammatical structure misrepresents differences of logical relations" (225).

This trait weakens the force of the book's quite simple argument, that Woolf responded to the revolution in theory of knowledge through her own "philosophical" aesthetics, an aesthetics influenced by Roger Fry's mediation of Cambridge philosophy. To say that "Woolf's art makes explicit the philosophical implications of Post-Impressionism that are implicit in Fry's account of it" (291) is a worthy, if unremarkable, thesis. To argue that Fry's aesthetics are rooted in analytic philosophy is a helpful contribution to understanding an important aspect of modernism. But *The Phantom Table* makes much larger claims. Somehow, modernism has become Bloomsbury, and Bloomsbury has become Woolf. Surely, Joyce engages more directly with the analytic philosophers' arguments, with the refutation of Idealism (think, for example, of Stephen walking the beach in the "Proteus" chapter of *Ulysses*). And while it is true that Woolf's "interludes" of unperceived nature are a common element of her fiction, so too are such representations recurrent in the fiction of Katherine Mansfield. Also, as Christopher Reed has pointed out, "Fry had come to question or contradict virtually all the formalist principles that he—like his American descendants—made the foundation of modernism" by the end of his life (*A Roger Fry Reader* 305- 06). Elsewhere, Reed has commented that "our current understanding of the relationship between Woolf and formalism has suffered from a tendency to read the relevant texts without regard to their dates of issue, imposing a false stasis on what reveals itself as, actually, a remarkably dynamic relationship" ("Through" 13). Although passages in Banfield's book can surprise and delight by their juxtaposed phrases from Woolf, Russell, Fry, and Stephen, ultimately her representation is a static one that suppresses the kind of nuance and uncertainty that particularly characterizes Woolf's writing. To seek a single "philosophical system" by which to explain Woolf's work seems to me an aim refuted by Woolf's own critiques of systems, in *Three Guineas*, or in "A Society," for example.

There are a number of missteps that cause the book to creak: quoting from *To the Lighthouse*, Banfield follows the American edition's clearly wrong punctuation that has Mrs. Ramsay looking into a *boeuf en daube* that contains "bay leaves and . . . wine, and thought." The English edition follows "thought" with a comma, making it clear that the word is a verb not, as suits Banfield's purpose, a noun. There are also the errors and typos now predictable even in an expensive book published by one of the world's leading publishers: "Fear no more the heat of the sun" is not, as note 1 to chapter 5 tells us, from *Winter's Tale*.

The Phantom Table deserves to be read, to be argued with, to be integrated into that mosaic of critical discussion that is the dynamic field of Woolf studies, and, more largely, of modernist studies. It should be engaged by feminist critics for its skirting of gender (at one of the few points gender becomes an issue, it seems we have returned to "the androgynous mind" as Woolf's significant contribution to thought! [200]). It makes too large a claim, however, in suggesting that it describes "the epistemology of modernism."

—Mark Hussey, *Pace University*

Works Cited

Donaldson, Sandra M. "Where Does Q Leave Mr. Ramsay?" *Tulsa Studies in Women's Literature* 11 (Fall 1992): 329-36.
Reed, Christopher. *A Roger Fry Reader.* Chcago: U of Chicago P, 1996.
——. "Through Formalism: Feminism and Virginia Woolf's Relation to Bloomsbury Aesthetics." In Diane F. Gillespie, ed. *The Multiple Muses of Virginia Woolf.* Columbia: U of Missouri P, 1993: 1-35.
Woolf, Virginia. *To the Lighthouse.* [1927] San Diego: Harvest/HBJ, 1981

Modernism and Eugenics: Woolf, Eliot, Yeats and the Culture of Degeneration
Donald J. Childs (Cambridge: Cambridge UP, 2001) 266 pp

While many of the male modernist writers—Pound, Eliot, Yeats, Wyndham Lewis, Lawrence among other—aligned themselves with various right-wing movements and ideologies, the female modernists, including Virginia Woolf, have generally been exempted from such connections and are tallied on the progressive side of the page as pacifists, feminists, and/or anti-imperialists. Donald J. Childs has done a service, if a disturbing one, by including three chapters on Virginia Woolf in his recent study *Modernism and Eugenics: Woolf, Eliot, Yeats, and the Culture of Degeneration*. He outlines in his introductory chapter the context of eugenical thinking in which many of the writers of the modernist era were immersed, and argues that "although not all writers were eugenists or sympathetic to eugenics, eugenics touched upon the interests—if not the very lives—of many more of them than were eugenists" (12). His list includes, in addition to the three writers who are the subject of the study: George Bernard Shaw, D. H. Lawrence, H. G. Wells, Rebecca West, Arnold Bennett, J. M. Synge, Aldous Huxley, F. Scott Fitzgerald, C. P. Snow, Olive Schreiner, Marie Stopes, H. L. Mencken, and Jack London (13). But he also maintains that eugenical thinking "served" not only "Yeats's Irish nationalism . . . Lawrence's vitalism, and Eliot's conservatism" but also "Shaw's Fabian socialism [and] Woolf's feminism" (20). Quoting Jonathan Freedland,[1] Childs claims that "'eugenics is the dirty little secret of the British left'" (16), and persuasively explains that "After the Nazi atrocities in the name of eugenics in the 1930s and 1940s, most countries apart from Germany conveniently forgot their complicity in the eugenics movement of the early years of the twentieth century" (15). Articles on individual modernist writers outline connections between their works and eugenical thought,[2] but

[1]Jonathan Freedland, "The Dirty Little Secret of the Old British Left." *Guardian Weekly* 7 September 1977.

[2]See for example, David Bradshaw, "The Eugenics Movement in the 1930s and the Emergence of *On the Boiler*," *Yeats Annual #9*. Edited by Dierdre Toomey. London: Macmillan, 1992. 189-215.

Childs' study is the first full-length treatment of this issue in relation to literary modernism, and as such is a valuable contribution to the field.

Childs mines numerous biographical and non-fictional sources (letters, essays, book reviews, memoirs, prefaces and so on) to provide evidence for connections between these writers and eugenical thought, and for the most part succeeds in establishing links. He provides a mildly Foucauldian frame for reading texts of many types in juxtaposition as proof of the existence of a discourse that shored up the "bio-power" of the state and other authorities (13). Childs' method of interpreting the literary works in light of these links, however, constricts his focus to such a narrow gauge that the readings he gives are occasionally warpings of great magnitude. He claims that "[e]ven when we need to tease it out of sometimes recalcitrant poems, plays, novels, and essays, the voice of eugenical discourse is nonetheless present and nonetheless significant for its reticence about being seen and heard" (15). One of the strengths of this study is in connecting three prominent writers to the context of the eugenics movement; at the same time the highly speculative if admirably inventive readings of individual poems and other works seem almost like filler—Childs protests too much in his assertions of eugenical echoes in the works of these writers, some of which appear a bit dubious.

Eugenical discourse was prominent in England from the late 19th century until World War II, and was of a piece with modernist laments about a world in decline, a humanity degenerating. "Eugenics" as a term was coined by Charles Darwin's cousin, Francis Galton, "from the Greek *eugenes* meaning 'well-born' or 'good-in-stock'" in 1883.[3] The Eugenics Education Society was formed in 1907 to promote and popularize Galton's ideas and "reflected a growing concern, felt in all sections of the British intelligentsia, about the threats posed to social hygiene and national efficiency by the alleged multiplication of the unfit" (Bradshaw 190-91). Eugenicist concerns rested largely on statistics showing that the "inferior" groups and classes in British society were reproducing at a much more rapid rate than the "superior" groups and classes. Childs sees the eugenical movement as an attempt to place in human hands the responsibility for human evolution "recently orphaned by the death of God" (4). "Positive" eugenics included all those methods to encourage the "fit" to marry early and multiply, such as tax incentives, housing benefits, and so on (Soloway 122). The more sinister "negative" eugenics involved "the encouragement of family limitation among the diseased, the incompetent, and the chronic poor," as well as forced sterilization or confinement of the "congenitally defective" (Soloway 122, 145); its most extreme form was, of course, the extermination of the "unfit," the Nazi

[3]Richard Allen Soloway, *Birth Control and the Population Question in England, 1877-1930.* Chapel Hill and London: University of North Carolina Press, 1982.

solution to "race degeneration." Childs explains well in his introduction how pervasive eugenical ideas were in the early twentieth century, and how difficult it would have been for an intellectually engaged author to avoid them.

Childs' chapters on Yeats outline with specificity the poet's encounters with eugenicist ideas and their dovetailings with his own notions of aristocracy, class, and the need for the desirable Anglo-Irish line to be perpetuated. While Yeats did not join the Eugenics Society until 1936, Childs argues that he had met eugenical ideas and incorporated them into his own works long before this. For example, by tracing echoes between Allan Estlake's account of a Christian experiment in living in *The Oneida Community* and Yeats's unfinished novel *The Speckled Bird*, Childs shows that Yeats was familiar with the "attempt to carry out the principles of . . . scientific race improvement" early in his career (170). This novel and the plays of this early period display a yearning for "a generation-by-generation improvement of the race" that Childs attributes to Yeats's familiarity with the Oneida concept of "stirpiculture," the breeding of humans toward purity (180). Childs' interpretations of plays such as *The King's Threshold* and poems from *In the Seven Woods* cleverly argue that Yeats "sees women and poets as having parallel eugenical roles: their shared task is to educate and discipline man to direct his 'ruddy desire' toward beauty"; men are to pursue beautiful women of gracious living who will perpetuate the best in the race and keep aristocracy alive, and women are to choose their men rightly. In order to establish Yeats's long-standing eugenical beliefs, Childs gathers together the poet's thoughts about Maud Gonne and her dysgenic marriage to the alcoholic John MacBride, his concerns for the degeneration of "hysterical Ireland," and the use in his work of folkloric beliefs such as that

> the poets hung
> Images of the life that was in Eden
> About the child-bed of the world, that it,
> Looking upon those images, might bear
> Triumphant children. (189)

These disparate opinions and images do convincingly add up to a set of beliefs that made their most extreme appearance in Yeats's later works, especially *On the Boiler*.

Less persuasive is Childs' treatment of T. S. Eliot's works because at points he practices a biographical criticism of the most egregious speculation that undermines the credibility of much of the rest of his scholarship. The first chapter on Eliot is a very useful and cogent outline of intersections between his thought and that of some of his contemporaries—the Darwinian E. W. MacBride,

Henry Adams, G. B. Shaw, Henri Bergson, and others. Childs establishes Eliot's familiarity with eugenical debates and his position on their outskirts. While Eliot even wrote an essay critiquing pieces from *The Eugenics Review* (76), the links between his reading and his poetry are much less direct than Childs pretends. As Louis Menand writes about a recent study, *Painted Shadow: The Life of Vivienne Eliot, First Wife of T. S. Eliot:* "for Eliot bad sex was the symptom of a failure of civilization, and it is a fallacy to conclude that because sex in his poems is disgusting, Eliot was disgusted by sex";[4] I would add that it is also a leap to conclude that the model for the "bad sex" that appears in his works was his troubled relationship with Vivien. We hear, however, from Childs that "Eliot's prose poem 'Hysteria' . . . seems to be about Tom and Viv, and it seems to have been written shortly after Eliot learned about Rose Haigh-Wood's fear that her daughter [Vivien] might have inherited moral insanity." Childs reads this prose poem as displaying a "fear of woman's sexuality in general" and as revealing Eliot's "particular fear of Vivien's sexuality—his fear of her womb" (103). The imagery in another poem, "Ode," of "blood on the bed" Childs links with "Hysteria" in the following speculation: "'Ode's' bed linen may even be anticipated in 'Hysteria''s table linen—the 'pink and white check cloth' functioning as a displaced version of the more disturbing image of menstrual blood on the bedsheets," which Childs claims refers to Vivien Eliot's "frequent and irregular menstrual cycles" (104), a factor in the couple's childlessness. Childs' inventiveness here more than challenges his reader's belief in his arguments.

In the following chapter Childs draws on readings of *The Waste Land* as a poem about fertility to draw connections to the eugenical and feminist movements. He sees "Eliot's sense of the bacterial threat represented by prostitution [as] evident in *The Waste Land*, where prostitution and disease always go together" (125). This leads to some fine comments on contemporary feminism and the effects of World War I on fertility. Even in the midst of outlining these historical trends, Childs holds onto the idea that *The Waste Land* includes a "Tom-figure" and a "Viv-figure" whose sexual behavior is somehow evident in the scenes in the poem (135). Childs' reading of this much-interpreted modernist mainstay adds new layers to a "fertility" reading, but can't help but reduce the complexity of the poem to near an anti-prostitution treatise or a revelation of Tom and Viv's inadequate sex life.

Childs writes a biographical chapter about Woolf as well as Eliot, which considers her mental illness a "hereditary taint," and supposes that Woolf would have encountered eugenical ideas in numerous arenas. For example, Childs suggests that "it is likely that explicitly or implicitly eugenics informed much of

---

[4]"The Women Come and Go." Louis Menand. *The New Yorker.* 30 September 2002. 126-131.

[the] conversation" between Woolf and her doctor George Savage during their infrequent dinners together. More solid is the fact that some of Woolf's closer friends such as "Goldie" Lowes Dickinson, John Maynard Keynes, and Ottoline Morrell were "members of the Eugenics Education Society itself," and so might have made eugenical ideas available to Woolf (27). Childs also suggests that she would have encountered this influence in her intimate relations with Leonard: "It is quite likely . . . that Leonard himself represented [her doctors'] eugenical views to Woolf as part of his argument that the couple should not have children" (29). However they arrived in Woolf's range of opinions, two statements link her directly with positive and negative eugenics, and for those readers who have not focused on these statements before, they are most disturbing. In a diary entry of 1915, we find the following:

> On the towpath we met & had to pass a long line of imbeciles. The first was a very tall young man, just queer enough to look twice at, but no more; the second shuffled, & looked aside; & then one realised that every one in that long line was a miserable ineffective shuffling idiotic creature, with no forehead or no chin, & an imbecile grin, or a wild suspicious stare. It was perfectly horrible. They should certainly be killed. (*D1* 13)

Childs rightly proclaims this a "most negative eugenics" (23). Much later in her career, Woolf promoted positive eugenics in *Three Guineas* in a passage about the need to pay women a wage for motherhood: "Consider . . . what effect this would have upon the birth-rate, in the very class where births are desirable—the educated class" (qtd. in Childs 23). While the possibility of irony surely exists, especially in a text like *Three Guineas*, the limitations of Woolf's perspective as one of the "daughters of educated men" throughout this work gives a bit of credence to her comment. Woolf, then, despite her feminism, her pacifism, and her distance from the nationalism of a Yeats and the conservatism of an Eliot, could participate in eugenical discourse in what appears to be a rather unselfconscious manner.

Childs extends his understanding of Woolf's eugenicism to her fiction, and again finds eugenics in many passages in her imaginative works. He provides an intriguing reading of Clarissa Dalloway's daughter Elizabeth's unusually "Chinese" features as a reference to Cruikshank's *The Mongol in Our Midst*; this work raised the fear that humans were reverting to an earlier type, the Mongol, "because of a recessive hereditary unit in the blood of certain Europeans" (51). This insightful interpretation continues: "Woolf's concern about the hereditary nature of mental defect is so great and so deep-seated that it wells up in this passage—unconsciously displacing anxiety about her own tainted germ plasm . . . onto a word (Mongol) that can express both Clarissa's descriptive purpose and Woolf's personal eugenical anxiety" (51). The presumption that Childs has reached Woolf's unconscious anxieties diminishes an otherwise stimulating interpretation.

Much more helpful and insightful is Childs' reading of *A Room of One's Own* as a eugenical tract calling for the "literary and literal breeding of the super-woman" (60). While Childs does not account for the text's contradictions and ironies, he shows that a eugenical way of thinking influenced Woolf's "biological model of woman's literary genius" (74). And while we might not see Woolf as a full-fledged eugenicist of either the positive or negative type, her text "*A Room of One's Own* . . . represents an extension of the discourse of 'bio-power' into a site where it had not been seen before–the site of women's imaginative creativity" (74). Moments of interpretation like these, in conjunction with the eugenical context he provides, make Childs' book a very worthwhile contribution to modernist study.

—Loretta Stec, *San Francisco State University*

Vita Sackville-West: Selected Writings brings together a selection of
Sackville-West's poetry, shorter fiction and novels, essays on literature, fragments from her gardening books, as well as excerpts from her diaries, travel
narratives, and correspondence. In this eclectic collection, readers discover the
many facets to Sackville-West's sparkling prose and poetry, that for the most part
are no longer in print or have never been published. What emerges in this convergence of her work is an accessible introduction to the literary output and
complexity of one of British modernism's fascinating writers.

Mary Ann Caws's sampling of Sackville-West's writing reminds scholars
that she engaged those preoccupations of Britain's intellectuals and artists
regarding modernist aesthetics, and the future of human civilization. For
instance, in *Seducers in Ecuador*, previously out of print, Sackville-West celebrates Virginia Woolf's use of multiple perspectives in fiction, and in fact
dedicated the novella to her. As Caws notes, "*Seducers in Ecuador*, with its play
on varying views dependent on the color of one's glasses, is quite as Woolfian
[as] any of Woolf's stories, short or long" (11). This fascinating tale, which
Virginia "liked…very, very much" was, she reported to Vita, "the sort of thing I
should like to write myself" (*The Letters of Vita Sackville West to Virginia Woolf*
55). The main character, Lomax, becomes obsessed with how he can alter his life
as a result of wearing either blue, amber or black spectacles. Caws comments in
her introduction to *Seducers*, "Blue glasses were all the rage at the time that this
work was written" (278). The colored spectacles alter reality for the bored and
lonely Lomax and allow him to assume various subject positions, that, as
Kristine Beach, a student in my modernism seminar, noted, are far more exciting. He becomes the supposed rescuer of Miss Whitaker, the confidante of the
suicidal Bellamy, and the benefactor of the scientist Artivale. Lomax's blue
spectacles also invoke the work of Bertrand Russell and the Cambridge debates
regarding the nature of material phenomena, which Ann Banfield in *The
Phantom Table* has shown were central to Bloomsbury aesthetics. Russell
explained that physical objects must be understood in their multiple appearances:
"We can shut one eye, or put on blue spectacles, or look through a microscope.
All these operations…alter the visual appearance" of an object as well as our

understanding of material phenomena (*Our Knowledge of the External World* 77). Likewise, Lomax's question, "What is reality?," resonates throughout this enchanting novella.

Readers also get a sense from Caws's edition of Sackville-West's passion for science, particularly astronomy. In her diary dated May 1910, she reported that the weather in Switzerland might be attributed to "Halley's comet, through the tail of which I believe we are passing now" (25). Much later, while traveling through France with Woolf, Sackville-West noted that one evening during a storm, "We [she and Virginia] talked about science & religion for an hour—and the ultimate principle...." (145). In *Country Notes*, excerpted by Caws and which Woolf read and enjoyed, Sackville-West reflected on the remarkable unexpected appearance of the sky and trees during a partial solar eclipse (not the total solar eclipse of June 1927 viewed near Richmond with Woolf). She relished "standing outside the kitchen door, sharing [a piece of smoked glass] with other members of [her] small household" (199). Like her character Lomax, Sackville-West recalled how "a flowering tree" viewed through the smoked glass was "transmuted into a tree of a sinister loveliness unknown to any earthly botanist" (199). Indeed in her critical essay "Some Tendencies of Modern English Poetry," Sackville-West called for the revitalization of modernist poetry, and suggested that the new "enlarged conception of Time and the Universe may reflect itself in serious and steadfast poetry" of the future (177).

Sackville-West traveled widely, journeying from England to the Italian Dolomite Alps, across the sand dunes of Persia, to the desert southwest in the U. S. Not surprisingly, a good portion of Caws's edition highlights these extensive travels, including the selection of letters to Woolf, two excerpts from Sackville-West's published travel narratives, and a journal of her and Harold Nicolson's lecture tour of the U. S. A section of the poetry also is dedicated to "Travel Poems."

In July 1924, while hiking in the Italian Dolomites, Sackville-West wrote to Virginia Woolf from a mountain village in the Tre Croci pass (5,936 ft.), as she was working on her manuscript for *Seducers*. She described the village as nestled between "two rocky peaks of uncompromising majesty [which] soar into the sky immediately outside one's window, and where an amphitheatre of mountains encloses one's horizons..." (86). She further noted, "Today I climbed up to the eternal snows, and there found bright yellow poppies braving alike the glacier and the storm; and was ashamed before their courage" (86). Woolf later reworked this account in her short story "The Symbol," which echoes multiple elements of Sackville-West's letter, including a character who writes to her sister about the amphitheatre of mountains just outside the cottage window and the brave flowers that survive at incredible heights on the mountain ridges.

Sackville-West made two trips through Persia, today known as Iran, from January to May in 1926 and in 1927. Her accounts of those excursions, published by the Hogarth Press in *Passenger to Teheran* (1926) and *Twelve Days* (1928), offer readers a snapshot of Egypt and Persia as they were in the mid-1920s. During her first trip to Persia with Dorothy Wellesley, Sackville-West ventured along the Nile to Luxor, Egypt; on to New Delhi, India; then alone by sea through the Persian Gulf; across the desert to the Persian Mountains, then on to Moscow (*Passenger to Teheran* 19). As it happened, she arrived at Luxor in early 1926 roughly three years after the tomb of Tutankhamen had been opened by Howard Carter. Nigel Nicolson points out that during this trip, Woolf was his mother's "chief correspondent" (*Passenger* 17). Among this correspondence are some of the more passionate letters exchanged between the two women, inspired by the newness of their intimate relationship and, it seems, by both writers' desire for ancient civilizations, mountain vistas, and brilliant views of sweeping landscapes. Five of these letters appear in Caws's text.

Sackville-West's account of visiting ancient archeological ruins forged in her mind questions central to Bloomsbury aesthetics. The excerpt from *Passenger to Teheran* includes a brilliant account of Sackville-West's moonlight visit to the Temple of Amen, considered the greatest of the Egyptian temples at Karnak: "Piled on fantastic ruin, obelisks pricked the sky; the colossal aisle [of columns] soared. . . " (112). As she stood in that ancient moonlit temple observing the "familiar constellations wryly tilted overhead," she noted "that the aesthetic value of a building was [dependent on] its site" even as a painting's aesthetics are determined by its frame (111).

Travel at times was precarious, as she would report to Woolf: "Well, I have been stuck in a river, crawled between ramparts of snow, attacked by a bandit, been baked and frozen alternately…. Worn a silk dress one day, and a sheepskin and fur cap the next…" (*Letters of Vita* 112). Nevertheless, she claimed, "I have discovered my true function in life: I am a snob. A geographical snob" (*Letters of Vita* 111). While aboard ship in the Red Sea in February 1926, Sackville-West jotted another letter to Woolf: "I come up on deck at dawn when there is no one about…and watch the sun rising straight ahead, out of the east, and the sky and sea are like the first morning of Genesis…. I want nine lives at least. . . . And nine planets to explore" (Caws 88-89). Thus in her travel narratives and correspondence did Sackville-West chart, invent and expand shimmering landscapes for Woolf, and for her readers.

Caws has transcribed and included nearly all of the journal for Vita and Harold Nicolson's lecture tour in 1933 in the U. S. Of some note from this previously unpublished text are Vita's meetings with Robinson Jeffers and Mabel Dodge Luhan, and with Orville Wright whom she described as "an uncommunicative but agreeably modest little grey man who shows us some photographs of his brother and of their early flights" (159). All told Vita surmised for Woolf, "the distance [she and Harold] shall have travelled. . . comes to over 33,000 miles—We've been to 72 different cities, and have spent 63 nights in the train. I hope you are impressed by these statistics" (*Letters of Vita* 368).

A singular preoccupation for Bloomsbury and for Sackville-West's travel narratives focused on the ephemerality of human civilizations. In an excerpt from *Twelve Days*, Sackville-West recounts her visit to the remains of the palace of Darius at Persepolis, once a capital of the ancient Persian empire: "[T]he hand of man has never desecrated these ruins, no excavator's pick has ever rung upon these stones; tumbled and desolate they lie to-day, as they lay after the might of Alexander had pushed them over. The heat of the Persian summers has passed over them and bleached them; they have flushed in the light of many sunrises and bared themselves to the silver of many moons. . ." (141). In that same text, Sackville-West reflects, "It seems not irrelevant to wonder whether . . . London, Paris, [and] New York [will perhaps someday] lie with the wild flowers blowing over their stones. . ." (143). Certainly woven into her descriptions of Persia's ancient cities is the modernist anxiety about the possible demise of human civilization that so preoccupied Virginia and Leonard Woolf, T. S. Eliot, and Clive Bell.

Other fascinating selections include three short stories, three critical essays, a collection of photographs, and more than a dozen poems not discussed here. There are excerpts from Sackville-West's novels *Challenge* (1924) and *All Passion Spent* (1931), and, as Caws points out, a wonderfully poignant autobiographical account of Vita as a youth in "Thirty Clocks Strike the Hour."

A prolific writer and editor herself, Caws has published on modernist British women writers in *Women of Bloomsbury: Virginia, Vanessa, and Carrington* (Routledge 1990), and has a new text titled *Virginia Woolf: Illustrated Lives* (Penguin 2001). While Caws has provided introductions to the selected texts, some explanatory notes, and there is also a brief foreword by Nigel Nicolson, this is not a critical edition in the usual sense. Often Caws's praise for Sackville-West glosses over the writer's literary and personal limitations. Nonetheless, her project to inspire interest in Sackville-West is admirable. Those teaching courses in British modernism, modern British women writers, or looking for supplementary material for a Woolf seminar will find this edition a delight for students, and a valuable course text.

—Holly Henry, *California State University, San Bernardino*

Works Cited

Banfield, Ann. *The Phantom Table: Woolf, Fry, Russell and the Epistemology of Modernism.* Cambridge: Cambridge UP, 2000.

Russell, Bertrand. *Our Knowledge of the External World.* London: Open Court, 1914.

Sackville-West, Vita. *The Letters of Vita Sackville-West to Virginia Woolf.* Eds. Louise DeSalvo and Mitchell Leaska. New York: William and Morrow Company, 1985.

——. *Passenger to Teheran.* East Sussex: Cockbird Press, 1990.

——. *Twelve Days: An Account of a Journey Across the Bakhtiari Mountains of South-western Persia.* London: Michael Haag, 1928.

Woolf, Virginia. *The Diary of Virginia Woolf.* Ed. Anne Olivier Bell. New York: Harcourt, 1977-1984.

——. *The Letters of Virginia Woolf.* Eds. Nigel Nicolson and Joanne Trautmann. New York: Harcourt, 1975-80.

Virginia Woolf: Becoming a Writer.
Katherine Dalsimer (New Haven and London: Yale UP, 2001) xvii + 206 pp.

Musing on the role that traumatic events played in the genesis of her creative work, Virginia Woolf wrote that she supposed the "shock-receiving capacity" is what made her a writer: "it is a token of some real thing behind appearances; and I make it real by putting it into words. It is only by putting it into words that I make it whole; this wholeness means that it has lost its power to hurt me; it gives me, perhaps because by doing so I take away the pain, a great delight to put the severed parts together" ("Sketch" 72). Foremost among the shocks she received were, of course, the deaths in her immediate family that occurred in rapid succession in her adolescence and early twenties: her mother in 1895, when Woolf was thirteen; her half-sister Stella in 1897; her father in 1904; her favorite brother Thoby in 1906. The effect of these losses, and Woolf's obsessive retelling and rewriting of her relationship to the "invisible presences" who continued to haunt her for the rest of her life, form the topic of Katherine Dalsimer's *Virginia Woolf: Becoming a Writer*. A clinical psychologist, Dalsimer sets out to create not a biography but a case study of how writing served Woolf "in the period when she was becoming a writer, the way it served her in the face of the 'sledge-hammer blows' that life dealt" (xvii). Woolf was fascinated by the workings of memory, and memory, Dalsimer observes, is a means of maintaining ties with the dead. Yet memory "tells a changing story" (xiv). Dalsimer's study juxtaposes the multiple versions of the same events that Woolf created over the course of her lifetime: in a shuttling pattern, she charts Woolf's movement "backward and forward over an earlier period of her life, from different ages, perspectives, and vantage points, reading the work of her maturity as well as her early writings" (xiii).

Dalsimer's sustained focus on this crucial set of years in Woolf's development uncovers surprising discrepancies in her written accounts of them. To some extent, the version of her childhood that Woolf created in such fictional and biographical texts as *To the Lighthouse* and "A Sketch of the Past" have come to dominate our understanding of this period of her life: the "merry crowded world" of childhood and its cast of characters—the mother who was central to its maintenance, the domineering and egotistical father, the abusive and insensitive half-brothers—are all now standard elements of Woolf's biography. But as

Dalsimer points out, these texts—one written in middle-age, the other near the end of Woolf's life—clash at many points with the portrayal of family life developed in the "Hyde Park Gate News," the weekly newspaper generated by the Stephen children beginning in 1891, when Woolf was nine, and continuing with little interruption until its abrupt cessation with Julia Stephen's death in 1895. "Preserved in the pages," Dalsimer writes, " . . . is a picture of family life that is robust, exuberant, and merry—before it would be shattered by death and before memory itself would be colored by grief and rage" (38). Hence while it comes as no surprise that Julia Stephen favored her sons, it comes as more of a surprise that the Stephens' children—particularly Woolf—mocked this "notorious" favoritism from the very beginning; that Julia, rather than central, as Woolf would later have it, comes off as peripheral, detached, and aloof; that the offensive half-brothers of later report are fully integrated into "the natural rhythms of family life" (33); and, perhaps most surprising of all, that the tyrannical father of Woolf's later accounts turns out to be playful, attentive, involved—not at all the egocentric "Victorian" two generations removed from Woolf and her siblings, but rather "a man of considerable vitality, very much engaged in the day-to-day life of his family . . . .as eager as the children themselves" (35, 36). It was Leslie who loved reading aloud to the children; Leslie who took them on walks and outings to the zoo; Leslie who—in contrast to that detestable wet blanket Woolf created in Mr. Ramsay—defied his wife's admonitions and took his children to the annual regatta at St. Ives, despite predictions of rain ("when in the course of the afternoon it began to rain again he decided, to the great joy of the children, that they would all stay on anyway," Dalsimer writes [37]). As Dalsimer notes in a later portion of the book, Woolf's portraits of her father remain full of contradictions: "He is gentle and fierce, adorable and intolerable. Woolf's writings about her father . . . reflect the way a life is told and retold and a relationship is altered in response to the currents of the present" (99). What remains constant is the bond she sustained with him through the acts of reading and writing.

Dalsimer follows this analysis of the "Hyde Park Gate News" with a detailed examination of Woolf's emergence as a writer, first in the private diaries she began to keep in her adolescence and then in her tentative early attempts to establish herself as an essayist and reviewer. Significantly, each of these developments followed the death of a parent and a serious mental breakdown on Woolf's part. These chapters are some of the most compelling in the book, as Dalsimer demonstrates how Woolf turned to writing first as a way to stabilize her shaky hold on reality, then as a reliable source of pleasure, consolation, and solace. Even in her first journal, begun in the aftermath of her mother's death and witness to Stella's disintegration and death, "there is always a tone of pleasure surrounding the *act of writing* itself," Dalsimer notes. "The very implements of writing are endowed with spirit and animation" (54; italics in the original). Like Lily Briscoe, Woolf discovers in artistry "the one dependable thing in a world of strife, ruin, chaos." Dalsimer also shows how these adolescent journals, ostensibly factual journals and early essay attempts, conceal an "insistent subtext" in what initially appear to be scribbles, fragments written upside down or on the backs of pages or both. These fragments, read in context with one another, form "a strong depressive undertow beneath the placid surface of the diary—pulling toward a past that is irretrievably lost, with tormenting questions of guilt and blame, and a yearning for death" (66, 67). The final essay at the end of one journal, written shortly before her father's death, confirms this assessment, as Woolf takes up a brief newspaper report of an anonymous suicide, a woman who drowned herself in the Serpentine and whose suicide note read "No father, no mother, no work." Woolf's imaginative elaboration of this report, Dalsimer argues, reveals not only her belief that no other ties in life can be as sustaining as parental ties (77), but Woolf's now certainty that work is not simply an economic necessity, but a psychic one as well, and "the most reliable way she had to deaden sorrow" (78).

Hence in the aftermath of the breakdown following her father's death Woolf repeatedly insists upon the necessity for work and for writing, and from the beginning her writing repeatedly circled back to her family and to her terrible losses. Here Dalsimer reads through early essays and reviews to show how characteristic themes and preoccupations emerged simultaneously as Woolf sought solace in her writing. "She bristled at stereotypes about women's writing and at the suggestion that the traditional role of women was more estimable than that of the writer," Dalsimer observes. "And she wrote compellingly about the way in which women who fulfill this traditional role, even those who are thought to do so beautifully, are lost to history, lost, indeed, to memory" (93). Dalsimer will eventually link this preoccupation with the lost history of women to Woolf's own sense that the history of Julia Stephen herself was lost to her, that Woolf's final attempts to memorialize her mother in "A Sketch of the Past" resulted in Woolf's admission that her memories of her mother were simply too meager to suffice. Dalsimer also reads some of Woolf's earliest attempts at memoir—a piece on her father that was included in F. W. Maitland's biography of Sir Leslie Stephen, and a second piece on hers and Vanessa's childhood, "Reminiscences"—against this later memoir to demonstrate Woolf's growing awareness of the role memory plays in shaping her portrait of her parents. Whereas Woolf wishes for an electrical device whereby she could "turn up August 1890" ("Sketch," 67)—a device whereby she could not only remember but actually recover the past—she finally must acknowledge that "in fact the past is not so retrievable as she had wished, and death itself does not make memories any less mutable" (118).

Dalsimer frames her analysis of the diaries and early essays and reviews with chapters on *To the Lighthouse* and *The Voyage Out*. These chapters unfortunately add little to existing scholarship on these much-studied texts; in fact Dalsimer seems to rely too heavily upon a limited number of earlier analyses in formulating her readings. Hence she concludes of *The Voyage Out* that, "[a]s much as the published text suggests a fear of male sexuality and of marriage, the earlier manuscripts suggest a powerful erotic pull toward women, specifically toward an older woman who is a maternal figure, and a fear of her imagined power" (170), a conclusion reached earlier by Madeline Moore and Ellen Bayuk Rosenman, among others. Nor is it clear why Dalsimer believes this novel "the one least read" (130) of Woolf's *corpus*, or why she believes it "difficult to read" (171). Similar limitations mar her reading of *To the Lighthouse*. Dalsimer seems herself too invested in Woolf's masterful portrait of Mrs. Ramsay to give due weight to other portions of the book: she dismisses the portrait of Mr. Ramsay as one of "woodenness, the abstractness of an allegorical figure, wearing his significance on his sleeve" (14) and reads the completion of Lily's painting as "wan and pale" in comparison to the more "vivid" and "convincingly imagined" dinner party created by Mrs. Ramsay (16). Dalsimer's dismissiveness towards Lily's painting is all the more surprising given her focus on the way in which artistry served Woolf as a means of countering loss and tragedy: Elizabeth Abel's Kleinian reading of Lily's painting as a form of boundary renegotiation and creative reparation to the lost mother and Jane Lilienfeld's juxtaposition of Lily's painting with the stages of grief and mourning are just two readings that counter Dalsimer's assessment of Lily's achievement. This chapter in particular would have benefitted from a broader familiarity with Woolf criticism in general and analyses of gender and mother-daughter conflict and resolution in particular, including those by Margaret Homans, Marianne Hirsch, and Ellen Bayuk Rosenman, to name just a few. (Dalsimer's apparently deliberate decision to limit most citations to bibliographical entries is an unfortunate one; at points where her work echoed that of other critics I found myself wishing for explicit acknowledgment of her indebtedness as well as some explanation of how her work differed.)

Dalsimer's study would also have benefitted from an explicit engagement with the theoretical issues that underpin her study. Early on she writes that "a rich psychoanalytic literature on early loss . . . informs all that follows" (6 n1), but she neither summarizes that body of work nor explains how its findings illuminate her own interpretations. Some theoretical background on memory might also have been helpful, particularly in light of Dalsimer's recuperation of George and Gerald Duckworth in her reading of the "Hyde Park Gate News." Dalsimer sidesteps Woolf's later allegations of sexual abuse, stating that "Much has been written about Woolf's later allegations . . . so much that . . . it has become impossible to consider the issue apart from all that has been made of it" (34 n 2); she then refers the reader to Hermione Lee's discussion of this controversy in her recent biography. But surely in a study of the nature of memory it is Dalsimer's responsibility to look at the "issue . . . [and] all that has been made of it": the way in which trauma impacts memory is much to the point here. Dalsimer's refusal to consider these particular shifts in memory has the unfortunate effect of privileging the childhood version of events, in which the Duckworth brothers form part of the "natural rhythms of family life" (33), and that "natural" family life is "merry" and "robust." Yet it is inconceivable that Woolf could ever have discussed her half-brothers' behavior in the pages of the "Hyde Park Gate News." This is one place where Dalsimer's otherwise astute identification of silencing and censoring factors in Woolf's memories falters.

Still, Dalsimer's book has much to offer those interested in the vicissitudes of memory and mourning in Woolf's life and work. Her focus on the changing nature of Woolf's fictional and biographical portraits of her parents and her childhood offer a much-needed corrective to those of us who have preferred only one of the multiple versions Woolf created over the course of her life. Dalsimer's weaving together of the work of the maturity with the juvenilia and diaries from which it emerged is especially impressive. Above all, she reminds us that for Woolf writing was a psychic necessity, the means by which the severed pieces of her past could coalesce. In a letter to Violet Dickinson following her father's death and her subsequent breakdown, Woolf wrote, "I am longing to begin work. I know I can write, and one of these days I mean to produce a good book. What do you think? Life interests me intensely, and writing is I know my natural means of expression" (qtd. in Dalsimer, 83). What Dalsimer shows is the process by which writing became Woolf's "natural means of expression" in the face of shattering loss and psychic disintegration.

—Patricia Moran, *University of California, Davis*

Feminism Beyond Modernism Elizabeth Flynn (Carbondale: Southern Illinois
UP, 2002) xv + 215pp

Elizabeth Flynn sets high goals for her book *Feminism Beyond Modernism*
as she strives to define two very large concepts, feminism and modernism, by
breaking them down into manageable parcels and setting up a sort of grid
through which she can examine the boxes which emerge as she crisscrosses the
categories of modernism, antimodernism, and postmodernism with feminism.
Her ultimate aim is praiseworthy and important: she suggests that "feminist traditions will be better understood if they are named, at least provisionally, if they
are related to other intellectual and historical traditions, and if they are represented in nonreductive ways" (4). To a great degree, Flynn achieves this goal,
bringing to her readers a clear, well-organized description of various modes of
both feminism and modernism. In the interest of such clarity and organization,
Flynn does, at times, appear to be somewhat reductive, perhaps a necessary
drawback in the process of tackling complex, contested topics and rendering
them accessible to a wide audience.

Flynn is a professor of reading and composition at Michigan Technological
University. Her appointment in a Humanities Department allows her opportunities to teach in several related disciplines, including literature and feminist
theory. Although she does not make this claim when she describes herself in her
preface, her strengths and primary interests are in rhetoric and composition. At
least this is what her book would lead you to believe, as she works her way
through philosophy and literature in the early and middle chapters of the book to
arrive, ultimately, at lengthy considerations of rhetoric and composition theory
and practice. For Woolf scholars, the first two thirds of her book, where she clas-
sifies feminism and modernism and discusses authors, will be of most interest.

The first part of Flynn's book is concerned with defining the categories of
modernism, anti-modernism, and postmodernism. Briefly, she defines modernism not as a literary movement but as a philosophy, associating it with the
Enlightenment. Seeing modernism as associated with democratic processes and
practices, universal human rights, rationality, human perfectibility, and science,
she also feels it is connected to imperialism, slavery, and the creation of an
underclass. While she does not blame modernist feminists for the negative
aspects, she clearly disassociates herself from modernism by critiquing it so

stringently from the outset of the book. Modernist feminists, explains Flynn, are "universalist, insisting that men and women have the same innate capacities but that women have been deprived of a right to develop these capacities because of prejudicial laws and policies" (20). Under the label of modernism, she discusses thinkers such as Kant, Locke, Wollstonecraft, Mill, Marx, Engels, James, de Beauvoir, Freud, and others. She sees two branches of feminism—Marxist feminism and psychoanalytic feminism—as being of the modernist school.

Antimodernism, according to Flynn, rejects and opposes modernism. She sees antimodernism as subjective, relativistic, and spiritual. Having roots in Romanticism, antimodernism's practitioners run the gamut from Wordsworth and Coleridge to Stanley Fish. Flynn situates radical feminists and cultural feminists within the antimodern category. Focusing on Mary Daly and Dale Spender, Flynn explains how radical feminists reject "androcentric" traditions and institutions. Cultural feminists such as Sara Ruddick, Carol Gilligan, and Evelyn Fox Keller "implicitly privilege subjective experience over objective analysis" (33). Cultural feminists see women as communal and connected, unlike men, and argue for gynocentric ways of living. Flynn criticizes antimodernist feminism for essentializing difference and construing gender roles too rigidly.

This critique leads Flynn directly to postmodernism, of course, which she describes as uncertain, contingent, ambivalent, and questioning. An important point, which she makes repeatedly, is that postmodernism does not reject or repudiate modernism, the way antimodernism does, but that it questions and problematizes modernism without opposing or negating it. Critics and thinkers deemed postmodern include Bakhtin, Lyotard, Derrida, Foucault, Kristeva, and Butler. Flynn values postmodernist feminism for being more inclusive and less elitist than the other types of modernism. After criticizing both modernism and antimodernism for their privileging of white, middle-class perspectives (a complaint she levies repeatedly), she finds postmodernism as having the most potential for change in the future.

That Flynn favors postmodernism becomes clear in her chapter "Reading Global Feminisms." By her own admission, Flynn uses the "real world" examples of responses to women's issues in non-Western cultures in order to demonstrate, in part, the limitations of both modernist and antimodernist world views. In this interesting chapter, Flynn analyzes discourse surrounding women's lives in non-Western countries. She explains how some of this discourse is modernist and some is antimodernist, revealing the weaknesses and problems in each approach. She concludes this chapter with a sub-section titled "Postmodern Hybrids," in which she praises commentators who are able to blend Western feminism and modernism with the "particularities of indigenous cultures." Flynn is particularly effective in this chapter as she uses examples from both academic and mainstream publications to show how the categories she has established function in relation to studies of groups of actual people rather than of literature or philosophies. This chapter provides a bridge between the first one which set up her categories and the next, a study of particular feminist authors, giving her project a real world sensibility and urgency.

Thus, when we come to Flynn's section on feminist authors, we feel convinced of the importance of her work. Woolf scholars will begin this section with anticipation and interest, as it is here Flynn discusses Woolf, Adrienne Rich, and Alice Walker. Unlike Rich and Walker, Woolf gets an entire chapter of her own, the only author to receive such extensive treatment in the book. Flynn titles this chapter, "Woolf's (Anti)Modern Reading," and aims to demonstrate that Woolf combines elements of both modernism and antimodernism in her writings about reading. Sensitively analyzing several essays in which Woolf discusses the reading process, Flynn explains that Woolf is modernist when she "portrays reading as a matter of recuperating relatively stable and determinate meanings" (59) but antimodernist when she comes across as a radical or cultural feminist and describes reading as "a political activity directly related to women's exclusion from traditional, patriarchal institutions" (60). When Woolf focuses on the emotional elements of reading, Flynn argues, she is being antimodernist, but when she advocates reading critically, she is being modernist. Woolf departs from male critics such as Roger Fry and Percy Lubbock who emphasize formalism and detachment in reading by making space for emotional, open responses to literature. Flynn breaks down Woolf's antimodernism into both radical feminism and cultural feminism, explaining how Woolf is radical feminist when she critiques the traditional canon, male critics, and other patriarchal institutions, and cultural feminist when she privileges common readers, particularly female, nonprofessional readers. Interestingly, Flynn's argument that Woolf is at times modernist and antimodernist would seem to lead to an assessment of Woolf as postmodernist, according to Flynn's own paradigms, because she does not repudiate modernism but moves beyond it. Yet Flynn assiduously avoids associating Woolf with postmodernism, relegating the mention of Pamela Caughie's book *Virginia Woolf and Postmodernism* to a footnote and pointing out there that Caughie herself does not call Woolf a postmodernist. Similarly, she begins the chapter on Woolf by quoting two Woolf scholars who seem to be heading in the direction of calling Woolf a postmodernist (in terms of the definition Flynn establishes). Kate Flint says that Woolf's views on reading are full of "ambivalences" which "demand a continually mobile response from the readers of her own fictions" and Michèle Barrett argues that Woolf cannot be categorized because she "confound[s] . . . classification" (57). Yet because of the large investment Flynn has made in setting up her grid, she cannot share this attitude that Woolf is unclassifiable. Her description of Woolf's reading as a "*curious* blend of the modern and antimodern*" (emphasis added) does not tip Flynn off to consider that Woolf appears curious to her perhaps because her categories do not work well for Woolf.

Flynn reserves her label of postmodernism not for an author (Rich and Walker, while seen as "more hard-hitting" than Woolf are ultimately still only antimodernist) but for a rhetorician, Louise Rosenblatt. The final section of Flynn's book is devoted to chapters on Rosenblatt and the fields of rhetoric and composition. Rosenblatt, Flynn argues, begins as a modernist but eventually her work "enables the development of postmodern and postmodernist feminist perspectives on reading and writing" (115). Flynn's last chapter is about postmodernist-feminist teaching practices in contemporary classrooms; it's clear that she finds in these spaces the apotheosis of her categories. Reading between the lines, one can almost hear Flynn's voice saying "it doesn't get much better than this."

The problem for Woolf scholars and other literary critics may be that the justification for the shift from discussion of writers to rhetoricians is not very convincing, despite the fact that Flynn provides a lengthy argument in favor of the equal status of rhetoric and composition studies in literature departments. But her insistence on the treatment of rhetoric and composition studies as equivalent to literary studies seems a begging of the question that leads one to reconsider the entire paradigm she sets up, exposing its arbitrariness. Woolf seems pigeonholed into the box Flynn wants her fit. In the process of shoehorning Woolf into this category, Flynn overlooks two important aspects of the treatment of reading in Woolf's *oeuvre*, the way her literary texts posit readers, and the depiction of readers within her books. These considerations would necessarily widen Flynn's conception of Woolf as an "(anti)modernist"; thus she cannot make them.

Although Flynn writes close to twenty pages about Woolf, she does not do her justice, I feel. Compared to other authors and philosophers discussed in the book, Woolf does well as the vast majority get barely a mention (with the exception of Rosenblatt.) Instead, most writers are used cumulatively, in order to build an argument and support Flynn's argumentative structure. On one hand, Flynn provides an important service, as she gives thumbnail sketches of a great number of thinkers and also offers good overviews of literary and philosophical trends in her footnotes. In this way, the book reads much like a series of introductory lectures for an undergraduate class; the lectures are clear, well organized, and accessible. On the other hand, the very traits that make the book suitable for students and those in fields not related to the book are what make it less useful

for those already well-versed in literary modernism, feminism, and Woolf studies. If you are interested in the connections among feminism, modernism(s), and
rhetoric and composition studies, this book has much to offer you. If you are
interested in sophisticated perceptions of modernism or of Woolf, there are many
other books that will suit your purposes better. A good place to start finding
those books is in Flynn's footnotes for *Feminism Beyond Modernism*.

—June Cummins, *San Diego State University*

Home Matters: Longing and Belonging,
Nostalgia and Mourning in Women's Fiction.
Roberta Rubenstein (New York: Palgrave, 2001) ix + 210 pp.

Roberta Rubenstein devotes very few pages to Virginia Woolf in her book, but she has done a great service for Woolf scholars nonetheless: she has broken Virginia Woolf out of the usual modernist triangles. It's not that those triangles—Woolf, Joyce, and Lawrence; Woolf, Hardy, and Lawrence; Woolf, West, and Barnes—aren't important or useful. And it's not that other authors haven't tried to create triangles outside the moderns—Krista Ratcliffe's study of Woolf, Daly, and Rich comes to mind. But it's liberating to see Woolf matter-of-factly combined with so many American women writers across generations and cultures: Barbara Kingsolver, Julia Alvarez, Anne Tyler, Paule Marshall, Gloria Naylor, and Toni Marshall. Paradoxically, then, one effect of this study of loss and mourning is a sense of plenty and richness. Woolf's venture into such mixed company succeeds, and Rubenstein, one hopes, has started a trend.

Rubenstein's introductory chapter on Virginia Woolf and Doris Lessing originally appeared in Ruth Saxton and Jean Tobin's collection, *Woolf and Lessing: Breaking the Mold*, so its specific argument may already be familiar to Woolf scholars. In it, she uses Woolf's *To the Lighthouse* and "A Sketch of the Past" and Lessing's *Going Home*, *Martha Quest*, *The Golden Notebook*, *Briefing for a Descent into Hell*, *Memoirs for a Survivor*, and *African Laughter* to contrast the two writers' autobiographical portrayals of their mothers and homes. Rubenstein establishes a tension between these two writers' responses to the past—Woolf tries to make of it something permanent whereas Lessing tries to repair or re-invent it—that functions well as an introduction to and a foundation for the rest of a study that examines memory, nostalgia, and yearning. But her conclusion about Woolf's attitude to the past rests on a shaky premise, that Woolf idealizes Julia Stephen in her portrayal of Mrs. Ramsay in the first part of *To the Lighthouse*. Rubenstein uses psychoanalytic theorists and critics to support her view that neither Woolf nor the characters she creates criticize Mrs. Ramsay in "The Window," but fails to rebut or even note the many critics who argue exactly the opposite. As my students often demonstrate, Mrs. Ramsay's power to seduce readers remains strong. But surely Woolf risks that reaction to expose the dynamics of that power, its patriarchal source, and its cost? After all, the text provides evidence against Rubenstein's claim that Mrs. Ramsay comes under no

critical scrutiny from within or without: Mrs. Ramsay's daughters have rebellious thoughts; the fairy tale can be read as an indictment; Lily does not just
worship and want to merge, but also laughs at Mrs. Ramsay's assumption of
superiority; Lily criticizes both Mrs. Ramsay's beliefs and methods at the dinner
table; and Mrs. Ramsay questions her own manipulations and motivations. Such
evidence suggests an author who questions her own idealizing impulses, an
author who works to undercut reverence, an author who creates a portrayal of her
mother from the point of view of "oneself grown up and on equal terms" (*L*3 572;
letter from Vanessa).

Rubenstein almost lost me with her insistence that Woolf unambiguously
idealizes Julia Stephen in her portrait of Mrs. Ramsay. Further, to give just one
example, Woolf's repetition of "I see now" in "A Sketch of the Past" (83) may
indicate a more fluid "fix" on the past than Rubenstein wants to suggest in her
comparison of Woolf and Lessing. (A small quibble—why use the 1976 edition
of *Moments of Being* instead of the 1985 revised edition?) But it would be unfortunate if this particular argument or the relatively brief space devoted to Woolf
in the book prevented Woolf scholars from reading the rest of it. Not only does
Rubenstein set up her argument about six contemporary American writers with
Woolf and Lessing—"there are no twentieth-century American literary fore-
mothers who have had an influence comparable to that of Woolf and Lessing"
(6-7)—but she illuminates a different kind of influence. Not focused on "a room
of one's own" or on breaking out of patriarchal domesticity, Rubenstein explores
the ways in which home matters to the eight writers in her study. In doing so,
she uses feminism to question the feminist assumption that home (and mother)
are always and only traps. Along the way, she creates a quietly powerful work.

Roberta Rubenstein takes seriously an eclectic group of contemporary
female writers, some of whom others might dismiss as either too popular or as
too tied to identity politics to be considered "good." She also crosses geograph-
ic, ethnic, and generational borders. In her most provocative rebellion, however,
she argues that nostalgia for home may not be regressive but restorative and asks
her readers to re-think their definitions of home and nostalgia. Nostalgia and its
concomitant attempt to *fix* the past—both secure it and repair it—do not necessarily mean sentimentality or stagnation in the texts Rubenstein examines.
Instead, nostalgia, in various complicated ways, plays an integral part in the
mourning process, necessary to healing and even to maturity, which, as she
points out, *means* "[r]esolving mourning—whether for lost parents, lost ancestors, lost selves, lost youth and possibilities, lost lives, lost places, lost cultures"
(164).

The reader's initial skepticism about this thesis testifies to the strength of the
70s feminist portrayal of home that Rubenstein tackles, but Rubenstein's slow

and careful building of her case, beginning with Doris Lessing and Virginia Woolf and then moving through *Animal Dreams*, *The Bean Trees*, *Pigs in Heaven*, *How the García Girls Lost Their Accents*, *Ladder of Years*, *Praisesong for the Widow*, *Jazz*, *Mama Day*, and *Paradise*, ultimately persuades. Looking first at reactions to the absence of the mother in Woolf's *To the Lighthouse* and various texts by Lessing, she then moves to displacements of/from home in Kingsolver and Alvarez. The strong middle section examines how the longing for home is related to aging and cultural loss in Tyler, Marshall, and Morrison. Finally, she examines the nostalgia for paradise in Gloria Naylor and Toni Morrison and reveals some of the paradoxes implicit in their maternal worlds.

The cumulative effect of this study's argument is its major strength. The earlier threads Rubenstein establishes—the contrast between memory as a lie that distorts in Lessing and memory as a scene that endures in Woolf and the "relationship between private history and cultural displacement" (77) in Kingsolver and Alvarez—weave their way through her discussions of the dislocations of aging and its effect on women's longing for belonging in Tyler, Marshall, and Morrison and cultural mourning in Marshall and Morrison. In turn, all those threads become the background for her examination of women's problematic longing for a maternal paradise in Naylor and Morrison. The book thus grows organically, with every new addition supplementing and complicating what went before and underlying and supporting what comes after; by the end, the reader feels deeply satisfied by the subtle and tightly woven tapestry in front of her.

At the same time, any single chapter can stand alone—the individual readings of the novels are rich, absorbing, and thought-provoking. For example, Rubenstein's discussion of Mama Day and the awe and ambivalence we feel in the face of that character's power made me greedily wish Rubenstein had included yet another text in her book: how does Naylor's portrayal of George Andrews' birth in *Bailey's Café*, written subsequent to the portrayal of his death in *Mama Day*, comment on Mama Day's actions? Furthermore, Rubenstein's chapters seem remarkably adaptable for teaching. Want some good insights into *Mama Day*? Some historical context for *When the García Girls Lost Their Accents*? An explanation of how the stages of grief play themselves out in *Ladder of Years*? A discussion of Morrison's modernist narrative cues and postmodernist narrative voices in *Jazz*? The chapters in this book can help.

Other strengths include Rubenstein's comparative work; she illuminates intriguing similarities and differences among the works in her clusters and then between and among all eight works. She also shows how the writers in her study range across and through literary traditions, noting, for example, how Kingsolver synthesizes and juxtaposes Western and Native American mythologies in her use of Homer, *The Waste Land*, and Pueblo and Navajo traditions. Although she occasionally mentions an echo of Woolf or Lessing in a contemporary novel, such comparisons and comments are not used to validate inclusion in the book or to highlight influence or indebtedness. Rather, Rubenstein wants to illustrate the pervasiveness of the "longing for belonging" in women's fiction, the ways in which "we are all [. . .] exiles from childhood," and thus, the way in which nostalgia, or homesickness, "is the existential condition of adulthood" (4-5).

Refreshing in its approach, liberating in its mix of "classic" and contemporary authors, generally solid in its interpretation, and convincing in its overall argument, this book is also a real pleasure to read. Rubenstein's attention to and enjoyment of language is clear throughout, and the resulting prose is complex without being filled with jargon, mentally challenging without being a thicket, and serious without being deadly. Re-stating her argument, however, does not do Rubenstein's fresh and sometimes playful language justice, so I would like to quote a portion of her last chapter here:

> Although it may be true that one "can't go home again," the eight writers considered in this study express a variety of ways to return imaginatively, through memory and art, to the original home—the place that represents emotional succor, intimacy, and plenitude. If the past may be understood as the home/homeland from which we are all exiles, literary nostalgia expresses a reparative vision, memorializing the imagination's subversive desire to "fix" the past. Mother is our first home, the original safe house—or the idealized fantasy of such a person and place—by which all later spaces of belonging are measured. Retracing the path from rupture back (or forward) to rapture represents, for the characters whose homesickness or nostalgia shapes a number of these narratives, the impulse to secure but also to recover, repair, restore, or discover a more enduring meaning in events that shape the unfoldings of time, emotional history, and memory. (159-160)

Some of her titles reflect the same playfulness: "Fixing the Past, Re-Placing Nostalgia," for example, or "Is Mother Home?" In addition, the scholarly apparatus is complete, something I mention because we can no longer take it for granted: the press has provided footnotes, works cited, *and* an index, plus it has added bold-faced index entries for the authors featured in the book, a lovely touch.

Woolf scholars will probably not buy this book just for Rubenstein's reading of Woolf's *To the Lighthouse*, but they certainly should consider it if they teach a wide variety of 20th century British and American women writers. Roberta Rubenstein's courageous thesis, creative border crossings, complex argument, insightful readings of contemporary texts, numerous teaching applications, and lively language all make this book well worth the price.

—Beth Rigel Daugherty, *Otterbein College*

Notes on Contributors

Evelyn Haller is Professor and Chair of English at Doane College in Crete, Nebraska. Her recent publications include "Willa Cather and Leon Bakst, Her Portraitist Who Was Designer to Diaghilev's Russian Ballet" in *Willa Cather's New York: New Essays on Cather in the City* edited by Merrill Skaggs, and "Ways To Access the Landscape, Soundscape, and Lifescape of Ireland in the Poetry of W. B. Yeats" in *The South Carolina Review*, spring 2001. "Her Father's Gifts: Books in English Pound Gave His Daughter That She Might Learn His Mother Tongue and More" is forthcoming in *Paideuma*. She is an Associate Fellow of the Center for Great Plains Studies at the University of Nebraska-Lincoln. Her two books in progress are discussions of Woolf's art through her use of various cultures, tentatively titled "Virginia Woolf's Harmonious Sphere: Her Merging of Many Cultures," and of Cather's use of art, including architecture, dance, and material culture, tentatively titled "The Inland Seas: Willa Cather's Intermingling of the Arts." Haller is also at work on a poetry collection tentatively titled "The Maker of Hours."

Jane Lilienfeld is a Professor of English at Lincoln University, an historically Black college in Jefferson City, MO. She has published essays on Willa Cather, Colette, Margaret Atwood, James Joyce, and feminist theory in addition to her work on Virginia Woolf. Her book *Reading Alcoholisms: Theorizing Character and Narrative in Selected Novels of Thomas Hardy, James Joyce, and Virginia Woolf* won a *Choice* Award as an outstanding academic book of 2000. With Jeffrey Oxford, she co-edited an anthology entitled *The Languages of Addiction*. Awarded a Canadian Studies Grant from the Canadian Government, Lilienfeld studied the manuscripts of Alice Munro at the University of Calgary in the summer of 2001. Her work on Alice Munro is part of her current project, tentatively entitled "Circumventing Circumstance: World Wide Women Tell Stories."

Amy Lilly recently completed her dissertation, entitled "'This Way to the Exhibition': Woolf, Joyce, Rhys, and the 1930s Fascist Culture of Exhibitions," at the University of Iowa.

Lisa Low is an independent scholar who has published a number of essays on Virginia Woolf. She is also co-editor with Anthony John Harding of *Milton, The Metaphysicals, and Romanticism.*

Jeanette McVicker is Professor of English at SUNY Fredonia. Her scholarly interests include modernism, poststructuralist theory, globalization and the profession, and postmodern American literature and culture. She directed the Women's Studies Program 1996-2000 and currently directs the Journalism Program. Her work has appeared in *Women's Studies On Its Own*; *boundary 2*; *Crossings*; *Woolf Studies Annual* and, with Laura Davis, she co-edited the *Selected Papers* from the 7th and 8th Annual Conferences on Virginia Woolf

Jeffrey Oxford received his PhD from Texas Tech University and is Associate Professor of Foreign Languages at the University of North Texas in Denton. He is the author of *Vicente Blasco Ibáñez: Color Symbolism in Selected Novels* and *Conversar para aprender*, editor of *La barraca* and co-editor of *The Languages of Addiction* and *Eduardo Mendoza: A New Look*. As well, he is author of various articles and presentations on naturalism and its manifestations in nineteenth- and twentieth-century peninsular Spanish literature.

Merry M. Pawlowski is Chair and Professor of English, California State University, Bakersfield, and co-director, with Vara Neverow, of the Center for Virginia Woolf Studies housed at CSUB. Her most recent book is an edited collection, *Virginia Woolf and Fascism: Resisting the Dictators' Seduction*, which will be translated into Italian under the auspices of Selene Press in 2003. She has published extensively on Woolf and on modernism, and has published several articles on Joseph Conrad and Henry James. She is currently working on a book project which examines Woolf and lesser-known women writers in the 30s within the framework of feminist theorizing of the state.

Natalya Reinhold received her PhD in English from Exeter University, UK and is Dr of Philology, Moscow, Russia. She has authored numerous publications on twentieth-century English literature, comparative studies and translation. Among them are *English Modernism: Psychological Prose*, published essays-cum-interviews with Iris Murdoch, Piers Paul Read, John Fowles and Martin Amis, translations of Virginia Woolf's essays on Russian writers and *A Room of One's*

Own, literary criticism of T. S. Eliot, et al. She is currently head and professor of the Department for Translation Studies at the Russian State University of the Humanities in Moscow.

Kathryn Simpson is Lecturer in English at the University of Birmingham, England, where she teaches courses on nineteenth and twentieth century fiction and film. Her research interests focus on the interrelationships of sexuality and creativity in the work of Virginia Woolf, H. D., and Gertrude Stein. She is currently working on an exploration of the reader's role in generating the lesbian erotics in Stein's writing, and researching the operation of the sexual economies at work in Modernist women's texts with a focus on the idea of the gift.

Miriam L. Wallace is Associate Professor of British and American literature at New College of Florida. While her current research focuses on novels by English "Jacobins" or political radicals of the 1790s, Professor Wallace has had a longstanding interest in Virginia Woolf; "The Politics of Body and Style: Theorizing Alternate Subjectivity in *The Waves*" was published in *Narrative* (2000). Her publications in the eighteenth century include "Gender Bending and Corporeal Limitations: The Modern Body in *Tristram Shandy*," in *Studies in Eighteenth-Century Culture*, and "Mary Hays's 'Female Philosopher': Constructing Revolutionary Subjects" in the collection *Rebellious Hearts: British Women and the French Revolution*, and "Wit and Revolution: Cultural Resistance in Elizabeth Inchbald's *A Simple Story*" in *European Romantic Review*. She won an NEH College Teacher's Grant for work on her book-in-progress, "Revolutionary Subjects in the English 'Jacobin' Novel, 1790-1810" in 2001-02.

Policy

*W*oolf
*S*tudies
*A*nnual invites articles on the work and life of Virginia Woolf and her milieu. The Annual intends to represent the breadth and eclecticism of critical approaches to Woolf, and particularly welcomes new perspectives and contexts of inquiry. Articles discussing relations between Woolf and other writers and artists are also welcome.

Articles are sent for review anonymously to a member of the Editorial Board and at least one other reader. Manuscripts should not be under consideration elsewhere or have been previously published. Final decisions are made by the Editorial Board.

Preparation of Copy

1. Articles are typically between 25 and 30 pages, and do not exceed 8000 words.

2. A separate page should include the article's title, author's name, address, telephone & fax numbers, and e-mail address. The author's name and identifying references should not appear on the manuscript.

3. A photocopy of any illustrations should accompany the manuscript. (Black-and-white photographs will be required for accepted work.)

4. Manuscripts should be prepared according to most recent MLA style.

5. Three copies of the manuscript and an abstract of up to 150 words should be sent to: Mark Hussey, English Dept., Pace University, One Pace Plaza, New York NY 10038-1598. Only materials accompanied by a self-addressed, stamped envelope (or international reply coupon) will be returned.

6. Authors of accepted manuscripts will be asked to submit two hard copies and an electronic version. Authors are responsible for all necessary permissions fees.

Please address inquiries to: Mark Hussey, English Department, 41 Park Row Rm. 1510, New York, NY 10038. Email: mhussey@pace.edu
Fax: (212) 346-1754.

Printed in the United States
1319200004B/40-75

9 780944 473627